BESCHERELLE

Complete Guide to Conjugating

12 000 French Verbs

New edition, revised by **Chantal Contant, linguist**
Université du Québec à Montréal

Translated by **Egan Valentine, PhD**
Université du Québec à Trois-Rivières

Hurtubise

Les Éditions Hurtubise bénéficient du soutien financier des institutions suivantes pour leurs activités d'édition :

- Gouvernement du Canada par l'entremise du Programme d'aide au développement de l'industrie de l'édition (PADIÉ) ;
- Société de développement des entreprises culturelles du Québec (SODEC) ;
- Gouvernement du Québec par l'entremise du programme de crédit d'impôt pour l'édition de livres.

Les Éditions Hurtubise receives financial support from the following organisms for its publishing activities:

- The Government of Canada through its Book Publishing Industry Development Program (BPIDP)
- The Société de développement des entreprises culturelles du Québec (SODEC)
- The Government of Quebec through its tax credit for book publishing

Maquette de couverture / Cover design - Eykel Design
Conception graphique et réalisation de l'intérieur / Interior design and layout - Folio infographie
Adaptation / Adaptation - Chantal Contant
Traduction / Translation - Egan Valentine
Collaboration à la traduction / Translation collaborators - Douglas L. Rideout, Doreen Preston
Recherche / Research - Frédéric Lehoux, Karine Gauthier
Révision linguistique / Proof-reading - Marie-Ève Lefebvre, Maureen-Claude LaPerriere, Edward Collister
Édition / Chief editor - Loïc Hervouet
Direction éditoriale / Editorial director - Corinne Audinet

ISBN 978-2-89647-183-6

Dépôt legal - 2e trimestre 2009 / Legal deposit - 2nd quarter, 2009
Bibliothèque et Archives nationales du Québec
Bibliothèque et Archives du Canada / Library and Archives Canada

Diffusion-distribution au Canada / Distribution in Canada
Distribution HMH
1815, av. De Lorimier
Montréal (Québec) H2K 3W6
Téléphone / Telephone: 514-523-1523
Télécopieur / Fax: 514-523-9969

Imprimé en France / Printed in France
www.editionshurtubise.com

FOREWORD

What is conjugation?

Conjugation is a pattern or arrangement of verb forms reflecting person, number, tense, aspect, mood and voice. To conjugate a verb is to list its inflected forms. The complexity of French conjugation has earned it a bad name, and undeservedly so. Admittedly, French does have a significant number of verb forms: as many as 96 for the active voice alone. But similar analogies can be made with many other languages. Moreover, most of these forms are easy to construct. For example, compound forms are rather straight-forward. Three ingredients are necessary: the correct past participle of the verb, the appropriate auxiliary and the correct conjugation of the auxiliary. As will be seen later on, the simple forms (those without an auxiliary) are paradoxically slightly more difficult. But these difficulties can be easily overcome.

How is the *Complete Guide to Conjugating* organized?

The *Complete Guide to Conjugating* provides quickly accessible information on all verb forms used in French.

- **Grammar of the Verb** (paragraphs 1 to 60)

Using standard French terminology currently employed in the classroom, this section provides complete information on **verb morphology** (the description of the structure of the forms), **verb syntax** (relationship of the verb with other units in the sentence, with specific reference to **agreement**), and **values** of the verb forms. Knowing how verb forms differ is essential. How is the information contained in the *passé simple* different from that in the *imparfait* or the *passé composé*? Therein, perhaps, lies the true "complexity" of French conjugation. An index at the end of this section provides easy reference to the grammatical terms used.

- **93 Conjugation Tables** (numbered 61 to 153)

The tables provide all the simple and compound forms for each model verb used to exemplify conjugation patterns. The structure of the forms is described in the section entitled Grammar of the Verb.

- **Alphabetical List of French Verbs**

The third section of this book provides a compendium comprised of verbs gleaned from the French-speaking world and listed in alphabetical order. For each verb, meaning, construction and sometimes agreement are indicated. Cross-references to the 93 conju-gation tables make it easy to solve conjugation queries.

Which verbs can be found in the *Complete Guide to Conjugating*?

French verbs evolve constantly: as verbs that are no longer useful disappear, newly coined verbs appear.

- **Neologisms or Newly Coined Verbs**

This new edition of the *Complete Guide to Conjugating* contains newly coined verbs: more or less technical or technology-related terms like *clavarder* (= to chat) or terms such as *staffer* (= to staff), confined to popular usage.

- **Verbs from the Francophonie [The French-speaking World]**

Another feature of this book is the inclusion of verbs peculiar to Quebec and French Canada (as attested to by *Antidote* – the French correction software, and the *Franqus – français québécois d'usage standard*, a dictionary developed by the Université de Sherbrooke) and verbs typically used in Belgium and Francophone Africa.

Does the spelling of verbs evolve?

Over the years, spelling has always been subject to change: *veoir* has become *voir, j'avois* has been replaced by *j'avais, commencea* by *commença, obeïr* by *obéir*… And change continues today.

The overall changes or orthographic rectifications recommended by the *Conseil supérieur de la langue française** [Superior Council of the French Language] and endorsed by the *Académie française*** [French Academy] include modified spellings to replace those deemed irregular: *assoir* can now be written without the *e* (the same applied to *voir*); the past participle *absous* has become *absout* to bring it in line with the feminine form *absoute*, etc. In the tables contained in this book, these changes are clearly pointed out and indicated as variants.

What terminology is used in this edition?

Every attempt has been made to ensure accessibility and clarity. In addition to the features mentioned above, grammatical explanations have been adapted and cogent comparisons made with English Grammar when considered useful. Both English and French terminology and nomenclature are used throughout this book. In the conjugation tables, the verb tenses are designated by their French names. In the annotations and explanations of grammar points, French names are used for those forms specific to the French language. For example, reference is made to the *passé composé*, the *passé simple*, the *imparfait*, etc. However, English terms (the present, the indicative, the past participle, etc.) are used when referring to or discussing generic grammatical notions and concepts. Nevertheless, the term "sentence complement" – not generally used in English – has been borrowed from French (*complément de phrase*). On page 254, after the alphabetical list, is a glossary of selected terms.

* An organization in a number of French-speaking countries that advises the government on issues relating to the usage of the French language.

** An eminent body in France which regulates the French language by determining standards of acceptable grammar, vocabulary, etc.

CONTENTS

GRAMMAR OF THE VERB

CONJUGATION TABLES

ALPHABETICAL LIST OF VERBS

The numbers 1 to 60 refer to paragraphs. Subsequent numbers refer to conjugation tables.

GRAMMAR OF THE VERB

The numbers indicated refer to paragraphs.

THE VERB

Chapter I

DEFINITION OF THE VERB

In French, as in other languages, words fall into several categories. Along with verbs, also exist nouns, determiners, adjectives, adverbs, prepositions, etc.
In French, verbs are distinctly different from nouns, and they exhibit various characteristics.

1 Conjugation

Verb **conjugation** is a systematic arrangement of various verb forms. These varying forms indicate person, number, tense and aspect, mood and voice.

The forms *elle travaille, nous travaillions, ils travaillèrent, qu'il travaillât, travaillez!* differ not only with respect to oral and written language but also with respect to the information they convey.

THE DIFFERENT TYPES OF VERBS

The classification used below takes both the meaning and the function of the verb into account. For classification according to verb form, see paragraphs 18 - 20.

2 The verbs *être* and *avoir*

These two verbs are distinctly different from other French verbs. They can be used in two different ways.

- ***Être* and *avoir*: basic lexical verbs**
  They can be used like other verbs with their specific meanings and constructions. *Être* can sometimes be used in the sense of "exist":

  Et la lumière fut.

  Être can be used to introduce an attribute:

  La conjugaison est très amusante. (très amusante: Adj-Phr attribute)

  Alice est médecin. (médecin: NP attribute)

  Mon meilleur ami est le président de l'association. (le président de l'association: NP attribute)

  Avoir is used with a direct complement and indicates that the subject "has" (or "possesses") the designated direct complement:

  J'ai deux livres de grammaire française. (deux livres de grammaire française: NP direct complement)

- ***Être* and *avoir* used as auxiliary verbs (see paragraph 15)**
  In addition to their use as basic lexical verbs, *être* and *avoir* are also used as auxiliary verbs. They help to conjugate other verbs in various contexts:

  – Passive voice (of direct transitive verbs) is formed with *être* and the past participle of the main verb:

  Le café est cultivé dans plusieurs pays d'Afrique. (est cultivé: passive form)

  – Compound tenses of all verbs use *avoir* or *être* as auxiliaries with the past participle. To determine the appropriate choice of auxiliary, see paragraph 15.

  Paul est parti pour Regina, mais il est arrivé à Winnipeg. (est parti: *passé composé*; est arrivé: *passé composé*)

  Julie avait mangé, mais n'avait rien bu. Elle s'est évanouie. (avait mangé: *plus-que-parfait*; n'avait rien bu: *plus-que-parfait*; s'est évanouie: *passé composé*)

– Compound tenses in the passive use both auxiliaries: *être* for the passive, and *avoir* for compound tenses:

Jocelyn a été reçu à l'hôtel de ville.
passé composé passive

– Double compound verb tenses are constructed with the usual auxiliary verb which is itself part of a compound structure and with another auxiliary. Note that the auxiliary *être* is placed in the front position in a reflexive construction.

Dès que Sylvain a eu fini son travail, il est parti.

Dès qu'elle a été née, on l'a aimée.

– Double compound verb tenses in the passive – as a rule rather infrequent – are constructed with the auxiliary *être* for the passive and the auxiliary *avoir* which is itself part of a compound structure with *avoir* as an auxiliary. This usage produces a structure with three successive auxiliaries, two of which are past participles.

Dès que le ministre a eu été opéré, il a repris ses responsabilités.

- **Use of the auxiliary *être* in compound tenses**
  – *Être* is an auxiliary to some verbs when they do not take a direct complement (see paragraph 4). These verbs are identified accordingly (with the mention **être**) in the alphabetical list (see the section at the end). Also, see paragraph 15.
  Aller, *arriver*, *devenir*, *mourir*, etc. are conjugated with *être*:

  Il est arrivé à Vancouver et il est devenu célèbre.

  – *Être* is also used as the auxiliary verb in pronominal constructions (see paragraphs 9 and 39):

  Elle s'est soignée, puis elle s'est lavé les mains.

For agreement of the past participle, see paragraphs 36 to 45.

- **Use of the auxiliary *avoir* in compound tenses**
  Avoir is the auxiliary used for all verbs which do not take the auxiliary *être*, notably direct transitive verbs (see paragraph 4).

  Avoir is used as an auxiliary to the verb *être*:

  L'accident a été très grave.
  passé composé of the verb *être*

  Avoir is used as an auxiliary to itself (*avoir* with the verb *avoir*):

  Le livre a eu beaucoup de succès.
  passé composé of the verb *avoir*

  For verbs conjugated sometimes with *être* sometimes with *avoir*, see paragraph 15.

- ***Être* and *avoir* - Frequency of use**
  As an auxiliary the verb *avoir* is more frequently used than the verb *être*. However, the verb *être* is far more frequently used as an ordinary verb (non-auxiliary use). In fact, it is the most frequently used verb in the French language; *avoir* follows next. Because of its prominent rank in the language, it is the first verb presented in the conjugation tables.

3 Semi-auxiliaries

The following verbs could be considered semi-auxiliaries:

- *aller* and *venir*;
- *devoir, pouvoir, savoir* and *vouloir*;
- *faire*.

- **Use of *aller* and *venir***
  Aller and *venir* followed by the infinitive constitute periphrastic verbal constructions expressing the *futur proche* and the *passé récent* respectively:

  Je vais partir. — *futur proche*
  Je viens d'arriver. — *passé récent*

- **Use of *devoir, pouvoir, savoir* and *vouloir***

  Some verbs can be used to modify the meaning of other verbs; they can add information. Examples of such verbs are *devoir*, which expresses necessity, sometimes probability; *pouvoir*, which expresses possibility; *savoir*, which expresses capability; and *vouloir* which expresses willingness. These are called **modal periphrases**.

  Il doit travailler, mais il veut se reposer.

  Elle sait lire, mais elle ne peut écrire aucun mot.

- **Use of *faire***

  Faire followed directly by the infinitive constitutes a factitive (or causative) construction. The subject of the sentence does not perform the action but causes the complement to perform the action.

  Alexandre Dumas faisait parfois écrire ses livres par d'autres auteurs.

  Used pronominally, and followed by an infinitive, it can have a passive sense:

  Mon ami s'est fait déranger par le bruit des camions.

4 Transitive, intransitive and attributive verbs

Many verbs indicate action performed by the subject: *travailler, manger, marcher, aller, monter…*

Others – fewer in number – indicate the state or an attribute of the subject; they are called **attributive verbs**.

- **Intransitive verbs**

  Some verbs express an action but are not accompanied by a direct complement: *aller, dormir, marcher, mugir…* Such verbs are called **intransitive verbs**. They may be followed by a complement:

  Ils s'endormiront vers minuit.
  sentence complement

- **Transitive verbs**

  Other verbs may express an action and be accompanied by a complement. Such verbs are referred to as **transitive verbs**.

  Simon construit sa maison.
  direct complement (sa maison)

  Ce tableau plaira à Véronique.
  indirect complement (à Véronique)

- **Direct transitive verbs**

  Some verbs take a direct complement (DC). In other words, there is no preposition before the complement.

  Les abeilles produisent le miel, les sauterelles détruisent les récoltes.
  DC of the verb *produire* (le miel) — **DC of the verb *détruire*** (les récoltes)

  If the verb is put into the passive, the direct complement becomes the subject:

  Le miel est produit par les abeilles.
  subject (Le miel)

  N.B. A word of caution about direct complements.
  Unlike French verbs, English verbs sometimes appear to have two direct complements because both complements come directly after the verb without any prepositions:

  We gave the waiter a generous tip.
  ind. compl. (NP) (the waiter) — **dir. compl. (NP)** (a generous tip)

  In English both complements can become the subject in the passive construction: "The waiter was given a generous tip." or "A generous tip was given to the waiter." In French only the direct complement can become the subject in a passive construction.

REM: Similarly, care should be taken not to confuse the direct complement with other complements which appear to be direct:

Il boit la nuit. — **complement of time** (la nuit)
Il mange le jour. — **complement of time** (le jour)

Despite their physical similarity, a direct complement and a sentence complement are grammatically different:

The sentence complement can be relocated elsewhere in the sentence without any change in the meaning.

A sentence complement cannot be the subject of a passive construction: ⊗ *La nuit est bue par lui* is not grammatically correct in French.

- **Indirect transitive verbs**

  With other verbs, the complement is introduced by a preposition, generally *à* or *de*. These verbs are called **indirect transitive verbs**. Their complement is called an indirect complement (IC).

  Elle ressemble à sa mère.* — **IC of the verb *ressembler*** (à sa mère)

  Elle parle de linguistique. — **IC of the verb *parler*** (de linguistique)

  * The English equivalent of this verb is direct transitive: "She resembles her mother". Some indirect transitive constructions in French have English counterparts that are direct transitive. A few examples are: *contrevenir (à), (dé) plaire (à), désobéir (à), échouer (à), renoncer (à), subvenir (à), succéder (à)*. On the other hand, some French verbs which are not followed by a preposition have English counterparts which require a preposition to introduce the complement: *habiter* = "live in", *attendre* = "wait for", *payer* = "pay for".

- **Attributive verbs**

  Attributive verbs introduce a noun phrase (NP) or an adjective phrase (Adj-Phr) which indicates a characteristic or attribute of the subject:

  Pierre est content: il deviendra pilote de ligne.

  Adj-Phr (content) — **NP** (pilote de ligne)

  Être and other variants expressing forms of existence: *sembler, paraître, devenir, rester…* are referred to as attributive verbs.

THE SIX VERB CATEGORIES

Conjugation provides information on various notions or concepts: person, number, tense and aspect, mood and voice. These notions are called **grammatical categories of the verb**, and combine with each other to produce various verb forms:

Ils chantèrent.

This single example indicates simultaneously person (3rd), number (plural), tense and aspect (*passé simple*), mood (indicative) and voice (active form).

5 Person

Variations according to person are specific to the verb and the personal pronoun. Agreement with the subject gives the verb its agreement markers (see paragraphs 25 and 26). They indicate the agent (the person or thing about which something is being said), usually the doer of the action expressed by the verb.

Je travaille. Nous travaillons.

The 1st person *je* is always the one speaking and is therefore the subject of the verb.

The 2nd person *tu* is the person spoken to.

Tu connais beaucoup de gens.
personal pronoun

The 3rd person *il* or *elle* indicates that the subject is not part of the exchange taking place between the first two persons. Unlike the first two persons, who are human beings (or personified as in cases where an animal is made to speak or one is speaking to an object), the 3rd person can designate either an animate or an inanimate object. The subject of the verb in the 3rd person can be either a personal pronoun in the 3rd person, a noun, or a pronoun in a category other than that of personal pronoun:

Elle sourit.	*Marc-André est agité.*	*Tout est fini.*
personal pronoun	**proper noun**	**indefinite pronoun**

- **Impersonal verbs**

  Impersonal verbs are conjugated in the 3rd person singular only. French conjugation requires a personal pronoun before the conjugated verb (except in the imperative). In impersonal constructions, the pronoun *il* is always used but carries no meaning. In some cases, a word group follows the impersonal verb and can be interpreted as the "real subject" (complement of the impersonal verb).

  Il (personal pronoun) *arrive* *des aventures étranges* (complement of the impersonal verb) *à ces personnages.*

6 Number

Number is a common feature of verbs, nouns, determiners, adjectives and most pronouns. In the case of verbs, number is associated with person. The subject also plays a part in determining number, through agreement (see paragraph 26). Variations in number provide information on the number of persons or agents acting as subject: in French, only one person for the singular, at least two for the plural.

Je chante. Nous chantons.

- **The polite *vous* and the modest or emphatic *nous***

  In French, the 2nd person plural is also used as the "polite form".

  Que désirez-vous, Madame ? Monsieur, étiez-vous malade ?

  The 1st person plural is sometimes used by an individual to indicate modesty as in certain written works:

  Dans ce livre, nous ne parlerons pas de ces problèmes. (*nous* = I)

  The emphatic *nous* is sometimes used:

  Nous, maire de Toronto, prenons l'arrêté suivant.

The polite *vous* and the modest or emphatic *nous* require conjugation of the verb in the plural form but the singular form is used for past participle agreement.

Vous êtes élue à l'unanimité.

7 Tense and aspect

The verb provides a temporal indication of the reality it depicts. The two types of indication are: tense and aspect.

- **Tense**
  The action (state or event) is cast in a time frame with respect to the moment of the utterance. This moment in time, corresponding to the present, marks a distinct separation between what precedes it (the past) and what is ahead of it (the future).

  All these distinctions between the various moments in time in which an action can occur are referred to in French grammar as "tenses", a designation also used to refer to each of the series of forms such as the present, the *imparfait*, the future.

- **Aspect**
  The manner in which the verb's action (state or event) is considered, independently of its relationship to the present, is referred to as "aspect". For example, aspect indicates whether the time limits of the action have been taken into account or not.

Frédérique travailla. (***passé simple***)   *Frédérique travaillait.* (***imparfait***)

In these two sentences, the action is situated in the past. Nevertheless, the two sentences have different meanings. In the first sentence, the action of working (*travailler*) is seen as limited. It is possible to specify when it began and when it ended. In the second sentence, on the other hand, the time limits are not specified. The *passé simple*, therefore, exhibits what is referred to as a simple aspect, while the *imparfait*, a progressive aspect.

It is also possible to indicate whether the action is unfolding (i.e. "not yet finished") or whether it is finished. In the following sentences, the verb in the present tense indicates that the action is unfolding; it is being carried out.

Quand on est seul, on déjeune vite.
En ce moment, les élèves terminent leur travail.

However, in the following sentences, the *passé composé* does not situate the action in the past (preterite), but rather indicates that at the time of speaking, the action has already taken place (perfect).

Quand on est seul, on a vite déjeuné.
En ce moment, les élèves ont terminé leur travail.

REM: One of the peculiarities, and undoubtedly one of the difficulties, of French conjugation is that, unlike what may be observed in other languages, time and aspect are usually indicated by the same forms, under particularly complex conditions. The *passé composé* can have a double meaning; it can express either an aspectual value (perfect) or a temporal value (preterite). Since the physical form of the *passé composé* has more than one meaning, the notion of aspect is often not dealt with in most grammar books.

8 Mood

The word **mood** refers to the personal moods, involving "person" (see paragraph 5), and the impersonal moods, which do not include this category.

- **The personal moods: indicative, subjunctive, imperative**
  In French, these moods are the indicative, the subjunctive and the imperative. The indicative and the subjunctive are fully inflected (they exhibit complete conjugation) to show number and person. The imperative, however, exhibits only the 1st person plural and the 2nd person singular and plural. The conditional, long considered a distinct mood, is nowadays considered part of the indicative because of its form and meaning (paragraphs 51 and 52).

- **The impersonal moods: infinitive, participle, gerund**
  In French, there are three impersonal moods: the infinitive, the participle, the gerund. The forms of the infinitive and the participle are given in the conjugation tables. The gerund is identical in form to the present participle and is preceded by the preposition *en*:

  Il travaille en chantant.

9 Voice: active form, passive form, pronominal constructions

- **Definition**
  Voice indicates the relationship between the subject and the action expressed by the verb.

- **Active form**
  When the verb is in the active form, the subject is the **agent** of the action, i.e. it performs the action.

  Le gros chat dévore les petites souris.

- **Passive form**
  The passive form indicates that the subject is the patient or **recipient** of the action, in other words, not the doer.

  Les petites souris sont dévorées par le gros chat.

  The passive form is obtained through the following transformation: the direct complement of the verb in the active form (*les petites souris*) becomes the subject when the verb is changed to the passive form. Additionally, the subject of the active verb (*le gros chat*) becomes the complement of the passive verb (*par le gros chat*), sometimes called the "agentive complement" or "by-phrase". The auxiliary *être* is used with the verb.

- **Verbs used in the passive form**
  Change from the active to the passive form affects only direct transitive verbs. The other verbs (indirect transitive, intransitive and attributive verbs: see paragraph 4) do not have a passive form.

- **Passive value of pronominal constructions**
  The pronominal constructions (see paragraph 14) sometimes closely resemble the passive form:

  Ce livre se vend bien. — **pronominal construction** (se vend)
  La pizza se mange avec les mains. — **pronominal construction** (se mange)

  The verbs in the examples above exhibit a passive interpretation even though they have no agentive complement. Some languages, such as French, have only active voice and passive voice. The passive interpretation or value contained in certain pronominal constructions has prompted some grammarians to talk of the "reflexive" or "middle" voice.

- **Another value of the pronominal constructions: the reflexive value**
  The subject of the verb does something to itself.

  L'étudiant se prépare à l'examen. (= prepares himself or prepares)

  Elle se prépare un avenir radieux. (= prepares for herself)

  N.B. The corresponding usage in English is not necessarily reflexive; the verb does not always require the use of the form "-self": *Je me lave* = "I'm washing (myself)". The pronoun may be used for emphasis. Some grammarians refer to three categories of pronominal verbs: reflexive, reciprocal and pronominal (this latter category being neither reflexive nor reciprocal).

- **Another value of the pronominal constructions: reciprocal value**
  The subjects act on each other.

  « Deux pigeons s'aimaient d'amour tendre. » La Fontaine

  Les étudiantes s'échangent leur documentation.

- **Verbs that are essentially pronominal**
  Some verbs are used only pronominally. The reflexive pronoun is an integral part of the verb but it has no distinguishable reflexive interpretation. Examples of such verbs are *s'abstenir, s'arroger, se désister, s'évanouir, se repentir*... Other verbs such as *préparer, aimer, échanger,* in the examples given above, are "occasionally pronominal".

REM: For rules of agreement of the past participle of pronominal verbs, see paragraph 39.

VERB MORPHOLOGY

Chapter II

HOW TO DECONSTRUCT THE VERB FORM

To explain verb morphology is to describe the physical structure of the verb.

10 Stem and affixes: analyzing an example

The following example is based on the analysis of the physical structure *nous aimerons*.

- **The morphology of the structure *aimerons***
  How is this structure parsed (the word linguists use for "break up") into its parts or morphemes? If we compare *aimerons* to *amuserons* or *déciderons*, we notice that *-erons* is common to all three. We can therefore immediately separate the ending (flexion) *-erons* from the stem of the verb. Moreover, the ending (flexion) *-erons* can also be replaced with the ending of another verb form with a different value: *-ions* (*nous amus-ions*), *-èrent* (*ils décid-èrent*), etc. This possibility of replacing one ending with another confirms the existence of a juncture between *-erons* and the stem of the verb.

- **The stem *aim-***
  The morphemes *aim-*, *amus-* and *décid-* that precede the endings such as *-erons*, *-ions* or *-èrent* carry different lexical meanings. Dictionaries provide the specific meaning of verb stems.

- **The ending *-erons***
  Traditionally, in French, the suffixes added to the stem of a verb were called *désinence* or *terminaison*. These words simply indicated that the suffix was found at the end of the verb, a characteristic that is both obvious and of little use. Therefore, a more precise analysis and terminology must be developed. But first, is it possible to further parse *-erons*?

- **The morpheme *-ons***
  To parse *-erons*, the form *nous aimerons* must be compared to *nous aimions*. The morpheme *-ons* is common to both forms. Associated with the pronoun *nous*, the ending *-ons* indicates person (1st person) and number (plural). The ending (flexion) *-ons* can be replaced by *-ez* (*vous aimer-ez*) which changes the person (2nd person), or by *-ai* (*j'aimer-ai*) which changes the number (singular). The ending *-erons* can therefore be parsed into the morphemes *-er-* and *-ons*.

- **The morpheme *-er-***
  In forms such as *aimerons/aimerez* and *aimions/aimiez*, the morphemes *-er-* and *-i-* are placed between the stem and the morphemes (*-ons* and *-ez*), indicating person and number. To understand the function of these morphemes, the value of two different verb forms must be compared. The verb form *aimerons* places the action in the future while the verb form *aimions* places it in the past. Beyond this, both forms are identical. Thus, the morpheme *-er-* indicates the future and the morpheme *-i-* indicates the *imparfait*.

11 Affixes: definition

Now, the morphemes *-er-*, *-i-*, and *-ons* can be identified as **affixes**. And in the conjugation of the verb, the affix indicates tense, person and number … (see paragraphs 5, 6, 7). In spoken language, these affixes are often clearly audible: the *-er-*, *-i-* and *-ons* in *aimerons*, *aimions* and *aimerions* are pronounced. But, as is often the case, some affixes are apparent only in the written form; they do not have a distinct audible form, as in the case of the *-es* in *tu aim-es*, and *-ent* in *ils* or *elles aim-ent*. The importance of the written affixes is a specific characteristic of French grammar and spelling. In some cases, the affix can be marked by the absence of any written or spoken form. This is referred to as a "zero" affix as opposed to an explicit affix. For the 3rd person singular, the form *il défend* has a "zero" affix, which distinguishes it from the 1st and 2nd persons singular as well as the 1st and 2nd persons plural:

je or *tu défend-s* : **written affix** ***-s***
nous défend-ons : **written and audible affix** ***-ons***
il or *elle défend* : **zero affix**

12 Simple and compound forms

French verb forms can be either simple or compound.

- **Simple forms**
  In the simple form, such as *nous aimerons*, the affixes are attached to the stem of the lexical verb.

  Nous aim-er-ons.
  stem affixes

- **Compound forms**
  In the compound forms, the lexical verb is a past participle, a verbal element that is not conjugated. Here, the affixes are attached to the auxiliary verbs (*être* or *avoir,* see paragraphs 2 and 15). In *nous aurons aimé*, the compound verb form corresponding to *nous aimerons*, the past participle of the verb *aimer* (*aimé*) is used. It is not conjugated; the auxiliary *avoir* takes the affixes indicating tense, person and number (here, *-r-* indicates the future and *-ons* indicates the 1st person plural).

  Nous au-r-ons aimé.
  affixes

REM: For problems concerning agreement of the part participle in gender and number, see paragraphs 36 to 45.

- **Correspondence between simple and compound forms**
  A property of the French verb system is the correspondence between two series of verb forms, one "simple", the other "compound". For each simple verb form, there is a corresponding compound form, as the pattern below for the indicative mood shows.

INDICATIVE

SIMPLE FORMS		COMPOUND FORMS	
present	*il écrit*	*passé composé*	*il a écrit*
imparfait	*elle écrivait*	*plus-que-parfait*	*elle avait écrit*
passé simple	*il écrivit*	*passé antérieur*	*il eut écrit*
future	*elle écrira*	*futur antérieur*	*elle aura écrit*
present conditional	*il écrirait*	past conditional	*il aurait écrit*

The auxiliary in the verb forms *il a écrit, elle avait écrit, il eut écrit, elle aura écrit, il aurait écrit* is in the same tense as the lexical verb in the corresponding simple form. Thus, the present corresponds to the *passé composé*, the *imparfait* to the *plus-que-parfait*, the *passé simple* to the *passé antérieur*, the future to the *futur antérieur* and the present conditional to the past conditional. This parallel structure between the simple and compound forms characterizes all the moods: the present and *imparfait* of the subjunctive correspond to the past and *plus-que-parfait* of the subjunctive, as illustrated below:

SUBJUNCTIVE

SIMPLE FORMS		COMPOUND FORMS	
present	*qu'il écrive*	past	*qu'il ait écrit*
imparfait	*qu'elle écrivît*	*plus-que-parfait*	*qu'elle eût écrit*

The same applies to the imperative:

écris *aie écrit*

The same type of correspondence can be observed in impersonal moods:

INFINITIVE	*écrire*	*avoir écrit*
PARTICIPLE	*écrivant*	*ayant écrit*
GERUND	*en écrivant*	*en ayant écrit*

There are also forms called *surcomposées* (double compound forms), see paragraph 57.

13 Active and passive forms

In the case of transitive verbs with a direct complement, French has two voices: active voice and passive voice.

Ils aimeront. — active form   *Ils seront aimés.* — passive form

Elles aimeront. — active form   *Elles seront aimées.* — passive form

As with the compound forms, the passive forms present the lexical verb in the form of a past participle. In the passive, the past participle is marked for gender and number according to its subject because it is conjugated with *être* (see paragraph 37). As the examples above show, the past participles *aimés* and *aimées* carry the mark of the plural from *ils* and *elles*. In addition, *aimées* carries the mark of the feminine from *elles*.

The conjugated form is the auxiliary verb *être*. The auxiliary is conjugated in the same tense as the lexical verb in the corresponding active verb form. For direct transitive verbs, there are as many passive forms as active forms, even if they are less frequently used.

Among these forms, there are compound passive forms. For example, there is the *passé composé* in the passive voice, *ils ont été aimés*, and even a *surcomposée* in the passive voice, *ils ont eu été aimés* (see paragraph 2).

14 Pronominal constructions

Pronominal constructions are those whose verb is accompanied by a complement in the form of a reflexive personal pronoun (*je me…*, *tu te…*, *il/elle se…*, *nous nous…*, *vous vous…*, *ils/elles se…*).

Elle se promène dans le parc.
pronominal construction

Transitive and intransitive verbs (see paragraph 4) are sometimes used in pronominal constructions. The reflexive pronoun may itself be either the direct complement (DC) or the indirect complement (IC), or it may simply not have any logical function.

Ils se sont vus. (*se* = DC)   *Ils se sont donné la main.* (*se* = IC, *la main* = DC)

Ils se sont parlé. (*se* = IC)   *Ils se sont évanouis.* (*se* = no logical function)

For agreement of the past participle, see paragraph 39.
For value of the pronominal constructions, see paragraph 9.

15 Choice of auxiliary verb

Avoir and **être** are used as auxiliaries (see paragraph 2).

- **Compound tenses**

In compound verb tenses, most verbs use only one auxiliary: *avoir* or *être*.

– Pronominal verbs: always conjugated with *être*
In compound verb tenses, all pronominal verbs use the auxiliary *être* (see Table 64).

Tu te serais nui. Elle s'était mariée. Nous nous sommes promenés.

– Non-pronominal verbs: usually conjugated with *avoir*
Most verbs that are not pronominal are usually conjugated with *avoir*.
Moreover, all direct transitive verbs with a direct complement are conjugated with the auxiliary *avoir*.

Luc a déplacé le sofa. Tu lui aurais nui. Elle avait survécu.

– Some non-pronominal verbs: conjugated with *être*
A limited number of non-pronominal verbs is conjugated with *être* in compound tenses, as long as they are not followed by a direct complement.
In the alphabetical list at the end of this book, verbs whose compound tenses require the auxiliary *être* are clearly indicated.

- List of verbs always conjugated with *être*:
advenir, aller, arriver, décéder, demeurer (in the sense of "remain"), *devenir, intervenir, mourir, naître* or *naitre, obvenir, partir, parvenir, provenir, redevenir, repartir, rester, retomber, revenir, souvenir, survenir, venir.*
Note: These verbs never take a direct complement.

Je suis arrivé. Tu es intervenu. Elle est décédée.

- List of verbs conjugated with *être* when they are not direct transitive (when they have no direct complement):
descendre, entrer, monter, redescendre, remonter, rentrer, ressortir (in the sense of "go out" or "leave again"), *retourner, sortir, tomber.*

Elle est sortie avec Paul. *Elle a sorti les valises.*
(direct complement)

REM: Sometimes the verbs *descendre, monter, redescendre* and *remonter* are conjugated with *avoir* when they have no direct complement: *les prix ont monté hier.*

- List of verbs conjugated with *avoir* and *être*

  The following verbs can all be conjugated with *avoir* but when they have no direct complement, they behave as indicated below:
  - They are generally conjugated with the auxiliary *être*, but sometimes with *avoir*: *accourir, (ré)apparaître* or *(ré)apparaitre, échoir* (*avoir*: archaic or popular), *passer, ressusciter;*
  - They are usually conjugated with *avoir*, but sometimes with *être*: *choir* (*être*: archaic), *convenir de* (*être*: literary), *déménager, disparaître* or *disparaitre, échapper* (when it connotes inadvertance), *éclore, paraître* or *paraitre, reparaître* or *reparaitre, résulter, surgir* (*être*: formal);
  - They are invariably conjugated with *avoir* or *être*: *disconvenir, repasser, trépasser.*

- **Passive voice: *être***

  The passive is formed by using the auxiliary *être* followed by the past participle of the verb (see Table 63 and paragraph 9).

  Luc déplace le sofa. Le sofa est déplacé par Luc.

- **Past participle used as an adjective with *être***

  The past participle of some verbs normally conjugated with the auxiliary *avoir* can be used as an adjective accompanied by the verb *être*.

  Elle a bien changé en deux ans. (compound verb tense = *passé composé* of the verb *changer*)

  Elle est bien changée aujourd'hui. (past participle used as an adjective with *être* in the present)

  The first example is a compound verb tense and indicates a completed action; the second indicates a state, condition or result. In the second example *changée* is not used as a verb but as an adjective in the same way as *belle* or *gentille* could have been used in the same sentence.

  J'ai divorcé hier. (past action expressed by the *passé composé* of the verb *divorcer*)

  Je suis divorcé aujourd'hui. (*divorcé* is used as an adjective with the verb *être* in the present; in this sentence, *divorcé* could be replaced by the adjectives *veuf* or *célibataire*)

Verbs likely to behave the same way: *aborder, accoucher, accroître* or *accroitre, augmenter, avorter, baisser, changer, croître* or *croitre* (*être*: archaic), *croupir, déborder, déchoir, décroître* ou *décroitre* (*être*: archaic), *dégénérer, diminuer, divorcer, embellir, empirer, enlaidir, expirer, faillir, grandir, sonner, vieillir…*

16 Inversion, euphony and elision

The inversion of the pronoun can sometimes affect the physical form of the verb and modify the way it sounds (for harmony of sound, or euphony).

- When the singular pronouns *il, elle* or *on* are inverted, and the verb ends in a letter other than *-t* or *-d*, the letter *-t-* must be added between the verb and the pronoun.

  Mange-t-on ? Y a-t-il quelqu'un ? Reviendra-t-elle ? Vainc-t-il ?
  Revient-on ? Luc dort-il ? Descend-elle ?

- When the pronoun *je* is inverted and the verb ends in *-e* (rare or archaic structure), its ending is replaced by *-é* or, in accordance with the reformed spelling system, by *-è*.

  Dussé-je ? (or *Dussè-je ?*) *Aimé-je ? (or Aimè-je ?) Osé-je ?* (or *Osè-je ?*)
  Suis-je ? Puis-je ? Vais-je ? Serai-je ? Ai-je ?

- When the complement pronouns *y* or *en* are inverted immediately after the verb in the imperative, and the verb ends in either *-e* or *-a*, an *-s* is added.

  Vas-y. Apportes-en. Chantes-en. Penses-y. Aies-en toujours sur toi.
  Va-t'en. Apporte-lui-en. Chante en français. Pense. Ose en écrire.

- The pronouns *je, le, la, me, te, se* are elided in front of a vowel or a "silent **h**". This means that the **e** and **a** are replaced by an apostrophe. If the verb begins with a consonant or an aspirated **h**, elision does not occur. In the alphabetical list of verbs found at the end, the aspirated **h** is indicated with an asterisk (* **h**).

  J'hésite. Je hurle. Tu l'honores. Tu le heurtes.

The pattern exemplified in the case of *nous aimerons* (see paragraph 10) is easy to understand. It serves as a model for describing the morphology of a number of simple verb forms, as was explained for the non-compound verb forms. Yet, some difficulties do become apparent. These difficulties are sometimes related to the stem and sometimes to the affixes.

17 Fixed stem, variable stem

In the case of the verb *aimer*, the stem *aim-* is identical throughout the conjugation. This invariability of the stem is extremely frequent. In fact, except for irregular verbs, the majority of verbs have a fixed stem.

18 Verbs ending in *-er*

The verbs whose infinitive is indicated by the affix *-er* mark the 1st person singular of the present indicative with the affix *-e*, except for the verb *aller* (*je vais*). It is the only verb in *-er* that is irregular.

All the other verbs ending in *-er* (for example *aimer* and *travailler*) have a fixed stem, with a few rare exceptions, where the stem is generally very easy to identify. Thus, *achever* sometimes has the stem *achèv-* (*j'achèv-e*), and other times *achev-* (*nous achev-ons*). In fact, the presence of the affix *-e* makes the **silent *e*** in *ach**e**ver* become an **open *e*** (**è**). Similarly, the **closed *e*** (***é***) of *c**é**der* becomes an **open *e*** in *je c**è**d-e*. The sound "**e**" (or the absence of sound) is called **silent *e*** and it is represented by the unaccented letter *e* in certain words: *semer, lever, peser…*

The sound "***é***" is called **closed *e*** and the sound "**è**" is called **open *e***, because, to pronounce one or the other, the mouth must be either more closed or more open.

Envoyer and *renvoyer* are a little more complex. They alternate between three stems: *envoi-* [ɑ̃vwa] in *j'envoi-e*, *envoy-* [ɑ̃vwaj] in *nous envoy-ons* and *enver-* [ɑ̃vɛʀ] in *il enver-r-a* (see Table 80).

Almost all new verbs are formed based on verbs in *-er*, which are by far the most numerous.

19 Verbs conjugated like *finir*

The infinitive is marked by the affix *-r* which immediately follows the stem ending in *-i-*. The stem of these verbs remains unchanged throughout the conjugation, but in some cases has an "expanded" form *-ss-*: *je fini-s, il fini-t, il fini-r-a, ils fini-rent*, but *nous fini-ss-ons, ils fini-ss-aient, fini-ss-ant*. Once the form characterized by the expanded form in *-ss-* (present in the present indicative from the 1st person plural, the *imparfait*, the present participle, etc.) is assimilated, identifying the stem is simple (see Table 81).

More than 300 verbs are conjugated like *finir*.

20 Irregular verbs

These are all the other verbs (approximately 375):
- The verb *aller*, with its infinitive in *-er* (see Table 83);
- *-ir* verbs without an expanded form: *courir, nous cour-ons, ils cour-aient, ils cour-r-ont* (where the second *-r-* is not part of the stem, but is the mark of the future), *cour-ant*, etc. (see Tables 84 to 99);
- Verbs with an infinitive ending in *-oir*: *devoir, pouvoir*, the auxiliary *avoir*, etc. (see Tables 62 and 100 to 117);
- Verbs with an infinitive ending in *-re*: *coudre, exclure, plaire, vaincre*, the auxiliary *être*, etc. (see Tables 61 and 118 to 153).

- **Verbs with a single stem**
Some of these verbs, for example *courir* and *exclure*, have a stem that remains unchanged throughout the entire conjugation.

- **Verbs with a stem with two different forms**
Ouvrir has a stem with two different forms: *ouvr-* (*il ouvr-e, il ouvr-ait*) and *ouvri-* (*il ouvri-r-a*). *Écrire, lire, croire, vivre…* also have a stem with two different forms.

- **Verbs with a stem with three different forms**
Devoir has a stem with three forms: *doi-* (*il doi-t*), *doiv-* (*ils doiv-ent*) and *dev-* (*il dev-ait, dev-oir*). Other verbs with this same variation are *voir* (*voi-* in *il voi-t*, *voy-* in *nous voy-ons* and *ver-* in *il ver-r-a*), *dormir, boire…*

- **Verbs with a stem with four different forms**

  The stem of the verb *tenir* has the forms *tien-* (*il tien-t*), *ten-* (*nous ten-ons*), *tienn-* (*qu'il tienn-e*), *tiend-* (*je tiend-r-ai*). Other verbs with this variation are, amongst others, *prendre* and *savoir*.

  The verb *aller* first appears to belong to this class as can be observed in the variations of the stem *v-* (*je v-ais, tu v-as*), *all-* (*nous all-ons*), *i-* (*nous i-r-ons*) and *aill-* (*que j'aill-e*). However, compared to other verbs, the stem exhibits more variety. As a result of these completely different forms of the stem as well as the variety of affixes in the present, it is classified among the "highly irregular" verbs (see below).

- **Verbs with a stem with five different forms**

  This category includes *vouloir* (*veu-* in *il veu-t, voul-* in *nous voul-ons, veul-* in *ils veul-ent, voud-* in *je voud-r-ai, veuill-* in *veuill-ez*) and *pouvoir* (*peu-* in *il peu-t, pouv-* in *nous pouv-ons, peuv-* in *ils peuv-ent, pour-* in *je pour-r-ai* and *puiss-* in *qu'il puiss-e*).

- **Highly irregular verbs**

  Generally speaking, highly irregular verbs include *aller*, *faire* and *dire* as well as *être* and *avoir*.

  The stem of these verbs has a great number of forms (up to eight, according to some analyses, for the verb *être*), and the forms a verb's stem may take are often radically different.

  Often, it is impossible to separate the stem from the affix: where is the boundary that separates the stem from the affix in examples such as *il a* or *ils ont*? The verb *avoir* is considered to have a fused stem/affix.

REM: In determining the number of forms the stem may take, the *passé simple* and the past participle were not considered. For several irregular verbs, these two forms would have greatly increased the number of forms of the stem: *vivre* (the forms *véc-* in *il véc-ut* and *véc-u*), *devoir* (*d-* in *il d-ut* and *d-û*), *naître* (*naqu-* in *je naqu-is* and *n-* in n-é), etc.

AFFIXES

21 Affixes

- **What is an affix?**

Almost all verb forms can be broken down into various components: the stem (in black) and the affixes (in blue). The affix is attached to the stem of the verb (see paragraph 11).

The examples in the table below show the affixes added to the stem in the verb conjugation.

Some affixes are never placed in final position and indicate the tense of the verb (**-ai-**: the *imparfait*, **-r-**: the future…)

Other affixes are placed in final position: they indicate person and number (**-ons**: the first person plural…) and sometimes tense (see paragraphs 10 to 20).

- **Synoptic table**

INDICATIF

présent

aim-e	fini-s	ouvr-e	dor-s	met-s	veu-x	vai-s
aim-es	fini-s	ouvr-es	dor-s	met-s	veu-x	va-s
aim-e	fini-t	ouvr-e	dor-t	met	veu-t	v-a
aim-ons	fini-ss-ons	ouvr-ons	dorm-ons	mett-ons	voul-ons	all-ons
aim-ez	fini-ss-ez	ouvr-ez	dorm-ez	mett-ez	voul-ez	all-ez
aim-ent	fini-ss-ent	ouvr-ent	dorm-ent	mett-ent	veul-ent	v-ont

imparfait

aim-ai-s	fini-ss-ai-s	ouvr-ai-s
aim-ai-s	fini-ss-ai-s	ouvr-ai-s
aim-ai-t	fini-ss-ai-t	ouvr-ai-t
aim-i-ons	fini-ss-i-ons	ouvr-i-ons
aim-i-ez	fini-ss-i-ez	ouvr-i-ez
aim-ai-ent	fini-ss-ai-ent	ouvr-ai-ent

passé simple

aim-ai	fin-is	ouvr-is	voul-us	t-ins
aim-as	fin-is	ouvr-is	voul-us	t-ins
aim-a	fin-it	ouvr-it	voul-ut	t-int
aim-âmes	fin-îmes	ouvr-îmes	voul-ûmes	t-înmes
aim-âtes	fin-îtes	ouvr-îtes	voul-ûtes	t-întes
aim-èrent	fin-irent	ouvr-irent	voul-urent	t-inrent

futur simple

aim-er-ai	fini-r-ai	ouvri-r-ai
aim-er-as	fini-r-as	ouvri-r-as
aim-er-a	fini-r-a	ouvri-r-a
aim-er-ons	fini-r-ons	ouvri-r-ons
aim-er-ez	fini-r-ez	ouvri-r-ez
aim-er-ont	fini-r-ont	ouvri-r-ont

21

conditionnel présent

aim-er-ai-s	fini-r-ai-s	ouvri-r-ai-s
aim-er-ai-s	fini-r-ai-s	ouvri-r-ai-s
aim-er-ai-t	fini-r-ai-t	ouvri-r-ai-t
aim-er-i-ons	fini-r-i-ons	ouvri-r-i-ons
aim-er-i-ez	fini-r-i-ez	ouvri-r-i-ez
aim-er-ai-ent	fini-r-ai-ent	ouvri-r-ai-ent

SUBJONCTIF

présent

aim-e	fini-ss-e	ouvr-e	soi-s	ai-e
aim-es	fini-ss-es	ouvr-es	soi-s	ai-es
alm-e	fini-ss-e	ouvr-e	soi-t	ai-t
aim-i-ons	fini-ss-i-ons	ouvr-i-ons	soy-ons	ay-ons
aim-i-ez	fini-ss-i-ez	ouvr-i-ez	soy-ez	ay-ez
aim-ent	fini-ss-ent	ouvr-ent	soi-ent	ai-ent

imparfait

aim-a-ss-e	fin-i-ss-e	ouvr-i-ss-e	t-in-ss-e	voul-u-ss-e
aim-a-ss-es	fin-i-ss-es	ouvr-i-ss-es	t-in-ss-es	voul-u-ss-es
aim-â-t	fin-î-t	ouvr-î-t	t-în-t	voul-û-t
aim-a-ss-i-ons	fin-i-ss-i-ons	ouvr-i-ss-i-ons	t-in-ss-i-ons	voul-u-ss-i-ons
aim-a-ss-i-ez	fin-i-ss-i-ez	ouvr-i-ss-i-ez	t-in-ss-i-ez	voul-u-ss-i-ez
aim-a-ss-ent	fin-i-ss-ent	ouvr-i-ss-ent	t-in-ss-ent	voul-u-ss-ent

IMPÉRATIF

présent

aim-e	fini-s	ouvr-e	dor-s	vau-x	v-a
aim-ons	fini-ss-ons	ouvr-ons	dorm-ons	val-ons	all-ons
aim-ez	fini-ss-ez	ouvr-ez	dorm-ez	val-ez	all-ez

PARTICIPE

présent

aim-ant	fini-ss-ant	ouvr-ant

passé

aim-é	fin-i	dorm-i	ten-u	pri-s	écri-t
				clo-s	ouver-t
				inclu-s	mor-t

INFINITIF

présent

aim-e-r	fin-i-r	ouvr-i-r	voul-oi-r	croi-r-e

DEFECTIVE VERBS

22 Definition of defective verbs

Some verbs exhibit incomplete conjugation because certain forms are inexistent in their conjugation. Because of their inexistent or missing forms, these verbs are called **defective verbs.**

23 Classes of defective verbs

- **Verbs that are exclusively impersonal**
  These verbs, commonly known as impersonal verbs, are defective simply because they exist in the 3rd person singular only. Among them are meteorological verbs (such as *neiger, venter,* etc.) and a few other verbs such as *falloir* (*il faut*), *s'agir* (*il s'agit de*) and the impersonal expression *il y a,* that are generally followed by a complement.

- **Other defective verbs**
  Other verbs lack certain forms in their conjugation or have forms that have become obsolete (see Tables 91, 98, 99, 105, 112, 113, 115, 116, 117, 127, 132, 138, 141).

SPELLING REFORM

24 The French spelling reform of 1990

The 1990 spelling reform (or "orthographic rectifications") consists of a series of recommendations, which are increasingly being adopted by dictionaries, reference works and language-correction software. The aim of the reform was to regularize spelling by removing many of its intricacies. In 1990 the *Conseil supérieur de la langue française* [the Superior Council of the French Language] in Paris published a report prepared by experts to the *Journal officiel de la République française**. This report outlining the proposals for reform had been endorsed by the *Académie française* and other competent authorities of the major Francophonie member states.

These recommended forms are gradually coming into general use, replacing traditional spellings deemed irregular or outdated. For example, *célébrera* (future of the verb *célébrer*) can now be written *célèbrera* (the first **e** with an accent *aigu,* the second with an accent *grave* as in the adjective *célèbre*); the verb *asseoir,* which assumes the forms *assois, assoira,* etc., during conjugation, can now be spelt *assoir* (similarly to *voir* which has evolved from the old form *veoir*).

* The *Journal* is the official daily record, the gazette of the French government. It publishes legal information and includes laws, decrees, and administrative orders.

VERB AGREEMENT

Chapter III

DEFINITION OF VERB AGREEMENT

25 What is verb agreement? Analysis of an example

Le petit garçon promène son chien.

In this sentence, the noun *garçon* covers several morphological categories. At a very basic level, it indicates the masculine gender. It is used in the singular, the number used to refer to only one person or thing. Finally, it indicates the 3rd person and could be replaced by the 3rd person personal pronoun *il*.

The three morphological categories that the noun *garçon* covers are linked to the parts of the sentence it is related to. The article *le* and the adjective *petit* are markers of the two categories, masculine gender and singular number but not the 3rd person. The verb, on the other hand, indicates the 3rd person and the singular number, but not masculine gender, because it cannot mark this category.

AGREEMENT OF THE VERB

26 Agreement of the verb with its subject

The personal forms of the verb agree in person and number with their subject:

Les élèves	*travaillent.*	*Nous ne faisons rien.*	
3rd pers. pl.	3rd pers. pl.	1st pers. pl.	1st pers. pl.

- **Agreement in person**

  The verb is conjugated in the 1st and 2nd persons when the subject is a personal pronoun of one of these two persons (*je* and *tu* for the singular, *nous* and *vous* for the plural or an equivalent such as *Luc et toi*):

Je	*suis*	*grammairienne.*
1st pers. sing.	1st pers. sing.	
Tu	*as*	*de bonnes notions de conjugaison.*
2nd pers. sing.	2nd pers. sing.	
Nous	*adorons*	*la syntaxe.*
1st pers. pl.	1st pers. pl.	
Vous	*avez*	*compris la morphologie du verbe.*
2nd pers. pl.	2nd pers. pl.	
Luc et	*toi*	*mangez tard ce soir.*
3rd pers. sing.	2nd pers. sing.	2nd pers. pl.

  All the other types of subject require a 3rd person agreement:

Chantal	*frémit*	*en pensant à son examen.*
proper noun	3rd pers.	
Personne	*ne peut*	*négliger l'orthographe.*
indefinite pronoun	3rd pers.	
Fumer	*est*	*dangereux pour la santé.*
infinitive	3rd pers.	

- **Agreement in number**

  With respect to number, the subject in the singular determines the agreement in the singular, the subject in the plural determines the agreement in the plural:

La grammaire	*est vraiment passionnante.*
singular subject	singular verb
Les élèves	*travaillent.*
plural subject	plural verb
Ils	*se moquent du temps qui passe.*
plural subject	plural verb
Certains	*préfèrent le homard au caviar.*
plural subject	plural verb

REM: The polite *vous* (*vous de politesse*) and the modest *nous* (*nous de modestie*) used for emphasis require plural agreement with the verb, but agreement with the past participle is in the singular (see paragraph 6).

27 Agreement of verb and relative pronoun

The relative pronoun *qui* may be preceded by a personal pronoun in the 1st or 2nd person. In such a case, the agreement must be made with the personal pronoun:

C'est moi qui ai raison; c'est toi qui as tort.

1st person antecedent — **1st pers.** — **2nd person antecedent** — **2nd pers.**

28 Agreement with collective nouns (*foule, masse, centaine...*)

Nouns such as *foule, multitude, infinité, troupe, masse, majorité...* as well as collective numerals expressing approximation: *dizaine, douzaine, vingtaine, centaine...* are morphologically singular. When they are used alone, the agreement is singular:

La foule se déplace.

These collective nouns designate several beings or objects. When followed by a noun in the plural, the agreement of the verb may be plural:

Une foule de manifestants se déplace or *se déplacent.*

collective — **plural noun** — **singular** — **plural**

The agreement depends on the interpretation given. If the noun *foule* is considered to be the focus or head noun of the subject noun phrase (NP), it requires an agreement in the singular. If however *une foule de* is considered to be a complex determiner (replaceable by *des*), the noun *manifestants* becomes the focus of the NP subject, requiring a plural agreement. The interpretation depends on the meaning expressed by the verb. Often, as in the example above, both interpretations are possible.

29 Agreement with adverbs of quantity (*beaucoup, trop, peu...*)

The adverbs *beaucoup, peu, pas mal, trop, assez, plus, moins, tant, autant*, the interrogative (and exclamative) *combien*, the exclamative *que* and a few other adverbs (+ *de*) are often followed by a noun:

beaucoup d'élèves	*beaucoup de lait*
plural noun	singular noun
pas mal d'élèves	*pas mal de neige*
plural noun	singular noun

In this case, they have the same function as a determiner in the plural (*beaucoup d'élèves = des élèves*) or the singular (*beaucoup de lait = du lait*), and require agreement of the verb with the noun that is the focus of the noun phrase (NP), as the general rule stipulates.

Peu de	*candidates*	*ont fui.*	*Beaucoup de*	*lait écrémé*	*a été bu.*
complex determiner	plural noun focus of NP	plural	complex determiner	singular noun focus of NP	singular

Some of these adverbs may be used alone. In this case, the agreement is usually plural:

Peu ont échoué. *Beaucoup sont satisfaites de leur résultat.*

REM:
- The expression *la plupart* follows this same rule: *la plupart des élèves travaillent; la plupart travaillent.*
- The expression *plus d'un* requires an agreement in the singular, and *moins de deux* requires a plural agreement, simply because the focus is *un* in the first example, and *deux* in the second: *plus d'un est venu; moins de deux millions sont repartis.* Here the general rule is applied.

30 Agreement of impersonal verbs

The problem here is the absence of a "real subject", i.e. of an agent of the action. What is the subject of *il pleut* or *il fallait*? French has resolved this problem by imposing the 3rd person singular pronoun (see paragraph 5) and, as a result, a singular agreement. This singular agreement is maintained even when the verb has a complement (or "real subject"):

Il pleut des cordes.
complement of the impersonal verb

31 Subject-verb agreement with several subjects

Frequently, the verb has as subject several noun phrases (NP), or several pronouns that are joined or juxtaposed. The general principle is that the verb with several subjects (at least two in French) is conjugated in the plural.

Le général et le colonel *ne s'entendent pas bien.*
singular singular plural

Sonia et René *ont fait de la linguistique.*
singular singular plural

Celui-ci et celui-là *travailleront correctement.*
singular singular plural

Elle et lui *ne font rien.*
singular singular plural

32 Agreement with subjects joined by *ou* and *ni... ni*

These two cases do not seem to pose any problems: there are at least two subjects, and a plural agreement seems inevitable.
Nevertheless, some schools of grammar explain this in the following ways:

- **Subjects joined with *ou***
When two subjects are linked with *ou*, the agreement is made in the singular when *ou* is exclusive. A singular agreement is therefore required for:

Une valise ou un gros sac m'est indispensable.
(= I need only one of the two objects, to the exclusion of the other)

A plural agreement applies in the following example:

Une valise ou un sac facile à porter ne se trouvent pas partout.
(= the two objects are equally difficult to find)

This reasoning is acceptable, despite its subtlety and the difficulties inherent in its practical application. This is apparent in agreement with *l'un ou l'autre* and *tel ou tel*, which is done mainly in the singular because the *ou* is exclusive.

- **Subjects joined with *ni... ni***
In practice, the singular or the plural agreement may be used.

Ni Henri V ni Charles XI n'a été roi or *n'ont été rois.*
subject subject singular plural

REM: The expression *ni l'un ni l'autre* takes a singular or plural agreement: *ni l'un ni l'autre ne travaille* or *ne travaillent.*

33 Agreement with subjects joined with *comme, ainsi que, de même que, autant que, au même titre que...*

The agreement is made in the plural when the expression linking the subjects functions as a coordinator (note the absence of commas):

Le latin comme le grec ancien sont des langues mortes. (= Latin and Greek)
plural

The agreement in the singular indicates that the expression which links the terms maintains its comparative value. In this case, the comparison is isolated by commas:

Mexico, au même titre que Tokyo et São Paulo, est une mégapole.
singular

34 Agreement with subjects of different persons

- **Agreement in number**
  When different subjects relate to different persons, the agreement is plural.

- **Agreement in person**
  The 1st person takes precedence over the other two:

  Toi et moi (= nous) *adorons la grammaire.*
  Toi, Marielle et moi (= nous) *passons notre temps à faire de la musique.*

  The 2nd person takes precedence over the 3rd person:
  Émilie et toi (= vous) *avez dévoré un énorme plat de choucroute.*

REM: If, however, we want to indicate the reference pronoun with which agreement is made, that pronoun is preceded by a comma: *Toi et moi, nous adorons la grammaire.*

35 Agreement of the verb *être* with the attribute (*c'était..., c'étaient...*)

Whenever the subject of the verb *être* is the demonstrative pronoun *ce* (or, sometimes, *ceci* or *cela,* often preceded by *tout*) and introduces an attribute in the plural (or a series of attributes that are juxtaposed or joined), it may, contrary to the general rule governing the agreement of the verb, take the plural marker, i.e. agree with the attribute:

Ce sont eux.
Tout ceci sont des vérités.
C'étaient un garçon et deux filles.

However, ⊗ *ce sont nous* and ⊗ *ce sont vous* are not accepted.

AGREEMENT OF THE PAST PARTICIPLE

36 Agreement of the past participle used without an auxiliary

The general rule derives from the status of the past participle: a verb used as an adjective and following the rules relating to the agreement of adjectives. It therefore takes the markers for gender and number from the noun or pronoun it modifies. The rule applies regardless of the function of the participle.

Les petites filles assises sur un banc regardaient les voitures.
feminine plural

Assises sur un banc, elles regardaient les voitures.
feminine plural

Elles se trouvaient assises sur un banc, regardant les voitures.
feminine plural

- ***Attendu, y compris, non compris, excepté, supposé, vu***
When these are placed before a noun phrase (i.e. before a noun determiner), these past participles serve as prepositions: they are invariable.

Vu les conditions atmosphériques, la cérémonie est reportée.
invariable participle — **noun phrase**

- ***Étant donné, passé, mis à part, fini***
These participles may agree at the beginning of the sentence:

Étant donné or *étant données les circonstances...*
feminine plural

Fini or *finies les folies!*
feminine plural

- ***Ci-joint, ci-annexé, ci-inclus***
  These are characteristic of administrative correspondence and in principle obey the following rules:
  - They are invariable at the beginning of a non-verbal sentence or before a noun without a determiner.

    Ci-joint la photocopie de mon chèque.
    Vous trouverez ci-joint copie de mon chèque.
  - They agree when placed after the noun (they thus become noun complements or attributes).

    Voir la photocopie ci-jointe. *La copie est ci-jointe.*
  - Even when they are placed in front, they agree if they are considered attributes of the noun accompanied by a determiner (attributes of the direct complement).

    Vous trouverez ci-jointe une photocopie de mon chèque.

37 Agreement of the past participle used with *être*: general rule

When used with the auxiliary *être*, the past participle must agree in gender and in number with the subject of the verb. This rule applies to verbs in the passive form and also to verbs which require the auxiliary *être* in their compound tenses. For pronominal verbs, see paragraph 39.

Les voyageurs sont bloqués sur l'autoroute par la neige.
passive form in the present

Quelques jeunes filles sont descendues sur la chaussée.
passé composé* of the verb *descendre

Il est arrivé deux trains hier.
impersonal form of the verb *arriver*

REM: The pronoun *on* usually determines the agreement of the past participle with the masculine singular: *On est arrivé*. However, the agreement can be made in the plural, masculine for the most part, feminine when the persons designated by *on* are all female: *On est reparties*. The agreement in the feminine singular is more unusual and indicates that *on* refers to only one female: *Alors, on est devenue hôtelière ?*

38 Agreement of the past participle used with *avoir*: general rule

The past participle conjugated with the auxiliary *avoir* never agrees with the subject of the verb.

Claudine n'aurait jamais mangé cela.
feminine subject **invariable past participle**

When preceeded by a direct complement (see paragraph 4), the past participle must agree with this complement:

Ces histoires, il les a souvent racontées. (*les* = *ces histoires* = feminine plural)
direct complement **past participle feminine plural**

The past participle *racontées* agrees in number and gender with the direct complement *les* that immediately precedes it, while this personal pronoun represents the feminine plural noun phrase *ces histoires*.

The rule relating to agreement of the past participle with the preceding direct complement applies only in a few situations. However, two strict conditions need to be met, conditions which are not infrequent:

1- The verb must have a direct complement, and therefore excludes intransitive verbs, attributives and even transitive verbs constructed without a direct complement.
2- The direct complement must be placed before the past participle, which is usually seen only in:

- interrogative or exclamatory statements (with *quel, quelle, quels, quelles, lequel, laquelle, lesquels, lesquelles, que de…, combien de…*) where the direct complement is placed at the beginning of the sentence:

  Quelles grammaires avez-vous consultées ? Laquelle avez-vous lue ?
  Que de pommes j'ai mangées ! Combien de livres as-tu achetés ?

- sentences where the direct complement is a personal pronoun (*le, la, l', les, me, m', te, t', nous, vous*):

  Il nous a vus. *Je range les grammaires dès que je les ai consultées.*

- relative clauses where the relative pronoun is the direct complement *que* (or *qu'*):

  Les grammaires que j'ai achetées sont bien intéressantes.

39 Agreement of the past participle of pronominal verbs

- **The rule**

Although pronominal verbs are always conjugated with *être*, the past participle does not always agree with the subject of the verb. Furthermore, pronominal constructions may have several values (see paragraph 9) but these do not interfere with the rule on agreement. Agreement is determined by syntactic criteria (direct or indirect transitive verb, presence of a direct complement; see paragraph 14).

STEP 1: Is there a direct complement?

If the verb is a direct transitive verb (if it has a direct complement), the direct complement determines the agreement:

- If the direct complement is placed before the verb, the past participle agrees with this direct complement.
- If the direct complement is placed after the verb, the past participle is invariable.

This first step therefore requires the same analysis as in applying the rule of agreement with the auxiliary *avoir*: first, the direct complement must be identified. Note that direct transitive verbs are very common in French.
If the direct complement is placed before the verb, this complement will have the same forms as those mentioned in paragraph 38 (*quel, quelle, quels, quelles, lequel, laquelle, lesquels, lesquelles, que de…, combien de…, le, la, l', les, me, m', te, t', nous, vous, que, qu'*). For pronominal verbs, *se* and *s'* must be added to this list.
In the case of the verb *laver*, strictly speaking, one washes someone or something (direct transitive). The verb should therefore have a direct complement that can be easily identified:

Elles se sont lavé les cheveux. (DC = *les cheveux*, placed after the verb → invariable)
Elles se les sont lavés. (DC = *les*, placed before the verb → agreement with *les*, meaning *cheveux*)
Elles se sont lavées. (DC = *se*, placed before the verb → agreement with *se*, which represents *elles*)

Once the direct complement has been identified (as in the examples above), the appropriate procedure is followed and the analysis ends, as when the verb is used with *avoir*. However, if there is no direct complement, the verb is definitely not a direct transitive verb and further analysis must be done.

STEP 2: Is the reflexive pronoun an indirect complement?

It should be ascertained whether or not the reflexive pronoun (*me, te, se, nous, vous*) is an indirect complement. Fortunately, very few indirect transitive verbs

whose complement is introduced by the preposition **à** are found in reflexive constructions. The best-known examples are the following: *plaire à, déplaire à, mentir à, nuire à, ressembler à, sourire à, succéder à, suffire à, en vouloir à*... and often *téléphoner à, parler à, écrire à, répondre à*...
– If the reflexive pronoun is an indirect complement, the past participle remains invariable. The indirect transitive verbs in question are often the ones listed above.
– If the reflexive pronoun is not an indirect complement, it has no logical function (since it is neither the DC nor the IC of the verb). The past participle agrees therefore with the subject. This is a very frequent occurrence.

Elles se sont nui. (*se* = IC: *nuire à quelqu'un* → invariable)
Ils s'en sont voulu. (*se* = IC: *en vouloir à quelqu'un* → invariable)
Les rois et les reines se sont succédé. (*se* = IC: *succéder à quelqu'un* → invariable)
Ils se sont parlé. (*se* = IC: *parler à quelqu'un* → invariable)
Ils se sont évanouis. (*se* = no logical function: *évanouir à eux?* impossible → agreement with the subject)
Ils se sont enfuis. (*se* = no logical function: *enfuir à eux?* impossible → agreement with the subject)
Ils se sont méfiés d'elle. (*se* = no logical function: *méfier à eux?* impossible → agreement with the subject)

S'évanouir, se méfier or *s'enfuir* cannot be used transitively without the reflexive pronoun. In other words, these verbs followed by a direct complement are non-existent.
Note that the English equivalent functions differently; *s'évanouir* ("to faint") is intransitive, *s'enfuir* ("to flee") is also intransitive, but *se méfier* ("to distrust") is a direct transitive verb.

- **The six exceptions**
  The past participle of the verbs *se plaire, se complaire, se déplaire, se rire* is always invariable, regardless of the analysis. *Elles se sont plu à faire cela.* The past participle of *s'écrier* and *s'exclamer* always agrees with the subject, regardless of the analysis. These are the only exceptions.

- **Observations**
  The rule is not complicated in and of itself. It is often analysis of the verb and its complements that presents a problem to language users, as this must be done carefully. When a direct complement is present, the agreement is the same for pronominal and non-pronominal verbs:

Elles se sont lavé les cheveux.
DC placed after verb

Elles leur ont lavé les cheveux.
DC placed after verb

Elles se les sont lavés.
DC in front — agreement with this DC

Elles les leur ont lavés.
DC in front — agreement with this DC

Elles se sont lavées.
DC in front — agreement with this DC

Elles les ont lavé(e)s.
DC in front — agreement with this DC

When there is no direct complement, the invariability is the same for indirect transitive pronominal verbs and for indirect transitive non-pronominal verbs:

Elles se sont souri.
IC

Elles leur ont souri.
IC

Verbs whose reflexive pronouns have no logical function may be essentially pronominal (*s'évanouir, s'envoler*...) or occasionally pronominal (*se lever, s'apercevoir, se jouer de*...). It is not suggested that these verbs be learnt by heart as the list would be too long. They need to be analyzed. Note that the presence of a DC takes precedence, even with a verb that is essentially pronominal: the participle in *elles se sont arrogé ces droits* is invariable because the direct complement (*ces droits*) is in final position.

40 Agreement of the past participle of impersonal verbs

The past participle of impersonal verbs is almost always invariable since it is usually accompanied by a complement of the impersonal verb ("real subject") and not by a DC. Be careful not to confuse these two notions.

les soins qu'il leur avait fallu
qu'il: complement of the impersonal verb — fallu: invariable past participle

41 Agreement of the past participle after *en*, *l'* (for the generic *le*), *combien*

These three elements are analogous to pronouns but neglect both gender and number. They therefore do not determine participle agreement:

Des grammaires, j'en ai lu à foison!
invariable past participle

La crise dure plus longtemps qu'on ne l'avait prévu.
invariable past participle

Combien en as-tu lu ?
invariable past participle

42 Agreement with the complements of verbs such as *coucher, courir, vivre, valoir, mesurer, souffrir, durer, peser, coûter* (or *couter*)

These complements bear only some of the traits of direct complements. Therefore, they cannot be put in the passive. Even when they are placed in front of the past participle, they do not as a rule determine the agreement:

les heures que le voyage a duré (≠ ⊗ *ces heures ont été durées*)
les sommes que cela lui a coûté (≠ ⊗ *ces sommes ont été coûtées*)

However, these verbs are at times truly used transitively and therefore require agreement:

les trois bébés que l'infirmière a pesés (= *les trois bébés ont été pesés*)

These uses are often confused.

43 Agreement of the past participle followed by an infinitive

- **Past participle of a verb of movement (*emmener, envoyer*) or of perception or sensation (*écouter, entendre, sentir, voir*)**

les cantatrices que j'ai entendues chanter

Here, the agreement occurs because the pronoun *que*, representing *les cantatrices*, is the direct complement of *j'ai entendu(es)*.

In the example below, however, the agreement does not occur because the pronoun *que*, representing *les opérettes*, is the direct complement of *chanter*, and not of *entendre*:

les opérettes que j'ai entendu chanter

Rule:
Agreement occurs when the preceding complement is the complement of the compound form with the participle (case of *cantatrices*). Agreement is not made when the preceding complement is the complement of the infinitive (case of *opérettes*).

A good way of distinguishing these two cases is to replace the relative pronoun *que* with its antecedent. A distinction is therefore made between *j'ai entendu les cantatrices chanter* (where *cantatrices* is the direct complement of *j'ai entendu*) and *j'ai entendu chanter les opérettes* (where *opérettes* is the direct complement of *chanter* and not of *j'ai entendu*: *j'ai entendu les opérettes chanter* is not possible).

- **Past participle of *faire* or *laisser***
  The past participle of *faire* followed by an infinitive is invariable:

Les députés que le premier ministre a fait démissionner ont l'air sérieux.
masculine plural (députés) — DC (que) — invariable past participle (fait)

This is undoubtedly explained by the fact that *faire* in its feminine form would be obvious in speech: ⊗ *la petite fille que j'ai faite jouer* (such bizarre examples are found in literature).
Agreement may or may not be made with the past participle of *laisser* (agreement is strictly **written**) followed by an infinitive. In 1990, the *Conseil supérieur de la langue française* recommended that this past participle remain invariable in keeping with the pattern of *faire*. This past participle would therefore be written as follows:

Les musiciennes que j'ai laissé jouer s'améliorent.
feminine plural (musiciennes) — DC (que) — invariable past participle (laissé)

44 Agreement of the past participle followed by an adjective or another participle

The general rule applies here. The participle agrees with its direct complement if it comes before the direct complement:

Julie et Claire, je vous aurais crues plus scrupuleuses !
Une lettre que j'aurais préférée écrite à la main.

45 Agreement of the past participle of double compound forms

Only the last participle carries agreement. The other past participles remain invariable since they are only auxiliaries to the conjugation (see paragraph 57).

Dès qu'elle les a eu tués, elle a plumé ses canards.
Dès qu'elle a eu été nettoyée, la route a été asphaltée.

VALUES OF THE VERB FORMS

Chapter IV

VALUES OF THE VERB FORMS

46 Organization of the values of the verb forms

The values of the verb forms are based on their differences: the present is distinguished from the *imparfait* and from the *passé simple*, which themselves are distinct from each other. The subjunctive is distinguished from the indicative and the imperative.

REM: This chapter describes only the values related to aspect, tense and mood. The values of other categories related to the verb (person, number and voice) are described in paragraphs 5 to 9.

47 The present: the moment of speaking (or enunciation)

The present – which is the most frequently used verb form – occupies a central place by separating the future from the past.

The fundamental value of the present is to indicate – as its name suggests – the simultaneous link between the moment of enunciation and the lexical event. In *Claude travaille*, the lexical event *travailler* occurs (or is being done) at the same moment as the enunciation of the statement. This is where *Claude travaille* is distinguished from *Claude travaillait* (the lexical event occurs before the act of enunciation) and *Claude travaillera* (the lexical event occurs after the moment of enunciation).

However, in *Claude travaille*, it is obvious that the lexical event in question – what *Claude* is doing – has already begun (for at least a brief moment), and will extend beyond the moment of enunciation: the duration of the lexical event is greater than that which is necessary to say it. This possibility of extending beyond the moment of enunciation explains the different values of the present.

- **Present moment**
  The events are taking place at the moment of enunciation, and their duration is longer than the enunciation itself:

  Il pleut : je travaille.

- **Permanent, eternal or general truth**
  The temporal limits of the events can be very distant. However, the act of enunciation must be located somewhere between the moment the event started and the moment the event ended, even if these limits are so distant and so difficult to envision that the sentence takes on a non-temporal (or omnipresent) value:

  La Terre tourne autour du Soleil.
  L'argent ne fait pas le bonheur.
  Tous les humains sont mortels.

- **Repetitive or habitual events**
  The action or event is repeated over a given period of time – long or short – which includes the moment of enunciation:

  Le téléphone sonne.
  Le geyser jaillit toutes les deux heures.
  Je vais à la piscine deux fois par semaine.

- **Recent past and near future**
  In these two cases, the event is presented by the speaker as close in time to the moment of enunciation, in the past or the future. This proximity to the moment of enunciation (because, as explained above, the present can extend beyond the moment of enunciation) allows the present to be used:

  J'arrive à l'instant de Fredericton.
  Nous partons mercredi prochain pour Calgary.

The present is used when a future event is considered fully programmed at the moment of enunciation, even if, objectively, the event is fairly distant in the future:

Je prends ma retraite dans dix ans.

The present is also used in the future conditional structure. The verb of the main clause is in the future while the verb of the subordinate clause is in the present:

Si tu viens demain, j'en serai ravi.
present future

- **Narrative present or historical present**
Here, the described lexical event does not occur at the moment of enunciation, but the enunciator describes the event as if it were actually occurring, thus making the event seem more relevant, more present:

Champlain meurt le 25 décembre 1635.
present

48 The simple verb forms in the past tense: the *imparfait* and the *passé simple*

- **Comparing the value of the *imparfait* and the *passé simple***
Unlike other languages (for example, English and German), French has two simple verb forms in the past tense. In fact, the *passé simple*, in all its uses, and the *imparfait*, most of the time, have a past value that differentiates them from the present. Thus, the problem is to understand how these two past tense verb forms are different from one another.

Comparing the following two examples will illustrate the difference:
- In the utterance *il travaillait*, in the *imparfait*, the focus is not on the moment the event or action began or the moment it ended. This is why it is possible to say *il travaillait déjà en 1907*, while it is not possible to say ⊗ *il travailla déjà en 1907*, using the *passé simple*.
- The utterance *il travailla* indicates that the event or action – that might have lasted a long time – had a beginning and an end. Thus, it is possible to say *il travailla de 1902 à 1937*, while it is not normally possible to say, using the *imparfait*, ⊗ *il travaillait de 1902 à 1937*.

This phenomenon explains the different values expressed by a series of verbs in the *imparfait* and the *passé simple.*

The *imparfait* normally indicates simultaneous or alternating events:

Elle dansait, sautait et chantait. **(N.B.: she was performing all three actions at the same time)**

The *passé simple* generally indicates a series of events:

Elle dansa, sauta et chanta. **(N.B.: she performed one action after the other)**

When both verb forms are used in the same sentence, the *imparfait* establishes the background event (without temporal limits, or no clearly indicated beginning or end) against which another event (with temporal limits) occurs. This event that occurs against a background event is expressed with the *passé simple*:

L'avion volait à haute altitude quand l'incident survint.

- **Current use of the *imparfait* and the *passé simple***

  The *imparfait* is used in both written and spoken French, in all three grammatical persons (1st, 2nd, and 3rd). However, the *passé simple* is used, in contemporary French, almost exclusively in the 3rd person. Consequently, the use of the *passé simple* in the 1st and 2nd persons is considered archaic, especially in the plural: *nous arrivâmes, vous dormîtes.* In these situations, the *passé composé* is the preferred verb form: *nous sommes arrivés, vous avez dormi* (see paragraph 54). Although not totally absent from the spoken language, the *passé simple* is more a characteristic of the written language, especially literary language.

49 The future and the conditional

Unlike other languages (notably English and German), the future and the conditional in French are simple verb forms.

REM: The infinitive of the verb does not provide, with perfect certainty, the morphological forms for the future and the conditional. In the forms *travaillerai(s), finirai(s), coudrai(s),* the infinitive is identifiable; in *enverrai(s), courrai(s)* and *irai(s),* it is not.

50 The future

- **The temporal value of the future**
  The future signals an event that is situated at a future moment in relation to the moment of enunciation:

  Il neigera demain.

  The events occur one after the other in:

  Ils se marieront (d'abord) et auront (ensuite) beaucoup d'enfants.

  They are either simultaneous or alternative in:

  Au cours de leur soirée d'adieu, ils mangeront, boiront et danseront.
  (N.B.: the three events occur at the same time or one after the other)

- **The historical future (*futur historique*)**
  The historical future relates events that took place in the past as if they were to take place at a moment after the moment of enunciation. A historian could, in 2009, write:

  La Première Guerre mondiale finira par éclater en 1914.

- **Other ways of expressing the future: periphrastic constructions**
  The two periphrastic constructions using *aller* or *être sur le point de* + infinitive emphasize the imminence of the event (objective or presented as such). The periphrastic construction with *aller* is called the *futur proche* (see paragraph 3).

  Je vais partir.
  Je suis sur le point de craquer.

51 The conditional expressing both future and past

The morphological form of the conditional has both a mark of the future (the affix *-(e)r-*) and a mark of the past (the affixes *-ais*, *-ait*, *-aient*, and *-i-* of *-ions* and *-iez*, common both to the conditional and the *imparfait*). This in particular explains both the temporal and modal values:

- From a temporal point of view, the conditional expresses a future in the past. In a context where one event occurs after another event in the past, this posterior event is perceived as a future.
- From a modal point of view, it combines modal elements of the future and the *imparfait*, which gives it a hypothetical value.

52 Value of the conditional

- **Use in subordinate clauses**

The conditional is the substitute for the future when the event is seen from the past (when the event follows in time, comes after, a point or event in the past). In this usage, the hypothectical nuance often characteristic of the conditional is not present.

Olivier espérait que Martine viendrait.

verb in the past — **conditional**

In the sentence above, the conditional plays the same role as the future in the sentence below.

Olivier espère que Martine viendra.

verb in the present — **future**

- **Use in autonomous sentences**

The same temporal value of the conditional is observed, in autonomous sentences, to indicate future events in an event related using the past:

Jacques pensait à Marie : viendrait-elle le voir bientôt ?

(Compare to: *Jacques pense à Marie : viendra-t-elle le voir bientôt ?*)

REM: Like the future, the conditional is normally not used in the hypothetical conditional subordinate clause introduced by *si*. Some familiar examples of this use (⊗ *si je voudrais, je pourrais*), judged as incorrect, should be avoided. Yet, the conditional is correct in a subordinate clause used as a direct complement and introduced by *si* (indirect interrogative): *Je me demande si je pourrais le faire.*

53 The two fundamental values of compound verb forms

In relation to the simple verb forms that correspond to them (see paragraph 12), the compound verb forms have two values.

- **Accomplished (perfect) value**
The compound forms indicate an aspectual notion of accomplishment. In the present, the statement:

J'écris ma lettre de réclamation.

indicates that the event is in the process of being done: it is in a non-accomplished state.

But if, in the present moment of enunciation, it is important to indicate that the event has been accomplished, the compound verb form corresponding to the present is used:

J'ai écrit ma lettre de réclamation.

- **Temporal anteriority**
Put into perspective, in the same sentence, with the corresponding simple verb form, the compound verb form indicates anteriority in relation to the simple verb form:

Dès que j'ai écrit ma lettre de réclamation, je l'envoie.

In this situation, the anteriority in relation to the present arises necessarily from the past. This is a temporal past tense value.

The opposition between the simple and compound verb forms is valid for all moods: thus, the past subjunctive could express, according to the context, either an accomplished or anterior value.

54 The *passé composé*

The *passé composé* is a more contentious verb form in French. It has, in fact, two clearly differentiated values that are known traditionally by the same name: the *passé composé*.

- **Expressing an accomplished event in the present**
  In some of its uses, the *passé composé* expresses a present accomplishment (perfect). When it has this value, it is absolutely impossible to replace this verb form with another verb form in the past tense. In fact, it is impossible to replace the *passé composé* with the *imparfait* or the *passé simple* in the following sentence:

  Quand on est seul, on a vite déjeuné.

  The temporal indications furnished by the subordinate clause in the present indicate that the described event is situated in the present. It is therefore dealing with the aspectual value of a present accomplishment.

  This allows the *passé composé* to take on a value of near future as an accomplished lexical event at a point in the near future:

  J'ai terminé dans cinq minutes.
  passé composé

  This sentence signifies that, in five minutes, I will have accomplished the event that I will have finished. It is similar to the value of near future that the present can also take, but as a non-accomplished lexical event:

  Je termine dans cinq minutes.
  present

- **Expressing the past**
  The same morphological structure of the *passé composé* is able to mark a past action. The *passé composé* can thus, without any noticeable difference in meaning, be replaced by the *passé simple*.

  La journaliste a mangé à cinq heures.
  passé composé

  La journaliste mangea à cinq heures.
  passé simple

  These two sentences relate the exact same event. In this use of the past, the *passé composé* is in contrast with the *imparfait* in the same way as the *passé simple* is in contrast with the *imparfait*:

  Les élèves travaillaient quand Marie a fait irruption or *fit irruption.*
  imparfait — passé composé — passé simple

However, compared to the *passé simple*, the *passé composé* gives the impression of the presence of the enunciator.

55 The *plus-que-parfait* and the *passé antérieur*

The *plus-que-parfait* is the compound verb form that corresponds to the *imparfait*, and the *passé antérieur* is the compound verb form that corresponds to the *passé simple*. These two verb forms therefore have the two expected values: an accomplished value and an anterior value.

- **The accomplished aspectual value**
  The events expressed by the verb are presented as being accomplished at a moment in the past.

  Le 20 janvier, j'avais terminé mon travail.
  plus-que-parfait (j'avais terminé)

  Il eut fini en un instant.
  passé antérieur (eut fini)

- **The anterior temporal value**
  The events expressed in the *plus-que-parfait* or in the *passé antérieur* indicate anteriority in relation to those expressed in the *imparfait* or in the *passé simple*.

  Dès qu'il avait terminé son travail, il partait se promener.
  plus-que-parfait (avait terminé)

  The event *terminer le travail* is anterior, further in the past, than that of *se promener*.

  Quand elle eut écrit ses lettres, elle les envoya.
  passé antérieur (eut écrit)

  The event *écrire ses lettres* is anterior, further in the past, than that of *les envoyer*.

- **The *plus-que-parfait*: specific value**
  The *plus-que-parfait* has a past unreal modal value in the subordinate clause introduced by *si* in a hypothetical sentence:

  Si j'avais eu (hier) de l'argent, je t'en aurais donné.
  plus-que-parfait (avais eu) — **past conditional** (aurais donné)

- **The *passé antérieur*: specific uses**
  The *passé antérieur* has the same limits on its use as the *passé simple*: its use in the first and second grammatical persons has become very rare, and the third person is found mainly in the written language.

REM: The *passé antérieur* should not be confused with the *plus-que-parfait* in the subjunctive. In the third person singular, they are often confused in spoken language, and, in the written language, they are only distinguishable from each other by the presence of a circumflex:

il eut écrit – qu'il eût écrit
elle fut revenue – qu'elle fût revenue

56 The *futur antérieur* and the past conditional

The *futur antérieur* and the past conditional are compound verb forms that correspond, respectively, to the future and present conditional. Their values conform to those expressed by the general opposition of compound verb forms to simple verb forms: accomplished aspectual value and anterior temporal value.

- **Values of the *futur antérieur***
  The *futur antérieur* indicates an accomplished event in the future:

J'aurai terminé mon roman à la fin du mois.

It also indicates anteriority in relation to the future:

Dès que Jacques aura fini son travail, il viendra nous voir.

futur antérieur — **future**

- **Temporal values of the past conditional**
  In a subordinate clause where the verb of the main clause is in the past, the past conditional is used instead of the *futur antérieur*. In the sentence:

Il prétend qu'il aura fini aujourd'hui.

verb in the present — ***futur antérieur***

corresponds to:

Il prétendait qu'il aurait fini aujourd'hui.

verb in the past — **past conditional**

- **Modal values of the past conditional**
  In a hypothetical context, the past conditional indicates, in the sentence, a past unreal:

  Si j'avais eu de l'argent hier, je t'en aurais donné.

  plus-que-parfait — **past conditional**

  The individual who pronounces this sentence did not have any money and, as a result, had none to give: this is why it is called a past unreal.

REM: In this type of use, the past conditional as well as the *plus-que-parfait* of the indicative in the subordinate clause are sometimes, in literary usage, both replaced by the *plus-que-parfait* of the subjunctive:

Si j'eusse eu de l'argent, je t'en eusse donné.

This usage is antiquated, which explains the name past conditional 2nd form that once referred to this use of the form of the *plus-que-parfait* in the subjunctive.

REM: The past conditional is never, in principle, used in a subordinate clause expressing a hypothetical conditional introduced by *si*. However, in popular usage, it is sometimes found:

⊗ *« Si j'aurais su, j'aurais pas venu. »* Louis Pergaud

The above use is incorrect and must be avoided, both in the written and spoken languages. The past conditional is thus correct in a subordinate clause functioning as a direct complement introduced by *si* (indirect interrogative):

Je me suis toujours demandé si j'aurais su quoi répondre à cette question.

57 Double compound verb forms

The most frequent of these forms, still fairly rare, consisting of an auxiliary verb in a compound form (see paragraph 2), is the *passé surcomposé*. In modern usage, it is specifically used to indicate anteriority (prior event) to a *passé composé*:

Quand elle a eu terminé son devoir, elle est sortie de la salle.

The *plus-que-parfait surcomposé* is also found at times:

Dès qu'elle avait eu fini son devoir, elle était sortie.

The *futur antérieur surcomposé* is even rarer:

Elle sera sortie dès qu'elle aura eu fini.

58 Tense and mood: a fuzzy boundary

There is no clear boundary between the categories of tense and mood. Some temporal markers (the *imparfait*, the future, and even the present) express mood (modal) values. The conditional, which is today considered part of the indicative mood, was traditionally classified as a mood on its own. In addition, the traditional category of mood includes two series of forms with a clearly differentiated status: the personal moods (indicative, subjunctive, imperative) and impersonal moods (infinitive, participle and gerund). Finally, the categories of tense and mood merge: the subjunctive may be present or *imparfait*, a "past" may relate to the imperative or the participle, etc.

59 Approach to the notion of mood

In these conditions, it is difficult to give a precise definition for the concept of mood.

- **Personal moods**
  For the three personal moods, it is often said that they correspond to three different ways of seeing the action expressed by the verb: the indicative presents it as real, the subjunctive as hypothetical or unreal, and the imperative as an order. However, these differences are often contradicted by actual use. There is nothing real in the indicative *viendra*:

Paul s'est mis en tête l'idée fausse que Jeanne viendra le voir.

There is nothing hypothetical in the subjunctive *travaille*:

Bien qu'il travaille, Jean ne réussit pas.

And the imperative *travaillez* can be interpreted as a condition ("if you work, you will succed") more than a command:

Travaillez : vous réussirez.

- **Impersonal moods**
The three impersonal moods are more homogeneous. They allow the speaker to confer upon a verb (a verb with all its complements and, sometimes, its subject) the general functions normally assumed by a word from another class: noun for the infinitive, adjective for the participle and adverb for the gerund.

- **Moods and tense**
The indicative is characterized by its rich temporal system.

The subjunctive has only four verb tenses.

The imperative and the infinitive have only two tenses.

The participle has three forms: the simple form of the present participle (*travaillant*) and the corresponding compound form (*ayant travaillé*), called *passé composé* past participle, do not pose any particular problem. The third form, simple (*travaillé*), is called the past participle. This participle is used in compound verb forms.

60 INDEX OF GRAMMATICAL TERMS

CONJUGATION TABLES

❶ ❶

verbs ending in **-oindre** | **joindre**

INDICATIF

Présent		Passé composé		
je	joins	j'	ai	joint
tu	joins	tu	as	joint
elle	joint	elle	a	joint
nous	joignons	nous	avons	joint
vous	joignez	vous	avez	joint
ils	joignent	ils	ont	joint

Imparfait		Plus-que-parfait		
je	joignais	j'	avais	joint
tu	joignais	tu	avais	joint
elle	joignait	elle	avait	joint
nous	joignions	nous	avions	joint
vous	joigniez	vous	aviez	joint
ils	joignaient	ils	avaient	joint

Passé simple		Passé antérieur		
je	joignis	j'	eus	joint
tu	joignis	tu	eus	joint
elle	joignit	elle	eut	joint
nous	joignîmes	nous	eûmes	joint
vous	joignîtes	vous	eûtes	joint
ils	joignirent	ils	eurent	joint

Futur simple		Futur antérieur		
je	joindrai	j'	aurai	joint
tu	joindras	tu	auras	joint
elle	joindra	elle	aura	joint
nous	joindrons	nous	aurons	joint
vous	joindrez	vous	aurez	joint
ils	joindront	ils	auront	joint

Conditionnel présent		Conditionnel passé		
je	joindrais	j'	aurais	joint
tu	joindrais	tu	aurais	joint
elle	joindrait	elle	aurait	joint
nous	joindrions	nous	aurions	joint
vous	joindriez	vous	auriez	joint
ils	joindraient	ils	auraient	joint

SUBJONCTIF

Présent		Passé		
que je	joigne	que j'	aie	joint
que tu	joignes	que tu	aies	joint
qu' elle	joigne	qu' elle	ait	joint
que n.	joignions	que n.	ayons	joint
que v.	joigniez	que v.	ayez	joint
qu' ils	joignent	qu' ils	aient	joint

Imparfait		Plus-que-parfait		
que je	joignisse	que j'	eusse	joint
que tu	joignisses	que tu	eusses	joint
qu' elle	joignît	qu' elle	eût	joint
que n.	joignissions	que n.	eussions	joint
que v.	joignissiez	que v.	eussiez	joint
qu' ils	joignissent	qu' ils	eussent	joint

IMPÉRATIF

Présent	Passé	
joins	aie	joint
joignons	ayons	joint
joignez	ayez	joint

INFINITIF

Présent	Passé
joindre	avoir joint

PARTICIPE

Présent	Passé (composé)
joignant	ayant joint
	Passé
	joint

❷ ❻

❹ • ***Conditionnel passé 2ᵉ forme* (2nd form)**: same form as the *plus-que-parfait* of the subjunctive.

❺ • ***Futur proche***: *je vais joindre* (see Grammar of the verb, paragraphs 3 and 50).

- The derived forms of **joindre** (see List of irregular verbs, p. 96 to 98) and the archaic verbs **poindre** and **oindre** follow this pattern of conjugation.
- As an intransitive verb, in the sense of *make a first appeareance*, **poindre** is used almost exclusively in the 3rd person (*le jour point*, *il poindra*, *l'aube poindrait*, *elle a point*). In this context, there is a tendency however to use the regular verb **pointer** instead: *le jour pointe* (= "daylight appears / morning has broken").
- **Oindre** is no longer used except in the following forms: infinitive, *imparfait* of the indicative (*oignait*) and past participle (*oint*, *oints*, *ointe*, *ointes*).

❽

HOW TO USE THE CONJUGATION TABLE

❶ Verb tenses.
Simple and compound tenses are placed side by side for easy comparison and contrast.

❷ Blue is used to indicate stem change in the verb.
The stem change is highlighted in blue. For exemple, in the forms *joignons*, *joignez* and *joignent* of the *indicatif présent* of the verb **joindre**, the stem *join-* changes to *joign-*.

❸ Bold blue is used to facilitate recall of spelling difficulties.
Specific spelling complexities appear in **bold blue** as, for example, in the forms *joign**i**ons* and *joign**i**ez* (*indicatif imparfait*) to emphasize the *-gn**i**-* spelling, in contrast to *joignons* and *joignez* (*indicatif présent*) without the **i**. Note that, in spoken language, this difference is not readily distinguishable.

❹ The *conditionnel passé 2e forme* (2nd form).
As this form is the same as that of the *plus-que-parfait* of the subjunctive, a simple cross reference is made at the end of each table.

❺ The *futur proche* (near future).
Formed with two verbs, ALLER followed by the INFINITIVE (see Grammar of the verb, paragraphs 3 and 50), it refers to time close to the present (a sort of imminent future). The first person is given as an example.

❻ The conjunction *que*.
This is not really part of the verb but is used to introduce the subjunctive and to distinguish it from the indicative (although in many cases the forms are identical).

❼ Impersonal modes.
The infinitive and the participle are highlighted in blue.

❽ The past participle.
The tables show verb conjugation. To simplify presentation of the past participle, only the generic unmarked form – the masculine singular – is provided. For more information on marked forms – i.e. feminine and plural – see Alphabetical list and paragraphs 36 to 45 of the section entitled Grammar of the verb.

THE VERBS *ÊTRE* AND *AVOIR*

INDICATIF

Présent		Passé composé		
je	suis	j'	ai	été
tu	es	tu	as	été
elle	est	elle	a	été
nous	sommes	nous	avons	été
vous	êtes	vous	avez	été
ils	sont	ils	ont	été

Imparfait		Plus-que-parfait		
j'	étais	j'	avais	été
tu	étais	tu	avais	été
elle	était	elle	avait	été
nous	étions	nous	avions	été
vous	étiez	vous	aviez	été
ils	étaient	ils	avaient	été

Passé simple		Passé antérieur		
je	fus	j'	eus	été
tu	fus	tu	eus	été
elle	fut	elle	eut	été
nous	fûmes	nous	eûmes	été
vous	fûtes	vous	eûtes	été
ils	furent	ils	eurent	été

Futur simple		Futur antérieur		
je	serai	j'	aurai	été
tu	seras	tu	auras	été
elle	sera	elle	aura	été
nous	serons	nous	aurons	été
vous	serez	vous	aurez	été
ils	seront	ils	auront	été

Conditionnel présent		Conditionnel passé		
je	serais	j'	aurais	été
tu	serais	tu	aurais	été
elle	serait	elle	aurait	été
nous	serions	nous	aurions	été
vous	seriez	vous	auriez	été
ils	seraient	ils	auraient	été

SUBJONCTIF

Présent		Passé		
que je	sois	que j'	aie	été
que tu	sois	que tu	aies	été
qu' elle	soit	qu' elle	ait	été
que n.	soyons	que n.	ayons	été
que v.	soyez	que v.	ayez	été
qu' ils	soient	qu' ils	aient	été

Imparfait		Plus-que-parfait		
que je	fusse	que j'	eusse	été
que tu	fusses	que tu	eusses	été
qu' elle	fût	qu' elle	eût	été
que n.	fussions	que n.	eussions	été
que v.	fussiez	que v.	eussiez	été
qu' ils	fussent	qu' ils	eussent	été

IMPÉRATIF

Présent	Passé	
sois	aie	été
soyons	ayons	été
soyez	ayez	été

INFINITIF

Présent	Passé
être	avoir été

PARTICIPE

Présent	Passé (composé)
étant	ayant été
	Passé
	été

***Conditionnel passé 2e forme* (2nd form)**: same form as the *plus-que-parfait* of the subjunctive.
Futur proche: *je vais être* (see Grammar of the verb, paragraphs 3 and 50).

- **Être** is used as an auxiliary verb in the following contexts:
  1. in the passive voice: *il est aimé, il a été aimé* (see Table 63);
  2. in compound forms of pronominal verbs: *il s'est blessé* (see Table 64);
  3. with some verbs used intransitively; these appear on the alphabetical list of verbs at the end of this book with the indication **être**.
- Some verbs are conjugated sometimes with **être** sometimes with **avoir**; in the alphabetical list, the appropriate auxiliary is indicated (see also Grammar of the verb, paragraph 15).
- The past participle *été* is invariable.

62 avoir

INDICATIF

Présent		Passé composé		
j'	ai	j'	ai	eu
tu	as	tu	as	eu
elle	a	elle	a	eu
nous	avons	nous	avons	eu
vous	avez	vous	avez	eu
ils	ont	ils	ont	eu

Imparfait		Plus-que-parfait		
j'	avais	j'	avais	eu
tu	avais	tu	avais	eu
elle	avait	elle	avait	eu
nous	avions	nous	avions	eu
vous	aviez	vous	aviez	eu
ils	avaient	ils	avaient	eu

Passé simple		Passé antérieur		
j'	eus	j'	eus	eu
tu	eus	tu	eus	eu
elle	eut	elle	eut	eu
nous	eûmes	nous	eûmes	eu
vous	eûtes	vous	eûtes	eu
ils	eurent	ils	eurent	eu

Futur simple		Futur antérieur		
j'	aurai	j'	aurai	eu
tu	auras	tu	auras	eu
elle	aura	elle	aura	eu
nous	aurons	nous	aurons	eu
vous	aurez	vous	aurez	eu
ils	auront	ils	auront	eu

Conditionnel présent		Conditionnel passé		
j'	aurais	j'	aurais	eu
tu	aurais	tu	aurais	eu
elle	aurait	elle	aurait	eu
nous	aurions	nous	aurions	eu
vous	auriez	vous	auriez	eu
ils	auraient	ils	auraient	eu

SUBJONCTIF

Présent		Passé		
que j'	aie	que j'	aie	eu
que tu	aies	que tu	aies	eu
qu' elle	ait	qu' elle	ait	eu
que n.	ayons	que n.	ayons	eu
que v.	ayez	que v.	ayez	eu
qu' ils	aient	qu' ils	aient	eu

Imparfait		Plus-que-parfait		
que j'	eusse	que j'	eusse	eu
que tu	eusses	que tu	eusses	eu
qu' elle	eût	qu' elle	eût	eu
que n.	eussions	que n.	eussions	eu
que v.	eussiez	que v.	eussiez	eu
qu' ils	eussent	qu' ils	eussent	eu

IMPÉRATIF

Présent	Passé	
aie	aie	eu
ayons	ayons	eu
ayez	ayez	eu

INFINITIF

Présent	Passé
avoir	avoir eu

PARTICIPE

Présent	Passé (composé)
ayant	ayant eu
	Passé
	eu

***Conditionnel passé 2e forme* (2nd form)**: same form as the *plus-que-parfait* of the subjunctive.
Futur proche: *je vais avoir* (see Grammar of the verb, paragraphs 3 and 50).

- **Avoir** is a transitive verb when it has a direct complement: *j'ai un beau livre.*
  It is used as an auxiliary (in compound verb tenses) to direct transitive verbs which are not pronominal and also a number of indirect transitive verbs and intransitive verbs. In the alphabetical list at the end of this book, the small number of verbs which take the auxiliary **être** are indicated accordingly.

THE PASSIVE FORM: *ÊTRE AIMÉ*

63 conjugation pattern of a verb in the passive | être aimé

INDICATIF

Présent			Passé composé		
je	suis	aimé	j'	ai	été aimé
tu	es	aimé	tu	as	été aimé
elle	est	aimée	elle	a	été aimée
nous	sommes	aimés	nous	avons	été aimés
vous	êtes	aimés	vous	avez	été aimés
ils	sont	aimés	ils	ont	été aimés

Imparfait			Plus-que-parfait		
j'	étais	aimé	j'	avais	été aimé
tu	étais	aimé	tu	avais	été aimé
elle	était	aimée	elle	avait	été aimée
nous	étions	aimés	nous	avions	été aimés
vous	étiez	aimés	vous	aviez	été aimés
ils	étaient	aimés	ils	avaient	été aimés

Passé simple			Passé antérieur		
je	fus	aimé	j'	eus	été aimé
tu	fus	aimé	tu	eus	été aimé
elle	fut	aimée	elle	eut	été aimée
nous	fûmes	aimés	nous	eûmes	été aimés
vous	fûtes	aimés	vous	eûtes	été aimés
ils	furent	aimés	ils	eurent	été aimés

Futur simple			Futur antérieur		
je	serai	aimé	j'	aurai	été aimé
tu	seras	aimé	tu	auras	été aimé
elle	sera	aimée	elle	aura	été aimée
nous	serons	aimés	nous	aurons	été aimés
vous	serez	aimés	vous	aurez	été aimés
ils	seront	aimés	ils	auront	été aimés

Conditionnel présent			Conditionnel passé		
je	serais	aimé	j'	aurais	été aimé
tu	serais	aimé	tu	aurais	été aimé
elle	serait	aimée	elle	aurait	été aimée
nous	serions	aimés	nous	aurions	été aimés
vous	seriez	aimés	vous	auriez	été aimés
ils	seraient	aimés	ils	auraient	été aimés

SUBJONCTIF

Présent			Passé		
que je	sois	aimé	que j'	aie	été aimé
que tu	sois	aimé	que tu	aies	été aimé
qu' elle	soit	aimée	qu' elle	ait	été aimée
que n.	soyons	aimés	que n.	ayons	été aimés
que v.	soyez	aimés	que v.	ayez	été aimés
qu' ils	soient	aimés	qu' ils	aient	été aimés

Imparfait			Plus-que-parfait		
que je	fusse	aimé	que j'	eusse	été aimé
que tu	fusses	aimé	que tu	eusses	été aimé
qu' elle	fût	aimée	qu' elle	eût	été aimée
que n.	fussions	aimés	que n.	eussions	été aimés
que v.	fussiez	aimés	que v.	eussiez	été aimés
qu' ils	fussent	aimés	qu' ils	eussent	été aimés

IMPÉRATIF

Présent		Passé	
sois	aimé	aie	été aimé
soyons	aimés	ayons	été aimés
soyez	aimés	ayez	été aimés

INFINITIF

Présent	Passé
être aimé	avoir été aimé

PARTICIPE

Présent	Passé (composé)
étant aimé	ayant été aimé
	Passé
	été aimé

***Conditionnel passé 2e forme* (2nd form)**: same form as the *plus-que-parfait* of the subjunctive.
Futur proche: *je vais être aimé* (see Grammar of the verb, paragraphs 3 and 50).

- For information on the passive, see Grammar of the verb, paragraphs 2 and 9.
- In the passive, the past participle of the verb always agrees with the subject: *Elle est aimée.*

THE PROMINAL CONSTRUCTIONS: *SE LAVER*

64 conjugation pattern of a pronominal verb | se laver

INDICATIF

Présent			Passé composé			
je	me	lave	je	me	suis	lavé
tu	te	laves	tu	t'	es	lavé
elle	se	lave	elle	s'	est	lavée
n.	nous	lavons	n.	nous	sommes	lavés
v.	vous	lavez	v.	vous	êtes	lavés
ils	se	lavent	ils	se	sont	lavés

Imparfait			Plus-que-parfait			
je	me	lavais	je	m'	étais	lavé
tu	te	lavais	tu	t'	étais	lavé
elle	se	lavait	elle	s'	était	lavée
n.	nous	lavions	n.	nous	étions	lavés
v.	vous	laviez	v.	vous	étiez	lavés
ils	se	lavaient	ils	s'	étaient	lavés

Passé simple			Passé antérieur			
je	me	lavai	je	me	fus	lavé
tu	te	lavas	tu	te	fus	lavé
elle	se	lava	elle	se	fut	lavée
n.	nous	lavâmes	n.	nous	fûmes	lavés
v.	vous	lavâtes	v.	vous	fûtes	lavés
ils	se	lavèrent	ils	se	furent	lavés

Futur simple			Futur antérieur			
je	me	laverai	je	me	serai	lavé
tu	te	laveras	tu	te	seras	lavé
elle	se	lavera	elle	se	sera	lavée
n.	nous	laverons	n.	nous	serons	lavés
v.	vous	laverez	v.	vous	serez	lavés
ils	se	laveront	ils	se	seront	lavés

Conditionnel présent			Conditionnel passé			
je	me	laverais	je	me	serais	lavé
tu	te	laverais	tu	te	serais	lavé
elle	se	laverait	elle	se	serait	lavée
n.	nous	laverions	n.	nous	serions	lavés
v.	vous	laveriez	v.	vous	seriez	lavés
ils	se	laveraient	ils	se	seraient	lavés

SUBJONCTIF

Présent			Passé			
que je	me	lave	que je	me	sois	lavé
que tu	te	laves	que tu	te	sois	lavé
qu' elle	se	lave	qu' elle	se	soit	lavée
que n.	n.	lavions	que n.	n.	soyons	lavés
que v.	v.	laviez	que v.	v.	soyez	lavés
qu' ils	se	lavent	qu' ils	se	soient	lavés

Imparfait			Plus-que-parfait			
que je	me	lavasse	que je	me	fusse	lavé
que tu	te	lavasses	que tu	te	fusses	lavé
qu' elle	se	lavât	qu' elle	se	fût	lavée
que n.	n.	lavassions	que n.	n.	fussions	lavés
que v.	v.	lavassiez	que v.	v.	fussiez	lavés
qu' ils	se	lavassent	qu' ils	se	fussent	lavés

IMPÉRATIF

Présent	Passé	
lave-toi	sois-toi	lavé
lavons-nous	soyons-nous	lavés
lavez-vous	soyez-vous	lavés

INFINITIF

Présent	Passé
se laver	s'être lavé

PARTICIPE

Présent	Passé (composé)
se lavant	s'étant lavé
	Passé
	lavé

***Conditionnel passé 2e forme* (2nd form)**: same form as the *plus-que-parfait* of the subjunctive.
Futur proche: *je vais me laver* (see Grammar of the verb, paragraphs 3 and 50).

- For complete information on pronominal constructions, see Grammar of the verb, paragraphs 2, 9 and 14.
- In the alphabetical list at the end of this book, pronominal verbs are followed by the letter **P**. They are all conjugated with the auxiliary **être**.
- For agreement of the past participle of pronominal verbs, see Grammar of the verb, paragraph 39. The past participle of some pronominal verbs is always invariable: *ils se sont nui*. In the alphabetical list, these verbs are labeled **p. p. invariable**.

REGULAR VERBS

list of regular verbs

Regular verbs fall into two types or categories: ER-verbs (ending in -er) and IR-verbs (ending in -ir). The list below indicates the verb types used to exemplify the conjugation pattern of all regular verbs.

- **Regular verbs ending in** -er

65	aimer	verbs ending in **-er**
66	placer	verbs ending in **-cer**
67	manger	verbs ending in **-ger**
68	peser	verbs ending in **-e(.)er**
69	céder	verbs ending in **-é(.)er**
70	jeter	verbs ending in **-eter** doubling the *t* before a silent or mute *e*
71	acheter	verbs ending in **-eter** changing *e* to *è* before a silent or mute syllable
72	appeler	verbs ending in **-eler** doubling the *l* before a silent or mute *e*
73	modeler	verbs ending in **-eler** changing *e* to *è* before a silent or mute syllable
74	créer	verbs ending in **-éer**
75	siéger	verbs ending in **-éger**
76	crier	verbs ending in **-ier**
77	payer	verbs ending in **-ayer**
78	broyer	verbs ending in **-oyer** (except *envoyer* and *renvoyer*)
79	essuyer	verbs ending in **-uyer**
80	envoyer	–

- **Regular verbs ending in** -ir

81	finir	verbs ending in **-ir**
82	haïr	–

aimer

INDICATIF

Présent		Passé composé		
j'	aime	j'	ai	aimé
tu	aimes	tu	as	aimé
elle	aime	elle	a	aimé
nous	aimons	nous	avons	aimé
vous	aimez	vous	avez	aimé
ils	aiment	ils	ont	aimé

Imparfait		Plus-que-parfait		
j'	aimais	j'	avais	aimé
tu	aimais	tu	avais	aimé
elle	aimait	elle	avait	aimé
nous	aimions	nous	avions	aimé
vous	aimiez	vous	aviez	aimé
ils	aimaient	ils	avaient	aimé

Passé simple		Passé antérieur		
j'	aimai	j'	eus	aimé
tu	aimas	tu	eus	aimé
elle	aima	elle	eut	aimé
nous	aimâmes	nous	eûmes	aimé
vous	aimâtes	vous	eûtes	aimé
ils	aimèrent	ils	eurent	aimé

Futur simple		Futur antérieur		
j'	aimerai	j'	aurai	aimé
tu	aimeras	tu	auras	aimé
elle	aimera	elle	aura	aimé
nous	aimerons	nous	aurons	aimé
vous	aimerez	vous	aurez	aimé
ils	aimeront	ils	auront	aimé

Conditionnel présent		Conditionnel passé		
j'	aimerais	j'	aurais	aimé
tu	aimerais	tu	aurais	aimé
elle	aimerait	elle	aurait	aimé
nous	aimerions	nous	aurions	aimé
vous	aimeriez	vous	auriez	aimé
ils	aimeraient	ils	auraient	aimé

SUBJONCTIF

Présent		Passé		
que j'	aime	que j'	aie	aimé
que tu	aimes	que tu	aies	aimé
qu' elle	aime	qu' elle	ait	aimé
que n.	aimions	que n.	ayons	aimé
que v.	aimiez	que v.	ayez	aimé
qu' ils	aiment	qu' ils	aient	aimé

Imparfait		Plus-que-parfait		
que j'	aimasse	que j'	eusse	aimé
que tu	aimasses	que tu	eusses	aimé
qu' elle	aimât	qu' elle	eût	aimé
que n.	aimassions	que n.	eussions	aimé
que v.	aimassiez	que v.	eussiez	aimé
qu' ils	aimassent	qu' ils	eussent	aimé

IMPÉRATIF

Présent	Passé	
aime	aie	aimé
aimons	ayons	aimé
aimez	ayez	aimé

INFINITIF

Présent	Passé
aimer	avoir aimé

PARTICIPE

Présent	Passé (composé)
aimant	ayant aimé
	Passé
	aimé

***Conditionnel passé 2e forme* (2nd form)**: same form as the *plus-que-parfait* of the subjunctive.
Futur proche: *je vais aimer* (see Grammar of the verb, paragraphs 3 and 50).

- For verbs conjugated with the auxiliary **être**, see conjugation of the verb **aller** in Table 83.
- In the imperative - 2nd person singular, the verb takes an **s** before the pronouns **y** and **en**: *penses-y, chantes-en encore*, but *ose y mettre de l'ordre, chante en français.*
- In the interrogative, the following written forms exist: *Aimé-je ?* or *Aimè-je ?* also *Aime-t-il ?* (see Grammar of the verb, paragraph 16).

placer

INDICATIF

Présent		Passé composé		
je	place	j'	ai	placé
tu	places	tu	as	placé
elle	place	elle	a	placé
nous	plaçons	nous	avons	placé
vous	placez	vous	avez	placé
ils	placent	ils	ont	placé

Imparfait		Plus-que-parfait		
je	plaçais	j'	avais	placé
tu	plaçais	tu	avais	placé
elle	plaçait	elle	avait	placé
nous	placions	nous	avions	placé
vous	placiez	vous	aviez	placé
ils	plaçaient	ils	avaient	placé

Passé simple		Passé antérieur		
je	plaçai	j'	eus	placé
tu	plaças	tu	eus	placé
elle	plaça	elle	eut	placé
nous	plaçâmes	nous	eûmes	placé
vous	plaçâtes	vous	eûtes	placé
ils	placèrent	ils	eurent	placé

Futur simple		Futur antérieur		
je	placerai	j'	aurai	placé
tu	placeras	tu	auras	placé
elle	placera	elle	aura	placé
nous	placerons	nous	aurons	placé
vous	placerez	vous	aurez	placé
ils	placeront	ils	auront	placé

Conditionnel présent		Conditionnel passé		
je	placerais	j'	aurais	placé
tu	placerais	tu	aurais	placé
elle	placerait	elle	aurait	placé
nous	placerions	nous	aurions	placé
vous	placeriez	vous	auriez	placé
ils	placeraient	ils	auraient	placé

SUBJONCTIF

Présent		Passé		
que je	place	que j'	aie	placé
que tu	places	que tu	aies	placé
qu'elle	place	qu'elle	ait	placé
que n.	placions	que n.	ayons	placé
que v.	placiez	que v.	ayez	placé
qu' ils	placent	qu' ils	aient	placé

Imparfait		Plus-que-parfait		
que je	plaçasse	que j'	eusse	placé
que tu	plaçasses	que tu	eusses	placé
qu'elle	plaçât	qu'elle	eût	placé
que n.	plaçassions	que n.	eussions	placé
que v.	plaçassiez	que v.	eussiez	placé
qu' ils	plaçassent	qu' ils	eussent	placé

IMPÉRATIF

Présent	Passé	
place	aie	placé
plaçons	ayons	placé
placez	ayez	placé

INFINITIF

Présent	Passé
placer	avoir placé

PARTICIPE

Présent	Passé (composé)
plaçant	ayant placé
	Passé
	placé

***Conditionnel passé 2e forme* (2nd form)**: same form as the *plus-que-parfait* of the subjunctive.
Futur proche: *je vais placer* (see Grammar of the verb, paragraphs 3 and 50).

- Verbs ending in -**cer** take a cedilla under the **c** before the vowels **a** and **o**: *nous commençons, tu commenças*, to maintain the soft **c** [s] sound.
- For verbs ending in -**ecer**, see also Table 68. **Dépecer**: *je dépèce, nous dépeçons.*
- For verbs ending in -**écer**, see also Table 69. **Rapiécer**: *je rapièce, nous rapiéçons.*

INDICATIF

Présent		Passé composé		
je	mange	j'	ai	mangé
tu	manges	tu	as	mangé
elle	mange	elle	a	mangé
nous	man**ge**ons	nous	avons	mangé
vous	mangez	vous	avez	mangé
ils	mangent	ils	ont	mangé

Imparfait		Plus-que-parfait		
je	man**ge**ais	j'	avais	mangé
tu	man**ge**ais	tu	avais	mangé
elle	man**ge**ait	elle	avait	mangé
nous	mangions	nous	avions	mangé
vous	mangiez	vous	aviez	mangé
ils	man**ge**aient	ils	avaient	mangé

Passé simple		Passé antérieur		
je	man**ge**ai	j'	eus	mangé
tu	man**ge**as	tu	eus	mangé
elle	man**ge**a	elle	eut	mangé
nous	man**ge**âmes	nous	eûmes	mangé
vous	man**ge**âtes	vous	eûtes	mangé
ils	mangèrent	ils	eurent	mangé

Futur simple		Futur antérieur		
je	mangerai	j'	aurai	mangé
tu	mangeras	tu	auras	mangé
elle	mangera	elle	aura	mangé
nous	mangerons	nous	aurons	mangé
vous	mangerez	vous	aurez	mangé
ils	mangeront	ils	auront	mangé

Conditionnel présent		Conditionnel passé		
je	mangerais	j'	aurais	mangé
tu	mangerais	tu	aurais	mangé
elle	mangerait	elle	aurait	mangé
nous	mangerions	nous	aurions	mangé
vous	mangeriez	vous	auriez	mangé
ils	mangeraient	ils	auraient	mangé

SUBJONCTIF

Présent		Passé		
que je	mange	que j'	aie	mangé
que tu	manges	que tu	aies	mangé
qu' elle	mange	qu' elle	ait	mangé
que n.	mangions	que n.	ayons	mangé
que v.	mangiez	que v.	ayez	mangé
qu' ils	mangent	qu' ils	aient	mangé

Imparfait		Plus-que-parfait		
que je	man**ge**asse	que j'	eusse	mangé
que tu	man**ge**asses	que tu	eusses	mangé
qu' elle	man**ge**ât	qu'elle	eût	mangé
que n.	man**ge**assions	que n.	eussions	mangé
que v.	man**ge**assiez	que v.	eussiez	mangé
qu' ils	man**ge**assent	qu' ils	eussent	mangé

IMPÉRATIF

Présent	Passé	
mange	aie	mangé
man**ge**ons	ayons	mangé
mangez	ayez	mangé

INFINITIF

Présent	Passé
manger	avoir mangé

PARTICIPE

Présent	Passé (composé)
man**ge**ant	ayant mangé
	Passé
	mangé

***Conditionnel passé 2ᵉ forme* (2nd form)**: same form as the *plus-que-parfait* of the subjunctive.
Futur proche: *je vais manger* (See Grammar of the verb, paragraphs 3 and 50).

- Verbs ending in **-ger** retain the **e** after the **g** before the vowels **a** and **o**: *nous jugeons, tu jugeas*, to conserve the soft **g** sound [ʒ] throughout the conjugation.
(Verbs ending in **-guer** retain the **u** in all forms.)
- For verbs ending in **-éger**, see Table 75.

68 verbs with a silent or mute *e* in the penultimate syllable of the infinitive: verbs with -e(.)er — peser

INDICATIF

Présent		Passé composé		
je	pèse	j'	ai	pesé
tu	pèses	tu	as	pesé
elle	pèse	elle	a	pesé
nous	pesons	nous	avons	pesé
vous	pesez	vous	avez	pesé
ils	pèsent	ils	ont	pesé

Imparfait		Plus-que-parfait		
je	pesais	j'	avais	pesé
tu	pesais	tu	avais	pesé
elle	pesait	elle	avait	pesé
nous	pesions	nous	avions	pesé
vous	pesiez	vous	aviez	pesé
ils	pesaient	ils	avaient	pesé

Passé simple		Passé antérieur		
je	pesai	j'	eus	pesé
tu	pesas	tu	eus	pesé
elle	pesa	elle	eut	pesé
nous	pesâmes	nous	eûmes	pesé
vous	pesâtes	vous	eûtes	pesé
ils	pesèrent	ils	eurent	pesé

Futur simple		Futur antérieur		
je	pèserai	j'	aurai	pesé
tu	pèseras	tu	auras	pesé
elle	pèsera	elle	aura	pesé
nous	pèserons	nous	aurons	pesé
vous	pèserez	vous	aurez	pesé
ils	pèseront	ils	auront	pesé

Conditionnel présent		Conditionnel passé		
je	pèserais	j'	aurais	pesé
tu	pèserais	tu	aurais	pesé
elle	pèserait	elle	aurait	pesé
nous	pèserions	nous	aurions	pesé
vous	pèseriez	vous	auriez	pesé
ils	pèseraient	ils	auraient	pesé

SUBJONCTIF

Présent		Passé		
que je	pèse	que j'	aie	pesé
que tu	pèses	que tu	aies	pesé
qu' elle	pèse	qu' elle	ait	pesé
que n.	pesions	que n.	ayons	pesé
que v.	pesiez	que v.	ayez	pesé
qu' ils	pèsent	qu' ils	aient	pesé

Imparfait		Plus-que-parfait		
que je	pesasse	que j'	eusse	pesé
que tu	pesasses	que tu	eusses	pesé
qu' elle	pesât	qu' elle	eût	pesé
que n.	pesassions	que n.	eussions	pesé
que v.	pesassiez	que v.	eussiez	pesé
qu' ils	pesassent	qu' ils	eussent	pesé

IMPÉRATIF

Présent	Passé	
pèse	aie	pesé
pesons	ayons	pesé
pesez	ayez	pesé

INFINITIF

Présent	Passé
peser	avoir pesé

PARTICIPE

Présent	Passé (composé)
pesant	ayant pesé
	Passé
	pesé

***Conditionnel passé 2e forme* (2nd form)**: same form as the *plus-que-parfait* of the subjunctive.
Futur proche: *je vais peser* (see Grammar of the verb, paragraphs 3 and 50).

- Verbs in **-ecer** (see also Table 66), **-emer**, **-ener**, **-erer**, **-eser**, **-ever**, **-evrer**.
  With these verbs – like **lever** – the silent **e** in the penultimate syllable of the infinitive becomes an open **e** (**è**) before a silent syllable, including before the endings **-erai...**, **-erais...** of the future and the present conditional: *je lève, je lèverai, je lèverais*.
- For verbs ending in **-eler**, **-eter**, see Tables 70, 71, 72 and 73.

céder

INDICATIF

Présent		Passé composé		
je	cède	j'	ai	cédé
tu	cèdes	tu	as	cédé
elle	cède	elle	a	cédé
nous	cédons	nous	avons	cédé
vous	cédez	vous	avez	cédé
ils	cèdent	ils	ont	cédé

Imparfait		Plus-que-parfait		
je	cédais	j'	avais	cédé
tu	cédais	tu	avais	cédé
elle	cédait	elle	avait	cédé
nous	cédions	nous	avions	cédé
vous	cédiez	vous	aviez	cédé
ils	cédaient	ils	avaient	cédé

Passé simple		Passé antérieur		
je	cédai	j'	eus	cédé
tu	cédas	tu	eus	cédé
elle	céda	elle	eut	cédé
nous	cédâmes	nous	eûmes	cédé
vous	cédâtes	vous	eûtes	cédé
ils	cédèrent	ils	eurent	cédé

Futur simple		/VARIANTE	Futur antérieur		
je	céderai	/cèderai	j'	aurai	cédé
tu	céderas	/cèderas	tu	auras	cédé
elle	cédera	/cèdera	elle	aura	cédé
nous	céderons	/cèderons	nous	aurons	cédé
vous	céderez	/cèderez	vous	aurez	cédé
ils	céderont	/cèderont	ils	auront	cédé

Conditionnel présent		/VARIANTE	Conditionnel passé		
je	céderais	/cèderais	j'	aurais	cédé
tu	céderais	/cèderais	tu	aurais	cédé
elle	céderait	/cèderait	elle	aurait	cédé
nous	céderions	/cèderions	nous	aurions	cédé
vous	céderiez	/cèderiez	vous	auriez	cédé
ils	céderaient	/cèderaient	ils	auraient	cédé

SUBJONCTIF

Présent		Passé		
que je	cède	que j'	aie	cédé
que tu	cèdes	que tu	aies	cédé
qu'elle	cède	qu'elle	ait	cédé
que n.	cédions	que n.	ayons	cédé
que v.	cédiez	que v.	ayez	cédé
qu'ils	cèdent	qu'ils	aient	cédé

Imparfait		Plus-que-parfait		
que je	cédasse	que j'	eusse	cédé
que tu	cédasses	que tu	eusses	cédé
qu'elle	cédât	qu'elle	eût	cédé
que n.	cédassions	que n.	eussions	cédé
que v.	cédassiez	que v.	eussiez	cédé
qu'ils	cédassent	qu'ils	eussent	cédé

IMPÉRATIF

Présent	Passé
cède	aie cédé
cédons	ayons cédé
cédez	ayez cédé

INFINITIF

Présent	Passé
céder	avoir cédé

PARTICIPE

Présent	Passé (composé)
cédant	ayant cédé
	Passé
	cédé

***Conditionnel passé 2e forme* (2nd form)**: same form as the *plus-que-parfait* of the subjunctive.
Futur proche: *je vais céder* (see Grammar of the verb, paragraphs 3 and 50).

- Verbs ending in **-éber**, **-ébrer**, **-écer** (see also Table 66), **-écher**, **-écrer**, **-éder**, **-égler**, **-égner**, **-égrer**, **-éguer**, **-éjer**, **-éler**, **-émer**, **-éner**, **-éper**, **-équer**, **-érer**, **-éser**, **-éter**, **-étrer**, **-éver**, **-évrer**, **-éyer**, etc.
- With these verbs, the closed **e** (**é**) in the penultimate syllable of the infinitive becomes an open **e** (**è**) before the silent syllable: *je cède*. Traditionally, these verbs retain the closed **e** (**é**) in the future and the present conditional, despite the tendency to pronounce it as if it were more open. The French spelling reform approves the use of an open **e** (**è**) in the future and the present conditional. The *Académie française* [French Academy] endorses the form: *je cèderai*.

70 verbs ending in **-eter** which double the *t* before a silent *e* | jeter

INDICATIF

Présent		Passé composé		
je	je**tt**e	j'	ai	jeté
tu	je**tt**es	tu	as	jeté
elle	je**tt**e	elle	a	jeté
nous	jetons	nous	avons	jeté
vous	jetez	vous	avez	jeté
ils	je**tt**ent	ils	ont	jeté

Imparfait		Plus-que-parfait		
je	jetais	j'	avais	jeté
tu	jetais	tu	avais	jeté
elle	jetait	elle	avait	jeté
nous	jetions	nous	avions	jeté
vous	jetiez	vous	aviez	jeté
ils	jetaient	ils	avaient	jeté

Passé simple		Passé antérieur		
je	jetai	j'	eus	jeté
tu	jetas	tu	eus	jeté
elle	jeta	elle	eut	jeté
nous	jetâmes	nous	eûmes	jeté
vous	jetâtes	vous	eûtes	jeté
ils	jetèrent	ils	eurent	jeté

Futur simple		Futur antérieur		
je	je**tt**erai	j'	aurai	jeté
tu	je**tt**eras	tu	auras	jeté
elle	je**tt**era	elle	aura	jeté
nous	je**tt**erons	nous	aurons	jeté
vous	je**tt**erez	vous	aurez	jeté
ils	je**tt**eront	ils	auront	jeté

Conditionnel présent		Conditionnel passé		
je	je**tt**erais	j'	aurais	jeté
tu	je**tt**erais	tu	aurais	jeté
elle	je**tt**erait	elle	aurait	jeté
nous	je**tt**erions	nous	aurions	jeté
vous	je**tt**eriez	vous	auriez	jeté
ils	je**tt**eraient	ils	auraient	jeté

SUBJONCTIF

Présent		Passé		
que je	je**tt**e	que j'	aie	jeté
que tu	je**tt**es	que tu	aies	jeté
qu' elle	je**tt**e	qu' elle	ait	jeté
que n.	jetions	que n.	ayons	jeté
que v.	jetiez	que v.	ayez	jeté
qu' ils	je**tt**ent	qu' ils	aient	jeté

Imparfait		Plus-que-parfait		
que je	jetasse	que j'	eusse	jeté
que tu	jetasses	que tu	eusses	jeté
qu' elle	jetât	qu' elle	eût	jeté
que n.	jetassions	que n.	eussions	jeté
que v.	jetassiez	que v.	eussiez	jeté
qu' ils	jetassent	qu' ils	eussent	jeté

IMPÉRATIF

Présent	Passé	
je**tt**e	aie	jeté
jetons	ayons	jeté
jetez	ayez	jeté

INFINITIF

Présent	Passé
jeter	avoir jeté

PARTICIPE

Présent	Passé (composé)
jetant	ayant jeté
	Passé
	jeté

***Conditionnel passé 2e forme* (2nd form)**: same form as the *plus-que-parfait* of the subjunctive.
Futur proche: *je vais jeter* (see Grammar of the verb, paragraphs 3 and 50).

- Several verbs ending in **-eter** double the **t** before a silent **e**: *je jette*. Other verbs do not double the consonant before the silent **e** but take a grave accent over the **e** preceding the **t**: *j'achète* (see the list of traditional examples in Table 71). However, the French spelling reform authorizes the use of the **è** for all verbs in **-eter** except **jeter** and verbs in the same family (*interjeter, projeter, rejeter*). Hence the following: *elle époussète* (or *elle époussette*) but *elle rejette*.

acheter

INDICATIF

Présent		Passé composé		
j'	achète	j'	ai	acheté
tu	achètes	tu	as	acheté
elle	achète	elle	a	acheté
nous	achetons	nous	avons	acheté
vous	achetez	vous	avez	acheté
ils	achètent	ils	ont	acheté

Imparfait		Plus-que-parfait		
j'	achetais	j'	avais	acheté
tu	achetais	tu	avais	acheté
elle	achetait	elle	avait	acheté
nous	achetions	nous	avions	acheté
vous	achetiez	vous	aviez	acheté
ils	achetaient	ils	avaient	acheté

Passé simple		Passé antérieur		
j'	achetai	j'	eus	acheté
tu	achetas	tu	eus	acheté
elle	acheta	elle	eut	acheté
nous	achetâmes	nous	eûmes	acheté
vous	achetâtes	vous	eûtes	acheté
ils	achetèrent	ils	eurent	acheté

Futur simple		Futur antérieur		
j'	achèterai	j'	aurai	acheté
tu	achèteras	tu	auras	acheté
elle	achètera	elle	aura	acheté
nous	achèterons	nous	aurons	acheté
vous	achèterez	vous	aurez	acheté
ils	achèteront	ils	auront	acheté

Conditionnel présent		Conditionnel passé		
j'	achèterais	j'	aurais	acheté
tu	achèterais	tu	aurais	acheté
elle	achèterait	elle	aurait	acheté
nous	achèterions	nous	aurions	acheté
vous	achèteriez	vous	auriez	acheté
ils	achèteraient	ils	auraient	acheté

SUBJONCTIF

Présent		Passé		
que j'	achète	que j'	aie	acheté
que tu	achètes	que tu	aies	acheté
qu' elle	achète	qu' elle	ait	acheté
que n.	achetions	que n.	ayons	acheté
que v.	achetiez	que v.	ayez	acheté
qu' ils	achètent	qu' ils	aient	acheté

Imparfait		Plus-que-parfait		
que j'	achetasse	que j'	eusse	acheté
que tu	achetasses	que tu	eusses	acheté
qu' elle	achetât	qu' elle	eût	acheté
que n.	achetassions	que n.	eussions	acheté
que v.	achetassiez	que v.	eussiez	acheté
qu' ils	achetassent	qu' ils	eussent	acheté

IMPÉRATIF

Présent	Passé	
achète	aie	acheté
achetons	ayons	acheté
achetez	ayez	acheté

INFINITIF

Présent	Passé
acheter	avoir acheté

PARTICIPE

Présent	Passé (composé)
achetant	ayant acheté
	Passé
	acheté

***Conditionnel passé 2ᵉ forme* (2nd form)**: same form as the *plus-que-parfait* of the subjunctive.
Futur proche: *je vais acheter* (see Grammar of the verb, paragraphs 3 and 50).

- Verbs ending in **-eter** which are conjugated like **acheter** always take a grave accent on the **e** (**è**) which precedes the mute syllable. Traditionally, verbs of this type are: *acheter (préacheter, racheter), bégueter, caleter, corseter, crocheter, émoucheter, fileter, fureter, haleter, moueter, rapiéceter* and *rapièceter*.
- In accordance with the French spelling reform, all other verbs ending in **-eter** except **jeter** (and its derived forms) can be conjugated by changing the **e** to **è**.

72 verbs ending in -eler which double the *l* before a silent *e* — appeler

INDICATIF

Présent		Passé composé		
j'	appe**ll**e	j'	ai	appelé
tu	appe**ll**es	tu	as	appelé
elle	appe**ll**e	elle	a	appelé
nous	appelons	nous	avons	appelé
vous	appelez	vous	avez	appelé
ils	appe**ll**ent	ils	ont	appelé

Imparfait		Plus-que-parfait		
j'	appelais	j'	avais	appelé
tu	appelais	tu	avais	appelé
elle	appelait	elle	avait	appelé
nous	appelions	nous	avions	appelé
vous	appeliez	vous	aviez	appelé
ils	appelaient	ils	avaient	appelé

Passé simple		Passé antérieur		
j'	appelai	j'	eus	appelé
tu	appelas	tu	eus	appelé
elle	appela	elle	eut	appelé
nous	appelâmes	nous	eûmes	appelé
vous	appelâtes	vous	eûtes	appelé
ils	appelèrent	ils	eurent	appelé

Futur simple		Futur antérieur		
j'	appe**ll**erai	j'	aurai	appelé
tu	appe**ll**eras	tu	auras	appelé
elle	appe**ll**era	elle	aura	appelé
nous	appe**ll**erons	nous	aurons	appelé
vous	appe**ll**erez	vous	aurez	appelé
ils	appe**ll**eront	ils	auront	appelé

Conditionnel présent		Conditionnel passé		
j'	appe**ll**erais	j'	aurais	appelé
tu	appe**ll**erais	tu	aurais	appelé
elle	appe**ll**erait	elle	aurait	appelé
nous	appe**ll**erions	nous	aurions	appelé
vous	appe**ll**eriez	vous	auriez	appelé
ils	appe**ll**eraient	ils	auraient	appelé

SUBJONCTIF

Présent		Passé		
que j'	appe**ll**e	que j'	aie	appelé
que tu	appe**ll**es	que tu	aies	appelé
qu'elle	appe**ll**e	qu'elle	ait	appelé
que n.	appelions	que n.	ayons	appelé
que v.	appeliez	que v.	ayez	appelé
qu' ils	appe**ll**ent	qu' ils	aient	appelé

Imparfait		Plus-que-parfait		
que j'	appelasse	que j'	eusse	appelé
que tu	appelasses	que tu	eusses	appelé
qu'elle	appelât	qu'elle	eût	appelé
que n.	appelassions	que n.	eussions	appelé
que v.	appelassiez	que v.	eussiez	appelé
qu' ils	appelassent	qu' ils	eussent	appelé

IMPÉRATIF

Présent	Passé	
appe**ll**e	aie	appelé
appelons	ayons	appelé
appelez	ayez	appelé

INFINITIF

Présent	Passé
appeler	avoir appelé

PARTICIPE

Présent	Passé (composé)
appelant	ayant appelé
	Passé
	appelé

***Conditionnel passé 2e forme* (2nd form)**: same form as the *plus-que-parfait* of the subjunctive.
Futur proche: *je vais appeler* (see Grammar of the verb, paragraphs 3 and 50).

- Several verbs ending in **-eler** double the **l** before a mute **e**: *j'appelle*. Other verbs do not double the consonant; instead they take a grave accent on the **e** preceding the **l**: *je modèle* (see the list of these traditional examples in Table 73). However, the spelling reform admits the use of the **è** for all verbs in **-eler** except **appeler**, **interpeller** (or **interpeler**) and verbs of the same family (*rappeler*...). Hence the forms *il ruissèle* (or *il ruisselle*) but *il appelle*.

modeler

INDICATIF

Présent		Passé composé		
je	modèle	j'	ai	modelé
tu	modèles	tu	as	modelé
elle	modèle	elle	a	modelé
nous	modelons	nous	avons	modelé
vous	modelez	vous	avez	modelé
ils	modèlent	ils	ont	modelé

Imparfait		Plus-que-parfait		
je	modelais	j'	avais	modelé
tu	modelais	tu	avais	modelé
elle	modelait	elle	avait	modelé
nous	modelions	nous	avions	modelé
vous	modeliez	vous	aviez	modelé
ils	modelaient	ils	avaient	modelé

Passé simple		Passé antérieur		
je	modelai	j'	eus	modelé
tu	modelas	tu	eus	modelé
elle	modela	elle	eut	modelé
nous	modelâmes	nous	eûmes	modelé
vous	modelâtes	vous	eûtes	modelé
ils	modelèrent	ils	eurent	modelé

Futur simple		Futur antérieur		
je	modèlerai	j'	aurai	modelé
tu	modèleras	tu	auras	modelé
elle	modèlera	elle	aura	modelé
nous	modèlerons	nous	aurons	modelé
vous	modèlerez	vous	aurez	modelé
ils	modèleront	ils	auront	modelé

Conditionnel présent		Conditionnel passé		
je	modèlerais	j'	aurais	modelé
tu	modèlerais	tu	aurais	modelé
elle	modèlerait	elle	aurait	modelé
nous	modèlerions	nous	aurions	modelé
vous	modèleriez	vous	auriez	modelé
ils	modèleraient	ils	auraient	modelé

SUBJONCTIF

Présent		Passé		
que je	modèle	que j'	aie	modelé
que tu	modèles	que tu	aies	modelé
qu' elle	modèle	qu' elle	ait	modelé
que n.	modelions	que n.	ayons	modelé
que v.	modeliez	que v.	ayez	modelé
qu' ils	modèlent	qu' ils	aient	modelé

Imparfait		Plus-que-parfait		
que je	modelasse	que j'	eusse	modelé
que tu	modelasses	que tu	eusses	modelé
qu' elle	modelât	qu' elle	eût	modelé
que n.	modelassions	que n.	eussions	modelé
que v.	modelassiez	que v.	eussiez	modelé
qu' ils	modelassent	qu' ils	eussent	modelé

IMPÉRATIF

Présent	Passé	
modèle	aie	modelé
modelons	ayons	modelé
modelez	ayez	modelé

INFINITIF

Présent	Passé
modeler	avoir modelé

PARTICIPE

Présent	Passé (composé)
modelant	ayant modelé
	Passé
	modelé

***Conditionnel passé 2e forme* (2nd form)**: same form as the *plus-que-parfait* of the subjunctive.
Futur proche: *je vais modeler* (see Grammar of the verb, paragraphs 3 and 50).

- Verbs ending in **-eler** conjugated like **modeler** always take a grave accent on the **e** preceding a mute **e**. Traditionally such verbs are: *babeler, celer (déceler, receler), ciseler (aciseler), démanteler, drapeler, écarteler, embreler, s'encasteler, épinceler, geler (congeler, décongeler, dégeler, recongeler, regeler, surgeler), handeler, harceler, marteler, modeler (remodeler), peler.*
- According to the spelling reform, all other verbs ending in **-eler** except **appeler**, **interpeller** (or **interpeler**) and their derived forms can be conjugated with the **è**.

INDICATIF

Présent		Passé composé		
je	crée	j'	ai	créé
tu	crées	tu	as	créé
elle	crée	elle	a	créé
nous	créons	nous	avons	créé
vous	créez	vous	avez	créé
ils	créent	ils	ont	créé

Imparfait		Plus-que-parfait		
je	créais	j'	avais	créé
tu	créais	tu	avais	créé
elle	créait	elle	avait	créé
nous	créions	nous	avions	créé
vous	créiez	vous	aviez	créé
ils	créaient	ils	avaient	créé

Passé simple		Passé antérieur		
je	créai	j'	eus	créé
tu	créas	tu	eus	créé
elle	créa	elle	eut	créé
nous	créâmes	nous	eûmes	créé
vous	créâtes	vous	eûtes	créé
ils	créèrent	ils	eurent	créé

Futur simple		Futur antérieur		
je	créerai	j'	aurai	créé
tu	créeras	tu	auras	créé
elle	créera	elle	aura	créé
nous	créerons	nous	aurons	créé
vous	créerez	vous	aurez	créé
ils	créeront	ils	auront	créé

Conditionnel présent		Conditionnel passé		
je	créerais	j'	aurais	créé
tu	créerais	tu	aurais	créé
elle	créerait	elle	aurait	créé
nous	créerions	nous	aurions	créé
vous	créeriez	vous	auriez	créé
ils	créeraient	ils	auraient	créé

SUBJONCTIF

Présent		Passé		
que je	crée	que j'	aie	créé
que tu	crées	que tu	aies	créé
qu'elle	crée	qu'elle	ait	créé
que n.	créions	que n.	ayons	créé
que v.	créiez	que v.	ayez	créé
qu' ils	créent	qu' ils	aient	créé

Imparfait		Plus-que-parfait		
que je	créasse	que j'	eusse	créé
que tu	créasses	que tu	eusses	créé
qu'elle	créât	qu'elle	eût	créé
que n.	créassions	que n.	eussions	créé
que v.	créassiez	que v.	eussiez	créé
qu' ils	créassent	qu' ils	eussent	créé

IMPÉRATIF

Présent	Passé	
crée	aie	créé
créons	ayons	créé
créez	ayez	créé

INFINITIF

Présent	Passé
créer	avoir créé

PARTICIPE

Présent	Passé (composé)
créant	ayant créé
	Passé
	créé

***Conditionnel passé 2e forme* (2nd form)**: same form as the *plus-que-parfait* of the subjunctive.
Futur proche: *je vais créer* (see Grammar of the verb, paragraphs 3 and 50).

- These are regular verbs. Their only distinctive feature is the double **e** with some persons in the following: present indicative, *passé simple*, future, present conditional, present imperative, present subjunctive, past participle (masculine form), and the triple **e** in the feminine form of the past participle: *créée*.
- With verbs ending in **-éer**, the **e** remains closed (**é**): *je crée, tu crées…*

INDICATIF

Présent		Passé composé		
je	siège	j'	ai	siégé
tu	sièges	tu	as	siégé
elle	siège	elle	a	siégé
nous	siégeons	nous	avons	siégé
vous	siégez	vous	avez	siégé
ils	siègent	ils	ont	siégé

Imparfait		Plus-que-parfait		
je	siégeais	j'	avais	siégé
tu	siégeais	tu	avais	siégé
elle	siégeait	elle	avait	siégé
nous	siégions	nous	avions	siégé
vous	siégiez	vous	aviez	siégé
ils	siégeaient	ils	avaient	siégé

Passé simple		Passé antérieur		
je	siégeai	j'	eus	siégé
tu	siégeas	tu	eus	siégé
elle	siégea	elle	eut	siégé
nous	siégeâmes	nous	eûmes	siégé
vous	siégeâtes	vous	eûtes	siégé
ils	siégèrent	ils	eurent	siégé

Futur simple		/VARIANTE	Futur antérieur		
je	siégerai	/siègerai	j'	aurai	siégé
tu	siégeras	/siègeras	tu	auras	siégé
elle	siégera	/siègera	elle	aura	siégé
nous	siégerons	/siègerons	nous	aurons	siégé
vous	siégerez	/siègerez	vous	aurez	siégé
ils	siégeront	/siègeront	ils	auront	siégé

Conditionnel présent		/VARIANTE	Conditionnel passé		
je	siégerais	/siègerais	j'	aurais	siégé
tu	siégerais	/siègerais	tu	aurais	siégé
elle	siégerait	/siègerait	elle	aurait	siégé
nous	siégerions	/siègerions	nous	aurions	siégé
vous	siégeriez	/siègeriez	vous	auriez	siégé
ils	siégeraient	/siègeraient	ils	auraient	siégé

SUBJONCTIF

Présent		Passé		
que je	siège	que j'	aie	siégé
que tu	sièges	que tu	aies	siégé
qu' elle	siège	qu' elle	ait	siégé
que n.	siégions	que n.	ayons	siégé
que v.	siégiez	que v.	ayez	siégé
qu' ils	siègent	qu' ils	aient	siégé

Imparfait		Plus-que-parfait		
que je	siégeasse	que j'	eusse	siégé
que tu	siégeasses	que tu	eusses	siégé
qu' elle	siégeât	qu' elle	eût	siégé
que n.	siégeassions	que n.	eussions	siégé
que v.	siégeassiez	que v.	eussiez	siégé
qu' ils	siégeassent	qu' ils	eussent	siégé

IMPÉRATIF

Présent	Passé	
siège	aie	siégé
siégeons	ayons	siégé
siégez	ayez	siégé

INFINITIF

Présent	Passé
siéger	avoir siégé

PARTICIPE

Présent	Passé (composé)
siégeant	ayant siégé
	Passé
	siégé

***Conditionnel passé 2e forme* (2nd form)**: same form as the *plus-que-parfait* of the subjunctive.
Futur proche: *je vais siéger* (see Grammar of the verb, paragraphs 3 and 50).

- In verbs ending in **-éger**:
  - The **é** of the stem becomes **è** before a mute **e** even in the future and the present conditional.
  - To keep the soft **g** sound [ʒ], they retain the **e** after the **g** in front of the vowels **a** and **o**.

INDICATIF

Présent		Passé composé		
je	crie	j'	ai	crié
tu	cries	tu	as	crié
elle	crie	elle	a	crié
nous	crions	nous	avons	crié
vous	criez	vous	avez	crié
ils	crient	ils	ont	crié

Imparfait		Plus-que-parfait		
je	criais	j'	avais	crié
tu	criais	tu	avais	crié
elle	criait	elle	avait	crié
nous	criions	nous	avions	crié
vous	criiez	vous	aviez	crié
ils	criaient	ils	avaient	crié

Passé simple		Passé antérieur		
je	criai	j'	eus	crié
tu	crias	tu	eus	crié
elle	cria	elle	eut	crié
nous	criâmes	nous	eûmes	crié
vous	criâtes	vous	eûtes	crié
ils	crièrent	ils	eurent	crié

Futur simple		Futur antérieur		
je	crierai	j'	aurai	crié
tu	crieras	tu	auras	crié
elle	criera	elle	aura	crié
nous	crierons	nous	aurons	crié
vous	crierez	vous	aurez	crié
ils	crieront	ils	auront	crié

Conditionnel présent		Conditionnel passé		
je	crierais	j'	aurais	crié
tu	crierais	tu	aurais	crié
elle	crierait	elle	aurait	crié
nous	crierions	nous	aurions	crié
vous	crieriez	vous	auriez	crié
ils	crieraient	ils	auraient	crié

SUBJONCTIF

Présent		Passé		
que je	crie	que j'	aie	crié
que tu	cries	que tu	aies	crié
qu' elle	crie	qu' elle	ait	crié
que n.	criions	que n.	ayons	crié
que v.	criiez	que v.	ayez	crié
qu' ils	crient	qu' ils	aient	crié

Imparfait		Plus-que-parfait		
que je	criasse	que j'	eusse	crié
que tu	criasses	que tu	eusses	crié
qu' elle	criât	qu' elle	eût	crié
que n.	criassions	que n.	eussions	crié
que v.	criassiez	que v.	eussiez	crié
qu' ils	criassent	qu' ils	eussent	crié

IMPÉRATIF

Présent	Passé	
crie	aie	crié
crions	ayons	crié
criez	ayez	crié

INFINITIF

Présent	Passé
crier	avoir crié

PARTICIPE

Présent	Passé (composé)
criant	ayant crié
	Passé
	crié

***Conditionnel passé 2e forme* (2nd form)**: same form as the *plus-que-parfait* of the subjunctive.
Futur proche: *je vais crier* (see Grammar of the verb, paragraphs 3 and 50).

- These are regular verbs. They exhibit no distinctive feature except for the fact that they have a double **i** in the 1st and 2nd persons in the plural of the *imparfait* of the indicative and the present subjunctive: *criions, criiez*. The double **i** results from the combination of the final **i** of the stem with the initial **i** of the endings of the *imparfait* of the indicative and of the present subjunctive.

INDICATIF

Présent		Passé composé		
je	paie / paye	j'	ai	payé
tu	paies / payes	tu	as	payé
elle	paie / paye	elle	a	payé
nous	payons	nous	avons	payé
vous	payez	vous	avez	payé
ils	paient / payent	ils	ont	payé

Imparfait		Plus-que-parfait		
je	payais	j'	avais	payé
tu	payais	tu	avais	payé
elle	payait	elle	avait	payé
nous	pay**i**ons	nous	avions	payé
vous	pay**i**ez	vous	aviez	payé
ils	payaient	ils	avaient	payé

Passé simple		Passé antérieur		
je	payai	j'	eus	payé
tu	payas	tu	eus	payé
elle	paya	elle	eut	payé
nous	payâmes	nous	eûmes	payé
vous	payâtes	vous	eûtes	payé
ils	payèrent	ils	eurent	payé

Futur simple		Futur antérieur		
je	pai**e**rai / pay**e**rai	j'	aurai	payé
tu	pai**e**ras / pay**e**ras	tu	auras	payé
elle	pai**e**ra / pay**e**ra	elle	aura	payé
nous	pai**e**rons / pay**e**rons	nous	aurons	payé
vous	pai**e**rez / pay**e**rez	vous	aurez	payé
ils	pai**e**ront / pay**e**ront	ils	auront	payé

Conditionnel présent		Conditionnel passé		
je	pai**e**rais / pay**e**rais	j'	aurais	payé
tu	pai**e**rais / pay**e**rais	tu	aurais	payé
elle	pai**e**rait / pay**e**rait	elle	aurait	payé
nous	pai**e**rions / pay**e**rions	nous	aurions	payé
vous	pai**e**riez / pay**e**riez	vous	auriez	payé
ils	pai**e**raient / pay**e**raient	ils	auraient	payé

SUBJONCTIF

Présent		Passé		
que je	paie / paye	que j'	aie	payé
que tu	paies / payes	que tu	aies	payé
qu'elle	paie / paye	qu'elle	ait	payé
que n.	pay**i**ons	que n.	ayons	payé
que v.	pay**i**ez	que v.	ayez	payé
qu'ils	paient / payent	qu'ils	aient	payé

Imparfait		Plus-que-parfait		
que je	payasse	que j'	eusse	payé
que tu	payasses	que tu	eusses	payé
qu'elle	payât	qu'elle	eût	payé
que n.	payassions	que n.	eussions	payé
que v.	payassiez	que v.	eussiez	payé
qu'ils	payassent	qu'ils	eussent	payé

IMPÉRATIF

Présent	Passé	
paye / paie	aie	payé
payons	ayons	payé
payez	ayez	payé

INFINITIF

Présent	Passé
payer	avoir payé

PARTICIPE

Présent	Passé (composé)
payant	ayant payé
	Passé
	payé

***Conditionnel passé 2e forme* (2nd form)**: same form as the *plus-que-parfait* of the subjunctive.
Futur proche: *je vais payer* (see Grammar of the verb, paragraphs 3 and 50).

- Verbs in **-ayer** may: 1. keep the **y** throughout the conjugation; 2. replace the **y** by an **i** before a silent **e**, i.e. before the endings **-e**, **-es**, **-ent**, **-erai** (**-eras...**), **-erais** (**-erait...**): *je paye* (pronounced [pɛj]) or *je paie* (pronounced [pɛ]).
- Note that the **i** is always present after the **y** in the first two persons of the *imparfait* of the indicative and of the present subjunctive.
- Verbs in **-eyer** (**grasseyer**, **faseyer**, **capeyer**...) keep the **y** throughout the conjugation.
- The verb **bayer** maintains the **y** throughout the conjugation.

78 verbs ending in -oyer[1] | broyer

INDICATIF

Présent		Passé composé		
je	broi**e**	j'	ai	broyé
tu	broi**es**	tu	as	broyé
elle	broi**e**	elle	a	broyé
nous	broyons	nous	avons	broyé
vous	broyez	vous	avez	broyé
ils	broi**ent**	ils	ont	broyé

Imparfait		Plus-que-parfait		
je	broyais	j'	avais	broyé
tu	broyais	tu	avais	broyé
elle	broyait	elle	avait	broyé
nous	broy**i**ons	nous	avions	broyé
vous	broy**i**ez	vous	aviez	broyé
ils	broyaient	ils	avaient	broyé

Passé simple		Passé antérieur		
je	broyai	j'	eus	broyé
tu	broyas	tu	eus	broyé
elle	broya	elle	eut	broyé
nous	broyâmes	nous	eûmes	broyé
vous	broyâtes	vous	eûtes	broyé
ils	broyèrent	ils	eurent	broyé

Futur simple		Futur antérieur		
je	broi**er**ai	j'	aurai	broyé
tu	broi**er**as	tu	auras	broyé
elle	broi**er**a	elle	aura	broyé
nous	broi**er**ons	nous	aurons	broyé
vous	broi**er**ez	vous	aurez	broyé
ils	broi**er**ont	ils	auront	broyé

Conditionnel présent		Conditionnel passé		
je	broi**er**ais	j'	aurais	broyé
tu	broi**er**ais	tu	aurais	broyé
elle	broi**er**ait	elle	aurait	broyé
nous	broi**er**ions	nous	aurions	broyé
vous	broi**er**iez	vous	auriez	broyé
ils	broi**er**aient	ils	auraient	broyé

SUBJONCTIF

Présent		Passé		
que je	broi**e**	que j'	aie	broyé
que tu	broi**es**	que tu	aies	broyé
qu' elle	broi**e**	qu' elle	ait	broyé
que n.	broy**i**ons	que n.	ayons	broyé
que v.	broy**i**ez	que v.	ayez	broyé
qu' ils	broi**ent**	qu' ils	aient	broyé

Imparfait		Plus-que-parfait		
que je	broyasse	que j'	eusse	broyé
que tu	broyasses	que tu	eusses	broyé
qu' elle	broyât	qu' elle	eût	broyé
que n.	broyassions	que n.	eussions	broyé
que v.	broyassiez	que v.	eussiez	broyé
qu' ils	broyassent	qu' ils	eussent	broyé

IMPÉRATIF

Présent	Passé	
broi**e**	aie	broyé
broyons	ayons	broyé
broyez	ayez	broyé

INFINITIF

Présent	Passé
broyer	avoir broyé

PARTICIPE

Présent	Passé (composé)
broyant	ayant broyé
	Passé
	broyé

1. Exceptions: **envoyer** and **renvoyer** are irregular in the future and the present conditional (see Table 80).

   Conditionnel passé 2e forme **(2nd form)**: same form as the *plus-que-parfait* of the subjunctive.
   Futur proche: *je vais broyer* (see Grammar of the verb, paragraphs 3 and 50).

- Verbs in **-oyer** change the **y** of the stem to **i** before a silent **e** (endings **-e**, **-es**, **-ent**, **-erai...**, **-erais...**): *je broie, je broierai.*
- Note that there is always an **i** after the **y** in the first two persons of the plural of the *imparfait* of the indicative and the present subjunctive.

INDICATIF

Présent		Passé composé		
j'	essuie	j'	ai	essuyé
tu	essuies	tu	as	essuyé
elle	essuie	elle	a	essuyé
nous	essuyons	nous	avons	essuyé
vous	essuyez	vous	avez	essuyé
ils	essuient	ils	ont	essuyé

Imparfait		Plus-que-parfait		
j'	essuyais	j'	avais	essuyé
tu	essuyais	tu	avais	essuyé
elle	essuyait	elle	avait	essuyé
nous	essuyions	nous	avions	essuyé
vous	essuyiez	vous	aviez	essuyé
ils	essuyaient	ils	avaient	essuyé

Passé simple		Passé antérieur		
j'	essuyai	j'	eus	essuyé
tu	essuyas	tu	eus	essuyé
elle	essuya	elle	eut	essuyé
nous	essuyâmes	nous	eûmes	essuyé
vous	essuyâtes	vous	eûtes	essuyé
ils	essuyèrent	ils	eurent	essuyé

Futur simple		Futur antérieur		
j'	essuierai	j'	aurai	essuyé
tu	essuieras	tu	auras	essuyé
elle	essuiera	elle	aura	essuyé
nous	essuierons	nous	aurons	essuyé
vous	essuierez	vous	aurez	essuyé
ils	essuieront	ils	auront	essuyé

Conditionnel présent		Conditionnel passé		
j'	essuierais	j'	aurais	essuyé
tu	essuierais	tu	aurais	essuyé
elle	essuierait	elle	aurait	essuyé
nous	essuierions	nous	aurions	essuyé
vous	essuieriez	vous	auriez	essuyé
ils	essuieraient	ils	auraient	essuyé

SUBJONCTIF

Présent		Passé		
que j'	essuie	que j'	aie	essuyé
que tu	essuies	que tu	aies	essuyé
qu' elle	essuie	qu' elle	ait	essuyé
que n.	essuyions	que n.	ayons	essuyé
que v.	essuyiez	que v.	ayez	essuyé
qu' ils	essuient	qu' ils	aient	essuyé

Imparfait		Plus-que-parfait		
que j'	essuyasse	que j'	eusse	essuyé
que tu	essuyasses	que tu	eusses	essuyé
qu' elle	essuyât	qu' elle	eût	essuyé
que n.	essuyassions	que n.	eussions	essuyé
que v.	essuyassiez	que v.	eussiez	essuyé
qu' ils	essuyassent	qu' ils	eussent	essuyé

IMPÉRATIF

Présent	Passé	
essuie	aie	essuyé
essuyons	ayons	essuyé
essuyez	ayez	essuyé

INFINITIF

Présent	Passé
essuyer	avoir essuyé

PARTICIPE

Présent	Passé (composé)
essuyant	ayant essuyé
	Passé
	essuyé

***Conditionnel passé 2e forme* (2nd form)**: same form as the *plus-que-parfait* of the subjunctive.
Futur proche: *je vais essuyer* (see Grammar of the verb, paragraphs 3 and 50).

- Verbs in **-uyer** change the **y** of the stem to **i** before a silent **e** (endings **-e**, **-es**, **-ent**, **-erai...**, **-erais...**): *j'essuie, j'essuierai.*
- Note that there is always an **i** after the **y** in the first two persons of the plural of the *imparfait* of the indicative and the present subjunctive.

80 envoyer

INDICATIF

Présent		Passé composé		
j'	envo**ie**	j'	ai	envoyé
tu	envo**ies**	tu	as	envoyé
elle	envo**ie**	elle	a	envoyé
nous	envoyons	nous	avons	envoyé
vous	envoyez	vous	avez	envoyé
ils	envo**ie**nt	ils	ont	envoyé

Imparfait		Plus-que-parfait		
j'	envoyais	j'	avais	envoyé
tu	envoyais	tu	avais	envoyé
elle	envoyait	elle	avait	envoyé
nous	envo**yi**ons	nous	avions	envoyé
vous	envo**yi**ez	vous	aviez	envoyé
ils	envoyaient	ils	avaient	envoyé

Passé simple		Passé antérieur		
j'	envoyai	j'	eus	envoyé
tu	envoyas	tu	eus	envoyé
elle	envoya	elle	eut	envoyé
nous	envoyâmes	nous	eûmes	envoyé
vous	envoyâtes	vous	eûtes	envoyé
ils	envoyèrent	ils	eurent	envoyé

Futur simple		Futur antérieur		
j'	enve**rr**ai	j'	aurai	envoyé
tu	enve**rr**as	tu	auras	envoyé
elle	enve**rr**a	elle	aura	envoyé
nous	enve**rr**ons	nous	aurons	envoyé
vous	enve**rr**ez	vous	aurez	envoyé
ils	enve**rr**ont	ils	auront	envoyé

Conditionnel présent		Conditionnel passé		
j'	enve**rr**ais	j'	aurais	envoyé
tu	enve**rr**ais	tu	aurais	envoyé
elle	enve**rr**ait	elle	aurait	envoyé
nous	enve**rr**ions	nous	aurions	envoyé
vous	enve**rr**iez	vous	auriez	envoyé
ils	enve**rr**aient	ils	auraient	envoyé

SUBJONCTIF

Présent		Passé		
que j'	envo**ie**	que j'	aie	envoyé
que tu	envo**ies**	que tu	aies	envoyé
qu' elle	envo**ie**	qu' elle	ait	envoyé
que n.	envo**yi**ons	que n.	ayons	envoyé
que v.	envo**yi**ez	que v.	ayez	envoyé
qu' ils	envo**ie**nt	qu' ils	aient	envoyé

Imparfait		Plus-que-parfait		
que j'	envoyasse	que j'	eusse	envoyé
que tu	envoyasses	que tu	eusses	envoyé
qu' elle	envoyât	qu' elle	eût	envoyé
que n.	envoyassions	que n.	eussions	envoyé
que v.	envoyassiez	que v.	eussiez	envoyé
qu' ils	envoyassent	qu' ils	eussent	envoyé

IMPÉRATIF

Présent	Passé	
envo**ie**	aie	envoyé
envoyons	ayons	envoyé
envoyez	ayez	envoyé

INFINITIF

Présent	Passé
envoyer	avoir envoyé

PARTICIPE

Présent	Passé (composé)
envoyant	ayant envoyé
	Passé
	envoyé

***Conditionnel passé 2e forme* (2nd form)**: same form as the *plus-que-parfait* of the subjunctive.
Futur proche: *je vais envoyer* (see Grammar of the verb, paragraphs 3 and 50).

- **Renvoyer** follows the same conjugation pattern.

finir

INDICATIF

Présent		Passé composé		
je	finis	j'	ai	fini
tu	finis	tu	as	fini
elle	finit	elle	a	fini
nous	finissons	nous	avons	fini
vous	finissez	vous	avez	fini
ils	finissent	ils	ont	fini

Imparfait		Plus-que-parfait		
je	finissais	j'	avais	fini
tu	finissais	tu	avais	fini
elle	finissait	elle	avait	fini
nous	finissions	nous	avions	fini
vous	finissiez	vous	aviez	fini
ils	finissaient	ils	avaient	fini

Passé simple		Passé antérieur		
je	finis	j'	eus	fini
tu	finis	tu	eus	fini
elle	finit	elle	eut	fini
nous	finîmes	nous	eûmes	fini
vous	finîtes	vous	eûtes	fini
ils	finirent	ils	eurent	fini

Futur simple		Futur antérieur		
je	finirai	j'	aurai	fini
tu	finiras	tu	auras	fini
elle	finira	elle	aura	fini
nous	finirons	nous	aurons	fini
vous	finirez	vous	aurez	fini
ils	finiront	ils	auront	fini

Conditionnel présent		Conditionnel passé		
je	finirais	j'	aurais	fini
tu	finirais	tu	aurais	fini
elle	finirait	elle	aurait	fini
nous	finirions	nous	aurions	fini
vous	finiriez	vous	auriez	fini
ils	finiraient	ils	auraient	fini

SUBJONCTIF

Présent		Passé		
que je	finisse	que j'	aie	fini
que tu	finisses	que tu	aies	fini
qu'elle	finisse	qu'elle	ait	fini
que n.	finissions	que n.	ayons	fini
que v.	finissiez	que v.	ayez	fini
qu'ils	finissent	qu'ils	aient	fini

Imparfait		Plus-que-parfait		
que je	finisse	que j'	eusse	fini
que tu	finisses	que tu	eusses	fini
qu'elle	finît	qu'elle	eût	fini
que n.	finissions	que n.	eussions	fini
que v.	finissiez	que v.	eussiez	fini
qu'ils	finissent	qu'ils	eussent	fini

IMPÉRATIF

Présent	Passé	
finis	aie	fini
finissons	ayons	fini
finissez	ayez	fini

INFINITIF

Présent	Passé
finir	avoir fini

PARTICIPE

Présent	Passé (composé)
finissant	ayant fini
	Passé
	fini

***Conditionnel passé 2e forme* (2nd form)**: same form as the *plus-que-parfait* of the subjunctive.
Futur proche: *je vais finir* (see Grammar of the verb, paragraphs 3 and 50).

- There are about 300 regular verbs in **-ir** which follow the same conjugation pattern.
- **Obéir** and **désobéir** – based on an archaic construction of direct transitive verbs – have retained a passive form: *Sera-t-elle obéie ?*
- The verb **maudire** follows this same pattern of conjugation although its infinitive ends in **-ire** and its past participle ends in **-t**: *maudi**t**, maudi**te***.
- The verb **amuïr** is conjugated along the same pattern and always carries the dieresis (never the circumflex) over the **i**.

82 haïr

INDICATIF

Présent		Passé composé		
je	hais	j'	ai	haï
tu	hais	tu	as	haï
elle	hait	elle	a	haï
nous	haïssons	nous	avons	haï
vous	haïssez	vous	avez	haï
ils	haïssent	ils	ont	haï

Imparfait		Plus-que-parfait		
je	haïssais	j'	avais	haï
tu	haïssais	tu	avais	haï
elle	haïssait	elle	avait	haï
nous	haïssions	nous	avions	haï
vous	haïssiez	vous	aviez	haï
ils	haïssaient	ils	avaient	haï

Passé simple		Passé antérieur		
je	haïs	j'	eus	haï
tu	haïs	tu	eus	haï
elle	haït	elle	eut	haï
nous	haïmes	nous	eûmes	haï
vous	haïtes	vous	eûtes	haï
ils	haïrent	ils	eurent	haï

Futur simple		Futur antérieur		
je	haïrai	j'	aurai	haï
tu	haïras	tu	auras	haï
elle	haïra	elle	aura	haï
nous	haïrons	nous	aurons	haï
vous	haïrez	vous	aurez	haï
ils	haïront	ils	auront	haï

Conditionnel présent		Conditionnel passé		
je	haïrais	j'	aurais	haï
tu	haïrais	tu	aurais	haï
elle	haïrait	elle	aurait	haï
nous	haïrions	nous	aurions	haï
vous	haïriez	vous	auriez	haï
ils	haïraient	ils	auraient	haï

SUBJONCTIF

Présent		Passé		
que je	haïsse	que j'	aie	haï
que tu	haïsses	que tu	aies	haï
qu' elle	haïsse	qu' elle	ait	haï
que n.	haïssions	que n.	ayons	haï
que v.	haïssiez	que v.	ayez	haï
qu' ils	haïssent	qu' ils	aient	haï

Imparfait		Plus-que-parfait		
que je	haïsse	que j'	eusse	haï
que tu	haïsses	que tu	eusses	haï
qu' elle	haït	qu' elle	eût	haï
que n.	haïssions	que n.	eussions	haï
que v.	haïssiez	que v.	eussiez	haï
qu' ils	haïssent	qu' ils	eussent	haï

IMPÉRATIF

Présent	Passé	
hais	aie	haï
haïssons	ayons	haï
haïssez	ayez	haï

INFINITIF

Présent	Passé
haïr	avoir haï

PARTICIPE

Présent	Passé (composé)
haïssant	ayant haï
	Passé
	haï

***Conditionnel passé 2e forme* (2nd form)**: same form as the *plus-que-parfait* of the subjunctive.
Futur proche: *je vais haïr* (see Grammar of the verb, paragraphs 3 and 50).

- **Haïr** and **entrehaïr** are the only verbs that follow this pattern.
- **Haïr** and **entrehaïr** carry a dieresis over the **i** throughout their conjugation, except in the 1st, 2nd and 3rd persons singular of the present indicative and the 2nd person singular of the present imperative, and is pronounced [ɛ].
- The *passé simple* and the *imparfait* of the subjunctive maintain the dieresis (never the circumflex) for all grammatical persons.

IRREGULAR VERBS

list of irregular verbs

These verbs are grouped in the same order as those in the conjugation tables showing fully conjugated verbs or conjugation patterns (in blue) but not necessarily with the corresponding auxiliary verb.

83 aller
84 tenir
abstenir (s')
appartenir
contenir
détenir
entretenir
maintenir
obtenir
retenir
soutenir
venir
advenir
bienvenir
circonvenir
contrevenir
convenir
devenir
disconvenir
intervenir
obvenir
parvenir
prévenir
provenir
redevenir
ressouvenir (se)
revenir
souvenir
subvenir
survenir

85 acquérir
conquérir
enquérir (s')
quérir
reconquérir
requérir
86 sentir
consentir
pressentir
ressentir
mentir
démentir
partir
départir
repartir
répartir [1]
repentir (se)
sortir
ressortir [2]
87 vêtir [3]
dévêtir
revêtir
survêtir
88 couvrir
découvrir
redécouvrir
recouvrir
ouvrir
entrouvrir
rentrouvrir
rouvrir
offrir
souffrir

89 cueillir
accueillir
recueillir
90 assaillir
saillir [4]
tressaillir
défaillir
91 faillir
92 bouillir
débouillir
racabouillir
rebouillir
93 dormir
endormir
rendormir
94 courir
accourir
concourir
discourir
encourir
parcourir
recourir
secourir
95 mourir
96 servir [5]
desservir
resservir
97 fuir
enfuir (s')
98 ouïr
99 gésir

100 recevoir
apercevoir
concevoir
décevoir
entrapercevoir
percevoir
101 voir
entrevoir
prévoir [6]
revoir
102 pourvoir
dépourvoir
103 savoir
104 devoir
redevoir
105 pouvoir
106 émouvoir
mouvoir
promouvoir
107 pleuvoir
repleuvoir
108 falloir
109 valoir
équivaloir
prévaloir
revaloir
110 vouloir
revouloir
111 seoir
112 asseoir/assoir
rasseoir/rassoir
113 messeoir/messoir

1. The verb **répartir**, in the sense of "distribute" or "allocate", follows the same conjugation pattern as **finir** (see Table 81).
2. The verb **ressortir**, when it means *être du ressort de* (= "fall within the competence of, be under the responsibility of"), is conjugated like **finir** (see Table 81).
3. **Vêtir** has varying forms not observed in other verbs derived from it.
4. The verb **saillir** has varying patterns of conjugation (see notes in Table 90).
5. **Asservir** is conjugated like **finir** (see Table 81).
6. **Prévoir** is conjugated like a regular verb in the future and the conditional (like **pourvoir**).

114 surseoir/sursoir
115 choir
116 échoir
117 déchoir
118 rendre
défendre
descendre
condescendre
redescendre
fendre
pourfendre
refendre
pendre
appendre
dépendre
rependre
suspendre
tendre
attendre
détendre
distendre
entendre
étendre
prétendre
réentendre
retendre
sous-entendre
sous-tendre
vendre
mévendre
revendre
épandre
répandre
fondre
confondre
morfondre (se)
parfondre
refondre
tréfondre
pondre
répondre
correspondre
tondre
retondre
surtondre
perdre
éperdre
reperdre
mordre
démordre
remordre
tordre
détordre
distordre
retordre
sourdre [1]
119 prendre
apprendre
comprendre
déprendre (se)
désapprendre
entreprendre
éprendre (s')
méprendre (se)
r(é)apprendre
reprendre
surprendre
120 rompre
corrompre
interrompre
foutre
contrefoutre (se)
refoutre
121 battre
abattre
combattre
contrebattre
débattre
ébattre (s')
embattre
entrebattre (s')
rabattre
rebattre
soubattre
122 mettre
admettre
commettre
compromettre
décommettre
démettre
émettre
entremettre (s')
mainmettre
omettre
permettre
promettre
réadmettre
remettre
retransmettre
soumettre
transmettre
123 peindre
dépeindre
repeindre
astreindre
épreindre
étreindre
restreindre
retreindre
rétreindre
atteindre
ceindre
enceindre
empreindre
enfreindre
feindre
geindre
teindre
déteindre
éteindre
reteindre
aveindre
124 joindre
adjoindre
conjoindre
disjoindre
enjoindre
rejoindre
oindre
poindre
125 craindre
contraindre
plaindre
126 vaincre
convaincre
127 traire
abstraire
distraire
extraire
rentraire
retraire
raire
soustraire
braire
128 faire
contrefaire
défaire
forfaire
malfaire
méfaire
parfaire
redéfaire
refaire
satisfaire
stupéfaire
surfaire

1. **Sourdre** is a defective verb.

129 plaire
complaire
déplaire
taire [1]
130 paraître/paraitre
apparaître/apparaitre
comparaître/comparaitre
disparaître/disparaitre
réapparaître/réapparaitre
recomparaître/recomparaitre
reparaître/reparaitre
transparaître/transparaitre
connaître/connaitre
méconnaître/méconnaitre
reconnaître/reconnaitre
131 naître/naitre
renaître/renaitre
132 paître/paitre
133 repaître/repaitre
134 croître/croitre
135 croire
accroire [2]
mécroire
136 décroître/décroitre
accroître/accroitre
recroître/recroitre
137 boire
emboire (s')
138 clore [3]
déclore
éclore
enclore
forclore
reclore
139 exclure
conclure
140 inclure
occlure
reclure
141 absoudre
dissoudre
142 résoudre
143 coudre
découdre
recoudre
144 moudre
émoudre
remoudre
145 suivre
ensuivre (s')
poursuivre
146 vivre
revivre
survivre
147 lire
élire
réélire
relire
148 dire [4, 5]
adire (s')
contredire
dédire
interdire
médire
prédire
redire [5]
149 rire
sourire
150 écrire
circonscrire
décrire
inscrire
prescrire
proscrire
récrire
réécrire
réinscrire
retranscrire
souscrire
transcrire
151 confire
déconfire
circoncire [6]
frire
suffire [7]
152 cuire
décuire
précuire
recuire
conduire
coproduire
déduire
éconduire
enduire
induire
introduire
méconduire (se)
produire
reconduire
réduire
réintroduire
reproduire
retraduire
séduire
surproduire
traduire
autodétruire (s')
construire
déconstruire
détruire
entredétruire (s')
instruire
reconstruire
nuire [8]
entrenuire (s') [8]
153 luire
reluire

1. **Taire** never takes a circumflex in the 3rd person singular of the present indicative.
2. **Accroire** is used only in the infinitive.
3. Some verbs of this family have an alternate form – without the circumflex – in the present indicative (example: *il éclôt* or *il éclot*).
4. **Maudire** is conjugated like **finir**.
5. **Dire** and **redire** are the only two verbs of this family with the ending **-ites** when used with the pronoun *vous*.
6. The past participle of **circoncire** ends in **-is**: *circoncis, circoncise, circoncises*.
7. The past participle of **suffire** ends in **-i** and is invariable: *suffi*.
8. The past participles of **nuire** and **entrenuire** end in **-i** and are invariable: *nui, entrenui*.

aller

INDICATIF

Présent		Passé composé		
je	vais	je	suis	allé
tu	vas	tu	es	allé
elle	va	elle	est	allée
nous	allons	nous	sommes	allés
vous	allez	vous	êtes	allés
ils	vont	ils	sont	allés

Imparfait		Plus-que-parfait		
j'	allais	j'	étais	allé
tu	allais	tu	étais	allé
elle	allait	elle	était	allée
nous	allions	nous	étions	allés
vous	alliez	vous	étiez	allés
ils	allaient	ils	étaient	allés

Passé simple		Passé antérieur		
j'	allai	je	fus	allé
tu	allas	tu	fus	allé
elle	alla	elle	fut	allée
nous	allâmes	nous	fûmes	allés
vous	allâtes	vous	fûtes	allés
ils	allèrent	ils	furent	allés

Futur simple		Futur antérieur		
j'	irai	je	serai	allé
tu	iras	tu	seras	allé
elle	ira	elle	sera	allée
nous	irons	nous	serons	allés
vous	irez	vous	serez	allés
ils	iront	ils	seront	allés

Conditionnel présent		Conditionnel passé		
j'	irais	je	serais	allé
tu	irais	tu	serais	allé
elle	irait	elle	serait	allée
nous	irions	nous	serions	allés
vous	iriez	vous	seriez	allés
ils	iraient	ils	seraient	allés

SUBJONCTIF

Présent		Passé		
que j'	aille	que je	sois	allé
que tu	ailles	que tu	sois	allé
qu' elle	aille	qu' elle	soit	allée
que n.	allions	que n.	soyons	allés
que v.	alliez	que v.	soyez	allés
qu' ils	aillent	qu' ils	soient	allés

Imparfait		Plus-que-parfait		
que j'	allasse	que je	fusse	allé
que tu	allasses	que tu	fusses	allé
qu' elle	allât	qu' elle	fût	allée
que n.	allassions	que n.	fussions	allés
que v.	allassiez	que v.	fussiez	allés
qu' ils	allassent	qu' ils	fussent	allés

IMPÉRATIF

Présent	Passé	
va	sois	allé
allons	soyons	allés
allez	soyez	allés

INFINITIF

Présent	Passé
aller	être allé

PARTICIPE

Présent	Passé (composé)
allant	étant allé
	Passé
	allé

***Conditionnel passé 2e forme* (2nd form)**: same form as the *plus-que-parfait* of the subjunctive.
Futur proche: *je vais aller* (see Grammar of the verb, paragraphs 3 and 50).

- Note the use of the auxiliary **être** in compound verb forms.
- In the 2nd person singular of the imperative, the verb **aller** (*va*) takes an **s** before the pronoun **y** for euphony (pleasantness of sound): *vas-y*, but *va y mettre bon ordre*. The interrogative form gives: *Va-t-il ?* as in *Aima-t-il ?* (see Grammar of the verb, paragraph 16).
- The verb **s'en aller** is conjugated like **aller**. In the compound verb forms, the auxiliary **être** is placed between **en** and the main verb (**aller**): *je m'en suis allé*. The forms of the imperative are *va-t'en* (the **e** of the reflexive pronoun **te** is elided), *allons-nous-en*, *allez-vous-en*.

tenir

INDICATIF

Présent		Passé composé		
je	tiens	j'	ai	tenu
tu	tiens	tu	as	tenu
elle	tient	elle	a	tenu
nous	tenons	nous	avons	tenu
vous	tenez	vous	avez	tenu
ils	tiennent	ils	ont	tenu

Imparfait		Plus-que-parfait		
je	tenais	j'	avais	tenu
tu	tenais	tu	avais	tenu
elle	tenait	elle	avait	tenu
nous	tenions	nous	avions	tenu
vous	teniez	vous	aviez	tenu
ils	tenaient	ils	avaient	tenu

Passé simple		Passé antérieur		
je	tins	j'	eus	tenu
tu	tins	tu	eus	tenu
elle	tint	elle	eut	tenu
nous	tînmes	nous	eûmes	tenu
vous	tîntes	vous	eûtes	tenu
ils	tinrent	ils	eurent	tenu

Futur simple		Futur antérieur		
je	tiendrai	j'	aurai	tenu
tu	tiendras	tu	auras	tenu
elle	tiendra	elle	aura	tenu
nous	tiendrons	nous	aurons	tenu
vous	tiendrez	vous	aurez	tenu
ils	tiendront	ils	auront	tenu

Conditionnel présent		Conditionnel passé		
je	tiendrais	j'	aurais	tenu
tu	tiendrais	tu	aurais	tenu
elle	tiendrait	elle	aurait	tenu
nous	tiendrions	nous	aurions	tenu
vous	tiendriez	vous	auriez	tenu
ils	tiendraient	ils	auraient	tenu

SUBJONCTIF

Présent		Passé		
que je	tienne	que j'	aie	tenu
que tu	tiennes	que tu	aies	tenu
qu'elle	tienne	qu'elle	ait	tenu
que n.	tenions	que n.	ayons	tenu
que v.	teniez	que v.	ayez	tenu
qu' ils	tiennent	qu' ils	aient	tenu

Imparfait		Plus-que-parfait		
que je	tinsse	que j'	eusse	tenu
que tu	tinsses	que tu	eusses	tenu
qu'elle	tînt	qu'elle	eût	tenu
que n.	tinssions	que n.	eussions	tenu
que v.	tinssiez	que v.	eussiez	tenu
qu' ils	tinssent	qu' ils	eussent	tenu

IMPÉRATIF

Présent	Passé	
tiens	aie	tenu
tenons	ayons	tenu
tenez	ayez	tenu

INFINITIF

Présent	Passé
tenir	avoir tenu

PARTICIPE

Présent	Passé (composé)
tenant	ayant tenu
	Passé
-	tenu

***Conditionnel passé 2e forme* (2nd form)**: same form as the *plus-que-parfait* of the subjunctive.
Futur proche: *je vais tenir* (see Grammar of the verb, paragraphs 3 and 50).

- **Tenir**, **venir** and their derived forms follow this pattern (see List of irregular verbs, p. 96 to 98).
- **Venir** and its derived forms take the auxiliary **être**. Exceptions are: **circonvenir**, **contrevenir**, **prévenir** and **subvenir**. The verb **disconvenir** takes both auxiliaries **avoir** and **être**. The verb **convenir** is conjugated with **avoir**, but **convenir de** may also be conjugated with **être** (literary usage).
- **Advenir** is used only in the 3rd person singular and plural; it is conjugated with the auxiliary **être**: *il est advenu*.

INDICATIF

Présent		Passé composé		
j'	acquiers	j'	ai	acquis
tu	acquiers	tu	as	acquis
elle	acquiert	elle	a	acquis
nous	acquérons	nous	avons	acquis
vous	acquérez	vous	avez	acquis
ils	acquièrent	ils	ont	acquis

Imparfait		Plus-que-parfait		
j'	acquérais	j'	avais	acquis
tu	acquérais	tu	avais	acquis
elle	acquérait	elle	avait	acquis
nous	acquérions	nous	avions	acquis
vous	acquériez	vous	aviez	acquis
ils	acquéraient	ils	avaient	acquis

Passé simple		Passé antérieur		
j'	acquis	j'	eus	acquis
tu	acquis	tu	eus	acquis
elle	acquit	elle	eut	acquis
nous	acquîmes	nous	eûmes	acquis
vous	acquîtes	vous	eûtes	acquis
ils	acquirent	ils	eurent	acquis

Futur simple		Futur antérieur		
j'	acquerrai	j'	aurai	acquis
tu	acquerras	tu	auras	acquis
elle	acquerra	elle	aura	acquis
nous	acquerrons	nous	aurons	acquis
vous	acquerrez	vous	aurez	acquis
ils	acquerront	ils	auront	acquis

Conditionnel présent		Conditionnel passé		
j'	acquerrais	j'	aurais	acquis
tu	acquerrais	tu	aurais	acquis
elle	acquerrait	elle	aurait	acquis
nous	acquerrions	nous	aurions	acquis
vous	acquerriez	vous	auriez	acquis
ils	acquerraient	ils	auraient	acquis

SUBJONCTIF

Présent		Passé		
que j'	acquière	que j'	aie	acquis
que tu	acquières	que tu	aies	acquis
qu' elle	acquière	qu' elle	ait	acquis
que n.	acquérions	que n.	ayons	acquis
que v.	acquériez	que v.	ayez	acquis
qu' ils	acquièrent	qu' ils	aient	acquis

Imparfait		Plus-que-parfait		
que j'	acquisse	que j'	eusse	acquis
que tu	acquisses	que tu	eusses	acquis
qu' elle	acquît	qu' elle	eût	acquis
que n.	acquissions	que n.	eussions	acquis
que v.	acquissiez	que v.	eussiez	acquis
qu' ils	acquissent	qu' ils	eussent	acquis

IMPÉRATIF

Présent	Passé	
acquiers	aie	acquis
acquérons	ayons	acquis
acquérez	ayez	acquis

INFINITIF

Présent	Passé
acquérir	avoir acquis

PARTICIPE

Présent	Passé (composé)
acquérant	ayant acquis
	Passé
	acquis

***Conditionnel passé 2e forme* (2nd form)**: same form as the *plus-que-parfait* of the subjunctive.
Futur proche: *je vais acquérir* (see Grammar of the verb, paragraphs 3 and 50).

- The derived forms of the verb **quérir** follow this pattern of conjugation (see List of irregular verbs, p. 96 to 98).
- The verb **quérir** is used only as an infinitive.
- Do not confuse the past participial noun **acquis** (*avoir de l'acquis*) with the verbal noun **acquit** from the verb **acquitter** (*par acquit, pour acquit*).
- Note the double **r** in the future and the present conditonal, and the absence of an accent on the **e** in this case: *j'acquerrai, j'acquerrais.*

86 sentir

INDICATIF

Présent		Passé composé		
je	sens	j'	ai	senti
tu	sens	tu	as	senti
elle	sent	elle	a	senti
nous	sentons	nous	avons	senti
vous	sentez	vous	avez	senti
ils	sentent	ils	ont	senti

Imparfait		Plus-que-parfait		
je	sentais	j'	avais	senti
tu	sentais	tu	avais	senti
elle	sentait	elle	avait	senti
nous	sentions	nous	avions	senti
vous	sentiez	vous	aviez	senti
ils	sentaient	ils	avaient	senti

Passé simple		Passé antérieur		
je	sentis	j'	eus	senti
tu	sentis	tu	eus	senti
elle	sentit	elle	eut	senti
nous	sentîmes	nous	eûmes	senti
vous	sentîtes	vous	eûtes	senti
ils	sentirent	ils	eurent	senti

Futur simple		Futur antérieur		
je	sentirai	j'	aurai	senti
tu	sentiras	tu	auras	senti
elle	sentira	elle	aura	senti
nous	sentirons	nous	aurons	senti
vous	sentirez	vous	aurez	senti
ils	sentiront	ils	auront	senti

Conditionnel présent		Conditionnel passé		
je	sentirais	j'	aurais	senti
tu	sentirais	tu	aurais	senti
elle	sentirait	elle	aurait	senti
nous	sentirions	nous	aurions	senti
vous	sentiriez	vous	auriez	senti
ils	sentiraient	ils	auraient	senti

SUBJONCTIF

Présent		Passé		
que je	sente	que j'	aie	senti
que tu	sentes	que tu	aies	senti
qu' elle	sente	qu' elle	ait	senti
que n.	sentions	que n.	ayons	senti
que v.	sentiez	que v.	ayez	senti
qu' ils	sentent	qu' ils	aient	senti

Imparfait		Plus-que-parfait		
que je	sentisse	que j'	eusse	senti
que tu	sentisses	que tu	eusses	senti
qu' elle	sentît	qu' elle	eût	senti
que n.	sentissions	que n.	eussions	senti
que v.	sentissiez	que v.	eussiez	senti
qu' ils	sentissent	qu' ils	eussent	senti

IMPÉRATIF

Présent	Passé	
sens	aie	senti
sentons	ayons	senti
sentez	ayez	senti

INFINITIF

Présent	Passé
sentir	avoir senti

PARTICIPE

Présent	Passé (composé)
sentant	ayant senti
	Passé
	senti

Conditionnel passé 2e forme **(2nd form)**: same form as the *plus-que-parfait* of the subjunctive.
Futur proche: *je vais sentir* (see Grammar of the verb, paragraphs 3 and 50).

- **Mentir**, **sentir**, **partir**, **se repentir**, **sortir** and their derived forms follow this pattern of conjugation (see List of irregular verbs, p. 96 to 98). Some of these verbs are conjugated with the auxiliary **être**.
- The past participle *menti* is invariable, but *démenti* is variable, hence the forms *démentie*, *démentis*, *démenties*.

vêtir

INDICATIF

Présent		Passé composé		
je	vêts	j'	ai	vêtu
tu	vêts	tu	as	vêtu
elle	vêt	elle	a	vêtu
nous	vêtons	nous	avons	vêtu
vous	vêtez	vous	avez	vêtu
ils	vêtent	ils	ont	vêtu

Imparfait		Plus-que-parfait		
je	vêtais	j'	avais	vêtu
tu	vêtais	tu	avais	vêtu
elle	vêtait	elle	avait	vêtu
nous	vêtions	nous	avions	vêtu
vous	vêtiez	vous	aviez	vêtu
ils	vêtaient	ils	avaient	vêtu

Passé simple		Passé antérieur		
je	vêtis	j'	eus	vêtu
tu	vêtis	tu	eus	vêtu
elle	vêtit	elle	eut	vêtu
nous	vêtîmes	nous	eûmes	vêtu
vous	vêtîtes	vous	eûtes	vêtu
ils	vêtirent	ils	eurent	vêtu

Futur simple		Futur antérieur		
je	vêtirai	j'	aurai	vêtu
tu	vêtiras	tu	auras	vêtu
elle	vêtira	elle	aura	vêtu
nous	vêtirons	nous	aurons	vêtu
vous	vêtirez	vous	aurez	vêtu
ils	vêtiront	ils	auront	vêtu

Conditionnel présent		Conditionnel passé		
je	vêtirais	j'	aurais	vêtu
tu	vêtirais	tu	aurais	vêtu
elle	vêtirait	elle	aurait	vêtu
nous	vêtirions	nous	aurions	vêtu
vous	vêtiriez	vous	auriez	vêtu
ils	vêtiraient	ils	auraient	vêtu

SUBJONCTIF

Présent		Passé		
que je	vête	que j'	aie	vêtu
que tu	vêtes	que tu	aies	vêtu
qu' elle	vête	qu' elle	ait	vêtu
que n.	vêtions	que n.	ayons	vêtu
que v.	vêtiez	que v.	ayez	vêtu
qu' ils	vêtent	qu' ils	aient	vêtu

Imparfait		Plus-que-parfait		
que je	vêtisse	que j'	eusse	vêtu
que tu	vêtisses	que tu	eusses	vêtu
qu' elle	vêtît	qu' elle	eût	vêtu
que n.	vêtissions	que n.	eussions	vêtu
que v.	vêtissiez	que v.	eussiez	vêtu
qu' ils	vêtissent	qu' ils	eussent	vêtu

IMPÉRATIF

Présent	Passé	
vêts	aie	vêtu
vêtons	ayons	vêtu
vêtez	ayez	vêtu

INFINITIF

Présent	Passé
vêtir	avoir vêtu

PARTICIPE

Présent	Passé (composé)
vêtant	ayant vêtu
	Passé
	vêtu

***Conditionnel passé 2e forme* (2nd form)**: same form as the *plus-que-parfait* of the subjunctive.
Futur proche: *je vais vêtir* (see Grammar of the verb, paragraphs 3 and 50).

- **Devêtir**, **survêtir** and **revêtir** follow this pattern of conjugation.
- Despite the forms given above, **vêtir** is sometimes conjugated like **finir**: present indicative (*je vêtis*), present subjunctive (*que je vêtisse*), *imparfait* of the indicative (*je vêtissais*), present imperative (*vêtis-toi, vêtissons-nous*), present participle (*vêtissant*). However, in derived forms of the verb (**dévêtir**, **revêtir**, **survêtir**), only those spellings indicated in the table are accepted: *il revêt, dévêts-toi, survêtant*.

INDICATIF

Présent		Passé composé		
je	couvre	j'	ai	couvert
tu	couvres	tu	as	couvert
elle	couvre	elle	a	couvert
nous	couvrons	nous	avons	couvert
vous	couvrez	vous	avez	couvert
ils	couvrent	ils	ont	couvert

Imparfait		Plus-que-parfait		
je	couvrais	j'	avais	couvert
tu	couvrais	tu	avais	couvert
elle	couvrait	elle	avait	couvert
nous	couvrions	nous	avions	couvert
vous	couvriez	vous	aviez	couvert
ils	couvraient	ils	avaient	couvert

Passé simple		Passé antérieur		
je	couvris	j'	eus	couvert
tu	couvris	tu	eus	couvert
elle	couvrit	elle	eut	couvert
nous	couvrîmes	nous	eûmes	couvert
vous	couvrîtes	vous	eûtes	couvert
ils	couvrirent	ils	eurent	couvert

Futur simple		Futur antérieur		
je	couvrirai	j'	aurai	couvert
tu	couvriras	tu	auras	couvert
elle	couvrira	elle	aura	couvert
nous	couvrirons	nous	aurons	couvert
vous	couvrirez	vous	aurez	couvert
ils	couvriront	ils	auront	couvert

Conditionnel présent		Conditionnel passé		
je	couvrirais	j'	aurais	couvert
tu	couvrirais	tu	aurais	couvert
elle	couvrirait	elle	aurait	couvert
nous	couvririons	nous	aurions	couvert
vous	couvririez	vous	auriez	couvert
ils	couvriraient	ils	auraient	couvert

SUBJONCTIF

Présent		Passé		
que je	couvre	que j'	aie	couvert
que tu	couvres	que tu	aies	couvert
qu' elle	couvre	qu' elle	ait	couvert
que n.	couvrions	que n.	ayons	couvert
que v.	couvriez	que v.	ayez	couvert
qu' ils	couvrent	qu' ils	aient	couvert

Imparfait		Plus-que-parfait		
que je	couvrisse	que j'	eusse	couvert
que tu	couvrisses	que tu	eusses	couvert
qu' elle	couvrît	qu' elle	eût	couvert
que n.	couvrissions	que n.	eussions	couvert
que v.	couvrissiez	que v.	eussiez	couvert
qu' ils	couvrissent	qu' ils	eussent	couvert

IMPÉRATIF

Présent	Passé	
couvre	aie	couvert
couvrons	ayons	couvert
couvrez	ayez	couvert

INFINITIF

Présent	Passé
couvrir	avoir couvert

PARTICIPE

Présent	Passé (composé)
couvrant	ayant couvert
	Passé
	couvert

***Conditionnel passé 2e forme* (2nd form)**: same form as the *plus-que-parfait* of the subjunctive.
Futur proche: *je vais couvrir* (see Grammar of the verb, paragraphs 3 and 50).

- **Couvrir**, **ouvrir**, **souffrir**, **offrir** and their derived forms follow this pattern of conjugation (see List of irregular verbs, p. 96 to 98).
- Note the similar endings in the present indicative, the present imperative, and the present subjunctive with those of verbs ending in **-er**.

cueillir

INDICATIF

Présent		Passé composé		
je	cueille	j'	ai	cueilli
tu	cueilles	tu	as	cueilli
elle	cueille	elle	a	cueilli
nous	cueillons	nous	avons	cueilli
vous	cueillez	vous	avez	cueilli
ils	cueillent	ils	ont	cueilli

Imparfait		Plus-que-parfait		
je	cueillais	j'	avais	cueilli
tu	cueillais	tu	avais	cueilli
elle	cueillait	elle	avait	cueilli
nous	cueillions	nous	avions	cueilli
vous	cueilliez	vous	aviez	cueilli
ils	cueillaient	ils	avaient	cueilli

Passé simple		Passé antérieur		
je	cueillis	j'	eus	cueilli
tu	cueillis	tu	eus	cueilli
elle	cueillit	elle	eut	cueilli
nous	cueillîmes	nous	eûmes	cueilli
vous	cueillîtes	vous	eûtes	cueilli
ils	cueillirent	ils	eurent	cueilli

Futur simple		Futur antérieur		
je	cueillerai	j'	aurai	cueilli
tu	cueilleras	tu	auras	cueilli
elle	cueillera	elle	aura	cueilli
nous	cueillerons	nous	aurons	cueilli
vous	cueillerez	vous	aurez	cueilli
ils	cueilleront	ils	auront	cueilli

Conditionnel présent		Conditionnel passé		
je	cueillerais	j'	aurais	cueilli
tu	cueillerais	tu	aurais	cueilli
elle	cueillerait	elle	aurait	cueilli
nous	cueillerions	nous	aurions	cueilli
vous	cueilleriez	vous	auriez	cueilli
ils	cueilleraient	ils	auraient	cueilli

SUBJONCTIF

Présent		Passé		
que je	cueille	que j'	aie	cueilli
que tu	cueilles	que tu	aies	cueilli
qu' elle	cueille	qu' elle	ait	cueilli
que n.	cueillions	que n.	ayons	cueilli
que v.	cueilliez	que v.	ayez	cueilli
qu' ils	cueillent	qu' ils	aient	cueilli

Imparfait		Plus-que-parfait		
que je	cueillisse	que j'	eusse	cueilli
que tu	cueillisses	que tu	eusses	cueilli
qu' elle	cueillît	qu' elle	eût	cueilli
que n.	cueillissions	que n.	eussions	cueilli
que v.	cueillissiez	que v.	eussiez	cueilli
qu' ils	cueillissent	qu' ils	eussent	cueilli

IMPÉRATIF

Présent	Passé	
cueille	aie	cueilli
cueillons	ayons	cueilli
cueillez	ayez	cueilli

INFINITIF

Présent	Passé
cueillir	avoir cueilli

PARTICIPE

Présent	Passé (composé)
cueillant	ayant cueilli
	Passé
	cueilli

***Conditionnel passé 2e forme* (2nd form)**: same form as the *plus-que-parfait* of the subjunctive.
Futur proche: *je vais cueillir* (see Grammar of the verb, paragraphs 3 and 50).

- **Accueillir** and **recueillir** follow this pattern of conjugation.
- Note the similarity of endings with those of verbs ending in **-er**, especially in the future and the present conditional: *je cueillerai*, like *j'aimerai*. (However, the *passé simple* is *je cueillis* as opposed to *j'aimai*.)

90 assaillir

INDICATIF

Présent		Passé composé		
j'	assaille	j'	ai	assailli
tu	assailles	tu	as	assailli
elle	assaille	elle	a	assailli
nous	assaillons	nous	avons	assailli
vous	assaillez	vous	avez	assailli
ils	assaillent	ils	ont	assailli

Imparfait		Plus-que-parfait		
j'	assaillais	j'	avais	assailli
tu	assaillais	tu	avais	assailli
elle	assaillait	elle	avait	assailli
nous	assaillions	nous	avions	assailli
vous	assailliez	vous	aviez	assailli
ils	assaillaient	ils	avaient	assailli

Passé simple		Passé antérieur		
j'	assaillis	j'	eus	assailli
tu	assaillis	tu	eus	assailli
elle	assaillit	elle	eut	assailli
nous	assaillîmes	nous	eûmes	assailli
vous	assaillîtes	vous	eûtes	assailli
ils	assaillirent	ils	eurent	assailli

Futur simple		Futur antérieur		
j'	assaillirai[1]	j'	aurai	assailli
tu	assailliras	tu	auras	assailli
elle	assaillira	elle	aura	assailli
nous	assaillirons	nous	aurons	assailli
vous	assaillirez	vous	aurez	assailli
ils	assailliront	ils	auront	assailli

Conditionnel présent		Conditionnel passé		
j'	assaillirais[1]	j'	aurais	assailli
tu	assaillirais	tu	aurais	assailli
elle	assaillirait	elle	aurait	assailli
nous	assaillirions	nous	aurions	assailli
vous	assailliriez	vous	auriez	assailli
ils	assailliraient	ils	auraient	assailli

SUBJONCTIF

Présent		Passé		
que j'	assaille	que j'	aie	assailli
que tu	assailles	que tu	aies	assailli
qu' elle	assaille	qu' elle	ait	assailli
que n.	assaillions	que n.	ayons	assailli
que v.	assailliez	que v.	ayez	assailli
qu' ils	assaillent	qu' ils	aient	assailli

Imparfait		Plus-que-parfait		
que j'	assaillisse	que j'	eusse	assailli
que tu	assaillisses	que tu	eusses	assailli
qu' elle	assaillît	qu' elle	eût	assailli
que n.	assaillissions	que n.	eussions	assailli
que v.	assaillissiez	que v.	eussiez	assailli
qu' ils	assaillissent	qu' ils	eussent	assailli

IMPÉRATIF

Présent	Passé	
assaille	aie	assailli
assaillons	ayons	assailli
assaillez	ayez	assailli

INFINITIF

Présent	Passé
assaillir	avoir assailli

PARTICIPE

Présent	Passé (composé)
assaillant	ayant assailli
	Passé
	assailli

1. **Saillir** behaves differently in the future and the present conditional. It is conjugated with an **e** instead of an **i**: *il saillera, il saillerait.*

***Conditionnel passé 2e forme* (2nd form)**: same form as the *plus-que-parfait* of the subjunctive.
Futur proche: *je vais assaillir* (see Grammar of the verb, paragraphs 3 and 50).

- **Tressaillir** and **défaillir** follow this pattern of conjugation.
- **Saillir** is used only in 3rd person, the infinitive and the present participle. Note, however:
  - in the sense of "protrude", "jut out" or "be prominent", it is conjugated like **assaillir** (pay attention to the exceptions in the future and the conditional);
  - in the sense of "gush forth" and in the sense of "copulate" or "cover" (zoology), it is conjugated like **finir** (see Table 81).

INDICATIF

Présent			Passé composé		
je	*faux*		j'	ai	failli
tu	*faux*		tu	as	failli
elle	*faut*		elle	a	failli
nous	*faillons*		nous	avons	failli
vous	*faillez*		vous	avez	failli
ils	*faillent*		ils	ont	failli
Imparfait			**Plus-que-parfait**		
je	*faillais*		j'	avais	failli
tu	*faillais*		tu	avais	failli
elle	*faillait*		elle	avait	failli
nous	*faillions*		nous	avions	failli
vous	*failliez*		vous	aviez	failli
ils	*faillaient*		ils	avaient	failli
Passé simple			**Passé antérieur**		
je	faillis		j'	eus	failli
tu	faillis		tu	eus	failli
elle	faillit		elle	eut	failli
nous	faillîmes		nous	eûmes	failli
vous	faillîtes		vous	eûtes	failli
ils	faillirent		ils	eurent	failli
Futur simple			**Futur antérieur**		
je	faillirai	*/ faudrai*	j'	aurai	failli
tu	failliras	*/ faudras*	tu	auras	failli
elle	faillira	*/ faudra*	elle	aura	failli
nous	faillirons	*/ faudrons*	nous	aurons	failli
vous	faillirez	*/ faudrez*	vous	aurez	failli
ils	failliront	*/ faudront*	ils	auront	failli
Conditionnel présent			**Conditionnel passé**		
je	faillirais	*/ faudrais*	j'	aurais	failli
tu	faillirais	*/ faudrais*	tu	aurais	failli
elle	faillirait	*/ faudrait*	elle	aurait	failli
nous	faillirions	*/ faudrions*	nous	aurions	failli
vous	failliriez	*/ faudriez*	vous	auriez	failli
ils	failliraient	*/ faudraient*	ils	auraient	failli

SUBJONCTIF

Présent			Passé		
que je	faillisse	*/ faille*	que j'	aie	failli
que tu	faillisses	*/ failles*	que tu	aies	failli
qu' elle	faillisse	*/ faille*	qu' elle	ait	failli
que n.	faillissions	*/ faillions*	que n.	ayons	failli
que v.	faillissiez	*/ failliez*	que v.	ayez	failli
qu' ils	faillissent	*/ faillent*	qu' ils	aient	failli
Imparfait			**Plus-que-parfait**		
que je	*faillisse*		que j'	eusse	failli
que tu	*faillisses*		que tu	eusses	failli
qu' elle	*faillît*		qu' elle	eût	failli
que n.	*faillissions*		que n.	eussions	failli
que v.	*faillissiez*		que v.	eussiez	failli
qu' ils	*faillissent*		qu' ils	eussent	failli

IMPÉRATIF

Présent	Passé
.	.
.	.
.	.

INFINITIF

Présent	Passé
faillir	avoir failli

PARTICIPE

Présent	Passé (composé)
faillant	ayant failli
	Passé
	failli

***Conditionnel passé 2e forme* (2nd form)**: same form as the *plus-que-parfait* of the subjunctive.
Futur proche: *je vais faillir* (see Grammar of the verb, paragraphs 3 and 50).

- The forms in italics are obsolete. The verb **faillir** has two distinct usages:
  1. In the sense of *manquer de* ("to have almost" or "very nearly done something"), the only forms used are the *passé simple* (*je faillis*), the future (*je faillirai*), the present conditional (*je faillirais*) and all compound verb forms such as *avoir failli*.
  2. These same forms are used in the sense of *manquer à* ("to fail to"): *je ne faillirai jamais à mon devoir*. This verb is also used in this sense in some fixed expressions: *le cœur me faut*. Do not confuse this verb with **falloir** (see Table 108) which also has the form *il faut*.
  Note: This verb is no longer used in the sense of "to go bankrupt". *Un failli* is a past participial noun.
- The verb **défaillir** is conjugated like **assaillir** (see Table 90).

92 bouillir

INDICATIF

Présent		Passé composé		
je	bous	j'	ai	bouilli
tu	bous	tu	as	bouilli
elle	bout	elle	a	bouilli
nous	bouillons	nous	avons	bouilli
vous	bouillez	vous	avez	bouilli
ils	bouillent	ils	ont	bouilli

Imparfait		Plus-que-parfait		
je	bouillais	j'	avais	bouilli
tu	bouillais	tu	avais	bouilli
elle	bouillait	elle	avait	bouilli
nous	bouillions	nous	avions	bouilli
vous	bouilliez	vous	aviez	bouilli
ils	bouillaient	ils	avaient	bouilli

Passé simple		Passé antérieur		
je	bouillis	j'	eus	bouilli
tu	bouillis	tu	eus	bouilli
elle	bouillit	elle	eut	bouilli
nous	bouillîmes	nous	eûmes	bouilli
vous	bouillîtes	vous	eûtes	bouilli
ils	bouillirent	ils	eurent	bouilli

Futur simple		Futur antérieur		
je	bouillirai	j'	aurai	bouilli
tu	bouilliras	tu	auras	bouilli
elle	bouillira	elle	aura	bouilli
nous	bouillirons	nous	aurons	bouilli
vous	bouillirez	vous	aurez	bouilli
ils	bouilliront	ils	auront	bouilli

Conditionnel présent		Conditionnel passé		
je	bouillirais	j'	aurais	bouilli
tu	bouillirais	tu	aurais	bouilli
elle	bouillirait	elle	aurait	bouilli
nous	bouillirions	nous	aurions	bouilli
vous	bouilliriez	vous	auriez	bouilli
ils	bouilliraient	ils	auraient	bouilli

SUBJONCTIF

Présent		Passé		
que je	bouille	que j'	aie	bouilli
que tu	bouilles	que tu	aies	bouilli
qu' elle	bouille	qu' elle	ait	bouilli
que n.	bouillions	que n.	ayons	bouilli
que v.	bouilliez	que v.	ayez	bouilli
qu' ils	bouillent	qu' ils	aient	bouilli

Imparfait		Plus-que-parfait		
que je	bouillisse	que j'	eusse	bouilli
que tu	bouillisses	que tu	eusses	bouilli
qu' elle	bouillît	qu' elle	eût	bouilli
que n.	bouillissions	que n.	eussions	bouilli
que v.	bouillissiez	que v.	eussiez	bouilli
qu' ils	bouillissent	qu' ils	eussent	bouilli

IMPÉRATIF

Présent	Passé	
bous	aie	bouilli
bouillons	ayons	bouilli
bouillez	ayez	bouilli

INFINITIF

Présent	Passé
bouillir	avoir bouilli

PARTICIPE

Présent	Passé (composé)
bouillant	ayant bouilli
	Passé
	bouilli

***Conditionnel passé 2e forme* (2nd form)**: same form as the *plus-que-parfait* of the subjunctive.
Futur proche: *je vais bouillir* (see Grammar of the verb, paragraphs 3 and 50).

- **Débouillir**, **racabouillir** and **rebouillir** follow the same pattern of conjugation.

INDICATIF

Présent		Passé composé		
je	dors	j'	ai	dormi
tu	dors	tu	as	dormi
elle	dort	elle	a	dormi
nous	dormons	nous	avons	dormi
vous	dormez	vous	avez	dormi
ils	dorment	ils	ont	dormi

Imparfait		Plus-que-parfait		
je	dormais	j'	avais	dormi
tu	dormais	tu	avais	dormi
elle	dormait	elle	avait	dormi
nous	dormions	nous	avions	dormi
vous	dormiez	vous	aviez	dormi
ils	dormaient	ils	avaient	dormi

Passé simple		Passé antérieur		
je	dormis	j'	eus	dormi
tu	dormis	tu	eus	dormi
elle	dormit	elle	eut	dormi
nous	dormîmes	nous	eûmes	dormi
vous	dormîtes	vous	eûtes	dormi
ils	dormirent	ils	eurent	dormi

Futur simple		Futur antérieur		
je	dormirai	j'	aurai	dormi
tu	dormiras	tu	auras	dormi
elle	dormira	elle	aura	dormi
nous	dormirons	nous	aurons	dormi
vous	dormirez	vous	aurez	dormi
ils	dormiront	ils	auront	dormi

Conditionnel présent		Conditionnel passé		
je	dormirais	j'	aurais	dormi
tu	dormirais	tu	aurais	dormi
elle	dormirait	elle	aurait	dormi
nous	dormirions	nous	aurions	dormi
vous	dormiriez	vous	auriez	dormi
ils	dormiraient	ils	auraient	dormi

SUBJONCTIF

Présent		Passé		
que je	dorme	que j'	aie	dormi
que tu	dormes	que tu	aies	dormi
qu' elle	dorme	qu' elle	ait	dormi
que n.	dormions	que n.	ayons	dormi
que v.	dormiez	que v.	ayez	dormi
qu' ils	dorment	qu' ils	aient	dormi

Imparfait		Plus-que-parfait		
que je	dormisse	que j'	eusse	dormi
que tu	dormisses	que tu	eusses	dormi
qu' elle	dormît	qu' elle	eût	dormi
que n.	dormissions	que n.	eussions	dormi
que v.	dormissiez	que v.	eussiez	dormi
qu' ils	dormissent	qu' ils	eussent	dormi

IMPÉRATIF

Présent	Passé	
dors	aie	dormi
dormons	ayons	dormi
dormez	ayez	dormi

INFINITIF

Présent	Passé
dormir	avoir dormi

PARTICIPE

Présent	Passé (composé)
dormant	ayant dormi
	Passé
	dormi

***Conditionnel passé 2ᵉ forme* (2nd form)**: same form as the *plus-que-parfait* of the subjunctive.
Futur proche: *je vais dormir* (see Grammar of the verb, paragraphs 3 and 50).

- **Endormir** and **rendormir** follow this conjugation pattern. Unlike **dormir**, they have a variable past participle: *(r)endormi, ie, is, ies.*

94 courir

INDICATIF

Présent		Passé composé		
je	cours	j'	ai	couru
tu	cours	tu	as	couru
elle	court	elle	a	couru
nous	courons	nous	avons	couru
vous	courez	vous	avez	couru
ils	courent	ils	ont	couru

Imparfait		Plus-que-parfait		
je	courais	j'	avais	couru
tu	courais	tu	avais	couru
elle	courait	elle	avait	couru
nous	courions	nous	avions	couru
vous	couriez	vous	aviez	couru
ils	couraient	ils	avaient	couru

Passé simple		Passé antérieur		
je	courus	j'	eus	couru
tu	courus	tu	eus	couru
elle	courut	elle	eut	couru
nous	courûmes	nous	eûmes	couru
vous	courûtes	vous	eûtes	couru
ils	coururent	ils	eurent	couru

Futur simple		Futur antérieur		
je	cou**rr**ai	j'	aurai	couru
tu	cou**rr**as	tu	auras	couru
elle	cou**rr**a	elle	aura	couru
nous	cou**rr**ons	nous	aurons	couru
vous	cou**rr**ez	vous	aurez	couru
ils	cou**rr**ont	ils	auront	couru

Conditionnel présent		Conditionnel passé		
je	cou**rr**ais	j'	aurais	couru
tu	cou**rr**ais	tu	aurais	couru
elle	cou**rr**ait	elle	aurait	couru
nous	cou**rr**ions	nous	aurions	couru
vous	cou**rr**iez	vous	auriez	couru
ils	cou**rr**aient	ils	auraient	couru

SUBJONCTIF

Présent		Passé		
que je	coure	que j'	aie	couru
que tu	coures	que tu	aies	couru
qu' elle	coure	qu' elle	ait	couru
que n.	courions	que n.	ayons	couru
que v.	couriez	que v.	ayez	couru
qu' ils	courent	qu' ils	aient	couru

Imparfait		Plus-que-parfait		
que je	courusse	que j'	eusse	couru
que tu	courusses	que tu	eusses	couru
qu' elle	courût	qu' elle	eût	couru
que n.	courussions	que n.	eussions	couru
que v.	courussiez	que v.	eussiez	couru
qu' ils	courussent	qu' ils	eussent	couru

IMPÉRATIF

Présent	Passé	
cours	aie	couru
courons	ayons	couru
courez	ayez	couru

INFINITIF

Présent	Passé
courir	avoir couru

PARTICIPE

Présent	Passé (composé)
courant	ayant couru
	Passé
	couru

***Conditionnel passé 2ᵉ forme* (2nd form)** same form as the *plus-que-parfait* of the subjunctive.
Futur proche: *je vais courir* (see Grammar of the verb, paragraphs 3 and 50).

- Derived forms of **courir** follow this conjugation pattern (see List of irregular verbs, p. 96 to 98).
- Note the double **r**: the first marks the stem, the second the affix of the future or the present conditional: *je courrai, je courrais*. The **i** of the infinitive has disappeared.

INDICATIF

Présent		Passé composé		
je	meurs	je	suis	mort
tu	meurs	tu	es	mort
elle	meurt	elle	est	morte
nous	mourons	nous	sommes	morts
vous	mourez	vous	êtes	morts
ils	meurent	ils	sont	morts

Imparfait		Plus-que-parfait		
je	mourais	j'	étais	mort
tu	mourais	tu	étais	mort
elle	mourait	elle	était	morte
nous	mourions	nous	étions	morts
vous	mouriez	vous	étiez	morts
ils	mouraient	ils	étaient	morts

Passé simple		Passé antérieur		
je	mourus	je	fus	mort
tu	mourus	tu	fus	mort
elle	mourut	elle	fut	morte
nous	mourûmes	nous	fûmes	morts
vous	mourûtes	vous	fûtes	morts
ils	moururent	ils	furent	morts

Futur simple		Futur antérieur		
je	mou**r**rai	je	serai	mort
tu	mou**r**ras	tu	seras	mort
elle	mou**r**ra	elle	sera	morte
nous	mou**r**rons	nous	serons	morts
vous	mou**r**rez	vous	serez	morts
ils	mou**r**ront	ils	seront	morts

Conditionnel présent		Conditionnel passé		
je	mou**r**rais	je	serais	mort
tu	mou**r**rais	tu	serais	mort
elle	mou**r**rait	elle	serait	morte
nous	mou**r**rions	nous	serions	morts
vous	mou**r**riez	vous	seriez	morts
ils	mou**r**raient	ils	seraient	morts

SUBJONCTIF

Présent		Passé		
que je	meure	que je	sois	mort
que tu	meures	que tu	sois	mort
qu' elle	meure	qu' elle	soit	morte
que n.	mourions	que n.	soyons	morts
que v.	mouriez	que v.	soyez	morts
qu' ils	meurent	qu' ils	soient	morts

Imparfait		Plus-que-parfait		
que je	mourusse	que je	fusse	mort
que tu	mourusses	que tu	fusses	mort
qu' elle	mourût	qu' elle	fût	morte
que n.	mourussions	que n.	fussions	morts
que v.	mourussiez	que v.	fussiez	morts
qu' ils	mourussent	qu' ils	fussent	morts

IMPÉRATIF

Présent	Passé	
meurs	sois	mort
mourons	soyons	morts
mourez	soyez	morts

INFINITIF

Présent	Passé
mourir	être mort

PARTICIPE

Présent	Passé (composé)
mourant	étant mort
	Passé
	mort

***Conditionnel passé 2e forme* (2nd form)**: same form as the *plus-que-parfait* of the subjunctive.
Futur proche: *je vais mourir* (see Grammar of the verb, paragraphs 3 and 50).

- Note the double **r** in the future and the present conditional: *je mourrai, je mourrais.*
- Note the use of the auxiliary **être** in the compound verb forms.
- Used pronominally, the verb **se mourir** has no compound forms.

96 servir

INDICATIF

Présent		Passé composé		
je	sers	j'	ai	servi
tu	sers	tu	as	servi
elle	sert	elle	a	servi
nous	servons	nous	avons	servi
vous	servez	vous	avez	servi
ils	servent	ils	ont	servi

Imparfait		Plus-que-parfait		
je	servais	j'	avais	servi
tu	servais	tu	avais	servi
elle	servait	elle	avait	servi
nous	servions	nous	avions	servi
vous	serviez	vous	aviez	servi
ils	servaient	ils	avaient	servi

Passé simple		Passé antérieur		
je	servis	j'	eus	servi
tu	servis	tu	eus	servi
elle	servit	elle	eut	servi
nous	servîmes	nous	eûmes	servi
vous	servîtes	vous	eûtes	servi
ils	servirent	ils	eurent	servi

Futur simple		Futur antérieur		
je	servirai	j'	aurai	servi
tu	serviras	tu	auras	servi
elle	servira	elle	aura	servi
nous	servirons	nous	aurons	servi
vous	servirez	vous	aurez	servi
ils	serviront	ils	auront	servi

Conditionnel présent		Conditionnel passé		
je	servirais	j'	aurais	servi
tu	servirais	tu	aurais	servi
elle	servirait	elle	aurait	servi
nous	servirions	nous	aurions	servi
vous	serviriez	vous	auriez	servi
ils	serviraient	ils	auraient	servi

SUBJONCTIF

Présent		Passé		
que je	serve	que j'	aie	servi
que tu	serves	que tu	aies	servi
qu' elle	serve	qu' elle	ait	servi
que n.	servions	que n.	ayons	servi
que v.	serviez	que v.	ayez	servi
qu' ils	servent	qu' ils	aient	servi

Imparfait		Plus-que-parfait		
que je	servisse	que j'	eusse	servi
que tu	servisses	que tu	eusses	servi
qu' elle	servît	qu' elle	eût	servi
que n.	servissions	que n.	eussions	servi
que v.	servissiez	que v.	eussiez	servi
qu' ils	servissent	qu' ils	eussent	servi

IMPÉRATIF

Présent	Passé	
sers	aie	servi
servons	ayons	servi
servez	ayez	servi

INFINITIF

Présent	Passé
servir	avoir servi

PARTICIPE

Présent	Passé (composé)
servant	ayant servi
	Passé
	servi

***Conditionnel passé 2e forme* (2nd form)**: same form as the *plus-que-parfait* of the subjunctive.
Futur proche: *je vais servir* (see Grammar of the verb, paragraphs 3 and 50).

- **Desservir** and **resservir** follow this pattern of conjugation.
  But **asservir** is conjugated like **finir** (see Table 81).

fuir

INDICATIF

Présent		Passé composé		
je	fuis	j'	ai	fui
tu	fuis	tu	as	fui
elle	fuit	elle	a	fui
nous	fuyons	nous	avons	fui
vous	fuyez	vous	avez	fui
ils	fuient	ils	ont	fui

Imparfait		Plus-que-parfait		
je	fuyais	j'	avais	fui
tu	fuyais	tu	avais	fui
elle	fuyait	elle	avait	fui
nous	fuyions	nous	avions	fui
vous	fuyiez	vous	aviez	fui
ils	fuyaient	ils	avaient	fui

Passé simple		Passé antérieur		
je	fuis	j'	eus	fui
tu	fuis	tu	eus	fui
elle	fuit	elle	eut	fui
nous	fuîmes	nous	eûmes	fui
vous	fuîtes	vous	eûtes	fui
ils	fuirent	ils	eurent	fui

Futur simple		Futur antérieur		
je	fuirai	j'	aurai	fui
tu	fuiras	tu	auras	fui
elle	fuira	elle	aura	fui
nous	fuirons	nous	aurons	fui
vous	fuirez	vous	aurez	fui
ils	fuiront	ils	auront	fui

Conditionnel présent		Conditionnel passé		
je	fuirais	j'	aurais	fui
tu	fuirais	tu	aurais	fui
elle	fuirait	elle	aurait	fui
nous	fuirions	nous	aurions	fui
vous	fuiriez	vous	auriez	fui
ils	fuiraient	ils	auraient	fui

SUBJONCTIF

Présent		Passé		
que je	fuie	que j'	aie	fui
que tu	fuies	que tu	aies	fui
qu'elle	fuie	qu'elle	ait	fui
que n.	fuyions	que n.	ayons	fui
que v.	fuyiez	que v.	ayez	fui
qu' ils	fuient	qu' ils	aient	fui

Imparfait		Plus-que-parfait		
que je	fuisse	que j'	eusse	fui
que tu	fuisses	que tu	eusses	fui
qu'elle	fuît	qu'elle	eût	fui
que n.	fuissions	que n.	eussions	fui
que v.	fuissiez	que v.	eussiez	fui
qu' ils	fuissent	qu' ils	eussent	fui

IMPÉRATIF

Présent	Passé	
fuis	aie	fui
fuyons	ayons	fui
fuyez	ayez	fui

INFINITIF

Présent	Passé
fuir	avoir fui

PARTICIPE

Présent	Passé (composé)
fuyant	ayant fui
	Passé
	fui

***Conditionnel passé 2ᵉ forme* (2nd form)**: same form as the *plus-que-parfait* of the subjunctive.
Futur proche: *je vais fuir* (see Grammar of the verb, paragraphs 3 and 50).

- **S'enfuir** follows this pattern of conjugation.

98 ouïr

INDICATIF

Présent			Passé composé		
j'	ois	/ouïs	j'	ai	ouï
tu	ois	/ouïs	tu	as	ouï
elle	oit	/ouït	elle	a	ouï
nous	oyons	/ouïssons	nous	avons	ouï
vous	oyez	/ouïssez	vous	avez	ouï
ils	oient	/ouïssent	ils	ont	ouï

Imparfait			Plus-que-parfait		
j'	oyais	/ouïssais	j'	avais	ouï
tu	oyais	/ouïssais	tu	avais	ouï
elle	oyait	/ouïssait	elle	avait	ouï
nous	oyions	/ouïssions	nous	avions	ouï
vous	oyiez	/ouïssiez	vous	aviez	ouï
ils	oyaient	/ouïssaient	ils	avaient	ouï

Passé simple		Passé antérieur		
j'	ouïs	j'	eus	ouï
tu	ouïs	tu	eus	ouï
elle	ouït	elle	eut	ouï
nous	ouïmes	nous	eûmes	ouï
vous	ouïtes	vous	eûtes	ouï
ils	ouïrent	ils	eurent	ouï

Futur simple			Futur antérieur		
j'	ouïrai	/orrai/oirai	j'	aurai	ouï
tu	ouïras	/orras/...	tu	auras	ouï
elle	ouïra	/orra/...	elle	aura	ouï
nous	ouïrons	/orrons/...	nous	aurons	ouï
vous	ouïrez	/orrez/...	vous	aurez	ouï
ils	ouïront	/orront/...	ils	auront	ouï

Conditionnel présent			Conditionnel passé		
j'	ouïrais	/orrais/oirais	j'	aurais	ouï
tu	ouïrais	/orrais/...	tu	aurais	ouï
elle	ouïrait	/orrait/...	elle	aurait	ouï
nous	ouïrions	/orrions/...	nous	aurions	ouï
vous	ouïriez	/orriez/...	vous	auriez	ouï
ils	ouïraient	/orraient/...	ils	auraient	ouï

SUBJONCTIF

Présent			Passé		
que j'	oie	/ouïsse	que j'	aie	ouï
que tu	oies	/ouïsses	que tu	aies	ouï
qu'elle	oie	/ouïsse	qu'elle	ait	ouï
que n.	oyions	/ouïssions	que n.	ayons	ouï
que v.	oyiez	/ouïssiez	que v.	ayez	ouï
qu' ils	oient	/ouïssent	qu' ils	aient	ouï

Imparfait		Plus-que-parfait		
que j'	ouïsse	que j'	eusse	ouï
que tu	ouïsses	que tu	eusses	ouï
qu'elle	ouït	qu'elle	eût	ouï
que n.	ouïssions	que n.	eussions	ouï
que v.	ouïssiez	que v.	eussiez	ouï
qu' ils	ouïssent	qu' ils	eussent	ouï

IMPÉRATIF

Présent		Passé	
ois	/ouïs	aie	ouï
oyons	/ouïssons	ayons	ouï
oyez	/ouïssez	ayez	ouï

INFINITIF

Présent	Passé
ouïr	avoir ouï

PARTICIPE

Présent	Passé (composé)
oyant	ayant ouï
	Passé
	ouï

***Conditionnel passé 2e forme* (2nd form)**: same form as the *plus-que-parfait* of the subjunctive.
Futur proche: *je vais ouïr* (see Grammar of the verb, paragraphs 3 and 50).

- The verb **ouïr** has fallen into disuse in favour of the verb **entendre**. It survives only in the infinitive, the imperative (*Oyez ! Oyez !* = "Hear ye!"), compound forms and in the expression *par ouï-dire* (= "by hearsay"). Note the masculine noun *le ouï-dire*. The archaic conjugation forms appear in italics above.
- Note the forms *j'ouïrai* (future) and *j'ouïrais* (present conditional) in which the endings are added to the infinitive as in the case of the verb **finir** (*je finirai, je finirais*).
- The presence of the diaresis in the *passé simple* and the *imparfait* of the subjunctive precludes the use of the circumflex.

INDICATIF

Présent /VARIANTE		Passé composé
je	gis	.
tu	gis	.
elle	gît /git	.
nous	gisons	.
vous	gisez	.
ils	gisent	.

Imparfait		Plus-que-parfait
je	gisais	.
tu	gisais	.
elle	gisait	.
nous	gisions	.
vous	gisiez	.
ils	gisaient	.

Passé simple	Passé antérieur
.	.
.	.
.	.
.	.
.	.
.	.

Futur simple	Futur antérieur
.	.
.	.
.	.
.	.
.	.
.	.

Conditionnel présent	Conditionnel passé
.	.
.	.
.	.
.	.
.	.
.	.

SUBJONCTIF

Présent	Passé
.	.
.	.
.	.
.	.
.	.
.	.

Imparfait	Plus-que-parfait
.	.
.	.
.	.
.	.
.	.
.	.

IMPÉRATIF

Présent	Passé
.	.
.	.
.	.

INFINITIF

Présent	Passé
gésir	.

PARTICIPE

Présent	Passé (composé)
gisant	.
	Passé
	.

***Conditionnel passé 2e forme* (2nd form)**: same form as the *plus-que-parfait* of the subjunctive.
Futur proche: *je vais gésir* (see Grammar of the verb, paragraphs 3 and 50).

- In accordance with the spelling reform, the form *git* can be written without the circumflex over the **i**.
- This verb which means "to be lying (in a horizontal position)" is used only in the forms given above.
  It is used primarily to refer to the lifeless, the very ill, the dead or objects that have been destroyed by the weather or war: *Nous gisions tous les deux sur le pavé d'un cachot, malades et privés de secours* (= "We both lay there…"). *Son cadavre gît maintenant dans le tombeau* (= "His dead body now lies…"). *Des colonnes gisant éparses.* (= "Fallen columns lay strewn about").* Ref. Graveside inscription: *Ci-gît* or *ci-git* (= "Here lies…").

* The participial form (*gisant*) is used here in a figurative sense. The proposed equivalent (replacing the participle by a finite verb in the past) is but one of a few possible options.

INDICATIF

Présent		Passé composé		
je	reçois	j'	ai	reçu
tu	reçois	tu	as	reçu
elle	reçoit	elle	a	reçu
nous	recevons	nous	avons	reçu
vous	recevez	vous	avez	reçu
ils	reçoivent	ils	ont	reçu

Imparfait		Plus-que-parfait		
je	recevais	j'	avais	reçu
tu	recevais	tu	avais	reçu
elle	recevait	elle	avait	reçu
nous	recevions	nous	avions	reçu
vous	receviez	vous	aviez	reçu
ils	recevaient	ils	avaient	reçu

Passé simple		Passé antérieur		
je	reçus	j'	eus	reçu
tu	reçus	tu	eus	reçu
elle	reçut	elle	eut	reçu
nous	reçûmes	nous	eûmes	reçu
vous	reçûtes	vous	eûtes	reçu
ils	reçurent	ils	eurent	reçu

Futur simple		Futur antérieur		
je	recevrai	j'	aurai	reçu
tu	recevras	tu	auras	reçu
elle	recevra	elle	aura	reçu
nous	recevrons	nous	aurons	reçu
vous	recevrez	vous	aurez	reçu
ils	recevront	ils	auront	reçu

Conditionnel présent		Conditionnel passé		
je	recevrais	j'	aurais	reçu
tu	recevrais	tu	aurais	reçu
elle	recevrait	elle	aurait	reçu
nous	recevrions	nous	aurions	reçu
vous	recevriez	vous	auriez	reçu
ils	recevraient	ils	auraient	reçu

SUBJONCTIF

Présent		Passé		
que je	reçoive	que j'	aie	reçu
que tu	reçoives	que tu	aies	reçu
qu' elle	reçoive	qu' elle	ait	reçu
que n.	recevions	que n.	ayons	reçu
que v.	receviez	que v.	ayez	reçu
qu' ils	reçoivent	qu' ils	aient	reçu

Imparfait		Plus-que-parfait		
que je	reçusse	que j'	eusse	reçu
que tu	reçusses	que tu	eusses	reçu
qu' elle	reçût	qu' elle	eût	reçu
que n.	reçussions	que n.	eussions	reçu
que v.	reçussiez	que v.	eussiez	reçu
qu' ils	reçussent	qu' ils	eussent	reçu

IMPÉRATIF

Présent	Passé	
reçois	aie	reçu
recevons	ayons	reçu
recevez	ayez	reçu

INFINITIF

Présent	Passé
recevoir	avoir reçu

PARTICIPE

Présent	Passé (composé)
recevant	ayant reçu
	Passé
	reçu

***Conditionnel passé 2e forme* (2nd form)**: same form as the *plus-que-parfait* of the subjunctive.
Futur proche: *je vais recevoir* (see Grammar of the verb, paragraphs 3 and 50).

- The **c** always takes a cedilla before **o** or **u**.
- **Apercevoir**, **concevoir**, **décevoir**, **entrapercevoir**, **percevoir** follow this pattern of conjugation.

voir

INDICATIF

Présent		Passé composé		
je	vois	j'	ai	vu
tu	vois	tu	as	vu
elle	voit	elle	a	vu
nous	voyons	nous	avons	vu
vous	voyez	vous	avez	vu
ils	voient	ils	ont	vu

Imparfait		Plus-que-parfait		
je	voyais	j'	avais	vu
tu	voyais	tu	avais	vu
elle	voyait	elle	avait	vu
nous	voyions	nous	avions	vu
vous	voyiez	vous	aviez	vu
ils	voyaient	ils	avaient	vu

Passé simple		Passé antérieur		
je	vis	j'	eus	vu
tu	vis	tu	eus	vu
elle	vit	elle	eut	vu
nous	vîmes	nous	eûmes	vu
vous	vîtes	vous	eûtes	vu
ils	virent	ils	eurent	vu

Futur simple		Futur antérieur		
je	verrai[1]	j'	aurai	vu
tu	verras	tu	auras	vu
elle	verra	elle	aura	vu
nous	verrons	nous	aurons	vu
vous	verrez	vous	aurez	vu
ils	verront	ils	auront	vu

Conditionnel présent		Conditionnel passé		
je	verrais[1]	j'	aurais	vu
tu	verrais	tu	aurais	vu
elle	verrait	elle	aurait	vu
nous	verrions	nous	aurions	vu
vous	verriez	vous	auriez	vu
ils	verraient	ils	auraient	vu

SUBJONCTIF

Présent		Passé		
que je	voie	que j'	aie	vu
que tu	voies	que tu	aies	vu
qu'elle	voie	qu'elle	ait	vu
que n.	voyions	que n.	ayons	vu
que v.	voyiez	que v.	ayez	vu
qu' ils	voient	qu' ils	aient	vu

Imparfait		Plus-que-parfait		
que je	visse	que j'	eusse	vu
que tu	visses	que tu	eusses	vu
qu'elle	vît	qu'elle	eût	vu
que n.	vissions	que n.	eussions	vu
que v.	vissiez	que v.	eussiez	vu
qu' ils	vissent	qu' ils	eussent	vu

IMPÉRATIF

Présent	Passé	
vois	aie	vu
voyons	ayons	vu
voyez	ayez	vu

INFINITIF

Présent	Passé
voir	avoir vu

PARTICIPE

Présent	Passé (composé)
voyant	ayant vu
	Passé
	vu

1. **Prévoir** is conjugated differently in the future and the present conditional: *je prévoirai…, je prévoirais…*

***Conditionnel passé 2e forme* (2nd form)**: same form as the *plus-que-parfait* of the subjunctive.
Futur proche: *je vais voir* (see Grammar of the verb, paragraphs 3 and 50).

- **Entrevoir** and **revoir** follow this pattern of conjugation.
- **Prévoir** also follows this pattern but is conjugated like a regular verb in the future and the present conditional (see Note 1 above).
- The verb **pourvoir** is conjugated differently (see Table 102).

102 pourvoir

INDICATIF

Présent		Passé composé		
je	pourvois	j'	ai	pourvu
tu	pourvois	tu	as	pourvu
elle	pourvoit	elle	a	pourvu
nous	pourvo**y**ons	nous	avons	pourvu
vous	pourvo**y**ez	vous	avez	pourvu
ils	pourvoient	ils	ont	pourvu

Imparfait		Plus-que-parfait		
je	pourvoyais	j'	avais	pourvu
tu	pourvoyais	tu	avais	pourvu
elle	pourvoyait	elle	avait	pourvu
nous	pourvo**yi**ons	nous	avions	pourvu
vous	pourvo**yi**ez	vous	aviez	pourvu
ils	pourvoyaient	ils	avaient	pourvu

Passé simple		Passé antérieur		
je	pourvus	j'	eus	pourvu
tu	pourvus	tu	eus	pourvu
elle	pourvut	elle	eut	pourvu
nous	pourvûmes	nous	eûmes	pourvu
vous	pourvûtes	vous	eûtes	pourvu
ils	pourvurent	ils	eurent	pourvu

Futur simple		Futur antérieur		
je	pourvoirai	j'	aurai	pourvu
tu	pourvoiras	tu	auras	pourvu
elle	pourvoira	elle	aura	pourvu
nous	pourvoirons	nous	aurons	pourvu
vous	pourvoirez	vous	aurez	pourvu
ils	pourvoiront	ils	auront	pourvu

Conditionnel présent		Conditionnel passé		
je	pourvoirais	j'	aurais	pourvu
tu	pourvoirais	tu	aurais	pourvu
elle	pourvoirait	elle	aurait	pourvu
nous	pourvoirions	nous	aurions	pourvu
vous	pourvoiriez	vous	auriez	pourvu
ils	pourvoiraient	ils	auraient	pourvu

SUBJONCTIF

Présent		Passé		
que je	pourvoie	que j'	aie	pourvu
que tu	pourvoies	que tu	aies	pourvu
qu' elle	pourvoie	qu' elle	ait	pourvu
que n.	pourvo**yi**ons	que n.	ayons	pourvu
que v.	pourvo**yi**ez	que v.	ayez	pourvu
qu' ils	pourvoient	qu' ils	aient	pourvu

Imparfait		Plus-que-parfait		
que je	pourvusse	que j'	eusse	pourvu
que tu	pourvusses	que tu	eusses	pourvu
qu' elle	pourvût	qu' elle	eût	pourvu
que n.	pourvussions	que n.	eussions	pourvu
que v.	pourvussiez	que v.	eussiez	pourvu
qu' ils	pourvussent	qu' ils	eussent	pourvu

IMPÉRATIF

Présent	Passé	
pourvois	aie	pourvu
pourvo**y**ons	ayons	pourvu
pourvo**y**ez	ayez	pourvu

INFINITIF

Présent	Passé
pourvoir	avoir pourvu

PARTICIPE

Présent	Passé (composé)
pourvoyant	ayant pourvu
	Passé
	pourvu

***Conditionnel passé 2e forme* (2nd form)**: same form as the *plus-que-parfait* of the subjunctive.
Futur proche: *je vais pourvoir* (see Grammar of the verb, paragraphs 3 and 50).

- **Dépourvoir** follows this conjugation pattern. It is mainly used pronominally (*je me suis dépourvu de tout)*, in the *passé simple*, the infinitive, the past participle and in compound forms.
- Note that **pourvoir** and **voir** have similar conjugation patterns (see Table 101) except in the future and the present conditional (*je pourvoirai, je pourvoirais*) and in the *passé simple* and the *imparfait* of the subjunctive (*je pourvus, que je pourvusse*).

INDICATIF

Présent		Passé composé		
je	sais	j'	ai	su
tu	sais	tu	as	su
elle	sait	elle	a	su
nous	savons	nous	avons	su
vous	savez	vous	avez	su
ils	savent	ils	ont	su
Imparfait		**Plus-que-parfait**		
je	savais	j'	avais	su
tu	savais	tu	avais	su
elle	savait	elle	avait	su
nous	savions	nous	avions	su
vous	saviez	vous	aviez	su
ils	savaient	ils	avaient	su
Passé simple		**Passé antérieur**		
je	sus	j'	eus	su
tu	sus	tu	eus	su
elle	sut	elle	eut	su
nous	sûmes	nous	eûmes	su
vous	sûtes	vous	eûtes	su
ils	surent	ils	eurent	su
Futur simple		**Futur antérieur**		
je	saurai	j'	aurai	su
tu	sauras	tu	auras	su
elle	saura	elle	aura	su
nous	saurons	nous	aurons	su
vous	saurez	vous	aurez	su
ils	sauront	ils	auront	su
Conditionnel présent		**Conditionnel passé**		
je	saurais	j'	aurais	su
tu	saurais	tu	aurais	su
elle	saurait	elle	aurait	su
nous	saurions	nous	aurions	su
vous	sauriez	vous	auriez	su
ils	sauraient	ils	auraient	su

SUBJONCTIF

Présent		Passé		
que je	sache	que j'	aie	su
que tu	saches	que tu	aies	su
qu'elle	sache	qu'elle	ait	su
que n.	sachions	que n.	ayons	su
que v.	sachiez	que v.	ayez	su
qu' ils	sachent	qu' ils	aient	su
Imparfait		**Plus-que-parfait**		
que je	susse	que j'	eusse	su
que tu	susses	que tu	eusses	su
qu'elle	sût	qu'elle	eût	su
que n.	sussions	que n.	eussions	su
que v.	sussiez	que v.	eussiez	su
qu' ils	sussent	qu' ils	eussent	su

IMPÉRATIF

Présent	Passé	
sache	aie	su
sachons	ayons	su
sachez	ayez	su

INFINITIF

Présent	Passé
savoir	avoir su

PARTICIPE

Présent	Passé (composé)
sachant	ayant su
	Passé
	su

***Conditionnel passé 2e forme* (2nd form)**: same form as the *plus-que-parfait* of the subjunctive.
Futur proche: *je vais savoir* (see Grammar of the verb, paragraphs 3 and 50).

- Note a somewhat archaic use of the subjunctive in the following expressions: *je ne sache pas qu'il soit venu; il n'est pas venu, que je sache.*

104 devoir

INDICATIF

Présent		Passé composé		
je	dois	j'	ai	dû
tu	dois	tu	as	dû
elle	doit	elle	a	dû
nous	devons	nous	avons	dû
vous	devez	vous	avez	dû
ils	doivent	ils	ont	dû

Imparfait		Plus-que-parfait		
je	devais	j'	avais	dû
tu	devais	tu	avais	dû
elle	devait	elle	avait	dû
nous	devions	nous	avions	dû
vous	deviez	vous	aviez	dû
ils	devaient	ils	avaient	dû

Passé simple		Passé antérieur		
je	dus	j'	eus	dû
tu	dus	tu	eus	dû
elle	dut	elle	eut	dû
nous	dûmes	nous	eûmes	dû
vous	dûtes	vous	eûtes	dû
ils	durent	ils	eurent	dû

Futur simple		Futur antérieur		
je	devrai	j'	aurai	dû
tu	devras	tu	auras	dû
elle	devra	elle	aura	dû
nous	devrons	nous	aurons	dû
vous	devrez	vous	aurez	dû
ils	devront	ils	auront	dû

Conditionnel présent		Conditionnel passé		
je	devrais	j'	aurais	dû
tu	devrais	tu	aurais	dû
elle	devrait	elle	aurait	dû
nous	devrions	nous	aurions	dû
vous	devriez	vous	auriez	dû
ils	devraient	ils	auraient	dû

SUBJONCTIF

Présent		Passé		
que je	doive	que j'	aie	dû
que tu	doives	que tu	aies	dû
qu' elle	doive	qu' elle	ait	dû
que n.	devions	que n.	ayons	dû
que v.	deviez	que v.	ayez	dû
qu' ils	doivent	qu' ils	aient	dû

Imparfait		Plus-que-parfait		
que je	dusse	que j'	eusse	dû
que tu	dusses	que tu	eusses	dû
qu' elle	dût	qu' elle	eût	dû
que n.	dussions	que n.	eussions	dû
que v.	dussiez	que v.	eussiez	dû
qu' ils	dussent	qu' ils	eussent	dû

IMPÉRATIF

Présent	Passé	
dois	aie	dû
devons	ayons	dû
devez	ayez	dû

INFINITIF

Présent	Passé
devoir	avoir dû

PARTICIPE

Présent	Passé (composé)
devant	ayant dû
	Passé
	dû

***Conditionnel passé 2e forme* (2nd form)**: same form as the *plus-que-parfait* of the subjunctive.
Futur proche: *je vais devoir* (see Grammar of the verb, paragraphs 3 and 50).

- The imperative form is hardly used.
- The past participle of **devoir** takes a circumflex in the masculine singular only: *dû*. The other forms take no accent: *due, dus, dues*.
- **Redevoir** follows this pattern. Traditionally the past participial forms are: *redû, redue, redus, redues*. The spelling reform recommends the accent be dropped in the masculine form of the past participle: *redu*.

INDICATIF

Présent		Passé composé		
je	peux / puis	j'	ai	pu
tu	peux	tu	as	pu
elle	peut	elle	a	pu
nous	pouvons	nous	avons	pu
vous	pouvez	vous	avez	pu
ils	peuvent	ils	ont	pu

Imparfait		Plus-que-parfait		
je	pouvais	j'	avais	pu
tu	pouvais	tu	avais	pu
elle	pouvait	elle	avait	pu
nous	pouvions	nous	avions	pu
vous	pouviez	vous	aviez	pu
ils	pouvaient	ils	avaient	pu

Passé simple		Passé antérieur		
je	pus	j'	eus	pu
tu	pus	tu	eus	pu
elle	put	elle	eut	pu
nous	pûmes	nous	eûmes	pu
vous	pûtes	vous	eûtes	pu
ils	purent	ils	eurent	pu

Futur simple		Futur antérieur		
je	pourrai	j'	aurai	pu
tu	pourras	tu	auras	pu
elle	pourra	elle	aura	pu
nous	pourrons	nous	aurons	pu
vous	pourrez	vous	aurez	pu
ils	pourront	ils	auront	pu

Conditionnel présent		Conditionnel passé		
je	pourrais	j'	aurais	pu
tu	pourrais	tu	aurais	pu
elle	pourrait	elle	aurait	pu
nous	pourrions	nous	aurions	pu
vous	pourriez	vous	auriez	pu
ils	pourraient	ils	auraient	pu

SUBJONCTIF

Présent		Passé		
que je	puisse	que j'	aie	pu
que tu	puisses	que tu	aies	pu
qu' elle	puisse	qu' elle	ait	pu
que n.	puissions	que n.	ayons	pu
que v.	puissiez	que v.	ayez	pu
qu' ils	puissent	qu' ils	aient	pu

Imparfait		Plus-que-parfait		
que je	pusse	que j'	eusse	pu
que tu	pusses	que tu	eusses	pu
qu' elle	pût	qu' elle	eût	pu
que n.	pussions	que n.	eussions	pu
que v.	pussiez	que v.	eussiez	pu
qu' ils	pussent	qu' ils	eussent	pu

IMPÉRATIF

Présent	Passé
.	.
.	.
.	.

INFINITIF

Présent	Passé
pouvoir	avoir pu

PARTICIPE

Présent	Passé (composé)
pouvant	ayant pu
	Passé
	pu

***Conditionnel passé 2e forme* (2nd form)**: same form as the *plus-que-parfait* of the subjunctive.
Futur proche: *je vais pouvoir* (see Grammar of the verb, paragraphs 3 and 50).

- **Pouvoir** takes a double **r** in the future and the present conditional, but unlike **mourir** and **courir** only one is pronounced.
- *Je puis* is more formal than *je peux*. In the first person however, the interrogative form is *Puis-je ?* not ⊗ *Peux-je ?*
- The construction *il se peut que* is used as a synonym for *il peut se faire que* to mean "it is possible that" and is normally followed by the subjunctive.
- There are no systematic imperative forms. However, note the following constructions: *Puisses-tu dire vrai !** (= "Would that that were true / If only that were true") or *Puissions-nous réussir !** (= "Would that we could succeed / If only we could succeed").

* Note that these forms are the same as the present subjunctive. The English counterpart using "would that" corresponds to a hypothetical construction that bears the meaning of "will" expressing desire, determination or choice.

106 émouvoir

INDICATIF

Présent		Passé composé		
j'	émeus	j'	ai	ému
tu	émeus	tu	as	ému
elle	émeut	elle	a	ému
nous	émouvons	nous	avons	ému
vous	émouvez	vous	avez	ému
ils	émeuvent	ils	ont	ému

Imparfait		Plus-que-parfait		
j'	émouvais	j'	avais	ému
tu	émouvais	tu	avais	ému
elle	émouvait	elle	avait	ému
nous	émouvions	nous	avions	ému
vous	émouviez	vous	aviez	ému
ils	émouvaient	ils	avaient	ému

Passé simple		Passé antérieur		
j'	émus	j'	eus	ému
tu	émus	tu	eus	ému
elle	émut	elle	eut	ému
nous	émûmes	nous	eûmes	ému
vous	émûtes	vous	eûtes	ému
ils	émurent	ils	eurent	ému

Futur simple		Futur antérieur		
j'	émouvrai	j'	aurai	ému
tu	émouvras	tu	auras	ému
elle	émouvra	elle	aura	ému
nous	émouvrons	nous	aurons	ému
vous	émouvrez	vous	aurez	ému
ils	émouvront	ils	auront	ému

Conditionnel présent		Conditionnel passé		
j'	émouvrais	j'	aurais	ému
tu	émouvrais	tu	aurais	ému
elle	émouvrait	elle	aurait	ému
nous	émouvrions	nous	aurions	ému
vous	émouvriez	vous	auriez	ému
ils	émouvraient	ils	auraient	ému

SUBJONCTIF

Présent		Passé		
que j'	émeuve	que j'	aie	ému
que tu	émeuves	que tu	aies	ému
qu' elle	émeuve	qu' elle	ait	ému
que n.	émouvions	que n.	ayons	ému
que v.	émouviez	que v.	ayez	ému
qu' ils	émeuvent	qu' ils	aient	ému

Imparfait		Plus-que-parfait		
que j'	émusse	que j'	eusse	ému
que tu	émusses	que tu	eusses	ému
qu' elle	émût	qu' elle	eût	ému
que n.	émussions	que n.	eussions	ému
que v.	émussiez	que v.	eussiez	ému
qu' ils	émussent	qu' ils	eussent	ému

IMPÉRATIF

Présent	Passé	
émeus	aie	ému
émouvons	ayons	ému
émouvez	ayez	ému

INFINITIF

Présent	Passé
émouvoir	avoir ému

PARTICIPE

Présent	Passé (composé)
émouvant	ayant ému
	Passé
	ému

***Conditionnel passé 2e forme* (2nd form)**: same form as the *plus-que-parfait* of the subjunctive.
Futur proche: *je vais émouvoir* (see Grammar of the verb, paragraphs 3 and 50).

- **Promouvoir** is conjugated like **émouvoir**.
- **Mouvoir** is conjugated like **émouvoir**. Traditionally, the masculine singular form of the past participle takes a circumflex: *mû*. The other forms: *mue, mus, mues* do not. The French spelling reform allows the past participle to be spelt without the circumflex: *mu*.

pleuvoir 107

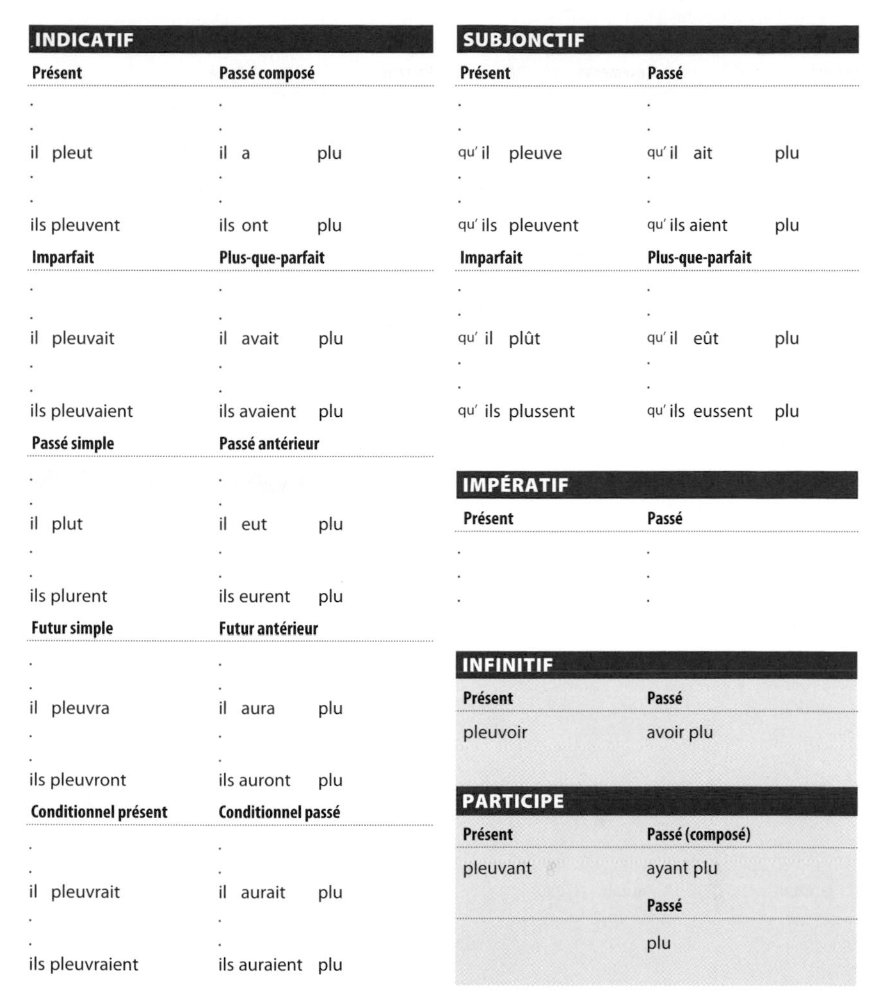

INDICATIF

Présent	Passé composé
.	.
.	.
il pleut	il a plu
.	.
.	.
ils pleuvent	ils ont plu

Imparfait	Plus-que-parfait
.	.
.	.
il pleuvait	il avait plu
.	.
.	.
ils pleuvaient	ils avaient plu

Passé simple	Passé antérieur
.	.
.	.
il plut	il eut plu
.	.
.	.
ils plurent	ils eurent plu

Futur simple	Futur antérieur
.	.
.	.
il pleuvra	il aura plu
.	.
.	.
ils pleuvront	ils auront plu

Conditionnel présent	Conditionnel passé
.	.
.	.
il pleuvrait	il aurait plu
.	.
.	.
ils pleuvraient	ils auraient plu

SUBJONCTIF

Présent	Passé
.	.
.	.
qu'il pleuve	qu'il ait plu
.	.
.	.
qu'ils pleuvent	qu'ils aient plu

Imparfait	Plus-que-parfait
.	.
.	.
qu'il plût	qu'il eût plu
.	.
.	.
qu'ils plussent	qu'ils eussent plu

IMPÉRATIF

Présent	Passé
.	.
.	.
.	.

INFINITIF

Présent	Passé
pleuvoir	avoir plu

PARTICIPE

Présent	Passé (composé)
pleuvant	ayant plu
	Passé
	plu

Conditionnel passé 2e forme **(2nd form)**: same form as the *plus-que-parfait* of the subjunctive.
Futur proche: *il va pleuvoir* (see Grammar of the verb, paragraphs 3 and 50).

- **Repleuvoir** follows the same pattern of conjugation.
- Although usually used in impersonal constructions, this verb is also used in the plural, but figuratively: *les coups de fusil pleuvent, les sarcasmes pleuvent sur lui, les honneurs pleuvaient sur sa personne*. The present participle also is used in a figurative sense only: *les coups pleuvant sur lui…*

108 impersonal verb | falloir

INDICATIF

Présent	Passé composé
.	.
.	.
il faut	il a fallu
.	.
.	.
.	.

Imparfait	Plus-que-parfait
.	.
.	.
il fallait	il avait fallu
.	.
.	.
.	.

Passé simple	Passé antérieur
.	.
.	.
il fallut	il eut fallu
.	.
.	.
.	.

Futur simple	Futur antérieur
.	.
.	.
il faudra	il aura fallu
.	.
.	.
.	.

Conditionnel présent	Conditionnel passé
.	.
.	.
il faudrait	il aurait fallu
.	.
.	.
.	.

SUBJONCTIF

Présent	Passé
.	.
.	.
qu'il faille	qu'il ait fallu
.	.
.	.
.	.

Imparfait	Plus-que-parfait
.	.
.	.
qu'il fallût	qu'il eût fallu
.	.
.	.
.	.

IMPÉRATIF

Présent	Passé
.	.
.	.
.	.

INFINITIF

Présent	Passé
falloir	avoir fallu

PARTICIPE

Présent	Passé (composé)
.	ayant fallu
	Passé
	fallu

***Conditionnel passé 2e forme* (2nd form)**: same form as the *plus-que-parfait* of the subjunctive.
Futur proche: *il va falloir* (see Grammar of the verb, paragraphs 3 and 50).

- In the expressions: *il s'en faut de beaucoup, tant s'en faut, peu s'en faut*, historically the form *faut* comes not from **falloir** but from **faillir** in the sense of "to lack" (see Table 91).

INDICATIF

Présent		Passé composé		
je	vaux	j'	ai	valu
tu	vaux	tu	as	valu
elle	vaut	elle	a	valu
nous	valons	nous	avons	valu
vous	valez	vous	avez	valu
ils	valent	ils	ont	valu

Imparfait		Plus-que-parfait		
je	valais	j'	avais	valu
tu	valais	tu	avais	valu
elle	valait	elle	avait	valu
nous	valions	nous	avions	valu
vous	valiez	vous	aviez	valu
ils	valaient	ils	avaient	valu

Passé simple		Passé antérieur		
je	valus	j'	eus	valu
tu	valus	tu	eus	valu
elle	valut	elle	eut	valu
nous	valûmes	nous	eûmes	valu
vous	valûtes	vous	eûtes	valu
ils	valurent	ils	eurent	valu

Futur simple		Futur antérieur		
je	vaudrai	j'	aurai	valu
tu	vaudras	tu	auras	valu
elle	vaudra	elle	aura	valu
nous	vaudrons	nous	aurons	valu
vous	vaudrez	vous	aurez	valu
ils	vaudront	ils	auront	valu

Conditionnel présent		Conditionnel passé		
je	vaudrais	j'	aurais	valu
tu	vaudrais	tu	aurais	valu
elle	vaudrait	elle	aurait	valu
nous	vaudrions	nous	aurions	valu
vous	vaudriez	vous	auriez	valu
ils	vaudraient	ils	auraient	valu

SUBJONCTIF

Présent		Passé		
que je	vaille[1]	que j'	aie	valu
que tu	vailles	que tu	aies	valu
qu'elle	vaille	qu'elle	ait	valu
que n.	valions	que n.	ayons	valu
que v.	valiez	que v.	ayez	valu
qu'ils	vaillent	qu'ils	aient	valu

Imparfait		Plus-que-parfait		
que je	valusse	que j'	eusse	valu
que tu	valusses	que tu	eusses	valu
qu'elle	valût	qu'elle	eût	valu
que n.	valussions	que n.	eussions	valu
que v.	valussiez	que v.	eussiez	valu
qu'ils	valussent	qu'ils	eussent	valu

IMPÉRATIF

Présent	Passé	
vaux	aie	valu
valons	ayons	valu
valez	ayez	valu

INFINITIF

Présent	Passé
valoir	avoir valu

PARTICIPE

Présent	Passé (composé)
valant	ayant valu
	Passé
	valu

1. **Prévaloir** is conjugated differently in the present subjunctive: *que je prévale…, que nous prévalions…*
Il ne faut pas que la coutume prévale sur la raison (Ac.).

***Conditionnel passé 2e forme* (2nd form)**: same form as the *plus-que-parfait* of the subjunctive.
Futur proche: *je vais valoir* (see Grammar of the verb, paragraphs 3 and 50).

- **Équivaloir** and **revaloir** are conjugated like **valoir**. The past participle *équivalu* is always invariable. The past participles *revalu* and *valu* are sometimes variable (see Grammar of the verb, paragraph 42).
- **Prévaloir** is conjugated like **valoir** except in the present subjunctive (see note above). When **prévaloir** is used pronominally, the participle agrees: *Elle s'est prévalue de ses droits.*

110 vouloir

INDICATIF

Présent		Passé composé		
je	veux	j'	ai	voulu
tu	veux	tu	as	voulu
elle	veut	elle	a	voulu
nous	voulons	nous	avons	voulu
vous	voulez	vous	avez	voulu
ils	veulent	ils	ont	voulu

Imparfait		Plus-que-parfait		
je	voulais	j'	avais	voulu
tu	voulais	tu	avais	voulu
elle	voulait	elle	avait	voulu
nous	voulions	nous	avions	voulu
vous	vouliez	vous	aviez	voulu
ils	voulaient	ils	avaient	voulu

Passé simple		Passé antérieur		
je	voulus	j'	eus	voulu
tu	voulus	tu	eus	voulu
elle	voulut	elle	eut	voulu
nous	voulûmes	nous	eûmes	voulu
vous	voulûtes	vous	eûtes	voulu
ils	voulurent	ils	eurent	voulu

Futur simple		Futur antérieur		
je	voudrai	j'	aurai	voulu
tu	voudras	tu	auras	voulu
elle	voudra	elle	aura	voulu
nous	voudrons	nous	aurons	voulu
vous	voudrez	vous	aurez	voulu
ils	voudront	ils	auront	voulu

Conditionnel présent		Conditionnel passé		
je	voudrais	j'	aurais	voulu
tu	voudrais	tu	aurais	voulu
elle	voudrait	elle	aurait	voulu
nous	voudrions	nous	aurions	voulu
vous	voudriez	vous	auriez	voulu
ils	voudraient	ils	auraient	voulu

SUBJONCTIF

Présent		Passé		
que je	veuille	que j'	aie	voulu
que tu	veuilles	que tu	aies	voulu
qu' elle	veuille	qu' elle	ait	voulu
que n.	voulions / *veuillions*	que n.	ayons	voulu
que v.	vouliez / *veuilliez*	que v.	ayez	voulu
qu' ils	veuillent	qu' ils	aient	voulu

Imparfait		Plus-que-parfait		
que je	voulusse	que j'	eusse	voulu
que tu	voulusses	que tu	eusses	voulu
qu' elle	voulût	qu' elle	eût	voulu
que n.	voulussions	que n.	eussions	voulu
que v.	voulussiez	que v.	eussiez	voulu
qu' ils	voulussent	qu' ils	eussent	voulu

IMPÉRATIF

Présent	Passé
veux / veuille	aie voulu
voulons / veuillons	ayons voulu
voulez / veuillez	ayez voulu

INFINITIF

Présent	Passé
vouloir	avoir voulu

PARTICIPE

Présent	Passé (composé)
voulant	ayant voulu
	Passé
	voulu

***Conditionnel passé 2ᵉ forme* (2nd form)**: same form as the *plus-que-parfait* of the subjunctive.
Futur proche: *je vais vouloir* (see Grammar of the verb, paragraphs 3 and 50).

- The imperatives *veux, voulons, voulez* are only used to urge someone to adopt a strong sense of will (as in the expression "to steel one's will"): *veux donc, malheureux, et tu seras sauvé*. The polite forms are: *veuille, veuillez* as in *veuillez agréer mes respectueuses salutations** (in the sense of *ayez la bonté de*...). When **vouloir** is used with the pronoun **en**, it means as to "feel resentful towards (someone)" or "hold something against (someone)": *ne m'en veux pas, ne m'en voulez pas*. Literary usage however would prefer the following forms: *ne m'en veuille pas, ne m'en veuillez pas*.
- In the present subjunctive, the forms *que nous voulions, que vous vouliez* are preferred to *que nous veuillions, que vous veuilliez*.

* Salutation at the end of a letter ("yours sincerely / truly; best regards").

INDICATIF

Présent	Passé composé
.	.
.	.
elle sied	.
.	.
.	.
ils siéent	.

Imparfait	Plus-que-parfait
.	.
.	.
elle seyait	.
.	.
.	.
ils seyaient	.

Passé simple	Passé antérieur
.	.
.	.
.	.
.	.
.	.
.	.

Futur simple	Futur antérieur
.	.
.	.
elle siéra	.
.	.
.	.
ils siéront	.

Conditionnel présent	Conditionnel passé
.	.
.	.
elle siérait	.
.	.
.	.
ils siéraient	.

SUBJONCTIF

Présent	Passé
.	.
.	.
qu'elle siée	.
.	.
.	.
qu'ils siéent	.

Imparfait	Plus-que-parfait
.	.
.	.
.	.
.	.
.	.
.	.

IMPÉRATIF

Présent	Passé
sieds	.
seyons	.
seyez	.

INFINITIF

Présent	Passé
seoir	.

PARTICIPE

Présent	Passé (composé)
séant / seyant	.
	Passé
	sis

Futur proche: *il va seoir* (see Grammar of the verb, paragraphs 3 and 50).

- This verb has no compound forms.
- The verb **seoir** generally has the same meaning as *convenir* (= "to be suited to" or "to suit"): *ce vêtement vous sied à merveille*. When it means "to be seated, to sit (at a meeting)", it takes the following forms:
  - Present participle: *séant* (sometimes used as a noun: *sur son séant*).
  - Past participle: *sis, sise* used almost exclusively in legal parlance instead of *situé, située*: *hôtel sis à Paris*.
  - The following pronominal imperatives are sometimes used: *sieds-toi, seyez-vous*.

asseoir/assoir

INDICATIF

Présent		Passé composé		
j'	assie**d**s	j'	ai	assis
tu	assie**d**s	tu	as	assis
elle	assie**d**	elle	a	assis
nous	asseyons	nous	avons	assis
vous	asseyez	vous	avez	assis
ils	asseyent	ils	ont	assis

Imparfait		Plus-que-parfait		
j'	asseyais	j'	avais	assis
tu	asseyais	tu	avais	assis
elle	asseyait	elle	avait	assis
nous	asse**yi**ons	nous	avions	assis
vous	asse**yi**ez	vous	aviez	assis
ils	asseyaient	ils	avaient	assis

Passé simple		Passé antérieur		
j'	assis	j'	eus	assis
tu	assis	tu	eus	assis
elle	assit	elle	eut	assis
nous	assîmes	nous	eûmes	assis
vous	assîtes	vous	eûtes	assis
ils	assirent	ils	eurent	assis

Futur simple		Futur antérieur		
j'	assiérai	j'	aurai	assis
tu	assiéras	tu	auras	assis
elle	assiéra	elle	aura	assis
nous	assiérons	nous	aurons	assis
vous	assiérez	vous	aurez	assis
ils	assiéront	ils	auront	assis

Conditionnel présent		Conditionnel passé		
j'	assiérais	j'	aurais	assis
tu	assiérais	tu	aurais	assis
elle	assiérait	elle	aurait	assis
nous	assiérions	nous	aurions	assis
vous	assiériez	vous	auriez	assis
ils	assiéraient	ils	auraient	assis

SUBJONCTIF

Présent		Passé		
que j'	asseye	que j'	aie	assis
que tu	asseyes	que tu	aies	assis
qu' elle	asseye	qu' elle	ait	assis
que n.	asse**yi**ons	que n.	ayons	assis
que v.	asse**yi**ez	que v.	ayez	assis
qu' ils	asseyent	qu' ils	aient	assis

Imparfait		Plus-que-parfait		
que j'	assisse	que j'	eusse	assis
que tu	assisses	que tu	eusses	assis
qu' elle	assît	qu' elle	eût	assis
que n.	assissions	que n.	eussions	assis
que v.	assissiez	que v.	eussiez	assis
qu' ils	assissent	qu' ils	eussent	assis

IMPÉRATIF

Présent	Passé	
assie**d**s	aie	assis
asseyons	ayons	assis
asseyez	ayez	assis

INFINITIF

Présent / VARIANTE	Passé
asse**oi**r / ass**oi**r	avoir assis

PARTICIPE

Présent	Passé (composé)
asseyant	ayant assis
	Passé
	assis

***Conditionnel passé 2e forme* (2nd form)**: same form as the *plus-que-parfait* of the subjunctive.
Futur proche: *je vais asseoir* or *je vais assoir* (see Grammar of the verb, paragraphs 3 and 50).

- The traditional spelling of this verb is **asseoir**. The French spelling reform has eliminated the **e** and admits the form **assoir**.
- This verb is conjugated primarily as a pronominal verb: **s'asseoir** or **s'assoir**.
- The forms in **-ie-** and **-ey-** are more literary than forms in **-oi-** (see next page).
- The future and the present conditional: *j'asseyerai…*, *j'asseyerais…* are no longer used.

SEE NEXT PAGE

asseoir/assoir

INDICATIF

Présent		Passé composé		
j'	assois	j'	ai	assis
tu	assois	tu	as	assis
elle	assoit	elle	a	assis
nous	asso**y**ons	nous	avons	assis
vous	asso**yez**	vous	avez	assis
ils	assoient	ils	ont	assis

Imparfait		Plus-que-parfait		
j'	assoyais	j'	avais	assis
tu	assoyais	tu	avais	assis
elle	assoyait	elle	avait	assis
nous	asso**yi**ons	nous	avions	assis
vous	asso**yi**ez	vous	aviez	assis
ils	assoyaient	ils	avaient	assis

Passé simple		Passé antérieur		
j'	assis	j'	eus	assis
tu	assis	tu	eus	assis
elle	assit	elle	eut	assis
nous	assîmes	nous	eûmes	assis
vous	assîtes	vous	eûtes	assis
ils	assirent	ils	eurent	assis

Futur simple		Futur antérieur		
j'	assoirai	j'	aurai	assis
tu	assoiras	tu	auras	assis
elle	assoira	elle	aura	assis
nous	assoirons	nous	aurons	assis
vous	assoirez	vous	aurez	assis
ils	assoiront	ils	auront	assis

Conditionnel présent		Conditionnel passé		
j'	assoirais	j'	aurais	assis
tu	assoirais	tu	aurais	assis
elle	assoirait	elle	aurait	assis
nous	assoirions	nous	aurions	assis
vous	assoiriez	vous	auriez	assis
ils	assoiraient	ils	auraient	assis

SUBJONCTIF

Présent		Passé		
que j'	assoie	que j'	aie	assis
que tu	assoies	que tu	aies	assis
qu' elle	assoie	qu' elle	ait	assis
que n.	asso**yi**ons	que n.	ayons	assis
que v.	asso**yi**ez	que v.	ayez	assis
qu' ils	assoient	qu' ils	aient	assis

Imparfait		Plus-que-parfait		
que j'	assisse	que j'	eusse	assis
que tu	assisses	que tu	eusses	assis
qu' elle	assît	qu' elle	eût	assis
que n.	assissions	que n.	eussions	assis
que v.	assissiez	que v.	eussiez	assis
qu' ils	assissent	qu' ils	eussent	assis

IMPÉRATIF

Présent	Passé	
assois	aie	assis
asso**y**ons	ayons	assis
asso**y**ez	ayez	assis

INFINITIF

Présent / VARIANTE	Passé
ass**eoi**r / ass**oi**r	avoir assis

PARTICIPE

Présent	Passé (composé)
assoyant	ayant assis
	Passé
	assis

***Conditionnel passé 2e forme* (2nd form)**: same form as the *plus-que-parfait* of the subjunctive.
Futur proche: *je vais asseoir* or *je vais assoir* (see Grammar of the verb, paragraphs 3 and 50).

- The traditional spelling of the infinitive contains an etymological **e**, unlike the present indicative (*j'assois*), the future (*j'assoirai*) and the present conditional (*j'assoirais*). The spelling reform admits **assoir** without the **e**.
- **Rasseoir** (or **rassoir**) follows either of these two patterns of conjugation.

SEE PREVIOUS PAGE

113 (to be unsuitable or unbecoming) messeoir/messoir

INDICATIF

Présent	Passé composé
.	.
.	.
elle messi**ed**	.
.	.
.	.
ils messi**ée**nt	.

Imparfait	Plus-que-parfait
.	.
.	.
elle messeyait	.
.	.
.	.
ils messeyaient	.

Passé simple	Passé antérieur
.	.
.	.
.	.
.	.
.	.
.	.

Futur simple	Futur antérieur
.	.
.	.
elle messiéra	.
.	.
.	.
ils messiéront	.

Conditionnel présent	Conditionnel passé
.	.
.	.
elle messiérait	.
.	.
.	.
ils messiéraient	.

SUBJONCTIF

Présent	Passé
.	.
.	.
qu'elle messi**ée**	.
.	.
.	.
qu'ils messi**ée**nt	.

Imparfait	Plus-que-parfait
.	.
.	.
.	.
.	.
.	.
.	.

IMPÉRATIF

Présent	Passé
.	.
.	.
.	.

INFINITIF

Présent	/ VARIANTE	Passé
mess**eoi**r	/ mess**oi**r	.

PARTICIPE

Présent	Passé (composé)
mess**é**ant / mess**ey**ant	.
	Passé
	.

Futur proche: *il va messeoir* or *il va messoir* (see Grammar of the verb, paragraphs 3 and 50).

- This verb has no compound forms.
- The traditional spelling is **messeoir**. With the spelling reform, it can be written **messoir** (without the **e** in the infinitive).

surseoir/sursoir 114

INDICATIF

Présent		Passé composé		
je	sursois	j'	ai	sursis
tu	sursois	tu	as	sursis
elle	sursoit	elle	a	sursis
nous	surso**y**ons	nous	avons	sursis
vous	surso**y**ez	vous	avez	sursis
ils	sursoient	ils	ont	sursis

Imparfait		Plus-que-parfait		
je	sursoyais	j'	avais	sursis
tu	sursoyais	tu	avais	sursis
elle	sursoyait	elle	avait	sursis
nous	surso**yi**ons	nous	avions	sursis
vous	surso**yi**ez	vous	aviez	sursis
ils	sursoyaient	ils	avaient	sursis

Passé simple		Passé antérieur		
je	sursis	j'	eus	sursis
tu	sursis	tu	eus	sursis
elle	sursit	elle	eut	sursis
nous	sursîmes	nous	eûmes	sursis
vous	sursîtes	vous	eûtes	sursis
ils	sursirent	ils	eurent	sursis

Futur simple		/ VARIANTE	Futur antérieur		
je	surs**eoi**rai	/ surs**oi**rai	j'	aurai	sursis
tu	surs**eoi**ras	/ surs**oi**ras	tu	auras	sursis
elle	surs**eoi**ra	/ surs**oi**ra	elle	aura	sursis
nous	surs**eoi**rons	/ surs**oi**rons	nous	aurons	sursis
vous	surs**eoi**rez	/ surs**oi**rez	vous	aurez	sursis
ils	surs**eoi**ront	/ surs**oi**ront	ils	auront	sursis

Conditionnel présent		/ VARIANTE	Conditionnel passé		
je	surs**eoi**rais	/ surs**oi**rais	j'	aurais	sursis
tu	surs**eoi**rais	/ surs**oi**rais	tu	aurais	sursis
elle	surs**eoi**rait	/ surs**oi**rait	elle	aurait	sursis
nous	surs**eoi**rions	/ surs**oi**rions	nous	aurions	sursis
vous	surs**eoi**riez	/ surs**oi**riez	vous	auriez	sursis
ils	surs**eoi**raient	/ surs**oi**raient	ils	auraient	sursis

SUBJONCTIF

Présent		Passé		
que je	sursoie	que j'	aie	sursis
que tu	sursoies	que tu	aies	sursis
qu' elle	sursoie	qu' elle	ait	sursis
que n.	surso**yi**ons	que n.	ayons	sursis
que v.	surso**yi**ez	que v.	ayez	sursis
qu' ils	sursoient	qu' ils	aient	sursis

Imparfait		Plus-que-parfait		
que je	sursisse	que j'	eusse	sursis
que tu	sursisses	que tu	eusses	sursis
qu' elle	sursît	qu' elle	eût	sursis
que n.	sursissions	que n.	eussions	sursis
que v.	sursissiez	que v.	eussiez	sursis
qu' ils	sursissent	qu' ils	eussent	sursis

IMPÉRATIF

Présent	Passé	
sursois	aie	sursis
surso**y**ons	ayons	sursis
surso**y**ez	ayez	sursis

INFINITIF

Présent / VARIANTE	Passé
surs**eoir** / surs**oir**	avoir sursis

PARTICIPE

Présent	Passé (composé)
sursoyant	ayant sursis
	Passé
	sursis

***Conditionnel passé 2e forme* (2nd form)**: same form as the *plus-que-parfait* of the subjunctive.
Futur proche: *je vais surseoir* or *je vais sursoir* (see Grammar of the verb, paragraphs 3 and 50).

- The traditional spelling of this verb is with an **e**. The French spelling reform allows the **e** to be dropped and recommends the spelling **sursoir**.
- **Surs(e)oir** has set the pattern for **-oi-** forms in **ass(e)oir** with the peculiarity that the **e** of the infinitive occurs in the traditional forms of the future and the present conditional: *je surseoirai…, je surseoirais…* The spelling reform has eliminated the **e** and regularized spelling in these two verb forms: *je sursoirai…, je sursoirais…*

115 choir

INDICATIF

Présent		Passé composé		
je	*chois*	j'	ai	chu
tu	*chois*	tu	as	chu
elle	choit	elle	a	chu
nous	*choyons*	nous	avons	chu
vous	*choyez*	vous	avez	chu
ils	choient	ils	ont	chu

Imparfait		Plus-que-parfait		
je	*choyais*	j'	avais	chu
tu	*choyais*	tu	avais	chu
elle	*choyait*	elle	avait	chu
nous	*choyions*	nous	avions	chu
vous	*choyiez*	vous	aviez	chu
ils	*choyaient*	ils	avaient	chu

Passé simple		Passé antérieur		
je	*chus*	j'	eus	chu
tu	*chus*	tu	eus	chu
elle	chut	elle	eut	chu
nous	*chûmes*	nous	eûmes	chu
vous	*chûtes*	vous	eûtes	chu
ils	churent	ils	eurent	chu

Futur simple			Futur antérieur		
je	*choirai*	*/cherrai*	j'	aurai	chu
tu	*choiras*	*/cherras*	tu	auras	chu
elle	*choira*	*/cherra*	elle	aura	chu
nous	*choirons*	*/cherrons*	nous	aurons	chu
vous	*choirez*	*/cherrez*	vous	aurez	chu
ils	*choiront*	*/cherront*	ils	auront	chu

Conditionnel présent			Conditionnel passé		
je	*choirais*	*/cherrais*	j'	aurais	chu
tu	*choirais*	*/cherrais*	tu	aurais	chu
elle	*choirait*	*/cherrait*	elle	aurait	chu
nous	*choirions*	*/cherrions*	nous	aurions	chu
vous	*choiriez*	*/cherriez*	vous	auriez	chu
ils	*choiraient*	*/cherraient*	ils	auraient	chu

SUBJONCTIF

Présent		Passé		
que je	*choie*	que j'	aie	chu
que tu	*choies*	que tu	aies	chu
qu'elle	*choie*	qu'elle	ait	chu
que n.	*choyions*	que n.	ayons	chu
que v.	*choyiez*	que v.	ayez	chu
qu'ils	*choient*	qu'ils	aient	chu

Imparfait		Plus-que-parfait		
que je	*chusse*	que j'	eusse	chu
que tu	*chusses*	que tu	eusses	chu
qu'elle	*chût*	qu'elle	eût	chu
que n.	*chussions*	que n.	eussions	chu
que v.	*chussiez*	que v.	eussiez	chu
qu'ils	*chussent*	qu'ils	eussent	chu

IMPÉRATIF

Présent	Passé	
chois	*aie*	*chu*
choyons	*ayons*	*chu*
choyez	*ayez*	*chu*

INFINITIF

Présent	Passé
choir	avoir chu

PARTICIPE

Présent	Passé (composé)
cheyant	ayant chu
	Passé
	chu

***Conditionnel passé 2e forme* (2nd form)**: same form as the *plus-que-parfait* of the subjunctive.
Futur proche: *il va choir* (see Grammar of the verb, paragraphs 3 and 50).

- The verb **choir** can also be conjugated with the auxiliary verb **être**, although use of the auxiliary **avoir** is currently more frequent.
- The forms in italics are obsolete.

INDICATIF

Présent			Passé composé		
.			.		
.			.		
elle	échoit	*/ échet*	elle	est	échue
.			.		
.			.		
ils	échoient	*/ échéent*	ils	sont	échus

Imparfait			Plus-que-parfait		
.			.		
.			.		
elle	échoyait	*/ échéait*	elle	était	échue
.			.		
.			.		
ils	échoyaient	*/ échéaient*	ils	étaient	échus

Passé simple		Passé antérieur		
.		.		
.		.		
elle	échut	elle	fut	échue
.		.		
.		.		
ils	échurent	ils	furent	échus

Futur simple			Futur antérieur		
.			.		
.			.		
elle	échoira	*/ écherra*	elle	sera	échue
.			.		
.			.		
ils	échoiront	*/ écherront*	ils	seront	échus

Conditionnel présent			Conditionnel passé		
.			.		
.			.		
elle	échoirait	*/ écherrait*	elle	serait	échue
.			.		
.			.		
ils	échoiraient	*/ écherraient*	ils	seraient	échus

SUBJONCTIF

Présent		Passé		
.		.		
.		.		
qu'elle	échoie	qu'elle	soit	échue
.		.		
.		.		
qu'ils	échoient	qu'ils	soient	échus

Imparfait		Plus-que-parfait		
.		.		
.		.		
qu'elle	échût	qu'elle	fût	échue
.		.		
.		.		
qu'ils	échussent	qu'ils	fussent	échus

IMPÉRATIF

Présent	Passé
.	.
.	.
.	.

INFINITIF

Présent	Passé
échoir	être échu

PARTICIPE

Présent	Passé (composé)
échéant	étant échu
	Passé
	échu

Conditionnel passé 2e forme **(2nd form)**: same form as the *plus-que-parfait* of the subjunctive.
Futur proche: *il va échoir* (see Grammar of the verb, paragraphs 3 and 50).

- **Échoir** is sometimes conjugated with the auxiliary verb **avoir** but this usage is archaic or popular.
- The forms in italics are obsolete. The form *il échet* is used mostly in legal documents.

117 déchoir

INDICATIF

Présent		Passé composé	
je déchois		j' ai	déchu
tu déchois		tu as	déchu
elle déchoit	/*déchet*	elle a	déchu
n. déchoyons		n. avons	déchu
v. déchoyez		v. avez	déchu
ils déchoient		ils ont	déchu

Imparfait	Plus-que-parfait	
je déchoyais	j' avais	déchu
tu déchoyais	tu avais	déchu
elle déchoyait	elle avait	déchu
n. déchoyions	n. avions	déchu
v. déchoyiez	v. aviez	déchu
ils déchoyaient	ils avaient	déchu

Passé simple	Passé antérieur	
je déchus	j' eus	déchu
tu déchus	tu eus	déchu
elle déchut	elle eut	déchu
n. déchûmes	n. eûmes	déchu
v. déchûtes	v. eûtes	déchu
ils déchurent	ils eurent	déchu

Futur simple		Futur antérieur	
je déchoirai	/*décherrai*	j' aurai	déchu
tu déchoiras	/*décherras*	tu auras	déchu
elle déchoira	/*décherra*	elle aura	déchu
n. déchoirons	/*décherrons*	n. aurons	déchu
v. déchoirez	/*décherrez*	v aurez	déchu
ils déchoiront	/*décherront*	ils auront	déchu

Conditionnel présent		Conditionnel passé	
je déchoirais	/*décherrais*	j' aurais	déchu
tu déchoirais	/*décherrais*	tu aurais	déchu
elle déchoirait	/*décherrait*	elle aurait	déchu
n. déchoirions	/*décherrions*	n. aurions	déchu
v. déchoiriez	/*décherriez*	v. auriez	déchu
ils déchoiraient	/*décherraient*	ils auraient	déchu

SUBJONCTIF

Présent	Passé	
que je déchoie	que j' aie	déchu
que tu déchoies	que tu aies	déchu
qu' elle déchoie	qu' elle ait	déchu
que n. déchoyions	que n. ayons	déchu
que v. déchoyiez	que v. ayez	déchu
qu' ils déchoient	qu' ils aient	déchu

Imparfait	Plus-que-parfait	
que je déchusse	que j' eusse	déchu
que tu déchusses	que tu eusses	déchu
qu' elle déchût	qu' elle eût	déchu
que n. déchussions	que n. eussions	déchu
que v. déchussiez	que v. eussiez	déchu
qu' ils déchussent	qu' ils eussent	déchu

IMPÉRATIF

Présent	Passé
déchois	*aie déchu*
déchoyons	*ayons déchu*
déchoyez	*ayez déchu*

INFINITIF

Présent	Passé
déchoir	avoir déchu

PARTICIPE

Présent	Passé (composé)
.	ayant déchu
	Passé
	déchu

***Conditionnel passé 2e forme* (2nd form)**: same form as the *plus-que-parfait* of the subjunctive.
Futur proche: *il va déchoir* (see Grammar of the verb, paragraphs 3 and 50).

- The forms in italics are obsolete.

rendre

INDICATIF

Présent		Passé composé		
je	ren**ds**	j'	ai	rendu
tu	ren**ds**	tu	as	rendu
elle	ren**d**	elle	a	rendu
nous	rendons	nous	avons	rendu
vous	rendez	vous	avez	rendu
ils	rendent	ils	ont	rendu

Imparfait		Plus-que-parfait		
je	rendais	j'	avais	rendu
tu	rendais	tu	avais	rendu
elle	rendait	elle	avait	rendu
nous	rendions	nous	avions	rendu
vous	rendiez	vous	aviez	rendu
ils	rendaient	ils	avaient	rendu

Passé simple		Passé antérieur		
je	rendis	j'	eus	rendu
tu	rendis	tu	eus	rendu
elle	rendit	elle	eut	rendu
nous	rendîmes	nous	eûmes	rendu
vous	rendîtes	vous	eûtes	rendu
ils	rendirent	ils	eurent	rendu

Futur simple		Futur antérieur		
je	rendrai	j'	aurai	rendu
tu	rendras	tu	auras	rendu
elle	rendra	elle	aura	rendu
nous	rendrons	nous	aurons	rendu
vous	rendrez	vous	aurez	rendu
ils	rendront	ils	auront	rendu

Conditionnel présent		Conditionnel passé		
je	rendrais	j'	aurais	rendu
tu	rendrais	tu	aurais	rendu
elle	rendrait	elle	aurait	rendu
nous	rendrions	nous	aurions	rendu
vous	rendriez	vous	auriez	rendu
ils	rendraient	ils	auraient	rendu

SUBJONCTIF

Présent		Passé		
que je	rende	que j'	aie	rendu
que tu	rendes	que tu	aies	rendu
qu' elle	rende	qu' elle	ait	rendu
que n.	rendions	que n.	ayons	rendu
que v.	rendiez	que v.	ayez	rendu
qu' ils	rendent	qu' ils	aient	rendu

Imparfait		Plus-que-parfait		
que je	rendisse	que j'	eusse	rendu
que tu	rendisses	que tu	eusses	rendu
qu' elle	rendît	qu' elle	eût	rendu
que n.	rendissions	que n.	eussions	rendu
que v.	rendissiez	que v.	eussiez	rendu
qu' ils	rendissent	qu' ils	eussent	rendu

IMPÉRATIF

Présent	Passé	
ren**ds**	aie	rendu
rendons	ayons	rendu
rendez	ayez	rendu

INFINITIF

Présent	Passé
rendre	avoir rendu

PARTICIPE

Présent	Passé (composé)
rendant	ayant rendu
	Passé
	rendu

1. Except for the conjugation of **prendre** and its derived forms (see Table 119).

***Conditionnel passé 2e forme* (2nd form)**: same form as the *plus-que-parfait* of the subjunctive.
Futur proche: *je vais rendre* (see Grammar of the verb, paragraphs 3 and 50).

- See List of irregular verbs, p. 96 to 98, for the numerous verbs conjugated like **rendre.**
- **Sourdre** is used only in the infinitive and in the 3rd person of the indicative forms.

119 prendre

INDICATIF

Présent		Passé composé		
je	prends	j'	ai	pris
tu	prends	tu	as	pris
elle	prend	elle	a	pris
nous	prenons	nous	avons	pris
vous	prenez	vous	avez	pris
ils	prennent	ils	ont	pris

Imparfait		Plus-que-parfait		
je	prenais	j'	avais	pris
tu	prenais	tu	avais	pris
elle	prenait	elle	avait	pris
nous	prenions	nous	avions	pris
vous	preniez	vous	aviez	pris
ils	prenaient	ils	avaient	pris

Passé simple		Passé antérieur		
je	pris	j'	eus	pris
tu	pris	tu	eus	pris
elle	prit	elle	eut	pris
nous	prîmes	nous	eûmes	pris
vous	prîtes	vous	eûtes	pris
ils	prirent	ils	eurent	pris

Futur simple		Futur antérieur		
je	prendrai	j'	aurai	pris
tu	prendras	tu	auras	pris
elle	prendra	elle	aura	pris
nous	prendrons	nous	aurons	pris
vous	prendrez	vous	aurez	pris
ils	prendront	ils	auront	pris

Conditionnel présent		Conditionnel passé		
je	prendrais	j'	aurais	pris
tu	prendrais	tu	aurais	pris
elle	prendrait	elle	aurait	pris
nous	prendrions	nous	aurions	pris
vous	prendriez	vous	auriez	pris
ils	prendraient	ils	auraient	pris

SUBJONCTIF

Présent		Passé		
que je	prenne	que j'	aie	pris
que tu	prennes	que tu	aies	pris
qu' elle	prenne	qu' elle	ait	pris
que n.	prenions	que n.	ayons	pris
que v.	preniez	que v.	ayez	pris
qu' ils	prennent	qu' ils	aient	pris

Imparfait		Plus-que-parfait		
que je	prisse	que j'	eusse	pris
que tu	prisses	que tu	eusses	pris
qu' elle	prît	qu' elle	eût	pris
que n.	prissions	que n.	eussions	pris
que v.	prissiez	que v.	eussiez	pris
qu' ils	prissent	qu' ils	eussent	pris

IMPÉRATIF

Présent	Passé	
prends	aie	pris
prenons	ayons	pris
prenez	ayez	pris

INFINITIF

Présent	Passé
prendre	avoir pris

PARTICIPE

Présent	Passé (composé)
prenant	ayant pris
	Passé
	pris

***Conditionnel passé 2ᵉ forme* (2nd form)**: same form as the *plus-que-parfait* of the subjunctive.
Futur proche: *je vais prendre* (see Grammar of the verb, paragraphs 3 and 50).

- The derived forms of the verb **prendre** (see List of irregular verbs, p. 96 to 98) follow this pattern of conjugation.

INDICATIF

Présent		Passé composé		
je	rom**ps**	j'	ai	rompu
tu	rom**ps**	tu	as	rompu
elle	rom**pt**	elle	a	rompu
nous	rompons	nous	avons	rompu
vous	rompez	vous	avez	rompu
ils	rompent	ils	ont	rompu

Imparfait		Plus-que-parfait		
je	rompais	j'	avais	rompu
tu	rompais	tu	avais	rompu
elle	rompait	elle	avait	rompu
nous	rompions	nous	avions	rompu
vous	rompiez	vous	aviez	rompu
ils	rompaient	ils	avaient	rompu

Passé simple		Passé antérieur		
je	rompis	j'	eus	rompu
tu	rompis	tu	eus	rompu
elle	rompit	elle	eut	rompu
nous	rompîmes	nous	eûmes	rompu
vous	rompîtes	vous	eûtes	rompu
ils	rompirent	ils	eurent	rompu

Futur simple		Futur antérieur		
je	romprai	j'	aurai	rompu
tu	rompras	tu	auras	rompu
elle	rompra	elle	aura	rompu
nous	romprons	nous	aurons	rompu
vous	romprez	vous	aurez	rompu
ils	rompront	ils	auront	rompu

Conditionnel présent		Conditionnel passé		
je	romprais	j'	aurais	rompu
tu	romprais	tu	aurais	rompu
elle	romprait	elle	aurait	rompu
nous	romprions	nous	aurions	rompu
vous	rompriez	vous	auriez	rompu
ils	rompraient	ils	auraient	rompu

SUBJONCTIF

Présent		Passé		
que je	rompe	que j'	aie	rompu
que tu	rompes	que tu	aies	rompu
qu'elle	rompe	qu'elle	ait	rompu
que n.	rompions	que n.	ayons	rompu
que v.	rompiez	que v.	ayez	rompu
qu' ils	rompent	qu' ils	aient	rompu

Imparfait		Plus-que-parfait		
que je	rompisse	que j'	eusse	rompu
que tu	rompisses	que tu	eusses	rompu
qu'elle	rompît	qu'elle	eût	rompu
que n.	rompissions	que n.	eussions	rompu
que v.	rompissiez	que v.	eussiez	rompu
qu' ils	rompissent	qu' ils	eussent	rompu

IMPÉRATIF

Présent	Passé	
rom**ps**	aie	rompu
rompons	ayons	rompu
rompez	ayez	rompu

INFINITIF

Présent	Passé
rompre	avoir rompu

PARTICIPE

Présent	Passé (composé)
rompant	ayant rompu
	Passé
	rompu

***Conditionnel passé 2ᵉ forme* (2nd form)**: same form as the *plus-que-parfait* of the subjunctive.
Futur proche: *je vais rompre* (see Grammar of the verb, paragraphs 3 and 50).

- The verbs **corrompre** and **interrompre** follow this pattern of conjugation.
- The verbs **foutre**, **refoutre** and **contrefoutre** also follow this pattern of conjugation and take a **t** in the 3rd person singular of the present indicative: *il fout, elle se contrefout.*

121 battre

INDICATIF

Présent		Passé composé		
je	bats	j'	ai	battu
tu	bats	tu	as	battu
elle	bat	elle	a	battu
nous	battons	nous	avons	battu
vous	battez	vous	avez	battu
ils	battent	ils	ont	battu

Imparfait		Plus-que-parfait		
je	battais	j'	avais	battu
tu	battais	tu	avais	battu
elle	battait	elle	avait	battu
nous	battions	nous	avions	battu
vous	battiez	vous	aviez	battu
ils	battaient	ils	avaient	battu

Passé simple		Passé antérieur		
je	battis	j'	eus	battu
tu	battis	tu	eus	battu
elle	battit	elle	eut	battu
nous	battîmes	nous	eûmes	battu
vous	battîtes	vous	eûtes	battu
ils	battirent	ils	eurent	battu

Futur simple		Futur antérieur		
je	battrai	j'	aurai	battu
tu	battras	tu	auras	battu
elle	battra	elle	aura	battu
nous	battrons	nous	aurons	battu
vous	battrez	vous	aurez	battu
ils	battront	ils	auront	battu

Conditionnel présent		Conditionnel passé		
je	battrais	j'	aurais	battu
tu	battrais	tu	aurais	battu
elle	battrait	elle	aurait	battu
nous	battrions	nous	aurions	battu
vous	battriez	vous	auriez	battu
ils	battraient	ils	auraient	battu

SUBJONCTIF

Présent		Passé		
que je	batte	que j'	aie	battu
que tu	battes	que tu	aies	battu
qu' elle	batte	qu' elle	ait	battu
que n.	battions	que n.	ayons	battu
que v.	battiez	que v.	ayez	battu
qu' ils	battent	qu' ils	aient	battu

Imparfait		Plus-que-parfait		
que je	battisse	que j'	eusse	battu
que tu	battisses	que tu	eusses	battu
qu' elle	battît	qu' elle	eût	battu
que n.	battissions	que n.	eussions	battu
que v.	battissiez	que v.	eussiez	battu
qu' ils	battissent	qu' ils	eussent	battu

IMPÉRATIF

Présent	Passé	
bats	aie	battu
battons	ayons	battu
battez	ayez	battu

INFINITIF

Présent	Passé
battre	avoir battu

PARTICIPE

Présent	Passé (composé)
battant	ayant battu
	Passé
	battu

***Conditionnel passé 2ᵉ forme* (2nd form)**: same form as the *plus-que-parfait* of the subjunctive.
Futur proche: *je vais battre* (see Grammar of the verb, paragraphs 3 and 50).

- The derived forms of **battre** (see List of irregular verbs, p. 96 to 98) follow this pattern of conjugation.

INDICATIF

Présent		Passé composé		
je	mets	j'	ai	mis
tu	mets	tu	as	mis
elle	met	elle	a	mis
nous	mettons	nous	avons	mis
vous	mettez	vous	avez	mis
ils	mettent	ils	ont	mis

Imparfait		Plus-que-parfait		
je	mettais	j'	avais	mis
tu	mettais	tu	avais	mis
elle	mettait	elle	avait	mis
nous	mettions	nous	avions	mis
vous	mettiez	vous	aviez	mis
ils	mettaient	ils	avaient	mis

Passé simple		Passé antérieur		
je	mis	j'	eus	mis
tu	mis	tu	eus	mis
elle	mit	elle	eut	mis
nous	mîmes	nous	eûmes	mis
vous	mîtes	vous	eûtes	mis
ils	mirent	ils	eurent	mis

Futur simple		Futur antérieur		
je	mettrai	j'	aurai	mis
tu	mettras	tu	auras	mis
elle	mettra	elle	aura	mis
nous	mettrons	nous	aurons	mis
vous	mettrez	vous	aurez	mis
ils	mettront	ils	auront	mis

Conditionnel présent		Conditionnel passé		
je	mettrais	j'	aurais	mis
tu	mettrais	tu	aurais	mis
elle	mettrait	elle	aurait	mis
nous	mettrions	nous	aurions	mis
vous	mettriez	vous	auriez	mis
ils	mettraient	ils	auraient	mis

SUBJONCTIF

Présent		Passé		
que je	mette	que j'	aie	mis
que tu	mettes	que tu	aies	mis
qu' elle	mette	qu' elle	ait	mis
que n.	mettions	que n.	ayons	mis
que v.	mettiez	que v.	ayez	mis
qu' ils	mettent	qu' ils	aient	mis

Imparfait		Plus-que-parfait		
que je	misse	que j'	eusse	mis
que tu	misses	que tu	eusses	mis
qu' elle	mît	qu' elle	eût	mis
que n.	missions	que n.	eussions	mis
que v.	missiez	que v.	eussiez	mis
qu' ils	missent	qu' ils	eussent	mis

IMPÉRATIF

Présent	Passé	
mets	aie	mis
mettons	ayons	mis
mettez	ayez	mis

INFINITIF

Présent	Passé
mettre	avoir mis

PARTICIPE

Présent	Passé (composé)
mettant	ayant mis
	Passé
	mis

***Conditionnel passé 2e forme* (2nd form)**: same form as the *plus-que-parfait* of the subjunctive.
Futur proche: *je vais mettre* (see Grammar of the verb, paragraphs 3 and 50).

- The derived forms of **mettre** (see List of irregular verbs, p. 96 to 98) follow this pattern of conjugation.

peindre

INDICATIF

Présent		Passé composé		
je	peins	j'	ai	peint
tu	peins	tu	as	peint
elle	peint	elle	a	peint
nous	peignons	nous	avons	peint
vous	peignez	vous	avez	peint
ils	peignent	ils	ont	peint

Imparfait		Plus-que-parfait		
je	peignais	j'	avais	peint
tu	peignais	tu	avais	peint
elle	peignait	elle	avait	peint
nous	peignions	nous	avions	peint
vous	peigniez	vous	aviez	peint
ils	peignaient	ils	avaient	peint

Passé simple		Passé antérieur		
je	peignis	j'	eus	peint
tu	peignis	tu	eus	peint
elle	peignit	elle	eut	peint
nous	peignîmes	nous	eûmes	peint
vous	peignîtes	vous	eûtes	peint
ils	peignirent	ils	eurent	peint

Futur simple		Futur antérieur		
je	peindrai	j'	aurai	peint
tu	peindras	tu	auras	peint
elle	peindra	elle	aura	peint
nous	peindrons	nous	aurons	peint
vous	peindrez	vous	aurez	peint
ils	peindront	ils	auront	peint

Conditionnel présent		Conditionnel passé		
je	peindrais	j'	aurais	peint
tu	peindrais	tu	aurais	peint
elle	peindrait	elle	aurait	peint
nous	peindrions	nous	aurions	peint
vous	peindriez	vous	auriez	peint
ils	peindraient	ils	auraient	peint

SUBJONCTIF

Présent		Passé		
que je	peigne	que j'	aie	peint
que tu	peignes	que tu	aies	peint
qu' elle	peigne	qu' elle	ait	peint
que n.	peignions	que n.	ayons	peint
que v.	peigniez	que v.	ayez	peint
qu' ils	peignent	qu' ils	aient	peint

Imparfait		Plus-que-parfait		
que je	peignisse	que j'	eusse	peint
que tu	peignisses	que tu	eusses	peint
qu' elle	peignît	qu' elle	eût	peint
que n.	peignissions	que n.	eussions	peint
que v.	peignissiez	que v.	eussiez	peint
qu' ils	peignissent	qu' ils	eussent	peint

IMPÉRATIF

Présent	Passé	
peins	aie	peint
peignons	ayons	peint
peignez	ayez	peint

INFINITIF

Présent	Passé
peindre	avoir peint

PARTICIPE

Présent	Passé (composé)
peignant	ayant peint
	Passé
	peint

***Conditionnel passé 2e forme* (2nd form)**: same form as the *plus-que-parfait* of the subjunctive.
Futur proche: *je vais peindre* (see Grammar of the verb, paragraphs 3 and 50).

- All verbs in **-eindre** (see List of irregular verbs, p. 96 to 98) follow this pattern of conjugation.

INDICATIF

Présent		Passé composé		
je	joins	j'	ai	joint
tu	joins	tu	as	joint
elle	joint	elle	a	joint
nous	joignons	nous	avons	joint
vous	joignez	vous	avez	joint
ils	joignent	ils	ont	joint

Imparfait		Plus-que-parfait		
je	joignais	j'	avais	joint
tu	joignais	tu	avais	joint
elle	joignait	elle	avait	joint
nous	joignions	nous	avions	joint
vous	joigniez	vous	aviez	joint
ils	joignaient	ils	avaient	joint

Passé simple		Passé antérieur		
je	joignis	j'	eus	joint
tu	joignis	tu	eus	joint
elle	joignit	elle	eut	joint
nous	joignîmes	nous	eûmes	joint
vous	joignîtes	vous	eûtes	joint
ils	joignirent	ils	eurent	joint

Futur simple		Futur antérieur		
je	joindrai	j'	aurai	joint
tu	joindras	tu	auras	joint
elle	joindra	elle	aura	joint
nous	joindrons	nous	aurons	joint
vous	joindrez	vous	aurez	joint
ils	joindront	ils	auront	joint

Conditionnel présent		Conditionnel passé		
je	joindrais	j'	aurais	joint
tu	joindrais	tu	aurais	joint
elle	joindrait	elle	aurait	joint
nous	joindrions	nous	aurions	joint
vous	joindriez	vous	auriez	joint
ils	joindraient	ils	auraient	joint

SUBJONCTIF

Présent		Passé		
que je	joigne	que j'	aie	joint
que tu	joignes	que tu	aies	joint
qu' elle	joigne	qu' elle	ait	joint
que n.	joignions	que n.	ayons	joint
que v.	joigniez	que v.	ayez	joint
qu' ils	joignent	qu' ils	aient	joint

Imparfait		Plus-que-parfait		
que je	joignisse	que j'	eusse	joint
que tu	joignisses	que tu	eusses	joint
qu' elle	joignît	qu' elle	eût	joint
que n.	joignissions	que n.	eussions	joint
que v.	joignissiez	que v.	eussiez	joint
qu' ils	joignissent	qu' ils	eussent	joint

IMPÉRATIF

Présent	Passé	
joins	aie	joint
joignons	ayons	joint
joignez	ayez	joint

INFINITIF

Présent	Passé
joindre	avoir joint

PARTICIPE

Présent	Passé (composé)
joignant	ayant joint
	Passé
	joint

***Conditionnel passé 2e forme* (2nd form):** same form as the *plus-que-parfait* of the subjunctive.
Futur proche: *je vais joindre* (see Grammar of the verb, paragraphs 3 and 50).

- The derived forms of **joindre** (see List of irregular verbs, p. 96 to 98) and the archaic verbs **poindre** and **oindre** follow this pattern of conjugation.
- As an intransitive verb, in the sense of "make a first appeareance", **poindre** is used almost exclusively in the 3rd person (*le jour point, il poindra, l'aube poindrait, elle a point*). In this context, there is a tendency however to use the regular verb **pointer** instead: *le jour pointe* (= "daylight appears / morning has broken").
- **Oindre** is no longer used except in the following forms: infinitive, *imparfait* of the indicative (*oignait*) and past participle (*oint, oints, ointe, ointes*).

craindre

INDICATIF

Présent		Passé composé		
je	crains	j'	ai	craint
tu	crains	tu	as	craint
elle	craint	elle	a	craint
nous	craignons	nous	avons	craint
vous	craignez	vous	avez	craint
ils	craignent	ils	ont	craint

Imparfait		Plus-que-parfait		
je	craignais	j'	avais	craint
tu	craignais	tu	avais	craint
elle	craignait	elle	avait	craint
nous	craignions	nous	avions	craint
vous	craigniez	vous	aviez	craint
ils	craignaient	ils	avaient	craint

Passé simple		Passé antérieur		
je	craignis	j'	eus	craint
tu	craignis	tu	eus	craint
elle	craignit	elle	eut	craint
nous	craignîmes	nous	eûmes	craint
vous	craignîtes	vous	eûtes	craint
ils	craignirent	ils	eurent	craint

Futur simple		Futur antérieur		
je	craindrai	j'	aurai	craint
tu	craindras	tu	auras	craint
elle	craindra	elle	aura	craint
nous	craindrons	nous	aurons	craint
vous	craindrez	vous	aurez	craint
ils	craindront	ils	auront	craint

Conditionnel présent		Conditionnel passé		
je	craindrais	j'	aurais	craint
tu	craindrais	tu	aurais	craint
elle	craindrait	elle	aurait	craint
nous	craindrions	nous	aurions	craint
vous	craindriez	vous	auriez	craint
ils	craindraient	ils	auraient	craint

SUBJONCTIF

Présent		Passé		
que je	craigne	que j'	aie	craint
que tu	craignes	que tu	aies	craint
qu' elle	craigne	qu' elle	ait	craint
que n.	craignions	que n.	ayons	craint
que v.	craigniez	que v.	ayez	craint
qu' ils	craignent	qu' ils	aient	craint

Imparfait		Plus-que-parfait		
que je	craignisse	que j'	eusse	craint
que tu	craignisses	que tu	eusses	craint
qu' elle	craignît	qu' elle	eût	craint
que n.	craignissions	que n.	eussions	craint
que v.	craignissiez	que v.	eussiez	craint
qu' ils	craignissent	qu' ils	eussent	craint

IMPÉRATIF

Présent	Passé	
crains	aie	craint
craignons	ayons	craint
craignez	ayez	craint

INFINITIF

Présent	Passé
craindre	avoir craint

PARTICIPE

Présent	Passé (composé)
craignant	ayant craint
	Passé
	craint

***Conditionnel passé 2e forme* (2nd form)**: same form as the *plus-que-parfait* of the subjunctive.
Futur proche: *je vais craindre* (see Grammar of the verb, paragraphs 3 and 50).

- **Contraindre** and **plaindre** follow this pattern of conjugation.

INDICATIF

Présent		Passé composé		
je	vain**cs**	j'	ai	vaincu
tu	vain**cs**	tu	as	vaincu
elle	vain**c**	elle	a	vaincu
nous	vainquons	nous	avons	vaincu
vous	vainquez	vous	avez	vaincu
ils	vainquent	ils	ont	vaincu

Imparfait		Plus-que-parfait		
je	vainquais	j'	avais	vaincu
tu	vainquais	tu	avais	vaincu
elle	vainquait	elle	avait	vaincu
nous	vainquions	nous	avions	vaincu
vous	vainquiez	vous	aviez	vaincu
ils	vainquaient	ils	avaient	vaincu

Passé simple		Passé antérieur		
je	vainquis	j'	eus	vaincu
tu	vainquis	tu	eus	vaincu
elle	vainquit	elle	eut	vaincu
nous	vainquîmes	nous	eûmes	vaincu
vous	vainquîtes	vous	eûtes	vaincu
ils	vainquirent	ils	eurent	vaincu

Futur simple		Futur antérieur		
je	vaincrai	j'	aurai	vaincu
tu	vaincras	tu	auras	vaincu
elle	vaincra	elle	aura	vaincu
nous	vaincrons	nous	aurons	vaincu
vous	vaincrez	vous	aurez	vaincu
ils	vaincront	ils	auront	vaincu

Conditionnel présent		Conditionnel passé		
je	vaincrais	j'	aurais	vaincu
tu	vaincrais	tu	aurais	vaincu
elle	vaincrait	elle	aurait	vaincu
nous	vaincrions	nous	aurions	vaincu
vous	vaincriez	vous	auriez	vaincu
ils	vaincraient	ils	auraient	vaincu

SUBJONCTIF

Présent		Passé		
que je	vainque	que j'	aie	vaincu
que tu	vainques	que tu	aies	vaincu
qu' elle	vainque	qu' elle	ait	vaincu
que n.	vainquions	que n.	ayons	vaincu
que v.	vainquiez	que v.	ayez	vaincu
qu' ils	vainquent	qu' ils	aient	vaincu

Imparfait		Plus-que-parfait		
que je	vainquisse	que j'	eusse	vaincu
que tu	vainquisses	que tu	eusses	vaincu
qu' elle	vainquît	qu' elle	eût	vaincu
que n.	vainquissions	que n.	eussions	vaincu
que v.	vainquissiez	que v.	eussiez	vaincu
qu' ils	vainquissent	qu' ils	eussent	vaincu

IMPÉRATIF

Présent	Passé	
vain**cs**	aie	vaincu
vainquons	ayons	vaincu
vainquez	ayez	vaincu

INFINITIF

Présent	Passé
vaincre	avoir vaincu

PARTICIPE

Présent	Passé (composé)
vainquant	ayant vaincu
	Passé
	vaincu

Conditionnel passé 2e forme **(2nd form)**: same form as the *plus-que-parfait* of the subjunctive.
Futur proche: *je vais vaincre* (see Grammar of the verb, paragraphs 3 and 50).

- Note that **vaincre** does not end with the letter **t** in the 3rd person singular of the present indicative: *il vainc.*
- Before a vowel (except in the case of **u**), the **c** becomes **qu**: *nous vainquons.*
- **Convaincre** follows this pattern of conjugation.
- The interrogative form is written: *Vainc-t-il ? Convainc-t-il ?* (see Grammar of the verb, paragraph 16).

traire

INDICATIF

Présent		Passé composé		
je	trais	j'	ai	trait
tu	trais	tu	as	trait
elle	trait	elle	a	trait
nous	tra**y**ons	nous	avons	trait
vous	tra**y**ez	vous	avez	trait
ils	traient	ils	ont	trait

Imparfait		Plus-que-parfait		
je	trayais	j'	avais	trait
tu	trayais	tu	avais	trait
elle	trayait	elle	avait	trait
nous	tra**yi**ons	nous	avions	trait
vous	tra**yi**ez	vous	aviez	trait
ils	trayaient	ils	avaient	trait

Passé simple		Passé antérieur		
.		j'	eus	trait
.		tu	eus	trait
.		elle	eut	trait
.		nous	eûmes	trait
.		vous	eûtes	trait
.		ils	eurent	trait

Futur simple		Futur antérieur		
je	trairai	j'	aurai	trait
tu	trairas	tu	auras	trait
elle	traira	elle	aura	trait
nous	trairons	nous	aurons	trait
vous	trairez	vous	aurez	trait
ils	trairont	ils	auront	trait

Conditionnel présent		Conditionnel passé		
je	trairais	j'	aurais	trait
tu	trairais	tu	aurais	trait
elle	trairait	elle	aurait	trait
nous	trairions	nous	aurions	trait
vous	trairiez	vous	auriez	trait
ils	trairaient	ils	auraient	trait

SUBJONCTIF

Présent		Passé		
que je	traie	que j'	aie	trait
que tu	traies	que tu	aies	trait
qu' elle	traie	qu' elle	ait	trait
que n.	tra**yi**ons	que n.	ayons	trait
que v.	tra**yi**ez	que v.	ayez	trait
qu' ils	traient	qu' ils	aient	trait

Imparfait	Plus-que-parfait		
.	que j'	eusse	trait
.	que tu	eusses	trait
.	qu' elle	eût	trait
.	que n.	eussions	trait
.	que v.	eussiez	trait
.	qu' ils	eussent	trait

IMPÉRATIF

Présent	Passé	
trais	aie	trait
tra**y**ons	ayons	trait
tra**y**ez	ayez	trait

INFINITIF

Présent	Passé
traire	avoir trait

PARTICIPE

Présent	Passé (composé)
trayant	ayant trait
	Passé
	trait

Conditionnel passé 2e forme **(2nd form)**: same form as the *plus-que-parfait* of the subjunctive.
Futur proche: *je vais traire* (see Grammar of the verb, paragraphs 3 and 50).

- The derived forms of **traire**, such as **extraire**, **distraire**, etc. (see List of irregular verbs, p. 96 to 98), follow this pattern of conjugation.
- The verbs **braire** and **raire** also follow this pattern of conjugation. They are used mostly in the 3rd person.
- Note that these verbs are not conjugated in the *passé simple* or the *imparfait* of the subjunctive.

INDICATIF

Présent

je	fais
tu	fais
elle	fait
nous	faisons
vous	faites
ils	font

Passé composé

j'	ai	fait
tu	as	fait
elle	a	fait
nous	avons	fait
vous	avez	fait
ils	ont	fait

Imparfait

je	faisais
tu	faisais
elle	faisait
nous	faisions
vous	faisiez
ils	faisaient

Plus-que-parfait

j'	avais	fait
tu	avais	fait
elle	avait	fait
nous	avions	fait
vous	aviez	fait
ils	avaient	fait

Passé simple

je	fis
tu	fis
elle	fit
nous	fîmes
vous	fîtes
ils	firent

Passé antérieur

j'	eus	fait
tu	eus	fait
elle	eut	fait
nous	eûmes	fait
vous	eûtes	fait
ils	eurent	fait

Futur simple

je	ferai
tu	feras
elle	fera
nous	ferons
vous	ferez
ils	feront

Futur antérieur

j'	aurai	fait
tu	auras	fait
elle	aura	fait
nous	aurons	fait
vous	aurez	fait
ils	auront	fait

Conditionnel présent

je	ferais
tu	ferais
elle	ferait
nous	ferions
vous	feriez
ils	feraient

Conditionnel passé

j'	aurais	fait
tu	aurais	fait
elle	aurait	fait
nous	aurions	fait
vous	auriez	fait
ils	auraient	fait

SUBJONCTIF

Présent

que je	fasse
que tu	fasses
qu' elle	fasse
que n.	fassions
que v.	fassiez
qu' ils	fassent

Passé

que j'	aie	fait
que tu	aies	fait
qu' elle	ait	fait
que n.	ayons	fait
que v.	ayez	fait
qu' ils	aient	fait

Imparfait

que je	fisse
que tu	fisses
qu' elle	fît
que n.	fissions
que v.	fissiez
qu' ils	fissent

Plus-que-parfait

que j'	eusse	fait
que tu	eusses	fait
qu' elle	eût	fait
que n.	eussions	fait
que v.	eussiez	fait
qu' ils	eussent	fait

IMPÉRATIF

Présent	Passé
fais	aie fait
faisons	ayons fait
faites	ayez fait

INFINITIF

Présent	Passé
faire	avoir fait

PARTICIPE

Présent	Passé (composé)
faisant	ayant fait

Passé

fait

***Conditionnel passé 2e forme* (2nd form)**: same form as the *plus-que-parfait* of the subjunctive.
Futur proche: *je vais faire* (see Grammar of the verb, paragraphs 3 and 50).

- The written form **fai-** is pronounced **fe** [fə] in the following forms: **fai***sons* [fəzɔ̃]; **fai***sais*, **fai***sait*, **fai***saient* [fəzɛ]; **fai***sions* [fəzjɔ̃]; **fai***siez* [fəzje]; **fai***sant* [fəzɑ̃].
  However, in these forms written with an **e**, pronunciation and spelling correspond: *je* **fe***rai*..., *je* **fe***rais*...
- Note the 2nd person plural in the present indicative and the imperative: *vous faites, faites*. The forms ⊗ *vous faisez*, ⊗ *faisez* are erroneous and are due to generalization or regularization of irregular forms.
- The derived forms of **faire** follow this pattern of conjugation (see List of irregular verbs, p. 96 to 98).

129 plaire

INDICATIF

Présent	/ VARIANTE	Passé composé		
je	plais	j'	ai	plu
tu	plais	tu	as	plu
elle	plaît / plait	elle	a	plu
nous	plaisons	nous	avons	plu
vous	plaisez	vous	avez	plu
ils	plaisent	ils	ont	plu

Imparfait		Plus-que-parfait		
je	plaisais	j'	avais	plu
tu	plaisais	tu	avais	plu
elle	plaisait	elle	avait	plu
nous	plaisions	nous	avions	plu
vous	plaisiez	vous	aviez	plu
ils	plaisaient	ils	avaient	plu

Passé simple		Passé antérieur		
je	plus	j'	eus	plu
tu	plus	tu	eus	plu
elle	plut	elle	eut	plu
nous	plûmes	nous	eûmes	plu
vous	plûtes	vous	eûtes	plu
ils	plurent	ils	eurent	plu

Futur simple		Futur antérieur		
je	plairai	j'	aurai	plu
tu	plairas	tu	auras	plu
elle	plaira	elle	aura	plu
nous	plairons	nous	aurons	plu
vous	plairez	vous	aurez	plu
ils	plairont	ils	auront	plu

Conditionnel présent		Conditionnel passé		
je	plairais	j'	aurais	plu
tu	plairais	tu	aurais	plu
elle	plairait	elle	aurait	plu
nous	plairions	nous	aurions	plu
vous	plairiez	vous	auriez	plu
ils	plairaient	ils	auraient	plu

SUBJONCTIF

Présent		Passé		
que je	plaise	que j'	aie	plu
que tu	plaises	que tu	aies	plu
qu'elle	plaise	qu'elle	ait	plu
que n.	plaisions	que n.	ayons	plu
que v.	plaisiez	que v.	ayez	plu
qu' ils	plaisent	qu' ils	aient	plu

Imparfait		Plus-que-parfait		
que je	plusse	que j'	eusse	plu
que tu	plusses	que tu	eusses	plu
qu'elle	plût	qu'elle	eût	plu
que n.	plussions	que n.	eussions	plu
que v.	plussiez	que v.	eussiez	plu
qu' ils	plussent	qu' ils	eussent	plu

IMPÉRATIF

Présent	Passé	
plais	aie	plu
plaisons	ayons	plu
plaisez	ayez	plu

INFINITIF

Présent	Passé
plaire	avoir plu

PARTICIPE

Présent	Passé (composé)
plaisant	ayant plu
	Passé
	plu

***Conditionnel passé 2e forme* (2nd form)**: same form as the *plus-que-parfait* of the subjunctive.
Futur proche: *je vais plaire* (see Grammar of the verb, paragraphs 3 and 50).

- **Complaire** and **déplaire** follow this pattern of conjugation.
- **Taire** is conjugated like **plaire**, except for the circumflex in the present indicative.
- Traditionally, *plaît*, *déplaît* and *complaît* (3rd person singular of the present indicative) are written with a circumflex. The French spelling reform admits these forms without the circumflex (*plait*, *déplait*, *complait*), as in the case of *tait* and *fait*.
- The past participles *plu*, *complu*, *déplu* are invariable but *tu* (from the verb **taire**) agrees with the subject: *Ils se sont tus*.

INDICATIF

Présent		/ VARIANTE	Passé composé		
je	parais		j'	ai	paru
tu	parais		tu	as	paru
elle	paraît	/ parait	elle	a	paru
nous	paraissons		nous	avons	paru
vous	paraissez		vous	avez	paru
ils	paraissent		ils	ont	paru

Imparfait		Plus-que-parfait		
je	paraissais	j'	avais	paru
tu	paraissais	tu	avais	paru
elle	paraissait	elle	avait	paru
nous	paraissions	nous	avions	paru
vous	paraissiez	vous	aviez	paru
ils	paraissaient	ils	avaient	paru

Passé simple		Passé antérieur		
je	parus	j'	eus	paru
tu	parus	tu	eus	paru
elle	parut	elle	eut	paru
nous	parûmes	nous	eûmes	paru
vous	parûtes	vous	eûtes	paru
ils	parurent	ils	eurent	paru

Futur simple		/ VARIANTE	Futur antérieur		
je	paraîtrai	/ paraitrai	j'	aurai	paru
tu	paraîtras	/ paraitras	tu	auras	paru
elle	paraîtra	/ paraitra	elle	aura	paru
nous	paraîtrons	/ paraitrons	nous	aurons	paru
vous	paraîtrez	/ paraitrez	vous	aurez	paru
ils	paraîtront	/ paraitront	ils	auront	paru

Conditionnel présent		/ VARIANTE	Conditionnel passé		
je	paraîtrais	/ paraitrais	j'	aurais	paru
tu	paraîtrais	/ paraitrais	tu	aurais	paru
elle	paraîtrait	/ paraitrait	elle	aurait	paru
nous	paraîtrions	/ paraitrions	nous	aurions	paru
vous	paraîtriez	/ paraitriez	vous	auriez	paru
ils	paraîtraient	/ paraitraient	ils	auraient	paru

SUBJONCTIF

Présent		Passé		
que je	paraisse	que j'	aie	paru
que tu	paraisses	que tu	aies	paru
qu'elle	paraisse	qu'elle	ait	paru
que n.	paraissions	que n.	ayons	paru
que v.	paraissiez	que v.	ayez	paru
qu' ils	paraissent	qu' ils	aient	paru

Imparfait		Plus-que-parfait		
que je	parusse	que j'	eusse	paru
que tu	parusses	que tu	eusses	paru
qu'elle	parût	qu'elle	eût	paru
que n.	parussions	que n.	eussions	paru
que v.	parussiez	que v.	eussiez	paru
qu' ils	parussent	qu' ils	eussent	paru

IMPÉRATIF

Présent	Passé	
parais	aie	paru
paraissons	ayons	paru
paraissez	ayez	paru

INFINITIF

Présent / VARIANTE	Passé
paraître / paraitre	avoir paru

PARTICIPE

Présent	Passé (composé)
paraissant	ayant paru
	Passé
	paru

***Conditionnel passé 2e forme* (2nd form)**: same form as the *plus-que-parfait* of the subjunctive.
Futur proche: *je vais paraître* or *je vais paraitre* (see Grammar of the verb, paragraphs 3 and 50).

- **Connaître** (or **connaitre**) and its derived forms as well as the derived forms of **paraître** (or **paraitre**) follow this pattern of conjugation (see List of irregular verbs, p. 96 to 98).
- Traditionally all verbs ending in **-aître** take a circumflex over the **i** preceeding the **t**. The spelling reform recommends elision of the circumflex (*paraitre, il parait; connaitre, elle connaitra*).

131 naître/naitre

INDICATIF

Présent	/ VARIANTE	Passé composé		
je nais		je	suis	né
tu nais		tu	es	né
elle naît	/ nait	elle	est	née
nous naissons		nous	sommes	nés
vous naissez		vous	êtes	nés
ils naissent		ils	sont	nés

Imparfait	Plus-que-parfait		
je naissais	j'	étais	né
tu naissais	tu	étais	né
elle naissait	elle	était	née
nous naissions	nous	étions	nés
vous naissiez	vous	étiez	nés
ils naissaient	ils	étaient	nés

Passé simple	Passé antérieur		
je naquis	je	fus	né
tu naquis	tu	fus	né
elle naquit	elle	fut	née
nous naquîmes	nous	fûmes	nés
vous naquîtes	vous	fûtes	nés
ils naquirent	ils	furent	nés

Futur simple	/ VARIANTE	Futur antérieur		
je naîtrai	/ naitrai	je	serai	né
tu naîtras	/ naitras	tu	seras	né
elle naîtra	/ naitra	elle	sera	née
nous naîtrons	/ naitrons	nous	serons	nés
vous naîtrez	/ naitrez	vous	serez	nés
ils naîtront	/ naitront	ils	seront	nés

Conditionnel présent	/ VARIANTE	Conditionnel passé		
je naîtrais	/ naitrais	je	serais	né
tu naîtrais	/ naitrais	tu	serais	né
elle naîtrait	/ naitrait	elle	serait	née
nous naîtrions	/ naitrions	nous	serions	nés
vous naîtriez	/ naitriez	vous	seriez	nés
ils naîtraient	/ naitraient	ils	seraient	nés

SUBJONCTIF

Présent		Passé		
que je	naisse	que je	sois	né
que tu	naisses	que tu	sois	né
qu' elle	naisse	qu' elle	soit	née
que n.	naissions	que n.	soyons	nés
que v.	naissiez	que v.	soyez	nés
qu' ils	naissent	qu' ils	soient	nés

Imparfait		Plus-que-parfait		
que je	naquisse	que je	fusse	né
que tu	naquisses	que tu	fusses	né
qu' elle	naquît	qu' elle	fût	née
que n.	naquissions	que n.	fussions	nés
que v.	naquissiez	que v.	fussiez	nés
qu' ils	naquissent	qu' ils	fussent	nés

IMPÉRATIF

Présent	Passé
nais	sois né
naissons	soyons nés
naissez	soyez nés

INFINITIF

Présent	/ VARIANTE	Passé
naître	/ naitre	être né

PARTICIPE

Présent	Passé (composé)
naissant	étant né

Passé

né

***Conditionnel passé 2e forme* (2nd form)**: same form as the *plus-que-parfait* of the subjunctive.
Futur proche: *je vais naître* or *je vais naitre* (see Grammar of the verb, paragraphs 3 and 50).

- **Renaître** (or **renaitre**) follows this pattern of conjugation. The compound forms and past participle of this verb are rarely used.
- Note the use of the auxiliary **être** with this verb.
- Traditionally, all verbs ending in **-aître** take a circumflex over the **i** preceding the **t**. The spelling reform recommends spelling it without the circumflex (*naitre, elle nait, elle naitra*...). However it retains the circumflex in the *imparfait* of the subjunctive (*qu'elle naquît*) to differentiate it from the *passé simple* which has no accent (*elle naquit*). The accent is also maintained with *nous* and *vous* in the *passé simple* to keep spelling consistent with the other French verbs.

INDICATIF

Présent		/ VARIANTE	Passé composé
je	pais		.
tu	pais		.
elle	paît	/ pait	.
nous	paissons		.
vous	paissez		.
ils	paissent		.

Imparfait		Plus-que-parfait
je	paissais	.
tu	paissais	.
elle	paissait	.
nous	paissions	.
vous	paissiez	.
ils	paissaient	.

Passé simple	Passé antérieur
.	.
.	.
.	.
.	.
.	.
.	.

Futur simple		/ VARIANTE	Futur antérieur
je	paîtrai	/ paitrai	.
tu	paîtras	/ paitras	.
elle	paîtra	/ paitra	.
nous	paîtrons	/ paitrons	.
vous	paîtrez	/ paitrez	.
ils	paîtront	/ paitront	.

Conditionnel présent		/ VARIANTE	Conditionnel passé
je	paîtrais	/ paitrais	.
tu	paîtrais	/ paitrais	.
elle	paîtrait	/ paitrait	.
nous	paîtrions	/ paitrions	.
vous	paîtriez	/ paitriez	.
ils	paîtraient	/ paitraient	.

SUBJONCTIF

Présent		Passé
que je	paisse	.
que tu	paisses	.
qu' elle	paisse	.
que n.	paissions	.
que v.	paissiez	.
qu' ils	paissent	.

Imparfait	Plus-que-parfait
.	.
.	.
.	.
.	.
.	.
.	.

IMPÉRATIF

Présent	Passé
pais	.
paissons	.
paissez	.

INFINITIF

Présent / VARIANTE	Passé
paître / paitre	.

PARTICIPE

Présent	Passé (composé)
paissant	.
	Passé
	pu

***Conditionnel passé 2e forme* (2nd form)**: same form as the *plus-que-parfait* of the subjunctive.
Futur proche: *je vais paître* or *je vais paitre* (see Grammar of the verb, paragraphs 3 and 50).

- This verb has no compound forms, only the simple forms given above. Note that the *passé simple* and the *imparfait* of the subjunctive do not exist.
- The past participle *pu* is invariable and is used only with regard to falconry.
- Traditionally all verbs in **-aître** take a circumflex over the **i** preceding the **t**. The spelling reform recommends elision of the circumflex (*paitre, il pait, elle paitra…*).

133 repaître/repaitre

INDICATIF

Présent		/VARIANTE	Passé composé		
je	repais		j'	ai	repu
tu	repais		tu	as	repu
elle	repaît	/repait	elle	a	repu
nous	repaissons		nous	avons	repu
vous	repaissez		vous	avez	repu
ils	repaissent		ils	ont	repu

Imparfait		Plus-que-parfait		
je	**repaissais**	j'	avais	repu
tu	repaissais	tu	avais	repu
elle	repaissait	elle	avait	repu
nous	repaissions	nous	avions	repu
vous	repaissiez	vous	aviez	repu
ils	repaissaient	ils	avaient	repu

Passé simple		Passé antérieur		
je	repus	j'	eus	repu
tu	repus	tu	eus	repu
elle	reput	elle	eut	repu
nous	repûmes	nous	eûmes	repu
vous	repûtes	vous	eûtes	repu
ils	repurent	ils	eurent	repu

Futur simple		/VARIANTE	Futur antérieur		
je	repaîtrai	/repaitrai	j'	aurai	repu
tu	repaîtras	/repaitras	tu	auras	repu
elle	repaîtra	/repaitra	elle	aura	repu
nous	repaîtrons	/repaitrons	nous	aurons	repu
vous	repaîtrez	/repaitrez	vous	aurez	repu
ils	repaîtront	/repaitront	ils	auront	repu

Conditionnel présent		/VARIANTE	Conditionnel passé		
je	repaîtrais	/repaitrais	j'	aurais	repu
tu	repaîtrais	/repaitrais	tu	aurais	repu
elle	repaîtrait	/repaitrait	elle	aurait	repu
nous	repaîtrions	/repaitrions	nous	aurions	repu
vous	repaîtriez	/repaitriez	vous	auriez	repu
ils	repaîtraient	/repaitraient	ils	auraient	repu

SUBJONCTIF

Présent		Passé		
que je	repaisse	que j'	aie	repu
que tu	repaisses	que tu	aies	repu
qu' elle	repaisse	qu' elle	ait	repu
que n.	repaissions	que n.	ayons	repu
que v.	repaissiez	que v.	ayez	repu
qu' ils	repaissent	qu' ils	aient	repu

Imparfait		Plus-que-parfait		
que je	repusse	que j'	eusse	repu
que tu	repusses	que tu	eusses	repu
qu' elle	repût	qu' elle	eût	repu
que n.	repussions	que n.	eussions	repu
que v.	repussiez	que v.	eussiez	repu
qu' ils	repussent	qu' ils	eussent	repu

IMPÉRATIF

Présent	Passé
repais	aie repu
repaissons	ayons repu
repaissez	ayez repu

INFINITIF

Présent /VARIANTE	Passé
repaître /repaitre	avoir repu

PARTICIPE

Présent	Passé (composé)
repaissant	ayant repu
	Passé
	repu

***Conditionnel passé 2e forme* (2nd form)**: same form as the *plus-que-parfait* of the subjunctive.
Futur proche: *je vais repaître* or *je vais repaitre* (see Grammar of the verb, paragraphs 3 and 50).

- **Repaître** (or **repaitre**) is archaic; modern usage prefers the pronominal form **se repaître** (or **se repaitre**).
- Traditionally, all verbs ending in **-aître** take a circumflex over the **i** preceding the **t**. The spelling reform recommends elision of the circumflex (*repaitre, il repait, elle repaitra*…).

INDICATIF

Présent		Passé composé		
je	croîs	j'	ai	crû
tu	croîs	tu	as	crû
elle	croît	elle	a	crû
nous	croissons	nous	avons	crû
vous	croissez	vous	avez	crû
ils	croissent	ils	ont	crû

Imparfait		Plus-que-parfait		
je	croissais	j'	avais	crû
tu	croissais	tu	avais	crû
elle	croissait	elle	avait	crû
nous	croissions	nous	avions	crû
vous	croissiez	vous	aviez	crû
ils	croissaient	ils	avaient	crû

Passé simple		Passé antérieur		
je	crûs	j'	eus	crû
tu	crûs	tu	eus	crû
elle	crût	elle	eut	crû
nous	crûmes	nous	eûmes	crû
vous	crûtes	vous	eûtes	crû
ils	crûrent	ils	eurent	crû

Futur simple		/ VARIANTE	Futur antérieur		
je	croîtrai	/ croitrai	j'	aurai	crû
tu	croîtras	/ croitras	tu	auras	crû
elle	croîtra	/ croitra	elle	aura	crû
nous	croîtrons	/ croitrons	nous	aurons	crû
vous	croîtrez	/ croitrez	vous	aurez	crû
ils	croîtront	/ croitront	ils	auront	crû

Conditionnel présent		/ VARIANTE	Conditionnel passé		
je	croîtrais	/ croitrais	j'	aurais	crû
tu	croîtrais	/ croitrais	tu	aurais	crû
elle	croîtrait	/ croitrait	elle	aurait	crû
nous	croîtrions	/ croitrions	nous	aurions	crû
vous	croîtriez	/ croitriez	vous	auriez	crû
ils	croîtraient	/ croitraient	ils	auraient	crû

SUBJONCTIF

Présent		Passé		
que je	croisse	que j'	aie	crû
que tu	croisses	que tu	aies	crû
qu' elle	croisse	qu' elle	ait	crû
que n.	croissions	que n.	ayons	crû
que v.	croissiez	que v.	ayez	crû
qu' ils	croissent	qu' ils	aient	crû

Imparfait		Plus-que-parfait		
que je	crûsse	que j'	eusse	crû
que tu	crûsses	que tu	eusses	crû
qu' elle	crût	qu' elle	eût	crû
que n.	crûssions	que n.	eussions	crû
que v.	crûssiez	que v.	eussiez	crû
qu' ils	crûssent	qu' ils	eussent	crû

IMPÉRATIF

Présent	Passé	
croîs	aie	crû
croissons	ayons	crû
croissez	ayez	crû

INFINITIF

Présent / VARIANTE	Passé
croître / croitre	avoir crû

PARTICIPE

Présent	Passé (composé)
croissant	ayant crû
	Passé
	crû

***Conditionnel passé 2e forme* (2nd form)**: same form as the *plus-que-parfait* of the subjunctive.
Futur proche: *je vais croître* or *je vais croitre* (see Grammar of the verb, paragraphs 3 and 50).

- Traditionally, the verb **croître** takes a circumflex over the **i** preceding the **t** and also to avoid possible confusion with the verb **croire** (*je croîs* = "I grow"; *je crois* = "I believe"). The spelling reform endorses the use of the circumflex only when it is necessary to avoid confusion. Since the infinitive, the future and the present conditional present no such risk, the accent is not mandatory in these forms.

135 croire

INDICATIF

Présent		Passé composé		
je	crois	j'	ai	cru
tu	crois	tu	as	cru
elle	croit	elle	a	cru
nous	croyons	nous	avons	cru
vous	croyez	vous	avez	cru
ils	croient	ils	ont	cru

Imparfait		Plus-que-parfait		
je	croyais	j'	avais	cru
tu	croyais	tu	avais	cru
elle	croyait	elle	avait	cru
nous	croyions	nous	avions	cru
vous	croyiez	vous	aviez	cru
ils	croyaient	ils	avaient	cru

Passé simple		Passé antérieur		
je	crus	j'	eus	cru
tu	crus	tu	eus	cru
elle	crut	elle	eut	cru
nous	crûmes	nous	eûmes	cru
vous	crûtes	vous	eûtes	cru
ils	crurent	ils	eurent	cru

Futur simple		Futur antérieur		
je	croirai	j'	aurai	cru
tu	croiras	tu	auras	cru
elle	croira	elle	aura	cru
nous	croirons	nous	aurons	cru
vous	croirez	vous	aurez	cru
ils	croiront	ils	auront	cru

Conditionnel présent		Conditionnel passé		
je	croirais	j'	aurais	cru
tu	croirais	tu	aurais	cru
elle	croirait	elle	aurait	cru
nous	croirions	nous	aurions	cru
vous	croiriez	vous	auriez	cru
ils	croiraient	ils	auraient	cru

SUBJONCTIF

Présent		Passé		
que je	croie	que j'	aie	cru
que tu	croies	que tu	aies	cru
qu'elle	croie	qu'elle	ait	cru
que n.	croyions	que n.	ayons	cru
que v.	croyiez	que v.	ayez	cru
qu' ils	croient	qu' ils	aient	cru

Imparfait		Plus-que-parfait		
que je	crusse	que j'	eusse	cru
que tu	crusses	que tu	eusses	cru
qu'elle	crût	qu'elle	eût	cru
que n.	crussions	que n.	eussions	cru
que v.	crussiez	que v.	eussiez	cru
qu' ils	crussent	qu' ils	eussent	cru

IMPÉRATIF

Présent	Passé	
crois	aie	cru
croyons	ayons	cru
croyez	ayez	cru

INFINITIF

Présent	Passé
croire	avoir cru

PARTICIPE

Présent	Passé (composé)
croyant	ayant cru
	Passé
	cru

***Conditionnel passé 2e forme* (2nd form)**: same form as the *plus-que-parfait* of the subjunctive.
Futur proche: *je vais croire* (see Grammar of the verb, paragraphs 3 and 50).

- **Mécroire** follows this pattern of conjugation.
- **Accroire** is used only in the infinitive.

INDICATIF

Présent	/ VARIANTE	Passé composé
je décrois		j' ai décru
tu décrois		tu as décru
elle décroît	/ décroit	elle a décru
nous décroissons		nous avons décru
vous décroissez		vous avez décru
ils décroissent		ils ont décru

Imparfait	Plus-que-parfait
je décroissais	j' avais décru
tu décroissais	tu avais décru
elle décroissait	elle avait décru
nous décroissions	nous avions décru
vous décroissiez	vous aviez décru
ils décroissaient	ils avaient décru

Passé simple	Passé antérieur
je décrus	j' eus décru
tu décrus	tu eus décru
elle décrut	elle eut décru
nous décrûmes	nous eûmes décru
vous décrûtes	vous eûtes décru
ils décrurent	ils eurent décru

Futur simple	/ VARIANTE	Futur antérieur
je décroîtrai	/ décroitrai	j' aurai décru
tu décroîtras	/ décroitras	tu auras décru
elle décroîtra	/ décroitra	elle aura décru
nous décroîtrons	/ décroitrons	nous aurons décru
vous décroîtrez	/ décroitrez	vous aurez décru
ils décroîtront	/ décroitront	ils auront décru

Conditionnel présent	/ VARIANTE	Conditionnel passé
je décroîtrais	/ décroitrais	j' aurais décru
tu décroîtrais	/ décroitrais	tu aurais décru
elle décroîtrait	/ décroitrait	elle aurait décru
nous décroîtrions	/ décroitrions	nous aurions décru
vous décroîtriez	/ décroitriez	vous auriez décru
ils décroîtraient	/ décroitraient	ils auraient décru

SUBJONCTIF

Présent	Passé
que je décroisse	que j' aie décru
que tu décroisses	que tu aies décru
qu' elle décroisse	qu' elle ait décru
que n. décroissions	que n. ayons décru
que v. décroissiez	que v. ayez décru
qu' ils décroissent	qu' ils aient décru

Imparfait	Plus-que-parfait
que je décrusse	que j' eusse décru
que tu décrusses	que tu eusses décru
qu' elle décrût	qu' elle eût décru
que n. décrussions	que n. eussions décru
que v. décruissiez	que v. eussiez décru
qu' ils décrussent	qu' ils eussent décru

IMPÉRATIF

Présent	Passé
décrois	aie décru
décroissons	ayons décru
décroissez	ayez décru

INFINITIF

Présent / VARIANTE	Passé
décroître / décroitre	avoir décru

PARTICIPE

Présent	Passé (composé)
décroissant	ayant décru

Passé
décru

***Conditionnel passé 2e forme* (2nd form)**: same form as the *plus-que-parfait* of the subjunctive.
Futur proche: *je vais décroître* or *je vais décroitre* (see Grammar of the verb, paragraphs 3 and 50).

- **Accroître** (or **accroitre**) and **recroître** (or **recroitre**) follow this pattern of conjugation.
- Traditionally, all verbs ending in **-oître** take a circumflex over the **i** preceding the **t**. The spelling reform recommends elision of the circumflex (*accroitre, il accroit, elle recroitra…*).
- Traditionally, the past participle of **recroître** takes a circumflex over the **u**. Hence *recrû* (but *accru* and *décru*). The spelling reform recommends elision of the circumflex: *recru*.

137 boire

INDICATIF

Présent		Passé composé		
je	bois	j'	ai	bu
tu	bois	tu	as	bu
elle	boit	elle	a	bu
nous	buvons	nous	avons	bu
vous	buvez	vous	avez	bu
ils	boivent	ils	ont	bu

Imparfait		Plus-que-parfait		
je	buvais	j'	avais	bu
tu	buvais	tu	avais	bu
elle	buvait	elle	avait	bu
nous	buvions	nous	avions	bu
vous	buviez	vous	aviez	bu
ils	buvaient	ils	avaient	bu

Passé simple		Passé antérieur		
je	bus	j'	eus	bu
tu	bus	tu	eus	bu
elle	but	elle	eut	bu
nous	bûmes	nous	eûmes	bu
vous	bûtes	vous	eûtes	bu
ils	burent	ils	eurent	bu

Futur simple		Futur antérieur		
je	boirai	j'	aurai	bu
tu	boiras	tu	auras	bu
elle	boira	elle	aura	bu
nous	boirons	nous	aurons	bu
vous	boirez	vous	aurez	bu
ils	boiront	ils	auront	bu

Conditionnel présent		Conditionnel passé		
je	boirais	j'	aurais	bu
tu	boirais	tu	aurais	bu
elle	boirait	elle	aurait	bu
nous	boirions	nous	aurions	bu
vous	boiriez	vous	auriez	bu
ils	boiraient	ils	auraient	bu

SUBJONCTIF

Présent		Passé		
que je	boive	que j'	aie	bu
que tu	boives	que tu	aies	bu
qu'elle	boive	qu'elle	ait	bu
que n.	buvions	que n.	ayons	bu
que v.	buviez	que v.	ayez	bu
qu' ils	boivent	qu' ils	aient	bu

Imparfait		Plus-que-parfait		
que je	busse	que j'	eusse	bu
que tu	busses	que tu	eusses	bu
qu'elle	bût	qu'elle	eût	bu
que n.	bussions	que n.	eussions	bu
que v.	bussiez	que v.	eussiez	bu
qu' ils	bussent	qu' ils	eussent	bu

IMPÉRATIF

Présent	Passé	
bois	aie	bu
buvons	ayons	bu
buvez	ayez	bu

INFINITIF

Présent	Passé
boire	avoir bu

PARTICIPE

Présent	Passé (composé)
buvant	ayant bu
	Passé
	bu

***Conditionnel passé 2e forme* (2nd form)**: same form as the *plus-que-parfait* of the subjunctive.
Futur proche: *je vais boire* (see Grammar of the verb, paragraphs 3 and 50).

- **S'emboire** (auxiliary **être**) follows this pattern of conjugation.

INDICATIF

Présent		Passé composé		
je	clos	j'	ai	clos
tu	clos	tu	as	clos
elle	clôt[1]	elle	a	clos
nous	*closons*	nous	avons	clos
vous	*closez*	vous	avez	clos
ils	closent	ils	ont	clos

Imparfait		Plus-que-parfait		
je	*closais*	j'	avais	clos
tu	*closais*	tu	avais	clos
elle	*closait*	elle	avait	clos
nous	*closions*	nous	avions	clos
vous	*closiez*	vous	aviez	clos
ils	*closaient*	ils	avaient	clos

Passé simple		Passé antérieur		
je	*closis*	j'	eus	clos
tu	*closis*	tu	eus	clos
elle	*closit*	elle	eut	clos
nous	*closîmes*	nous	eûmes	clos
vous	*closîtes*	vous	eûtes	clos
ils	*closirent*	ils	eurent	clos

Futur simple		Futur antérieur		
je	clorai	j'	aurai	clos
tu	cloras	tu	auras	clos
elle	clora	elle	aura	clos
nous	clorons	nous	aurons	clos
vous	clorez	vous	aurez	clos
ils	cloront	ils	auront	clos

Conditionnel présent		Conditionnel passé		
je	clorais	j'	aurais	clos
tu	clorais	tu	aurais	clos
elle	clorait	elle	aurait	clos
nous	clorions	nous	aurions	clos
vous	cloriez	vous	auriez	clos
ils	cloraient	ils	auraient	clos

SUBJONCTIF

Présent		Passé		
que je	close	que j'	aie	clos
que tu	closes	que tu	aies	clos
qu' elle	close	qu' elle	ait	clos
que n.	closions	que n.	ayons	clos
que v.	closiez	que v.	ayez	clos
qu' ils	closent	qu' ils	aient	clos

Imparfait		Plus-que-parfait		
que je	*closisse*	que j'	eusse	clos
que tu	*closisses*	que tu	eusses	clos
qu' elle	*closît*	qu' elle	eût	clos
que n.	*closissions*	que n.	eussions	clos
que v.	*closissiez*	que v.	eussiez	clos
qu' ils	*closissent*	qu' ils	eussent	clos

IMPÉRATIF

Présent	Passé	
clos	aie	clos
closons	ayons	clos
closez	ayez	clos

INFINITIF

Présent	Passé
clore	avoir clos

PARTICIPE

Présent	Passé (composé)
closant	ayant clos
	Passé
	clos

1. According to the *Académie française*, some verbs can be written without the circumflex over the **o** in the 3rd person singular of the present indicative: *elle enclot, il éclot, il déclot.*

Conditionnel passé 2e forme **(2nd form)**: same form as the *plus-que-parfait* of the subjunctive.
Futur proche: *je vais clore* (see Grammar of the verb, paragraphs 3 and 50).

- **Enclore** follows this pattern of conjugation. Both forms *il enclôt* or *il enclot* are correct.
- **Éclore** is used mostly in the 3rd person which is written *il éclôt* or *il éclot* (with or without the circumflex). The auxiliary *être* is admissible.
- **Déclore** is used mostly in the infinitive and the past participle. The 3rd person singular is written *il déclôt* or *il déclot.*
- **Reclore**, like **clore**, takes a circumflex in *il reclôt.*
- **Forclore** is used only in the infinitive and the past participle (*forclos, forclose, forcloses*).
- The forms in italics in the table are rare.

139 exclure

INDICATIF

Présent		Passé composé		
j'	exclus	j'	ai	exclu
tu	exclus	tu	as	exclu
elle	exclut	elle	a	exclu
nous	excluons	nous	avons	exclu
vous	excluez	vous	avez	exclu
ils	excluent	ils	ont	exclu

Imparfait		Plus-que-parfait		
j'	excluais	j'	avais	exclu
tu	excluais	tu	avais	exclu
elle	excluait	elle	avait	exclu
nous	excluions	nous	avions	exclu
vous	excluiez	vous	aviez	exclu
ils	excluaient	ils	avaient	exclu

Passé simple		Passé antérieur		
j'	exclus	j'	eus	exclu
tu	exclus	tu	eus	exclu
elle	exclut	elle	eut	exclu
nous	exclûmes	nous	eûmes	exclu
vous	exclûtes	vous	eûtes	exclu
ils	exclurent	ils	eurent	exclu

Futur simple		Futur antérieur		
j'	exclurai	j'	aurai	exclu
tu	excluras	tu	auras	exclu
elle	exclura	elle	aura	exclu
nous	exclurons	nous	aurons	exclu
vous	exclurez	vous	aurez	exclu
ils	excluront	ils	auront	exclu

Conditionnel présent		Conditionnel passé		
j'	exclurais	j'	aurais	exclu
tu	exclurais	tu	aurais	exclu
elle	exclurait	elle	aurait	exclu
nous	exclurions	nous	aurions	exclu
vous	excluriez	vous	auriez	exclu
ils	excluraient	ils	auraient	exclu

SUBJONCTIF

Présent		Passé		
que j'	exclue	que j'	aie	exclu
que tu	exclues	que tu	aies	exclu
qu' elle	exclue	qu' elle	ait	exclu
que n.	excluions	que n.	ayons	exclu
que v.	excluiez	que v.	ayez	exclu
qu' ils	excluent	qu' ils	aient	exclu

Imparfait		Plus-que-parfait		
que j'	exclusse	que j'	eusse	exclu
que tu	exclusses	que tu	eusses	exclu
qu' elle	exclût	qu' elle	eût	exclu
que n.	exclussions	que n.	eussions	exclu
que v.	exclussiez	que v.	eussiez	exclu
qu' ils	exclussent	qu' ils	eussent	exclu

IMPÉRATIF

Présent	Passé	
exclus	aie	exclu
excluons	ayons	exclu
excluez	ayez	exclu

INFINITIF

Présent	Passé
exclure	avoir exclu

PARTICIPE

Présent	Passé (composé)
excluant	ayant exclu
	Passé
	exclu

***Conditionnel passé 2e forme* (2nd form)**: same form as the *plus-que-parfait* of the subjunctive.
Futur proche: *je vais exclure* (see Grammar of the verb, paragraphs 3 and 50).

- Note the difference between *exclu(e)* and *inclus(e)*.
- **Conclure** is conjugated like **exclure**. The past participle of **conclure** is *conclu* (feminine = *conclue*).

INDICATIF

Présent		Passé composé		
j'	inclus	j'	ai	inclus
tu	inclus	tu	as	inclus
elle	inclut	elle	a	inclus
nous	incluons	nous	avons	inclus
vous	incluez	vous	avez	inclus
ils	incluent	ils	ont	inclus

Imparfait		Plus-que-parfait		
j'	incluais	j'	avais	inclus
tu	incluais	tu	avais	inclus
elle	incluait	elle	avait	inclus
nous	incluions	nous	avions	inclus
vous	incluiez	vous	aviez	inclus
ils	incluaient	ils	avaient	inclus

Passé simple		Passé antérieur		
j'	inclus	j'	eus	inclus
tu	inclus	tu	eus	inclus
elle	inclut	elle	eut	inclus
nous	inclûmes	nous	eûmes	inclus
vous	inclûtes	vous	eûtes	inclus
ils	inclurent	ils	eurent	inclus

Futur simple		Futur antérieur		
j'	inclurai	j'	aurai	inclus
tu	incluras	tu	auras	inclus
elle	inclura	elle	aura	inclus
nous	inclurons	nous	aurons	inclus
vous	inclurez	vous	aurez	inclus
ils	incluront	ils	auront	inclus

Conditionnel présent		Conditionnel passé		
j'	inclurais	j'	aurais	inclus
tu	inclurais	tu	aurais	inclus
elle	inclurait	elle	aurait	inclus
nous	inclurions	nous	aurions	inclus
vous	incluriez	vous	auriez	inclus
ils	incluraient	ils	auraient	inclus

SUBJONCTIF

Présent		Passé		
que j'	inclue	que j'	aie	inclus
que tu	inclues	que tu	aies	inclus
qu' elle	inclue	qu' elle	ait	inclus
que n.	incluions	que n.	ayons	inclus
que v.	incluiez	que v.	ayez	inclus
qu' ils	incluent	qu' ils	aient	inclus

Imparfait		Plus-que-parfait		
que j'	inclusse	que j'	eusse	inclus
que tu	inclusses	que tu	eusses	inclus
qu' elle	inclût	qu' elle	eût	inclus
que n.	inclussions	que n.	eussions	inclus
que v.	inclussiez	que v.	eussiez	inclus
qu' ils	inclussent	qu' ils	eussent	inclus

IMPÉRATIF

Présent	Passé	
inclus	aie	inclus
incluons	ayons	inclus
incluez	ayez	inclus

INFINITIF

Présent	Passé
inclure	avoir inclus

PARTICIPE

Présent	Passé (composé)
incluant	ayant inclus
	Passé
	inclus

***Conditionnel passé 2e forme* (2nd form)**: same form as the *plus-que-parfait* of the subjunctive.
Futur proche: *je vais inclure* (see Grammar of the verb, paragraphs 3 and 50).

- Note the difference between *inclus(e)* and *exclu(e)*.
- **Occlure** follows this pattern of conjugation.
- **Reclure** follows this pattern of conjugation. It is used almost exclusively in the infinitive and the past participle.

141 absoudre

INDICATIF

Présent		Passé composé		/ VARIANTE
j'	absous	j'	ai	absous / t
tu	absous	tu	as	absous / t
elle	absout	elle	a	absous / t
nous	absolvons	nous	avons	absous / t
vous	absolvez	vous	avez	absous / t
ils	absolvent	ils	ont	absous / t

Imparfait		Plus-que-parfait		/ VARIANTE
j'	absolvais	j'	avais	absous / t
tu	absolvais	tu	avais	absous / t
elle	absolvait	elle	avait	absous / t
nous	absolvions	nous	avions	absous / t
vous	absolviez	vous	aviez	absous / t
ils	absolvaient	ils	avaient	absous / t

Passé simple		Passé antérieur		/ VARIANTE
j'	*absolus*	j'	eus	absous / t
tu	*absolus*	tu	eus	absous / t
elle	*absolut*	elle	eut	absous / t
nous	*absolûmes*	nous	eûmes	absous / t
vous	*absolûtes*	vous	eûtes	absous / t
ils	*absolurent*	ils	eurent	absous / t

Futur simple		Futur antérieur		/ VARIANTE
j'	absoudrai	j'	aurai	absous / t
tu	absoudras	tu	auras	absous / t
elle	absoudra	elle	aura	absous / t
nous	absoudrons	nous	aurons	absous / t
vous	absoudrez	vous	aurez	absous / t
ils	absoudront	ils	auront	absous / t

Conditionnel présent		Conditionnel passé		/ VARIANTE
j'	absoudrais	j'	aurais	absous / t
tu	absoudrais	tu	aurais	absous / t
elle	absoudrait	elle	aurait	absous / t
nous	absoudrions	nous	aurions	absous / t
vous	absoudriez	vous	auriez	absous / t
ils	absoudraient	ils	auraient	absous / t

SUBJONCTIF

Présent		Passé		/ VARIANTE
que j'	absolve	que j'	aie	absous / t
que tu	absolves	que tu	aies	absous / t
qu' elle	absolve	qu' elle	ait	absous / t
que n.	absolvions	que n.	ayons	absous / t
que v.	absolviez	que v.	ayez	absous / t
qu' ils	absolvent	qu' ils	aient	absous / t

Imparfait		Plus-que-parfait		/ VARIANTE
que j'	*absolusse*	que j'	eusse	absous / t
que tu	*absolusses*	que tu	eusses	absous / t
qu' elle	*absolût*	qu' elle	eût	absous / t
que n.	*absolussions*	que n.	eussions	absous / t
que v.	*absolussiez*	que v.	eussiez	absous / t
qu' ils	*absolussent*	qu' ils	eussent	absous / t

IMPÉRATIF

Présent	Passé		/ VARIANTE
absous	aie	absous	/ absout
absolvons	ayons	absous	/ absout
absolvez	ayez	absous	/ absout

INFINITIF

Présent	Passé	/ VARIANTE
absoudre	avoir absous	/ absout

PARTICIPE

Présent	Passé (composé)	/ VARIANTE
absolvant	ayant absous	/ absout
	Passé	**/ VARIANTE**
	absou**s**	/ absou**t**

Conditionnel passé 2ᵉ forme **(2nd form)**: same form as the *plus-que-parfait* of the subjunctive.
Futur proche: *je vais absoudre* (see Grammar of the verb, paragraphs 3 and 50).

- **Absoudre**: *absous/absout* have replaced *absolu*, the old form of the past participle which survives in the language as an adjective meaning "absolute" or "uncompromising".
- **Dissoudre** is conjugated like **absoudre**; the past participle is *dissous/dissout*; it's distinct from the old past participle *dissolu* which has survived as an adjective in the sense of "dissolute" or "licentious".
- The past participles **absous** and **dissous** have been changed to **absout** and **dissout** by the French spelling reform, to bring them in line with the feminine forms **absoute** and **dissoute**.
- The *passé simple* and the *imparfait* of the subjunctive are rare.

INDICATIF

Présent		Passé composé		
je	résous	j'	ai	résolu
tu	résous	tu	as	résolu
elle	résout	elle	a	résolu
nous	résolvons	nous	avons	résolu
vous	résolvez	vous	avez	résolu
ils	résolvent	ils	ont	résolu

Imparfait		Plus-que-parfait		
je	résolvais	j'	avais	résolu
tu	résolvais	tu	avais	résolu
elle	résolvait	elle	avait	résolu
nous	résolvions	nous	avions	résolu
vous	résolviez	vous	aviez	résolu
ils	résolvaient	ils	avaient	résolu

Passé simple		Passé antérieur		
je	**résolus**	j'	eus	résolu
tu	résolus	tu	eus	résolu
elle	résolut	elle	eut	résolu
nous	résolûmes	nous	eûmes	résolu
vous	résolûtes	vous	eûtes	résolu
ils	résolurent	ils	eurent	résolu

Futur simple		Futur antérieur		
je	**résoudrai**	j'	aurai	résolu
tu	résoudras	tu	auras	résolu
elle	résoudra	elle	aura	résolu
nous	résoudrons	nous	aurons	résolu
vous	résoudrez	vous	aurez	résolu
ils	résoudront	ils	auront	résolu

Conditionnel présent		Conditionnel passé		
je	résoudrais	j'	aurais	résolu
tu	résoudrais	tu	aurais	résolu
elle	résoudrait	elle	aurait	résolu
nous	résoudrions	nous	aurions	résolu
vous	résoudriez	vous	auriez	résolu
ils	résoudraient	ils	auraient	résolu

SUBJONCTIF

Présent		Passé		
que je	résolve	que j'	aie	résolu
que tu	résolves	que tu	aies	résolu
qu' elle	résolve	qu' elle	ait	résolu
que n.	résolvions	que n.	ayons	résolu
que v.	résolviez	que v.	ayez	résolu
qu' ils	résolvent	qu' ils	aient	résolu

Imparfait		Plus-que-parfait		
que je	résolusse	que j'	eusse	résolu
que tu	résolusses	que tu	eusses	résolu
qu' elle	résolût	qu' elle	eût	résolu
que n.	résolussions	que n.	eussions	résolu
que v.	résolussiez	que v.	eussiez	résolu
qu' ils	résolussent	qu' ils	eussent	résolu

IMPÉRATIF

Présent	Passé	
résous	aie	résolu
résolvons	ayons	résolu
résolvez	ayez	résolu

INFINITIF

Présent	Passé
résoudre	avoir résolu

PARTICIPE

Présent	Passé (composé)
résolvant	ayant résolu
	Passé
	résolu

Conditionnel passé 2e forme **(2nd form)**: same form as the *plus-que-parfait* of the subjunctive.
Futur proche: *je vais résoudre* (see Grammar of the verb, paragraphs 3 and 50).

- The past participle of **résoudre** is *résolu*. An older version still exists: *résous/résout(e)*. It is very rarely used. Note also the existence of the adjective *résolu* (identical in form with the past participle) which means "determined".

143 coudre

INDICATIF

Présent		Passé composé		
je	couds	j'	ai	cousu
tu	couds	tu	as	cousu
elle	coud	elle	a	cousu
nous	cousons	nous	avons	cousu
vous	cousez	vous	avez	cousu
ils	cousent	ils	ont	cousu

Imparfait		Plus-que-parfait		
je	cousais	j'	avais	cousu
tu	cousais	tu	avais	cousu
elle	cousait	elle	avait	cousu
nous	cousions	nous	avions	cousu
vous	cousiez	vous	aviez	cousu
ils	cousaient	ils	avaient	cousu

Passé simple		Passé antérieur		
je	cousis	j'	eus	cousu
tu	cousis	tu	eus	cousu
elle	cousit	elle	eut	cousu
nous	cousîmes	nous	eûmes	cousu
vous	cousîtes	vous	eûtes	cousu
ils	cousirent	ils	eurent	cousu

Futur simple		Futur antérieur		
je	coudrai	j'	aurai	cousu
tu	coudras	tu	auras	cousu
elle	coudra	elle	aura	cousu
nous	coudrons	nous	aurons	cousu
vous	coudrez	vous	aurez	cousu
ils	coudront	ils	auront	cousu

Conditionnel présent		Conditionnel passé		
je	coudrais	j'	aurais	cousu
tu	coudrais	tu	aurais	cousu
elle	coudrait	elle	aurait	cousu
nous	coudrions	nous	aurions	cousu
vous	coudriez	vous	auriez	cousu
ils	coudraient	ils	auraient	cousu

SUBJONCTIF

Présent		Passé		
que je	couse	que j'	aie	cousu
que tu	couses	que tu	aies	cousu
qu' elle	couse	qu' elle	ait	cousu
que n.	cousions	que n.	ayons	cousu
que v.	cousiez	que v.	ayez	cousu
qu' ils	cousent	qu' ils	aient	cousu

Imparfait		Plus-que-parfait		
que je	cousisse	que j'	eusse	cousu
que tu	cousisses	que tu	eusses	cousu
qu' elle	cousît	qu' elle	eût	cousu
que n.	cousissions	que n.	eussions	cousu
que v.	cousissiez	que v.	eussiez	cousu
qu' ils	cousissent	qu' ils	eussent	cousu

IMPÉRATIF

Présent	Passé	
couds	aie	cousu
cousons	ayons	cousu
cousez	ayez	cousu

INFINITIF

Présent	Passé
coudre	avoir cousu

PARTICIPE

Présent	Passé (composé)
cousant	ayant cousu
	Passé
	cousu

***Conditionnel passé 2e forme* (2nd form)**: same form as the *plus-que-parfait* of the subjunctive.
Futur proche: *je vais coudre* (see Grammar of the verb, paragraphs 3 and 50).

- **Découdre** and **recoudre** follow this pattern of conjugation.

INDICATIF

Présent		Passé composé		
je	mouds	j'	ai	moulu
tu	mouds	tu	as	moulu
elle	moud	elle	a	moulu
nous	moulons	nous	avons	moulu
vous	moulez	vous	avez	moulu
ils	moulent	ils	ont	moulu

Imparfait		Plus-que-parfait		
je	moulais	j'	avais	moulu
tu	moulais	tu	avais	moulu
elle	moulait	elle	avait	moulu
nous	moulions	nous	avions	moulu
vous	mouliez	vous	aviez	moulu
ils	moulaient	ils	avaient	moulu

Passé simple		Passé antérieur		
je	moulus	j'	eus	moulu
tu	moulus	tu	eus	moulu
elle	moulut	elle	eut	moulu
nous	moulûmes	nous	eûmes	moulu
vous	moulûtes	vous	eûtes	moulu
ils	moulurent	ils	eurent	moulu

Futur simple		Futur antérieur		
je	moudrai	j'	aurai	moulu
tu	moudras	tu	auras	moulu
elle	moudra	elle	aura	moulu
nous	moudrons	nous	aurons	moulu
vous	moudrez	vous	aurez	moulu
ils	moudront	ils	auront	moulu

Conditionnel présent		Conditionnel passé		
je	moudrais	j'	aurais	moulu
tu	moudrais	tu	aurais	moulu
elle	moudrait	elle	aurait	moulu
nous	moudrions	nous	aurions	moulu
vous	moudriez	vous	auriez	moulu
ils	moudraient	ils	auraient	moulu

SUBJONCTIF

Présent		Passé		
que je	moule	que j'	aie	moulu
que tu	moules	que tu	aies	moulu
qu'elle	moule	qu'elle	ait	moulu
que n.	moulions	que n.	ayons	moulu
que v.	mouliez	que v.	ayez	moulu
qu' ils	moulent	qu' ils	aient	moulu

Imparfait		Plus-que-parfait		
que je	moulusse	que j'	eusse	moulu
que tu	moulusses	que tu	eusses	moulu
qu'elle	moulût	qu'elle	eût	moulu
que n.	moulussions	que n.	eussions	moulu
que v.	moulussiez	que v.	eussiez	moulu
qu' ils	moulussent	qu' ils	eussent	moulu

IMPÉRATIF

Présent	Passé	
mouds	aie	moulu
moulons	ayons	moulu
moulez	ayez	moulu

INFINITIF

Présent	Passé
moudre	avoir moulu

PARTICIPE

Présent	Passé (composé)
moulant	ayant moulu
	Passé
	moulu

***Conditionnel passé 2e forme* (2nd form)**: same form as the *plus-que-parfait* of the subjunctive.
Futur proche: *je vais moudre* (see Grammar of the verb, paragraphs 3 and 50).

- **Émoudre** and **remoudre** follow this pattern of conjugation.

145 suivre

INDICATIF

Présent		Passé composé		
je	suis	j'	ai	suivi
tu	suis	tu	as	suivi
elle	suit	elle	a	suivi
nous	suivons	nous	avons	suivi
vous	suivez	vous	avez	suivi
ils	suivent	ils	ont	suivi

Imparfait		Plus-que-parfait		
je	suivais	j'	avais	suivi
tu	suivais	tu	avais	suivi
elle	suivait	elle	avait	suivi
nous	suivions	nous	avions	suivi
vous	suiviez	vous	aviez	suivi
ils	suivaient	ils	avaient	suivi

Passé simple		Passé antérieur		
je	suivis	j'	eus	suivi
tu	suivis	tu	eus	suivi
elle	suivit	elle	eut	suivi
nous	suivîmes	nous	eûmes	suivi
vous	suivîtes	vous	eûtes	suivi
ils	suivirent	ils	eurent	suivi

Futur simple		Futur antérieur		
je	suivrai	j'	aurai	suivi
tu	suivras	tu	auras	suivi
elle	suivra	elle	aura	suivi
nous	suivrons	nous	aurons	suivi
vous	suivrez	vous	aurez	suivi
ils	suivront	ils	auront	suivi

Conditionnel présent		Conditionnel passé		
je	suivrais	j'	aurais	suivi
tu	suivrais	tu	aurais	suivi
elle	suivrait	elle	aurait	suivi
nous	suivrions	nous	aurions	suivi
vous	suivriez	vous	auriez	suivi
ils	suivraient	ils	auraient	suivi

SUBJONCTIF

Présent		Passé		
que je	suive	que j'	aie	suivi
que tu	suives	que tu	aies	suivi
qu'elle	suive	qu'elle	ait	suivi
que n.	suivions	que n.	ayons	suivi
que v.	suiviez	que v.	ayez	suivi
qu' ils	suivent	qu' ils	aient	suivi

Imparfait		Plus-que-parfait		
que je	suivisse	que j'	eusse	suivi
que tu	suivisses	que tu	eusses	suivi
qu'elle	suivît	qu'elle	eût	suivi
que n.	suivissions	que n.	eussions	suivi
que v.	suivissiez	que v.	eussiez	suivi
qu' ils	suivissent	qu' ils	eussent	suivi

IMPÉRATIF

Présent	Passé	
suis	aie	suivi
suivons	ayons	suivi
suivez	ayez	suivi

INFINITIF

Présent	Passé
suivre	avoir suivi

PARTICIPE

Présent	Passé (composé)
suivant	ayant suivi
	Passé
	suivi

***Conditionnel passé 2e forme* (2nd form)**: same form as the *plus-que-parfait* of the subjunctive.
Futur proche: *je vais suivre* (see Grammar of the verb, paragraphs 3 and 50).

- **S'ensuivre** (auxiliary **être**) and **poursuivre** follow this pattern of conjugation.
- **S'ensuivre** is used only in the infinitive, the present participle and the 3rd person forms (*il s'est ensuivi, il s'en est ensuivi* or *il s'en est suivi*).

vivre

INDICATIF

Présent		Passé composé		
je	vis	j'	ai	vécu
tu	vis	tu	as	vécu
elle	vit	elle	a	vécu
nous	vivons	nous	avons	vécu
vous	vivez	vous	avez	vécu
ils	vivent	ils	ont	vécu

Imparfait		Plus-que-parfait		
je	vivais	j'	avais	vécu
tu	vivais	tu	avais	vécu
elle	vivait	elle	avait	vécu
nous	vivions	nous	avions	vécu
vous	viviez	vous	aviez	vécu
ils	vivaient	ils	avaient	vécu

Passé simple		Passé antérieur		
je	vécus	j'	eus	vécu
tu	vécus	tu	eus	vécu
elle	vécut	elle	eut	vécu
nous	vécûmes	nous	eûmes	vécu
vous	vécûtes	vous	eûtes	vécu
ils	vécurent	ils	eurent	vécu

Futur simple		Futur antérieur		
je	vivrai	j'	aurai	vécu
tu	vivras	tu	auras	vécu
elle	vivra	elle	aura	vécu
nous	vivrons	nous	aurons	vécu
vous	vivrez	vous	aurez	vécu
ils	vivront	ils	auront	vécu

Conditionnel présent		Conditionnel passé		
je	vivrais	j'	aurais	vécu
tu	vivrais	tu	aurais	vécu
elle	vivrait	elle	aurait	vécu
nous	vivrions	nous	aurions	vécu
vous	vivriez	vous	auriez	vécu
ils	vivraient	ils	auraient	vécu

SUBJONCTIF

Présent		Passé		
que je	vive	que j'	aie	vécu
que tu	vives	que tu	aies	vécu
qu' elle	vive	qu' elle	ait	vécu
que n.	vivions	que n.	ayons	vécu
que v.	viviez	que v.	ayez	vécu
qu' ils	vivent	qu' ils	aient	vécu

Imparfait		Plus-que-parfait		
que je	vécusse	que j'	eusse	vécu
que tu	vécusses	que tu	eusses	vécu
qu' elle	vécût	qu' elle	eût	vécu
que n.	vécussions	que n.	eussions	vécu
que v.	vécussiez	que v.	eussiez	vécu
qu' ils	vécussent	qu' ils	eussent	vécu

IMPÉRATIF

Présent	Passé	
vis	aie	vécu
vivons	ayons	vécu
vivez	ayez	vécu

INFINITIF

Présent	Passé
vivre	avoir vécu

PARTICIPE

Présent	Passé (composé)
vivant	ayant vécu
	Passé
	vécu

***Conditionnel passé 2e forme* (2nd form)**: same form as the *plus-que-parfait* of the subjunctive.
Futur proche: *je vais vivre* (see Grammar of the verb, paragraphs 3 and 50).

- **Revivre** is conjugated like **vivre**.
- **Survivre** also is conjugated like **vivre**.

147 lire

INDICATIF

Présent		Passé composé		
je	lis	j'	ai	lu
tu	lis	tu	as	lu
elle	llt	elle	a	lu
nous	lisons	nous	avons	lu
vous	lisez	vous	avez	lu
ils	lisent	ils	ont	lu

Imparfait		Plus-que-parfait		
je	lisais	j'	avais	lu
tu	lisais	tu	avais	lu
elle	lisait	elle	avait	lu
nous	lisions	nous	avions	lu
vous	lisiez	vous	aviez	lu
ils	lisaient	ils	avaient	lu

Passé simple		Passé antérieur		
je	lus	j'	eus	lu
tu	lus	tu	eus	lu
elle	lut	elle	eut	lu
nous	lûmes	nous	eûmes	lu
vous	lûtes	vous	eûtes	lu
ils	lurent	ils	eurent	lu

Futur simple		Futur antérieur		
je	lirai	j'	aurai	lu
tu	liras	tu	auras	lu
elle	lira	elle	aura	lu
nous	lirons	nous	aurons	lu
vous	lirez	vous	aurez	lu
ils	liront	ils	auront	lu

Conditionnel présent		Conditionnel passé		
je	lirais	j'	aurais	lu
tu	lirais	tu	aurais	lu
elle	lirait	elle	aurait	lu
nous	lirions	nous	aurions	lu
vous	liriez	vous	auriez	lu
ils	liraient	ils	auraient	lu

SUBJONCTIF

Présent		Passé		
que je	lise	que j'	aie	lu
que tu	lises	que tu	aies	lu
qu' elle	lise	qu' elle	ait	lu
que n.	lisions	que n.	ayons	lu
que v.	lisiez	que v.	ayez	lu
qu' ils	lisent	qu' ils	aient	lu

Imparfait		Plus-que-parfait		
que je	lusse	que j'	eusse	lu
que tu	lusses	que tu	eusses	lu
qu' elle	lût	qu' elle	eût	lu
que n.	lussions	que n.	eussions	lu
que v.	lussiez	que v.	eussiez	lu
qu' ils	lussent	qu' ils	eussent	lu

IMPÉRATIF

Présent	Passé	
lis	aie	lu
lisons	ayons	lu
lisez	ayez	lu

INFINITIF

Présent	Passé
lire	avoir lu

PARTICIPE

Présent	Passé (composé)
lisant	ayant lu
	Passé
	lu

Conditionnel passé 2e forme **(2nd form)**: same form as the *plus-que-parfait* of the subjunctive.
Futur proche: *je vais lire* (see Grammar of the verb, paragraphs 3 and 50).

- **Élire**, **réélire** and **relire** follow this pattern of conjugation.

INDICATIF

Présent		Passé composé		
je	dis	j'	ai	dit
tu	dis	tu	as	dit
elle	dit	elle	a	dit
nous	disons	nous	avons	dit
vous	dites[1]	vous	avez	dit
ils	disent	ils	ont	dit

Imparfait		Plus-que-parfait		
je	disais	j'	avais	dit
tu	disais	tu	avais	dit
elle	disait	elle	avait	dit
nous	disions	nous	avions	dit
vous	disiez	vous	aviez	dit
ils	disaient	ils	avaient	dit

Passé simple		Passé antérieur		
je	dis	j'	eus	dit
tu	dis	tu	eus	dit
elle	dit	elle	eut	dit
nous	dîmes	nous	eûmes	dit
vous	dîtes	vous	eûtes	dit
ils	dirent	ils	eurent	dit

Futur simple		Futur antérieur		
je	dirai	j'	aurai	dit
tu	diras	tu	auras	dit
elle	dira	elle	aura	dit
nous	dirons	nous	aurons	dit
vous	direz	vous	aurez	dit
ils	diront	ils	auront	dit

Conditionnel présent		Conditionnel passé		
je	dirais	j'	aurais	dit
tu	dirais	tu	aurais	dit
elle	dirait	elle	aurait	dit
nous	dirions	nous	aurions	dit
vous	diriez	vous	auriez	dit
ils	diraient	ils	auraient	dit

SUBJONCTIF

Présent		Passé		
que je	dise	que j'	aie	dit
que tu	dises	que tu	aies	dit
qu' elle	dise	qu' elle	ait	dit
que n.	disions	que n.	ayons	dit
que v.	disiez	que v.	ayez	dit
qu' ils	disent	qu' ils	aient	dit

Imparfait		Plus-que-parfait		
que je	disse	que j'	eusse	dit
que tu	disses	que tu	eusses	dit
qu' elle	dît	qu' elle	eût	dit
que n.	dissions	que n.	eussions	dit
que v.	dissiez	que v.	eussiez	dit
qu' ils	dissent	qu' ils	eussent	dit

IMPÉRATIF

Présent	Passé	
dis	aie	dit
disons	ayons	dit
dites[1]	ayez	dit

INFINITIF

Présent	Passé
dire	avoir dit

PARTICIPE

Présent	Passé (composé)
disant	ayant dit
	Passé
	dit

1. **Contredire**, **dédire**, **interdire**, **médire** and **prédire** exhibit the following forms in the present indicative and the imperative: (*vous*) *contredisez*, *dédisez*, *interdisez*, *médisez*, *prédisez* (unlike **dire** and **redire**: *dites*, *redites*).

Conditionnel passé 2e forme **(2nd form)**: same form as the *plus-que-parfait* of the subjunctive.
Futur proche: *je vais dire* (see Grammar of the verb, paragraphs 3 and 50).

- **Redire** follows this pattern of conjugation.
- **Contredire**, **dédire**, **interdire**, **médire** and **prédire** are conjugated like **dire** except for the forms indicated under Note 1 above. **Maudire** is conjugated like **finir**: *nous maudissons*, *vous maudissez*, *ils maudissent*, *je maudissais*, etc., *maudissant*, except for the past participle: *maudit*, *maudite*.

149 | rire

INDICATIF

Présent		Passé composé		
je	ris	j'	ai	ri
tu	ris	tu	as	ri
elle	rit	elle	a	ri
nous	rions	nous	avons	ri
vous	riez	vous	avez	ri
ils	rient	ils	ont	ri

Imparfait		Plus-que-parfait		
je	riais	j'	avais	ri
tu	riais	tu	avais	ri
elle	riait	elle	avait	ri
nous	r**ii**ons	nous	avions	ri
vous	r**ii**ez	vous	aviez	ri
ils	riaient	ils	avaient	ri

Passé simple		Passé antérieur		
je	ris	j'	eus	ri
tu	ris	tu	eus	ri
elle	rit	elle	eut	ri
nous	rîmes	nous	eûmes	ri
vous	rîtes	vous	eûtes	ri
ils	rirent	ils	eurent	ri

Futur simple		Futur antérieur		
je	rirai	j'	aurai	ri
tu	riras	tu	auras	ri
elle	rira	elle	aura	ri
nous	rirons	nous	aurons	ri
vous	rirez	vous	aurez	ri
ils	riront	ils	auront	ri

Conditionnel présent		Conditionnel passé		
je	rirais	j'	aurais	ri
tu	rirais	tu	aurais	ri
elle	rirait	elle	aurait	ri
nous	ririons	nous	aurions	ri
vous	ririez	vous	auriez	ri
ils	riraient	ils	auraient	ri

SUBJONCTIF

Présent		Passé		
que je	rie	que j'	aie	ri
que tu	ries	que tu	aies	ri
qu' elle	rie	qu' elle	ait	ri
que n.	r**ii**ons	que n.	ayons	ri
que v.	r**ii**ez	que v.	ayez	ri
qu' ils	rient	qu' ils	aient	ri

Imparfait *(rare)*		Plus-que-parfait		
que je	risse	que j'	eusse	ri
que tu	risses	que tu	eusses	ri
qu' elle	rît	qu' elle	eût	ri
que n.	rissions	que n.	eussions	ri
que v.	rissiez	que v.	eussiez	ri
qu' ils	rissent	qu' ils	eussent	ri

IMPÉRATIF

Présent	Passé	
ris	aie	ri
rions	ayons	ri
riez	ayez	ri

INFINITIF

Présent	Passé
rire	avoir ri

PARTICIPE

Présent	Passé (composé)
riant	ayant ri
	Passé
	ri

***Conditionnel passé 2e forme* (2nd form)**: same form as the *plus-que-parfait* of the subjunctive.
Futur proche: *je vais rire* (see Grammar of the verb, paragraphs 3 and 50).

- Note the double **i** in 1st and 2nd persons plural of the *imparfait* of the indicative and the present subjunctive.
- **Sourire** follows this pattern of conjugation.
- The past participles of **rire** and **sourire** are invariable, even in pronominal constructions: *ri, souri. Ils se sont ri des difficultés* (= "They laughed at /off the difficulties"). *Elles se sont souri* (= "They smiled at each other").

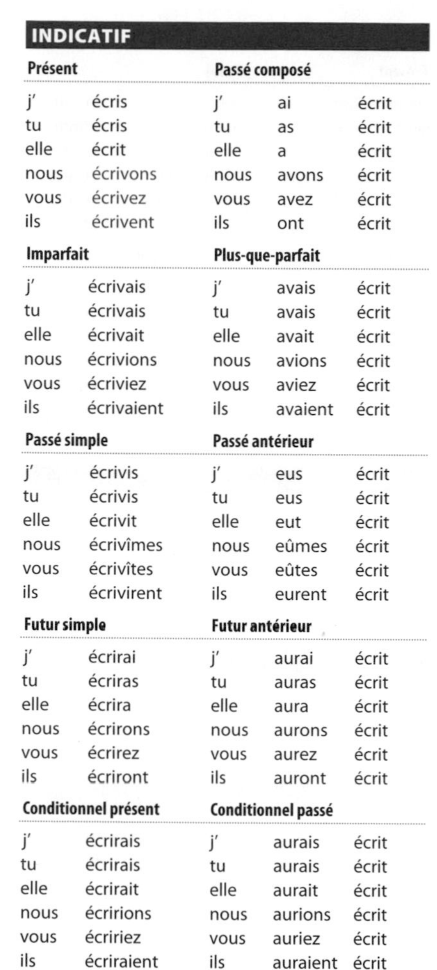

INDICATIF

Présent		Passé composé		
j'	écris	j'	ai	écrit
tu	écris	tu	as	écrit
elle	écrit	elle	a	écrit
nous	écrivons	nous	avons	écrit
vous	écrivez	vous	avez	écrit
ils	écrivent	ils	ont	écrit

Imparfait		Plus-que-parfait		
j'	écrivais	j'	avais	écrit
tu	écrivais	tu	avais	écrit
elle	écrivait	elle	avait	écrit
nous	écrivions	nous	avions	écrit
vous	écriviez	vous	aviez	écrit
ils	écrivaient	ils	avaient	écrit

Passé simple		Passé antérieur		
j'	écrivis	j'	eus	écrit
tu	écrivis	tu	eus	écrit
elle	écrivit	elle	eut	écrit
nous	écrivîmes	nous	eûmes	écrit
vous	écrivîtes	vous	eûtes	écrit
ils	écrivirent	ils	eurent	écrit

Futur simple		Futur antérieur		
j'	écrirai	j'	aurai	écrit
tu	écriras	tu	auras	écrit
elle	écrira	elle	aura	écrit
nous	écrirons	nous	aurons	écrit
vous	écrirez	vous	aurez	écrit
ils	écriront	ils	auront	écrit

Conditionnel présent		Conditionnel passé		
j'	écrirais	j'	aurais	écrit
tu	écrirais	tu	aurais	écrit
elle	écrirait	elle	aurait	écrit
nous	écririons	nous	aurions	écrit
vous	écririez	vous	auriez	écrit
ils	écriraient	ils	auraient	écrit

SUBJONCTIF

Présent		Passé		
que j'	écrive	que j'	aie	écrit
que tu	écrives	que tu	aies	écrit
qu' elle	écrive	qu' elle	ait	écrit
que n.	écrivions	que n.	ayons	écrit
que v.	écriviez	que v.	ayez	écrit
qu' ils	écrivent	qu' ils	aient	écrit

Imparfait		Plus-que-parfait		
que j'	écrivisse	que j'	eusse	écrit
que tu	écrivisses	que tu	eusses	écrit
qu' elle	écrivît	qu' elle	eût	écrit
que n.	écrivissions	que n.	eussions	écrit
que v.	écrivissiez	que v.	eussiez	écrit
qu' ils	écrivissent	qu' ils	eussent	écrit

IMPÉRATIF

Présent	Passé	
écris	aie	écrit
écrivons	ayons	écrit
écrivez	ayez	écrit

INFINITIF

Présent	Passé
écrire	avoir écrit

PARTICIPE

Présent	Passé (composé)
écrivant	ayant écrit
	Passé
	écrit

***Conditionnel passé 2e forme* (2nd form)**: same form as the *plus-que-parfait* of the subjunctive.
Futur proche: *je vais écrire* (see Grammar of the verb, paragraphs 3 and 50).

- **Récrire**, **réécrire**, **décrire** and derived forms ending in **-scrire** (see List of irregular verbs, p. 96 to 98) follow this pattern of conjugation.

151 confire

INDICATIF

Présent		Passé composé		
je	confis	j'	ai	confit
tu	confis	tu	as	confit
elle	confit	elle	a	confit
nous	confisons	nous	avons	confit
vous	confisez	vous	avez	confit
ils	confisent	ils	ont	confit

Imparfait		Plus-que-parfait		
je	confisais	j'	avais	confit
tu	confisais	tu	avais	confit
elle	confisait	elle	avait	confit
nous	confisions	nous	avions	confit
vous	confisiez	vous	aviez	confit
ils	confisaient	ils	avaient	confit

Passé simple		Passé antérieur		
je	confis	j'	eus	confit
tu	confis	tu	eus	confit
elle	confit	elle	eut	confit
nous	confîmes	nous	eûmes	confit
vous	confîtes	vous	eûtes	confit
ils	confirent	ils	eurent	confit

Futur simple		Futur antérieur		
je	confirai	j'	aurai	confit
tu	confiras	tu	auras	confit
elle	confira	elle	aura	confit
nous	confirons	nous	aurons	confit
vous	confirez	vous	aurez	confit
ils	confiront	ils	auront	confit

Conditionnel présent		Conditionnel passé		
je	confirais	j'	aurais	confit
tu	confirais	tu	aurais	confit
elle	confirait	elle	aurait	confit
nous	confirions	nous	aurions	confit
vous	confiriez	vous	auriez	confit
ils	confiraient	ils	auraientl	confit

SUBJONCTIF

Présent		Passé		
que je	confise	que j'	aie	confit
que tu	confises	que tu	aies	confit
qu' elle	confise	qu' elle	alt	conflt
que n.	confisions	que n.	ayons	confit
que v.	confisiez	que v.	ayez	confit
qu' ils	confisent	qu' ils	aient	confit

Imparfait		Plus-que-parfait		
que je	confisse	que j'	eusse	confit
que tu	confisses	que tu	eusses	confit
qu' elle	confît	qu' elle	eût	confit
que n.	confissions	que n.	eussions	confit
que v.	confissiez	que v.	eussiez	confit
qu' ils	confissent	qu' ils	eussent	confit

IMPÉRATIF

Présent	Passé	
confis	aie	confit
confisons	ayons	confit
confisez	ayez	confit

INFINITIF

Présent	Passé
confire	avoir confit

PARTICIPE

Présent	Passé (composé)
confisant	ayant confit
	Passé
	confit[1, 2]

1. The past participle of **circoncire** ends in **-s**: *circoncis, circoncise*.
2. The past participle of **suffire** ends in **-i**: *suffi* (always invariable).

Conditionnel passé 2e forme **(2nd form)**: same form as the *plus-que-parfait* of the subjunctive.
Futur proche: *je vais confire* (see Grammar of the verb, paragraphs 3 and 50).

- **Déconfire** is conjugated like **confire**.
- **Circoncire** and **suffire** follow the same pattern except for the past participle (see Notes 1 and 2 above).
- **Frire** is conjugated like **confire**. It is used only in the present indicative and the imperative in the singular: *je fris, tu fris, il frit, fris*; in the past participle: *frit, frite*; in compound forms using the auxiliary **avoir**; rarely in the future and the present conditional: *je frirai…, je frirais…* In cases where **frire** is defective (or the forms are rare), the causative construction *faire frire* (by prefixing the verb **faire**) is preferred: *ils font frire le poisson*.

INDICATIF

Présent		Passé composé		
je	cuis	j'	ai	cuit
tu	cuis	tu	as	cuit
elle	cuit	elle	a	cuit
nous	cuisons	nous	avons	cuit
vous	cuisez	vous	avez	cuit
ils	cuisent	ils	ont	cuit

Imparfait		Plus-que-parfait		
je	cuisais	j'	avais	cuit
tu	cuisais	tu	avais	cuit
elle	cuisait	elle	avait	cuit
nous	cuisions	nous	avions	cuit
vous	cuisiez	vous	aviez	cuit
ils	cuisaient	ils	avaient	cuit

Passé simple		Passé antérieur		
je	cuisis	j'	eus	cuit
tu	cuisis	tu	eus	cuit
elle	cuisit	elle	eut	cuit
nous	cuisîmes	nous	eûmes	cuit
vous	cuisîtes	vous	eûtes	cuit
ils	cuisirent	ils	eurent	cuit

Futur simple		Futur antérieur		
je	cuirai	j'	aurai	cuit
tu	cuiras	tu	auras	cuit
elle	cuira	elle	aura	cuit
nous	cuirons	nous	aurons	cuit
vous	cuirez	vous	aurez	cuit
ils	cuiront	ils	auront	cuit

Conditionnel présent		Conditionnel passé		
je	cuirais	j'	aurais	cuit
tu	cuirais	tu	aurais	cuit
elle	cuirait	elle	aurait	cuit
nous	cuirions	nous	aurions	cuit
vous	cuiriez	vous	auriez	cuit
ils	cuiraient	ils	auraient	cuit

SUBJONCTIF

Présent		Passé		
que je	cuise	que j'	aie	cuit
que tu	cuises	que tu	aies	cuit
qu' elle	cuise	qu' elle	ait	cuit
que n.	cuisions	que n.	ayons	cuit
que v.	cuisiez	que v.	ayez	cuit
qu' ils	cuisent	qu' ils	aient	cuit

Imparfait		Plus-que-parfait		
que je	cuisisse	que j'	eusse	cuit
que tu	cuisisses	que tu	eusses	cuit
qu' elle	cuisît	qu' elle	eût	cuit
que n.	cuisissions	que n.	eussions	cuit
que v.	cuisissiez	que v.	eussiez	cuit
qu' ils	cuisissent	qu' ils	eussent	cuit

IMPÉRATIF

Présent	Passé
cuis	aie cuit
cuisons	ayons cuit
cuisez	ayez cuit

INFINITIF

Présent	Passé
cuire	avoir cuit

PARTICIPE

Présent	Passé (composé)
cuisant	ayant cuit
	Passé
	cuit[1]

1. The past participle of **nuire** and **entrenuire** ends in **-i**: *nui, entrenui.*

***Conditionnel passé 2e forme* (2nd form)**: same form as the *plus-que-parfait* of the subjunctive.
Futur proche: *je vais cuire* (see Grammar of the verb, paragraphs 3 and 50).

- The verbs ending in **-cuire**, in **-duire** and in **-truire** follow this pattern of conjugation (see List of irregular verbs, p. 96 to 98).
- **Nuire** and **entrenuire** follow this pattern of conjugation, but their past participle ends in **-i** (as mentioned above) not in **-it**: *nui, entrenui*. Note that the past participles *nui* and *entrenui* are always invariable.

153 luire

INDICATIF

Présent		Passé composé		
je	luis	j'	ai	lui
tu	luis	tu	as	lui
elle	luit	elle	a	lui
nous	luisons	nous	avons	lui
vous	luisez	vous	avez	lui
ils	luisent	ils	ont	lui

Imparfait		Plus-que-parfait		
je	luisais	j'	avais	lui
tu	luisais	tu	avais	lui
elle	luisait	elle	avait	lui
nous	luisions	nous	avions	lui
vous	luisiez	vous	aviez	lui
ils	luisaient	ils	avaient	lui

Passé simple			Passé antérieur		
je	luis	/ *luisis*	j'	eus	lui
tu	luis	/ *luisis*	tu	eus	lui
elle	luit	/ *luisit*	elle	eut	lui
nous	luîmes	/ *luisîmes*	nous	eûmes	lui
vous	luîtes	/ *luisîtes*	vous	eûtes	lui
ils	luirent	/ *luisirent*	ils	eurent	lui

Futur simple		Futur antérieur		
je	luirai	j'	aurai	lui
tu	luiras	tu	auras	lui
elle	luira	elle	aura	lui
nous	luirons	nous	aurons	lui
vous	luirez	vous	aurez	lui
ils	luiront	ils	auront	lui

Conditionnel présent		Conditionnel passé		
je	luirais	j'	aurais	lui
tu	luirais	tu	aurais	lui
elle	luirait	elle	aurait	lui
nous	luirions	nous	aurions	lui
vous	luiriez	vous	auriez	lui
ils	luiraient	ils	auraient	lui

SUBJONCTIF

Présent		Passé		
que je	luise	que j'	aie	lui
que tu	luises	que tu	aies	lui
qu'elle	luise	qu'elle	ait	lui
que n.	luisions	que n.	ayons	lui
que v.	luisiez	que v.	ayez	lui
qu' ils	luisent	qu' ils	aient	lui

Imparfait		Plus-que-parfait		
que je	luisisse	que j'	eusse	lui
que tu	luisisses	que tu	eusses	lui
qu' elle	luisît	qu' elle	eût	lui
que n.	luisissions	que n.	eussions	lui
que v.	luisissiez	que v.	eussiez	lui
qu' ils	luisissent	qu' ils	eussent	lui

IMPÉRATIF

Présent	Passé	
luis	aie	lui
luisons	ayons	lui
luisez	ayez	lui

INFINITIF

Présent	Passé
luire	avoir lui

PARTICIPE

Présent	Passé (composé)
luisant	ayant lui
	Passé
	lui

***Conditionnel passé 2e forme* (2nd form)**: same form as the *plus-que-parfait* of the subjunctive.
Futur proche: *je vais luire* (see Grammar of the verb, paragraphs 3 and 50).

- **Reluire** is conjugated like **luire**.
- The past participles *lui* and *relui* are always invariable.
- The forms of the *passé simple* in italics are obsolete (*je luisis…, ils luisirent*). These are always replaced by *je luis…, ils luirent*.

Abbreviations used in the list

afr.: Africanism
belg.: Belgicism
D: defective verb
I: intransitive verb
impers.: impersonal verb
p. p.: past participle
P: pronominal verb
québ.: Quebecism
T: direct transitive
Ti: indirect transitive

Variants in spelling are indicated with brackets around the optional letter or hyphen or written both ways using a slash to separate the alternate spellings.
As a reminder, prepositions (*à*, *de*, etc.) governed by certain verbs appear with the entry.
For easy use, certain abbreviations are repeated at the bottom of every second page. Supplementary information is also provided. For example, on every second page, users are reminded that when a verb is used intransitively (and conjugated with *avoir*), the past participle is invariable.
Semantic information is provided in cases where a change in structure or auxiliary affects the meaning:

65 demeurer (habiter) I, *avoir – to live (somewhere), to dwell*
65 demeurer (continuer à être) I, *être – to remain*

ALPHABETICAL LIST OF VERBS

Glossary of Selected Terms (p. 254)
Bibliography (p. 256)

The numbers refer to conjugation tables.
The model verb (used to exemplify the conjugation pattern) appears in bold blue.

a

65 abaisser T – *to lower, to abase*
65 abaisser (s') P – *to lower oneself*
65 abandonner T – *to abandon, to leave, to give up*
65 abandonner (s') à P – *to give way to*
81 abasourdir T – *to dumbfound*
81 abâtardir T – *to debase, to deteriorate*
81 abâtardir (s') P – *to degenerate, to bastardize*
121 abattre I, T – *to knock down, to destroy*
121 abattre (s') P – *to collapse*
69 abcéder I – *to abscess, to form an abscess*
69 abcéder (s') P – *to become abscessed*
65 abdiquer I, T – *to abdicate*
65 aberrer I – *to aberrate*
81 abêtir T – *to stupefy, to stultify*
81 abêtir (s') P – *to grow stupid*
65 abhorrer T – *to abhor*
65 abîmer/abimer T – *to damage*
65 abîmer/abimer (s') P – *to get damaged, to sink*
65 abjurer I, T – *to renounce*
65 ablater T – *to ablate*
65 ablater (s') P – *to become ablated*
65 abloquer T – *to clamp*
81 abolir T – *to abolish, to wipe out*
65 abomber afr. I – *to speed, to put the pedal to the metal*
65 abominer T – *to loathe*
65 abonder I – *to abound, to be plentiful*
65 abonner T – *to subscribe to*
65 abonner (s') P – *to subscribe to, to take a subscription*
81 abonnir T – *to improve*
81 abonnir (s') P – *to improve oneself*
65 aborder I, T – *to approach, to touch land*
65 aborder (s') P – *to approach each other*
65 aboucher T – *to join up*
65 aboucher (s') P – *to join up with, to take up with*
65 abouler I, T – *to hand over, to come along*
65 abouler (s') P – *to arrive*
65 abouter T – *to join end to end*
81 aboutir à I, Ti – *to result in, to culminate in*
78 aboyer I, T – *to bark*
65 abraser T – *to abrade*
65 abraser (s') P – *to become abraded*
75 abréger T – *to shorten*
75 abréger (s') P – *to shorten, to become shorter*
65 abreuver T – *to water (animal), to soak (plant), to heap on (insults)*
65 abreuver (s') P – *to drink deep*
65 abricoter T – *to coat apricot jam on a cooked tart using a brush*
76 abrier québ. T – *to shelter*
76 abrier (s') québ. P – *to shelter, to cover oneself*
65 abriter T – *to shelter*
65 abriter (s') P – *to take shelter*
67 abroger T – *to repeal*
81 abrutir T – *to stupefy*
81 abrutir (s') P – *to degrade oneself*
65 absenter afr. T – *to be absent*
65 absenter (s') P – *to leave, to be away*
65 absorber T – *to absorb*
65 absorber (s') P – *to become absorbed in*
141 absoudre T – *to absolve*
84 abstenir (s') P – *to abstain*
127 abstraire T, D – *to abstract*
127 abstraire (s') P, D – *to isolate oneself*
65 abuser de T, Ti – *to take advantage of, to overdo*
65 abuser (s') P – *to be mistaken*
65 acagnarder (s') P – *to be lazy*
65 accabler T – *to overwhelm, to overpower, to condemn, to heap on (insults)*
65 accaparer T – *to monopolize, to hoard, to corner*
65 accastiller T – *to equip (ship)*
69 accéder à Ti – *to attain, to accede to*
69 accélérer I, T – *to accelerate*
69 accélérer (s') P – *to gather speed*
65 accentuer T – *to stress*
65 accentuer (s') P – *to increase*
65 accepter de T, Ti – *to agree*
65 accepter (s') P – *to accept oneself, to be accepted*
65 accessoiriser T – *to accessorize*
65 accidenter T – *to damage, to injure*
65 acclamer T – *to acclaim, to cheer*
65 acclimater T – *to acclimatize*
65 acclimater (s') P – *to become acclimatized*
65 accointer (s') P – *to make acquaintance*
65 accoler T – *to place side by side, to couple, to lean (something)*
65 accoler (s') P – *to take up with, to lean against*
65 accommoder T – *to accommodate*
65 accommoder (s') P – *to come to terms (with)*
65 accompagner T – *to accompany*
65 accompagner (s') P – *to be accompanied (with)*
81 accomplir T – *to accomplish, to fulfil*
81 accomplir (s') P – *to finish*
65 accorder T – *to grant, to concede, to tune (piano)*
65 accorder (s') P – *to agree with*
65 accorer T – *to shore*
65 accoster T – *to accost, to berth (boat)*
65 accoster (s') P – *to greet*
65 accoter T – *to bring a working face to its ultimate position (mining industry)*
65 accoter (s') P – *to lean against*
65 accoucher de I, T, Ti – *to give birth, to deliver*
65 accouder (s') P – *to lean on one's elbow*
65 accouer T– *to tie horses head to tail*
65 accoupler T – *to couple up with, to join, to connect, to form pairs*
65 accoupler (s') P – *to mate, to copulate*
81 accourcir I, T – *to shorten*
94 accourir I, *être* (or *avoir*) – *to come running, to rush in*
65 accoutrer T – *to accoutre, to dress, to outfit*
65 accoutrer (s') P – *to accoutre (oneself)*
65 accoutumer T – *to accustom*
65 accoutumer (s') P – *to become accustomed*
65 accréditer T – *to accredit, to substantiate*
65 accréditer (s') P – *to ingratiate oneself*
65 accrocher I, T – *to hook, to hang up, to collide with, to engage*
65 accrocher (s') P – *to hold on, to hold fast*
135 accroire T, D – *to delude*
used only prefixed with the verb "faire"
136 accroître/accroitre à T, Ti – *to top up, to accrue to*
136 accroître/accroitre (s') P – *to accrue*
81 accroupir (s') P – *to squat*
89 accueillir T – *to receive, to greet*

65 acculer T – *to drive to*
65 acculturer T – *to acculturate*
65 accumuler I, T – *to accumulate, to amass*
65 accumuler (s') P – *to accumulate, to amass*
65 accuser T – *to accuse, to blame, to acknowledge (letters), to show up*
65 accuser (s') P – *to accuse oneself, to accentuate*
65 acenser T – *to let, to lease*
69 acérer T – *to sharpen*
76 acétifier T – *to acetify*
65 acétyler T – *to create acetyl acid*
65 achalander T – *to provide with*
65 achaler québ. T – *to annoy*
65 acharner T – *to set on*
65 acharner (s') P – *to be intent on*
65 acheminer T – *to forward, to dispatch*
65 acheminer (s') P – *to proceed*
71 acheter I, T – *to buy, to bribe*
71 acheter (s') P – *to buy (for oneself), to be buyable*
68 achever T – *to end, to complete*
68 achever (s') P – *to draw to an end*
65 achopper sur Ti – *to stumble over*
65 achopper (s') P – *to stumble over*
65 achromatiser T – *to achromatize*
76 acidifier T – *to acidify*
76 acidifier (s') P – *to turn sour*
65 aciduler T – *to acidulate*
69 aciérer T – *to steel*
73 aciseler T – *to completely cover with earth or soil (wine)*
65 acoquiner (s') P – *to gang up*
85 acquérir T – *to acquire, to obtain, to purchase*
85 acquérir (s') P – *to accrue*
66 acquiescer à I, Ti – *to agree, to consent*
65 acquitter T – *to acquit*
65 acquitter (s') P – *to perform*
65 acter T – *to publish officially*
65 actionner T – *to operate, to actuate, to sue*
65 activer I, T – *to speed up, to activate*
65 activer (s') P – *to become activated, to keep busy*
65 actualiser T – *to update, to actualize*
65 adapter T – *to adapt*
65 adapter (s') P – *to adapt (oneself)*
65 additionner T – *to add, to add up*
65 additionner (s') P – *to add, to add up*
69 adhérer à Ti – *to adhere to, to join (party)*
65 adirer T, D – *to lose*
only in the infinitive
and the p. p. "adiré" – *misplaced, lost*
65 adjectiver T – *to use as an adjective*
65 adjectiviser T – *to adjectivize*
124 adjoindre T – *to associate*
124 adjoindre (s') P – *to take on*
67 adjuger T – *to award, to knock down (auction)*
67 adjuger (s') P – *to appropriate, to take possession of*
65 adjurer T – *to beseech*
122 admettre T – *to admit*
65 administrer T – *to administer, to manage*
65 administrer (s') P – *to manage (itself)*
65 admirer T – *to admire*
65 admirer (s') P – *to admire oneself*
65 admonester T – *to reprimand*
65 adoniser (s') P – *to beautify oneself*
65 adonner I – *to veer aft*
65 adonner (s') P – *to engage in*
65 adopter T – *to adopt, to take up (cause)*
65 adorer T – *to adore, to worship*
65 adorer (s') P – *to adore oneself*
65 adosser T – *to rest (support) the back against something*
65 adosser (s') P – *to lean against something, to lean something against something*
65 adouber I, T – *to dub (knight)*
81 adoucir T – *to sweeten, to soften, to mellow*
81 adoucir (s') P – *to get milder (weather)*
65 adresser T – *to address*
65 adresser (s') P – *to address*
65 adsorber T – *to adsorb*
65 aduler T – *to adulate*
69 adultérer T – *to adulterate, to debase*
84 advenir I, *être*, D – *to happen, to occur*
only in infinitive
and 3rd person
65 adverbialiser T – *to adverbialize*
69 aérer T – *to air, to aerate (water)*
69 aérer (s') P – *to take fresh air*
65 affabuler I, T – *to invent stories*
81 affadir T – *to make tasteless, to make insipid*
81 affadir (s') P – *to become tasteless, to become insipid*
81 affaiblir T – *to weaken, to reduce*
81 affaiblir (s') P – *to become weak, to lose strength*
65 affairer (s') P – *to bustle about*
65 affaisser T – *to sink, to weigh down*
65 affaisser (s') P – *to collapse, to subside*
65 affaler T – *to lower*
65 affaler (s') P – *to drop, to fall, to flop*
65 affamer T – *to starve*
67 afféager T – *to grant part of a noble ground of a domain, to hold in fief*
65 affecter T – *to affect, to feign*
65 affecter (s') P – *to assign oneself*
65 affectionner T – *to be fond of*
69 afférer I – *to relate to*
65 affermer T – *to lease*
81 affermir T – *to firm up, to consolidate*
81 affermir (s') P – *to become stronger*
65 afficher T – *to put up, to display, to advertise*
65 afficher (s') P – *to be seen (with), to show off*
65 affiler T – *to sharpen*
76 affilier T – *to affiliate*
76 affilier (s') P – *to be affiliated*
65 affiner T – *to refine, to improve*
65 affiner (s') P – *to improve, to ripen (cheese)*
65 affirmer T – *to affirm, to maintain*
65 affirmer (s') P – *to assert oneself*
65 affleurer I, T – *to break through the surface, to show through*

T: direct transitive (p. p. variable) – **Ti**: indirect transitive (p. p. invariable) – **I**: intransitive verb (p. p. invariable)
P: pronominal verb (auxiliary *être*) – **impers.**: impersonal verb – **D**: defective verb – *être*: verb conjugated with the auxiliary *être* – *être* or *avoir*: verbs conjugated with *être* or *avoir* (see paragraph 15)

67 affliger T – *to distress, to grieve*
67 affliger (s') P – *to grieve*
65 afflouer T – *to refloat*
65 affluer I – *to flow (water), to rush (blood), to be plentiful*
65 affoler T – *to throw into a panic*
65 affoler (s') P – *to panic*
67 affouager T – *to grant right of estovers*
65 affouiller T – *to scour, to wash away*
65 affourcher T – *to moor with two anchors*
67 affourrager T – *to supply fodder*
81 affranchir T – *to stamp (letter), to emancipate*
81 affranchir (s') P – *to exempt oneself*
69 affréter T – *to charter*
65 affriander T – *to tempt, to allure*
65 affricher T – *to leave fallow*
65 affrioler T – *to entice*
65 affriter T – *to treat (a cooking utensil)*
65 affronter T – *to face, to confront*
65 affronter (s') P – *to face up to, to confront*
65 affruiter I, T – *to bear fruit*
65 affubler T – *to rig out*
65 affubler (s') P – *to rig oneself out*
65 affurer T – *to gain, to win*
65 affûter/affuter T – *to sharpen, to grind*
65 africaniser T – *to Africanize*
65 africaniser (s') P – *to become Africanized*
66 agacer T – *to irritate, to jar, to probe*
66 agacer (s') de P – *to become irritated with*
66 agencer T – *to arrange, to organize*
66 agencer (s') P – *to combine, to harmonize*
65 agenouiller (s') P – *to kneel*
69 agglomérer T – *to agglomerate*
69 agglomérer (s') P – *to pile up*
65 agglutiner T – *to stick together, to agglutinate*
65 agglutiner (s') P – *to become agglutinated*
65 aggraver T – *to make worse, to aggravate*
65 aggraver (s') P – *to worsen*
65 agioter I – *to speculate*
81 agir I – *to act*
81 agir (s') P – *to be a matter of, to be about always used in impersonal expression* "il s'agit de": *it's about, this means ...*
65 agiter T – *to stir, to agitate*
65 agiter (s') P – *to be agitated, to fidget*
72 agneler I – *to lamb*
81 agonir T – *to revile, to hurl ... at*
65 agoniser I – *to be dying*
65 agrafer T – *to staple*
81 agrandir T – *to widen, to enlarge*
81 agrandir (s') P – *to grow, to expand*
74 agréer à T, Ti – *to accredit, to approve*
75 agréger T – *to aggregate*
75 agréger (s') P – *to become aggregated*
65 agrémenter T – *to embellish*
65 agresser T – *to attack*
65 agricher T – *to grab*
65 agriffer (s') P – *to become attached with claws*
65 agripper T – *to grip*
65 agripper (s') P – *to grip*
81 aguerrir T – *to harden*
81 aguerrir (s') P – *to become inured to*
65 aguicher T – *to excite*
65 ahaner I – *to labour*
65 aheurter (s') P – *to be angry with an obstacle*
81 ahurir T – *to dumbfound, to bewilder*
65 aicher T – *to bait*
65 aider à, de T, Ti – *to assist in, to help*
65 aider (s') P – *to help oneself*
81 aigrir I, T – *to embitter*
81 aigrir (s') P – *to become bitter*
65 aiguiller T – *to shunt (train), to direct*
70 aiguilleter T – *to lash*
65 aiguillonner T – *to goad, to urge on*
65 aiguiser T– *to sharpen*
65 aiguiser (s') P– *to sharpen*
65 ailler T – *to flavour with garlic*
65 aimanter T – *to magnetize*
65 aimanter (s') P – *to magnetize*
65 aimer T – *to love, to like*
65 aimer (s') P – *to like oneself, to make love*
65 airer I – *to nest*
65 ajointer T – *to join end to end*
65 ajourer T – *to ornament with openwork*
65 ajourner T – *to adjourn*
65 ajouter à T, Ti – *to add to*
65 ajouter (s') P – *to add, to add up*
65 ajuster T – *to adjust, to fit*
65 ajuster (s') P – *to adjust, to fit*
65 alambiquer T – *to convolute*
81 alanguir T – *to enfeeble*
81 alanguir (s') P – *to flag, to drop*
65 alarmer T – *to give the alarm, to alarm*
65 alarmer (s') P – *to take alarm*
65 alcaliniser T – *to alkalanize*
65 alcaliser T – *to make alkaline*
65 alcooliser T – *to alcoholize, to fortify (wine)*
65 alcooliser (s') P – *to drink to excess, to soak*
81 alentir T – *to make slower*
65 alerter T – *to warn*
69 aléser T – *to bore out*
65 aleviner T – *to spawn*
69 aliéner T – *to alienate, to estrange*
69 aliéner (s') P – *to alienate, to estrange*
65 aligner T – *to align, to line up*
65 aligner (s') P – *to fall into line*
65 alimenter T – *to feed, to nourish*
65 alimenter (s') P – *to feed*
65 aliter T – *to keep in bed*
65 aliter (s') P – *to be confined to bed*
65 allaiter I, T – *to nurse, to suckle*
69 allécher T – *to tempt, to make the mouth water*
75 alléger T – *to lighten*
81 allégir T – *to decrease in all the dimensions the volume of a body*
65 allégoriser T – *to allegorize*
69 alléguer T – *to allege, to plead*
83 aller I, *être* – *to go, to be going*
83 aller (s'en) P – *to go away, to depart*
76 allier T – *to ally, to combine*
76 allier (s') P – *to form alliance, to blend*
67 allonger I, T – *to lengthen*
67 allonger (s') P – *to strech out, to lie down*
65 allouer T – *to grant, to allocate*
65 allumer T – *to light, to switch on*
65 allumer (s') P – *to catch fire, to light up*

65 alluvionner I – *to deposit alluvium*
81 alourdir T – *to weigh down, to make heavy*
81 alourdir (s') P – *to weigh down, to make heavy*
65 alpaguer T – *to collar, to nab*
65 alphabétiser T – *to teach how to read and write, to alphabetize*
69 altérer T – *to distort, to change*
69 altérer (s') P – *to deteriorate*
65 alterner I, T – *to alternate, to rotate*
65 aluminer T – *to aluminate*
65 aluner T – *to soak into an alum solution*
81 alunir I – *to land on the moon*
65 amadouer T – *to coax, to wheedle, to soft-soap*
81 amaigrir T – *to make thin*
81 amaigrir (s') P – *to grow thin*
65 amalgamer T – *to combine, to amalgamate*
65 amalgamer (s') P – *to combine, to amalgamate*
65 amariner T – *to make sea worthy*
65 amariner (s') P – *to man a vessel, to find one's sea legs*
65 amarrer T – *to moor*
65 amarrer (s') P – *to moor*
65 amasser I, T – *to amass, to pile up*
65 amasser (s') P – *to amass, to pile up*
81 amatir T – *to mat*
66 ambiancer afr. I – *to liven up (the place)*
76 ambifier (s') afr. P – *to lighten (one's skin)*
65 ambitionner T – *to aspire to, to covet*
65 ambler I – *to amble, to pace*
65 ambrer T – *to amber*
65 améliorer T – *to improve, to better*
65 améliorer (s') P – *to get better*
67 aménager T – *to organize, to plan*
65 amender T – *to improve, to amend*
65 amender (s') P – *to amend one's way*
68 amener T – *to bring, to lead*
68 amener (s') P – *to turn up to come along*
65 amenuiser T – *to reduce, to thin*
65 amenuiser (s') P – *to thin down*
65 américaniser T – *to Americanize*
65 américaniser (s') P – *to become Americanized*
81 amerrir I – *to alight*
81 ameublir T – *to loosen*
65 ameuter T – *to assemble, to stir up*
65 ameuter (s') P – *to gather into a mob*
65 amidonner T – *to starch*
81 amincir I, T – *to thin down*
81 amincir (s') P – *to slim down*
65 aminer belg. I – *to aminate*
76 amnistier T – *to pardon, to amnisty*
65 amocher T – *to mess up, to make a mess of*
65 amocher (s') P – *to bash oneself up*
76 amodier T – *to farm out, to lease*
81 amoindrir T – *to reduce, to diminish*
81 amoindrir (s') P – *to reduce, to diminish*
81 amollir T – *to soften*
81 amollir (s') P – *to become soft*
72 amonceler T – *to accumulate*
72 amonceler (s') P – *to pile up*
66 amorcer I, T – *to begin, to bait*
66 amorcer (s') P – *to start moving*
66 amordancer T – *to treat (handle) a material by a caustic*
81 amortir T – *to deaden, to pay off (debt)*
81 amortir (s') P – *to be redeemed*
65 amouracher (s') P – *to be enamoured*
65 amourer afr. T – *to make love*
76 amplifier T – *to enlarge, to exaggerate*
76 amplifier (s') P – *to enlarge, to exaggerate*
65 amputer T – *to amputate*
81 amuïr (s') P – *to become mute, to be dropped (in pronunciation)*
65 amurer T – *to haul aboard the tack of, to tack*
65 amuser T – *to entertain, to amuse*
65 amuser (s') P – *to enjoy oneself*
76 analgésier T – *to kill pain*
65 analyser T – *to analyze*
65 analyser (s') P – *to be analyzed*
65 anastomoser T – *to anastomose*
65 anastomoser (s') P – *to anastomose*
65 anathématiser T – *to curse, to anathematize*
65 ancrer T – *to anchor*
65 ancrer (s') P – *to be established, to anchor oneself, to root, to rivet*
81 anéantir T – *to annihilate, to be dumbfounded*
81 anéantir (s') P – *to vanish*
76 anémier T – *to weaken*
76 anesthésier T – *to anaesthetize*
65 anglaiser T – *to dock a horse's tail*
65 angliciser T – *to anglicize*
65 angliciser (s') P – *to become anglicized*
65 angoisser I, T – *to distress, to be distressed*
65 angoisser (s') P – *to become distressed*
69 anhéler I – *to gasp*
65 animaliser T – *to animalize, to sensualize*
65 animer T – *to animate, to enliven, to give life to*
65 animer (s') P – *to come to life*
65 aniser T – *to flavor with aniseed*
65 ankyloser T – *to stiffen*
65 ankyloser (s') P – *to stiffen*
72 anneler T – *to arrange in ringlets*
65 annexer T – *to append, to annex*
65 annexer (s') P – *to append, to annex*
65 annihiler T – *to destroy, to annul*
65 annihiler (s') P – *to destroy oneself*
66 annoncer T – *to announce, to advertise*
66 annoncer (s') P – *to proclaim oneself, to be imminent*
65 annoter T – *to annotate*
65 annualiser T – *to annualize*
65 annuler T – *to annul, to cancel*
65 annuler (s') P – *to become annulled, to become cancelled*
81 anoblir T – *to ennoble*
81 anoblir (s') P – *to become ennobled*
65 anodiser T – *to anodize*
65 ânonner I, T – *to stumble, to blunder through*
81 anordir I – *to veer northward, to north*

T: direct transitive (p. p. variable) – **Ti**: indirect transitive (p. p. invariable) – **I**: intransitive verb (p. p. invariable) **P**: pronominal verb (auxiliary *être*) – **impers.**: impersonal verb – **D**: defective verb – *être*: verb conjugated with the auxiliary *être* – *être* or *avoir*: verbs conjugated with *être* or *avoir* (see paragraph 15)

65 antéposer T – *to place in front of*
65 anticiper I, T – *to anticipate, to forestall*
65 antidater T – *to antedate*
65 aoûter/aouter T – *to harden off*
65 apaiser T – *to appease, to pacify*
65 apaiser (s') P – *to calm down*
67 apanager T – *to grant appanage*
100 apercevoir T – *to perceive, to observe*
100 apercevoir (s') P – *to perceive, to observe*
65 apeurer T – *to frighten*
65 apiquer T – *to steeve, to top off*
78 apitoyer T – *to move, to pity*
78 apitoyer (s') P – *to feel pity, to feel sorry*
81 aplanir T – *to smooth, to plane*
81 aplanir (s') P – *to become smoother, to grow easier*
81 aplatir T – *to flatten*
81 aplatir (s') P – *to become flat, to lie down flat*
65 aplomber québ. T – *to plumb*
65 aplomber (s') québ. P – *to become plumbed*
76 apostasier I – *to apostatize*
65 aposter T – *to station*
65 apostiller T – *to add*
65 apostropher T – *to apostrophize, to upbraid*
65 apostropher (s') P – *to accost each other*
65 appairer T – *to pair up*
130 apparaître/apparaitre I – *to appear, to seem*
être *(or* avoir*)*
65 appareiller I, T – *to equip, to get under way*
65 appareiller (s') P – *to sail, to string up*
65 apparenter T – *to ally with, to marry into*
65 apparenter (s') P – *to ally to, to be related to, to marry into*
76 apparier T – *to pair off*
76 apparier (s') P – *to match*
apparoir I, D – *to appear*
only in the infinitive
and 3rd person singular
indicative present: "il appert" – *it appears*
84 appartenir à Ti – *to belong (to), to concern*
84 appartenir (s') P – *to be one's own master*
65 appâter T – *to pure, to force-feed*
81 appauvrir T – *to impoverish*
81 appauvrir (s') P – *to grow poor*
72 appeler à T, Ti – *to call, to ring somebody, to appoint, to assign*
72 appeler (s') P – *to be called (named)*
118 appendre T – *to suspend*
65 appertiser T – *to sterilize*
81 appesantir T – *to weigh down*
81 appesantir (s') P – *to grow heavier*
69 appéter T – *to crave for*
81 applaudir à I, T, Ti – *to applaud, to commend*
81 applaudir (s') P – *to congratulate oneself, to pat oneself on the back*
65 appliquer T – *to apply*
65 appliquer (s') P – *to apply oneself, to apply to*
65 appointer T – *to put on the pay roll*
65 appointer (s') P – *to sharpen*
81 appointir T – *to point*
65 apponter I – *to land on deck*
65 apporter T – *to bring, to cause*
65 apposer T – *to affix, to append*
76 apprécier T – *to appreciate, to appraise*
76 apprécier (s') P – *to like each other, to appreciate*
65 appréhender T – *to arrest, to dread*
119 apprendre T – *to learn, to teach, to hear of*
119 apprendre (s') P – *to be learned*
65 apprêter T – *to prepare*
65 apprêter (s') P – *to get ready*
65 apprivoiser T – *to tame*
65 apprivoiser (s') P – *to become tame*
65 approcher de I, T, Ti – *to come close, to draw near*
65 approcher (s') de P – *to approach, to come near*
81 approfondir T – *to deepen*
81 approfondir (s') P – *to grow deeper*
76 approprier T – *to appropriate*
76 approprier (s') P – *to take for oneself*
65 approuver T – *to approve of, to agree to*
65 approuver (s') P – *to become approved*
65 approvisionner T – *to supply with*
65 approvisionner (s') P – *to take in supplies*
79 appuyer I, T – *to press, to support*
79 appuyer (s') P – *to lean on, to rely on*
65 apurer T – *to audit, to check*
67 aquiger I – *to injure, to damage*
65 arabiser T – *to Arabicize*
65 araser T – *to level*
65 arbitrer T – *to arbitrate*
65 arborer T – *to display, to wear*
65 arboriser I – *to plant trees*
65 arc(-)bouter T – *to buttress*
65 arc(-)bouter (s') P – *to take a firm stand*
65 archaïser I – *to archaize*
65 architecturer T – *to architect*
65 archiver T – *to record, to file*
65 arçonner T – *to bend*
65 ardoiser T – *to slate* (roof)
65 argenter T – *to silver*
65 argenter (s') P – *to silverize*
65 argotiser I – *to speak slang*
65 argougner T – *to collar*
65 arguer/argüer de T, Ti – *to assert, to infer*
65 argumenter I – *to argue*
65 ariser T – *to reef*
65 armer T – *to arm, to fit out*
65 armer (s') P – *to arm, to fit out*
76 armorier T – *to emblazon*
65 arnaquer T – *to swindle, to racket*
65 aromatiser T – *to aromatize, to flavour*
75 arpéger I, T – *to play in arpeggios*
65 arpenter T – *to survey, to pace up and down*
65 arpigner T – *to touch (slang)*
65 arquebuser T – *to kill with an arquebus*
66 arquepincer T – *to collar, to arrest*
65 arquer I, T – *to bend*
65 arquer (s') P – *to bend*
65 arracher T – *to pull up, to tear out*
65 arracher (s') P – *to pull up, to tear out*
65 arraisonner T – *to stop and inspect (ship)*
67 arranger T – *to manage, to work out*
67 arranger (s') P – *to arrange*
65 arrenter T – *to lease land*
67 arrérager I – *to fall into arrears*
67 arrérager (s') P – *to fall into arrears*
65 arrêter I, T – *to stop, to arrest*
65 arrêter (s') P – *to come to a stop*

69 arriérer T – *to postpone, to delay, to fall behind (payments)*
65 arrimer T – *to stow, to secure*
65 arriser T – *to touch sail*
65 arriver I, *être* – *to arrive, to happen*
67 arroger (s') P – *to claim for oneself*
81 arrondir T – *to round off*
81 arrondir (s') P – *to become round*
65 arroser T – *to water, to spray, to bribe*
65 arroser (s') P – *to call for a drink, to drink to something*
65 arsouiller (s') P – *to get drunk*
65 articuler I, T – *to articulate, to hinge*
65 articuler (s') P – *to be jointed*
65 artiller I – *to provide a vessel with artillery*
65 ascensionner T – *to make an ascent*
65 aseptiser T – *to asepticize*
65 aspecter T – *to face*
67 asperger T – *to sprinkle, to splash*
67 asperger (s') P – *to splash*
65 asphalter T – *to asphalt*
76 asphyxier I, T – *to suffocate*
76 asphyxier (s') P – *to suffocate*
65 aspirer à T, Ti – *to inhale, to aspire*
81 assagir T – *to quieten, to settle down*
81 assagir (s') P – *to quieten, to settle down*
90 assaillir T – *to assault, to attack*
81 assainir T – *to clean up, to improve*
65 assaisonner T – *to season, to dress*
65 assarmenter T – *to shoot-thin a vine*
65 assassiner T – *to murder, to pester*
assavoir T, D – *to let be known only in infinitive*
69 assécher I, T – *to dry, to drain*
69 assécher (s') P – *to dry, to drain*
65 assembler T – *to gather, to assemble*
65 assembler (s') P – *to gather, to assemble*
68 assener T – *to strike*
69 asséner T – *to strike*
112 ass(e)oir T – *to sit, to establish*
112 ass(e)oir (s') P – *to sit down*
65 assermenter T – *to swear in*
81 asservir T – *to enslave, to subjugate*
81 asservir (s') P – *to submit*
65 assibiler T – *to assibilate*
65 assibiler (s') P – *to assibilate*
75 assiéger T – *to besiege, to mob*
65 assigner T – *to assign, to fix, to summon*
65 assimiler T – *to assimilate*
65 assimiler (s') P – *to become assimilated*
65 assister à T, Ti – *to attend, to witness*
76 associer T – *to associate, to connect*
76 associer (s') P – *to join, to share in*
65 assoiffer T – *to make thirsty*
112 assoir/asseoir T – *to sit, to establish*
112 assoir/asseoir (s') P – *to sit down*
65 assoler T – *to rotate crops*
81 assombrir T – *to darken*
81 assombrir (s') P – *to become dark, to cloud over*
65 assommer T – *to batter to death, to knock out, to bore (figurative)*
65 assommer (s') P – *to batter oneself or each other*
65 assoner I – *to assonate*
81 assortir T – *to match, to accompany*
81 assortir (s') P – *to match, to go together*
81 assoupir T – *to lull, to make drowsy*
81 assoupir (s') P – *to doze off*
81 assouplir T – *to soften*
81 assouplir (s') P – *to become supple*
81 assourdir I, T – *to deafen, to muffle*
81 assourdir (s') P – *to become voiceless or unvoiced*
81 assouvir T – *to satisfy, to assuage, to sate*
81 assouvir (s') P – *to be sated, to become sated*
81 assujettir T – *to subdue, to fasten*
81 assujettir (s') P – *to subject oneself*
65 assumer I, T – *to assume, to take upon oneself*
65 assumer (s') P – *to be self responsible*
65 assurer I, T – *to secure, to assure, to insure*
65 assurer (s') P – *to make sure, to contract an insurance*
65 asticoter T – *to tease*
65 astiquer T – *to polish*
123 astreindre T – *to compel*
123 astreindre (s') P – *to restrain oneself*
78 atermoyer I – *to put off, to procrastinate*
65 atomiser T – *to atomize*
65 atomiser (s') P – *to become atomized*
65 atriquer T – *to dress, to equip*
76 atrophier T – *to atrophy*
76 atrophier (s') P – *to waste away*
65 attabler T – *to seat at the table*
65 attabler (s') P – *to sit down at the table*
65 attacher I, T – *to fasten, to attach*
65 attacher (s') P – *to become attached, to link to, to stick*
65 attaquer T – *to attack, to prosecute, to contest*
65 attaquer (s') P – *to tackle, to take on*
65 attarder (s') P – *to linger, to stay behind*
123 atteindre à T, Ti – *to reach, to achieve*
72 atteler I, T – *to hitch up, to harness*
72 atteler (s') P – *to become hitched or harnessed, to buckle down to*
118 attendre I, T – *to wait*
118 attendre (s') P – *to wait for each other*
81 attendrir T – *to soften, to tenderize*
81 attendrir (s') P – *to be moved*
65 attenter à I, Ti – *to attempt on, to violate*
65 atténuer T – *to lessen, to diminish*
65 atténuer (s') P – *to lessen, to diminish*
65 atterrer T – *to overwhelm, to crush*
81 atterrir I – *to land, to touch ground*
65 attester T – *to testify, to attest*
81 attiédir T – *to cool down, to take the chill off*
81 attiédir (s') P – *to cool off*
65 attifer T – *to doll up*
65 attifer (s') P – *to doll up*
67 attiger I, T – *to exaggerate*
65 attirer T – *to draw, to attract*

T: direct transitive (p. p. variable) – **Ti**: indirect transitive (p. p. invariable) – **I**: intransitive verb (p. p. invariable) **P**: pronominal verb (auxiliary *être*) – **impers.**: impersonal verb – **D**: defective verb – *être*: verb conjugated with the auxiliary *être* – *être* or *avoir*: verbs conjugated with *être* or *avoir* (see paragraph 15)

65 attirer (s') P – *to win*
65 attiser T – *to fan, to stir up*
65 attitrer T – *to appoint*
65 attraper T – *to catch, to hold on to*
65 attraper (s') P – *to quarrel*
65 attribuer T – *to confer, to attribute*
65 attribuer (s') P – *to claim, to appropriate*
65 at(t)riquer T – *to dress (like a dog's dinner), to equip*
65 attrister T – *to sadden*
65 attrister (s') P – *to grow sad*
65 attrouper T – *to gather*
65 attrouper (s') P – *to flock*
65 auditionner I, T – *to audition*
65 augmenter I, T – *to increase*
65 augmenter (s') P – *to increase*
65 augurer I, T – *to foresee, to augur*
65 auner T – *to size up*
65 auréoler T – *to glorify*
65 auréoler (s') P – *to take an aura of*
76 aurifier T – *to stop with gold*
65 ausculter T – *to sound, to auscultate*
76 authentifier T – *to authenticate*
65 authentiquer T – *to legalize*
65 autocensurer (s') P – *to practice self-censorship*
67 autocorriger T – *to self-correct*
67 autocorriger (s') P – *to self-correct*
152 autodétruire (s') P – *to self-destruct*
65 autodéterminer (s') P – *to self-determine*
66 autofinancer T – *to self-finance*
66 autofinancer (s') P – *to self-finance*
76 autographier T – *to autograph*
65 autoguider (s') P – *to self direct*
65 automatiser T – *to automate*
65 autoproclamer (s') P – *to proclaim oneself*
76 autopsier T – *to carry out an autopsy*
65 autoriser T – *to authorize, to allow*
65 autoriser (s') P – *to permit oneself, to allow oneself*
65 autosuggestionner (s') P – *to auto-suggest*
65 autotomiser (s') P – *to autotomize*
81 avachir I, T – *to be out of shape, to slacken*
81 avachir (s') P – *to lose shape, to be sloppy*
65 avaler T – *to swallow*
65 avaliser T – *to endorse*
66 avancer I, T – *to advance, to progress, to bring forward, to put forward*
66 avancer (s') P – *to make one's way, to advance*
67 avantager T – *to favour*
76 avarier T – *to spoil, to go bad*
76 avarier (s') P – *to spoil, to go bad*
123 aveindre T – *to reach or attain*
65 aventurer T – *to risk*
65 aventurer (s') P – *to venture*
69 avérer T– *to turn out that, to prove to be*
69 avérer (s') P – *to prove*
81 avertir T – *to warn, to notify*
65 aveugler T – *to blind, to dazzle*
65 aveugler (s') P – *to blind oneself*
81 aveulir T – *to deaden*
81 aveulir (s') P – *to go to pieces*
81 avilir T – *to debase*
81 avilir (s') P – *to demean oneself, to stoop to*
65 aviner T – *to season*
65 aviser I, T – *to spot, to inform*
65 aviser (s') P – *to become informed*
65 avitailler T – *to take in supplies (ship), to (re)fuel*
65 avitailler (s') P – *to take in supplies, to (re)fuel*
65 aviver T – *to revive, to highten*
65 avocasser T – *to be a lawyer*
65 avoiner T – *to feed a horse with oats, to beat up*
62 avoir T – *to have, to get, to own*
65 avoisiner T – *to border on*
65 avoisiner (s') P – *to be near*
65 avorter I, T – *to abort*
65 avouer T – *to acknowledge, to admit*
65 avouer (s') P – *to confess*
78 avoyer T – *to set (the tooth points of a saw)*
65 axer T – *to centre on*
65 axiomatiser T – *to axiomatize*
65 azimuter T – *to locate the azimuth*
65 azimuther T – *to observe*
65 azurer T – *to tinge with blue*

b

73 babeler belg. I – *to chit-chat, to shoot the breeze*
65 babiller I – *to prattle, to babble, to gossip*
65 bâcher T – *to cover with tarpaulin*
65 bachoter I – *to cram*
65 bâcler I, T – *to botch*
65 bader T – *to gape, to gawk*
65 badigeonner T – *to whitewash, to daub*
65 badigeonner (se) P – *to daub (oneself) with*
65 badiner I – *to trifle with, to banter*
65 baffer T – *to slap, to cuff*
65 bafouer T – *to scoff, to jeer at*
65 bafouiller I, T – *to splutter*
65 bâfrer I, T – *to guzzle*
65 bagarrer I – *to wrangle, to scuffle*
65 bagarrer (se) P – *to wrangle, to scuffle*
65 bagoter I – *to make a move on, to step on it*
65 bagotter I – *to make a move on, to step on it*
65 bagouler I – *to be glib*
65 baguenauder I – *to go for a stroll*
65 baguenauder (se) P – *to mooch around*
65 baguer T – *to ring, to put a gold band*
65 baigner I, T – *to bathe, to give a bath*
65 baigner (se) P – *to go bathing, to have a bath*
65 bailler (la bailler belle) T – *to tell to the marines!*
65 bâiller (bâiller d'ennui) I – *to yawn, to gape*
65 bâillonner T – *to gag, to muzzle*
65 baiser I, T – *to kiss, to fuck*
65 baisser I, T – *to lower, to fade, to decline*
65 baisser (se) P – *to bend down, to stoop*
65 balader T – *to trail around*
65 balader (se) P – *to stroll around, to saunter*
65 balafrer T – *to gash, to slash*
66 balancer I, T – *to balance, to throw, to wawer*
66 balancer (se) P – *to swing*
65 balanstiquer T – *to get rid of, to throw away*
77 balayer T – *to sweep, to clear out*
76 balbutier I, T – *to mumble*
65 baleiner T – *to stiffen, to bone (a garment)*
65 baligander belg. I – *to roam, to wander*

65 baliser I, T – *to buoy, to mark out*
65 balkaniser T – *to Balkanize*
65 balkaniser (se) P – *to become Balkanized*
65 ballaster T – *to ballast*
65 baller I – *to dangle, to hang*
65 ballonner T – *to swell, to puff out*
65 ballot(t)er I, T – *to shake about, to toss*
65 bal(l)uchonner T – *to put in a bundle*
65 bal(l)uchonner (se) P – *to be put in a bundle*
65 balter belg. T – *to joke*
65 bambocher I – *to live it up*
65 banaliser T – *to trivialize, to make common place*
65 banaliser (se) P – *to become common place*
65 bananer T – *to get told off, to get thrashed*
65 bancher T – *to form panel settings*
65 bander I, T – *to bandage, to tie up, to have an erection*
65 bander (se) P – *to become tied up*
65 banner T – *to cover*
81 bannir T – *to banish, to expel*
65 banquer I – *to pay*
70 banqueter I – *to feast*
65 baptiser T – *to baptize, to christen*
65 baquer (se) P – *to have a bath*
65 baquer belg. T – *to bathe*
70 baqueter T – *to bale out*
65 baragouiner I, T – *to jabber*
65 baraquer I, T – *to lodge in barracks, to lodge in huts*
65 baratiner I, T – *to spin a yarn*
65 baratter T – *to churn milk*
65 barber T – *to bore*
65 barber (se) P – *to be bored*
76 barbifier T – *to shave*
76 barbifier (se) P – *to shave*
65 barboter I, T – *to splash about*
65 barbouiller T – *to smear, to daub*
65 barder I, T, impers. – *to bard*
69 baréter I – *to roar, to trumpet (elephant)*
65 barguigner I – *to hesitate*
65 barioler T – *to variegate, to daub with many colours*
65 barjaquer I – *to chat, to shoot the breeze*
65 barloquer belg. I – *to swing*
65 barouder I – *to flight guerilla-fashion*
65 barrer I, T – *to bar, to block, to cross (cheque)*
65 barrer (se) P – *to clear off*
65 barricader T – *to barricade*
65 barricader (se) P – *to barricade*
81 barrir I – *to trumpet (elephant)*
65 basaner T – *to tan*
65 basculer I, T – *to tilt, to seesaw*
65 baser T – *to base on*
65 baser (se) P – *to be based on*
65 bassiner T – *to bathe, to warm (a bed), to bore*
65 bastillonner T – *to fortify*
65 bastionner T – *to fortify*
65 bastonner T – *to fight*
65 bastonner (se) P – *to fight*
65 batailler I – *to battle, to fight*
65 batailler (se) P – *to fight*
72 bateler I – *to juggle*
65 bâter T – *to put a pack on a mule*
65 batifoler I – *to romp*
81 bâtir T – *to build, to construct*
81 bâtir (se) P – *to be built, to be put up*
65 bâtonner T – *to cane*
121 **battre** en I, T, Ti – *to beat*
"battre (en retraite)" – *to retreat*
121 battre (se) P – *to fight*
67 bauger (se) P – *to retire to its lair (boar)*
65 bavarder I – *to chat*
65 bavasser I – *to gossip*
65 baver I – *to drivel, to slobber*
65 bavocher I – *to blur*
65 bayer (aux corneilles) I – *to gape at the moon*
65 bazarder T – *to sell off, to get rid of*
76 béatifier T – *to beatify*
65 bêcher I, T – *to dig, to have a dig at*
70 bêcheveter T – *to place top-to-tail*
65 bécoter T – *to peck*
65 bécoter (se) P – *to kiss*
65 becquer T – *to peck at*
70 becqueter T – *to peck at, to eat*
65 becter T, D – *to eat*
used especially in the infinitive and the p. p.
65 bedonner I – *to get a paunch*
74 béer I, D – *to be (wide) open, to gape*
especially in the infinitive, the imparfait *of the indicative, the present participle* "béant" *and in the expression* "bouche bée" *(literal) flabbergasted (figurative)*
77 bégayer I, T – *to stammer*
71 bégueter I – *to bleat (goat)*
65 bêler I – *to bleat, to bawl*
65 bémoliser T – *to mark with a flat note (music)*
76 bénéficier de Ti – *to profit by*
81 bénir T – *to bless, to glorify*
"une union bénie" – *blessed union*
"l'eau bénite" – *holy water*
p. p. "béni, e, is, ies"
not to be confused with the adjective in "eau bénite"
70 béqueter T – *to peck at, to eat*
65 béquiller I, T – *to walk on crutches, to prop up*
66 bercer T – *to rock, to lull*
66 bercer (se) P – *to delude oneself, to harbour (illusions)*
65 berdeller belg. I, T – *to talk a lot*
65 berlurer I – *to deceive somebody*
65 berlurer (se) P – *to deceive oneself*
65 berner T – *to hoax*
65 besogner I – *to slave, to labour at*
76 bêtifier I, T – *to act the fool*
76 bêtifier (se) P – *to prattle stupidity*
65 bêtiser I – *to talk stupidly*
65 bétonner I, T – *to build in concrete*
65 beugler I, T – *to bellow, to bawl*

T: direct transitive (p. p. variable) – **Ti**: indirect transitive (p. p. invariable) – **I**: intransitive verb (p. p. invariable) **P**: pronominal verb (auxiliary *être*) – **impers.**: impersonal verb – **D**: defective verb – *être*: verb conjugated with the auxiliary *être* – *être* or *avoir*: verbs conjugated with *être* or *avoir* (see paragraph 15)

65 beurrer T – *to butter*
65 beurrer (se) P – *to get roaring drunk*
65 biaiser I, T – *to slant, to evade*
65 bibarder I – *to drink*
65 bibeloter I – *to collect curios*
65 biberonner I – *to booze*
65 bicher I – *to enjoy*
65 bichonner T – *to titivate, to pet*
65 bichonner (se) P – *to dress up, to spruce oneself up*
65 bichoter I – *to feel good*
impersonal expression: "ça bichote"
65 bidonner (se) P – *to split one's sides*
65 bidouiller T – *to jerryrig*
65 biffer T – *to cross out*
65 bifurquer I – *to branch off*
65 bigarrer T – *to mottle*
65 bigler I, T – *to squint, to look at*
65 biglouser I – *to squint*
65 bigophoner I – *to be on the blower, to be on the horn*
65 bigorner T – *to hit*
65 bigorner (se) P – *to fight*
65 bilaner afr. I – *to take stock*
65 biler (se) P – *to get worked up*
65 billebauder I – *to lose the scent (hounds)*
65 biller I – *to ball-test*
65 billonner T – *to ridge*
65 biloquer T – *to break land*
65 biner I, T – *to harrow, to hoe*
65 biquer belg. I – *to kiss*
65 biscuiter T – *to make biscuit pottery*
65 biseauter T – *to bevel*
65 bisegmenter T – *to bisect*
65 biser I, T – *to kiss*
65 bisquer I – *to sulk*
65 bisser T – *to give an encore, to ask for an encore*
65 bistourner T – *to wring, to wrench*
65 bistrer T – *to darken*
65 biter T – *to catch (understand)*
65 bitonner I – *to give birth*
65 bitter T – *to catch (understand)*
65 bitumer T – *to bituminize, to pave*
65 bituminer T – *to pave*
65 bit(t)urer (se) P – *to get plastered*
65 bivouaquer I – *to bivouac, to sleep in the open*
65 bizuter T – *to rag*
65 blablater I – *to talk bla-bla-bla*
65 blackbouler T – *to reject, to turn down*
65 blaguer I – *to joke, to make fun of*
65 blairer T – *to sniff, to stand*
65 blâmer T – *to blame*
65 blâmer (se) P – *to blame oneself*
81 blanchir I, T – *to wash, to turn white*
81 blanchir (se) P – *to whitewash oneself*
65 blaser T – *to make blasé, to make indifferent*
65 blaser (se) P – *to become indifferent*
65 blasonner T – *to blazon, to emblazon*
69 blasphémer I, T – *to profane, to swear*
69 blatérer I – *to bleat*
65 bleffer belg. I – *to drool*
81 blêmir I – *to turn pale, to grow dim*
69 bléser I – *to lisp*
65 blesser T – *to hurt, to injure, to wound*
65 blesser (se) P – *to hurt oneself, to feel hurt*
81 blettir I – *to become overripe*
81 bleuir I, T – *to turn blue*
65 bleuter T – *to blue*
65 blinder I, T – *to armour-plate*
65 blinder (se) P – *to reinforce, to become immune (figurative)*
65 blinquer belg. I, T – *to shine*
65 blobloter I – *to tremble, to shiver*
81 blondir I, T – *to turn yellow, to dye blond*
78 blondoyer I – *to have a yellow glimmer*
65 bloquer T – *to block, to jam*
65 bloquer (se) P – *to get jammed up*
81 blottir (se) P – *to cower, to huddle*
65 blouser I, T – *to be loose fitting, to cheat*
65 bluffer I, T – *to bluff*
65 bluter T – *to silt, to bolt*
65 bobiner T – *to wind, to spool, to coil*
65 bocarder T – *to stamp*
65 boetter T – *to bait*
137 boire I, T – *to drink, to absorb*
137 boire (se) P – *to be drunk (liquid), to be consumed*
65 boiser T – *to timber, to panel, to afforest*
65 boiter I – *to limp*
65 boitiller I – *to hobble*
65 bolcheviser T – *to Bolshevize*
65 bombarder T – *to bomb, to shell, to bombard*
65 bomber I, T – *to bulge out, to camber (road)*
65 bonder T – *to fill, to cram*
65 bondériser T – *to bonderize*
81 bondir I – *to leap, to spring, to bounce*
65 bondonner T – *to bung*
76 bonifier T – *to improve*
76 bonifier (se) P – *to improve*
65 bonimenter I – *to coax*
81 bonir T – *to tell*
81 bonnir T – *to tell*
65 bordéliser T – *to create havoc*
65 border T – *to border, to bound*
65 bordurer T – *to board*
65 borgnoter T – *to spy on*
65 borner T – *to mark out, to limit*
65 borner (se) P – *to restrict (oneself), to be content (to)*
78 bornoyer I, T – *to check an alignment with one eye closed*
72 bosseler T – *to dent*
65 bosser I, T – *to work hard, to slave*
65 bossuer T – *to dent*
65 bostonner I – *to play boston (cards), to dance the boston*
65 botaniser I – *to botanize*
72 botteler T – *to bundle, to bunch*
65 botter I, T – *to suit*
65 botter (se) P – *to put on boots*
65 bottiner I, T – *to ask emphatically*
65 boubouler I – *to hoot*
65 boucaner I, T – *to buccaneer, to cure (meat)*
65 boucharder T – *to bushhammer*
65 boucher T – *to stop, to cork (bottle), to fill*
65 boucher (se) P – *to get blocked*
65 bouchonner I, T – *to bundle up, to jam*
65 bouchonner (se) P – *to bundle up, to jam*
65 boucler I, T – *to buckle, to fasten, to curl (hair), to lock up*

65 boucler (se) P – *to buckle*
65 bouder I, T – *to sulk*
65 bouder (se) P – *to give the cold shoulder*
65 boudiner T – *to truss*
65 bouffer I, T – *to puff out, to eat (greedily)*
65 bouffer (se) P – *to have a go at one another*
81 bouffir I, T – *to swell, to become bloated*
65 bouffonner I – *to act the buffoon*
67 bouger I, T – *to move, to stir*
67 bouger (se) P – *to move, to do something*
65 bougonner I, T – *to grumble*
92 bouillir I, T – *to boil*
65 bouillonner I, T – *to bubble, to boil over*
65 bouillotter I – *to simmer*
67 boulanger I, T – *to make bread*
65 bouler I, T – *to roll on*
65 bouleverser T – *to upset, to bowl over*
65 bouliner T – *to tack*
65 boulocher I – *to pill*
65 boulonner I, T – *to bolt down, to swot*
65 boulot(t)er I, T – *to eat*
65 boumer I – *to go like a bomb*
impersonal expression:
"ça boume" – *everything's going fine*
65 bouquiner I, T – *to read, to browse through books*
65 bourder I – *to goof up, to lie*
65 bourdonner I – *to buzz, to hum*
65 bourgeonner I – *to bud*
65 bourlinguer I – *to knock about, to live rough*
72 bourreler T – *to torment*
65 bourrer I, T – *to stuff*
65 bourrer (se) P – *to stuff*
65 boursicoter I – *to dabble on the stock exchange*
65 boursouf(f)ler T – *to puff up, to swell*
65 boursouf(f)ler (se) P – *to blister*
65 bousculer T – *to jostle*
65 bousculer (se) P – *to jostle*
65 bousiller I, T – *to bungle, to botch*
65 boustifailler I – *to stuff oneself*
65 bouter T – *to drive out*
65 boutonner I, T – *to button, to fasten*
65 boutonner (se) P – *to button up*
65 bouturer T – *to propagate plants by cuttings*
65 boxer I, T – *to box, to spar*
65 boyauter (se) P – *to laugh ont's head off, to split one's sides*
65 boycotter T – *to boycott*
65 braconner I, T – *to poach*
65 brader T – *to sell off, to sell cheaply*
65 brailler I, T – *to bawl, to shout*
65 brailler (se) afr. P – *to get dressed properly*
127 braire I, T, D – *to bray*
65 braiser T – *to braise*
65 bramer I – *to troat (stag), to trumpet*
65 brancarder T – *to carry on a stretcher*
65 brancher I, T – *to be in the know*
65 brancher (se) P – *to plug in, to connect*
65 brandiller I, T – *to swing, to wag*
81 brandir T – *to brandish, to wave about*
65 branler I, T – *to shake, to be loose, to hang around*
65 branler (se) – *to masturbate*
65 branlocher T – *to masturbate, to jerk off*
65 braquer I, T – *to aim, to fix*
65 braquer (se) P – *to set one's mind against*
65 braser T – *to braze*
65 brasiller I – *to sizzle, to sputter, to sparkle (fire)*
65 brasser T – *to brew, to mix, to handle (business), to shuffle*
65 brasser (se) P – *to mix, to become mixed*
77 brasseyer T – *to brace, to trim the yards*
65 braver T – *to brave, to defy*
77 brayer T – *to pitch*
65 bredouiller I, T – *to mumble*
65 brêler T – *to lash, to bind*
65 breller T – *to lash, to bind*
65 brésiller I, T – *to crumble*
65 brésiller (se) P – *to crumble*
65 bretailler – *to draw (sword), to fight*
72 bretteler T – *to tooth*
65 bretter T – *to be a swashbuckler*
70 breveter T – *to patent*
65 bricoler I, T – *to do odd jobs, to tinker with*
65 brider T – *to bridle, to fasten up*
67 bridger I – *to play bridge*
65 briefer T – *to brief*
65 brif(f)er I, T – *to bolt (down), to damage*
65 brigander I, T – *to plunder*
65 briguer T – *to solicit, to canvass*
65 brillanter T – *to gloss*
65 brillantiner T – *to brilliantine*
65 briller I – *to shine, to glitter*
65 brimbaler I, T – *to dangle, to swing*
65 brimer T – *to bully, to persecute*
65 bringuebal(l)er I, T – *to shake about, to hang loose*
65 brinquebal(l)er I, T – *to shake about, to hang loose*
65 briquer T – *to scrub clean*
70 briqueter T – *to brick, to face*
65 briser I, T – *to break, to shatter*
65 briser (se) P – *to break, to shatter*
65 broadcaster T – *to broadcast*
65 brocanter I, T – *to deal in second hand goods*
65 brocarder T – *to jibe at, to lampoon*
65 brocher T – *to brocade, to sew (books)*
65 broder I, T – *to embroider, to embellish*
65 broncher I – *to stumble, to flinch*
65 bronzer I, T – *to tan, to bronze*
65 bronzer (se) P – *to sunbathe*
65 broquanter I – *to barter, to swap, to exchange*
65 broquer belg. I – *to bait (small fish)*
65 brosser I, T – *to brush, to scrub*
65 brosser (se) P – *to brush one's clothes, to do without*
65 brouetter T – *to barrow*
65 brouillasser – *to be foggy, to drizzle*
impersonal expression:
"il brouillasse" – *it is foggy*
65 brouiller T – *to blur, to mix up, to jumble*
65 brouiller (se) P – *to become blurred, to fall out with*
65 brouillonner I, T – *to draft, to botch*

T: direct transitive (p. p. variable) – **Ti**: indirect transitive (p. p. invariable) – **I**: intransitive verb (p. p. invariable)
P: pronominal verb (auxiliary *être*) – **impers.**: impersonal verb – **D**: defective verb – *être*: verb conjugated with the auxiliary *être* – *être* or *avoir*: verbs conjugated with *être* or *avoir* (see paragraph 15)

65 brouter I, T – *to graze*
78 broyer T – *to pound, to crunch, to grind*
65 bruiner impers. – *to drizzle*
impersonal expression:
"il bruine" – *it is drizzly*
81 bruire I, D – *to rustle, to whim, to murmur*
used especially in the present participle
"bruissant" *and 3rd person of*
the present and the imparfait *of the*
indicative "il bruit/ils bruissent,
il bruissait/ils bruissaient",
and the present subjunctive
"qu'il bruisse/qu'ils bruissent".
The p. p. "brui" *is invariable.*
65 bruisser I – *to rustle, to murmur*
65 bruiter T – *to produce sound effects*
65 brûler/bruler I, T – *to burn*
65 brûler/bruler (se) P – *to burn*
65 brumasser I – *to be misty*
impersonal expression:
"il brumasse" – *it's misty*
65 brumer I – *to be hazy*
impersonal expression:
"il brume" – *it's hazy*
65 bruncher I – *to brunch*
81 brunir I, T – *to burnish, to tan*
81 brunir (se) P – *to go darker*
65 brusquer T – *to precipitate, to rush, to be rough with*
65 brutaliser T – *to manhandle, to brutalize*
65 bûcher/bucher I, T – *to rough-hew, to work hard at*
71 budgeter T – *to budget*
69 budgéter T – *to budget*
65 budgétiser T – *to budget for*
65 buller I – *to laze around*
65 bureaucratiser T – *to bureaucratize*
65 bureaucratiser (se) P – *to become bureaucratized*
65 buriner T – *to engrave, to chisel*
65 buser afr. T – *to fail someone on an exam*
65 busquer – *to busk, to corset*
65 buter I, T – *to butt, to come up against, to kill*
65 buter (se) P – *to be stubborn*
65 butiner I, T – *to gather honey, to pilfer*
65 butter T – *to ridge (ground)*
65 butter (se) P – *to take shelter*
65 buvoter I – *to sip, to tipple*

C

65 cabaler I – *to plot*
65 cabaner T – *to capsize (boat)*
65 cabiner afr. I – *to relieve oneself*
65 câbler T – *to cable*
65 cabosser T – *to dent*
65 caboter I – *to coast*
65 cabotiner I – *to play-act*
65 cabrer T – *to rear up, to rebel*
65 cabrer (se) P – *to rear up, to rebel*
65 cabrioler I – *to caper, to cut capers*
65 cacaber I – *to call (bird)*
65 cacarder I – *to cackle, to gabble*
65 cacher T – *to hide, to conceal*
65 cacher (se) P – *to hide, to conceal*
70 cacheter T – *to seal*
65 cachetonner I – *to play bit parts*
65 cadastrer T – *to survey (land), to register (land)*
65 cadeauter afr. T – *to give as a gift*
65 cadenasser T – *to padlock*
66 cadencer T – *to give rhythm to*
65 cadoter afr. T – *to give a gift*
65 cadrer I, T – *to frame, to focus, to tally*
65 cafarder I, T – *to tell tales*
70 cafeter I, T – *to tell tales on, to tattle*
65 cafouiller I – *to muddle, to flounder*
65 cafter I, T – *to sneak*
65 cagnarder I – *to live from day to day, to loaf*
65 cagner I – *to refuse difficult or dangerous work*
65 caguer I – *to shit*
65 cahoter I, T – *to jolt, to jerk*
65 caillebotter T – *to clot, to curdle*
65 cailler I, T – *to curdle, to clot, to coagulate, to freeze*
65 cailler (se) P – *to curdle, to clot, to coagulate, to freeze*
70 cailleter I – *to chatter*
65 caillouter T – *to ballast, to gravel*
65 caïmanter afr. T – *to cram for an exam*
65 cajoler T – *to coax, to cajole*
65 calaminer (se) P – *to coke up*
65 calamistrer T – *to curl (hair)*
65 calancher I – *to die*
65 calandrer T – *to roll, to press, to mangle*
65 calciner T – *to burn up*
65 calculer I, T – *to calculate, to compute, to reckon*
66, 68 calecer T – *to screw, to fuck*
65 caler I, T – *to wedge, to clamp, to stall (car)*
65 caler (se) P – *to settle (oneself), to keep pace with*
71 caleter I – *to make off, to scarper, to buzz off*
71 caleter (se) P – *to make off, to scarper, to buzz off*
65 calfater T – *to caulk*
65 calfeutrer T – *to make draught-proof, to block up*
65 calfeutrer (se) P – *to shut oneself up*
65 calibrer T – *to grade, to gauge*
65 câliner T – *to cuddle, to make a fuss of*
76 calligraphier T – *to calligraph*
65 calmer T – *to calm, to soothe*
65 calmer (se) P – *to calm down, to abate*
81 calmir I – *to becalm*
76 calomnier T – *to slander, to libel*
67 calorifuger T – *to insulate*
65 calotter T – *to cuff*
65 calquer T – *to trace, to copy*
65 calter I – *to buzz off*
65 calter (se) P – *to make oneself scarce*
65 cambrer T – *to bend, to arch, to curve*
65 cambrer (se) P – *to draw oneself up*
65 cambrioler T – *to burgle, to break into*
65 cambuter I, T – *to trade (something) for something of lesser value*
65 cameloter I – *to deal in cheap goods*
69 camembérer afr. I – *to have smelly feet*
65 camer (se) P – *to be on drugs*
65 camionner T – *to truck, to convey*
65 camoufler T – *to disguise, to camouflage*
65 camoufler (se) P – *to camouflage (oneself)*
65 camper I, T – *to camp, to pitch camp, to place*

65 camper (se) P – *to take a firm stand*
65 canaliser T – *to channel*
65 canarder I, T – *to snipe*
65 cancaner I – *to gossip, to quack*
65 cancériser T – *to become cancerous*
81 candir (se) P – *to candy*
65 caner I – *to kick the bucket, to chicken out*
72 canneler T – *to flute, to corrugate*
65 canner I, T – *to cane*
65 cannibaliser T – *to cannibalize*
65 cannibaliser (se) P – *to cannibalize*
65 canoniser T – *to canonize*
65 canonner T – *to cannonade, to batter*
65 canoter I – *to boat, to row*
65 cantiner I – *to buy at a cantine*
65 cantonner I, T – *to quarter, to station, to confine*
65 cantonner (se) à P– *to confine (oneself) to*
65 canuler T – *to bore, to pester*
65 caoutchouter T – *to rubberize*
65 capahuter T – *to steal part of a loot*
65 caparaçonner T – *to caparison*
65 caparaçonner (se) P – *to caparison (oneself)*
74 capéer I – *to lie to*
72 capeler T – *to rig*
77 capeyer I – *to lie (navigation)*
65 capitaliser I, T – *to capitalise, to save*
65 capitonner T – *to pad, to upholster*
65 capitonner (se) P – *to become padded*
65 capituler I – *to capitulate, to surrender*
65 caponner I – *to funk, to cheat, (Afr.) to panic, to fear*
65 caporaliser T – *to militarize*
65 capoter I, T – *to capsize, to overturn, to put a hood on, to fail*
65 capsuler T – *to cap*
65 capter T – *to collect, to capt*
65 captiver T – *to captivate, to enthrall*
65 captiver (se) P – *to become captivated, to become enthralled*
65 capturer T – *to capture, to catch*
65 capuchonner T – *to cover up*
65 caquer T – *to salt-sure (herrlng)*
70 caqueter I – *to cackle, to gossip*
65 caracoler I – *to caper*
65 caractériser T – *to characterize, to mark*
65 caractériser (se) P – *to be characterized*
65 caramboler I, T – *to collide with, to cannon into*
65 caramboler (se) P – *to collide with*
65 caraméliser I, T – *to caramelize*
65 caraméliser (se) P – *to caramelize*
65 carapater (se) P – *to bolt, to scram*
65 carbonater T – *to carbonate*
65 carboniser T – *to char, to carbonize*
65 carburer I, T – *to carburet, to work*
65 carcailler I – *to call (quail)*
65 carder T – *to card*
66 carencer T – *to deprive*
69 caréner I, T – *to careen*
65 carer T – *to square*
65 caresser T – *to fondle, to caress*
65 caresser (se) P – *to caress each other, to play with oneself*
65 carguer T – *to take in (sail)*
65 caricaturer T – *to caricature*
76 carier T – *to decay, to rot*
76 carier (se) P – *to decay, to rot*
65 carillonner I, T – *to chime, to jingle*
65 carmer T – *to pay*
65 carminer T – *to dye carmine, to rouge*
76 carnifier (se) P – *to develop muscular-like tissue*
65 carotter I, T – *to do out of, to wangle*
65 caroubler T – *to pick a lock*
72 carreler T – *to tile, to pave*
65 carrer T – *to square*
65 carrer (se) P – *to ensconce oneself*
65 carrosser T – *to fit the body (chassis of car)*
78 carroyer T – *to square (off)*
65 carter T – *to card, to fasten on a card*
65 cartonner I, T – *to stiffen (with cardboard), to case (books)*
65 cascader I – *to cascade, to gag (a part)*
76 caséifier T – *to casefy*
65 casemater T – *to casemate*
65 caser T – *to stow away, to find a place for*
65 caser (se) P – *to settle down*
65 caserner T – *to quarter*
65 casquer I, T – *to fork out*
65 casse-croûter/casse-crouter I – *to snack, to have lunch*
65 casser I, T – *to break, to snap, to buzz off*
65 casser (se) P – *to break, to snap, to buzz off*
65 castagner I, T – *to fight, to have a punch-up*
65 castagner (se) P – *to fight, to have a punch-up*
65 castrer T – *to castrate*
65 cataloguer T – *to list*
65 catalyser T – *to catalyse*
65 catapulter T – *to catapult*
65 catastropher T – *to wreck, to overwhelm*
65 catcher I – *to wrestle*
65 catéchiser T – *to catechize*
65 catiner québ. I, T – *to play with dolls*
81 catir T – *to press, to gloss*
65 cauchemarder I – *to have nightmares*
65 causer I, T – *to cause, to chat*
65 cautériser T – *to cauterize*
65 cautionner T – *to answer for, to stand for, to go bail for*
65 cavacher afr. I – *to cavacha, to dance the cavacha*
65 cavalcader I – *to cavalcade*
65 cavaler I, T – *to run away, to clear off*
65 cavaler (se) P – *to clear off, to run off*
65 caver I, T – *to excavate*
65 caver (se) P – *to excavate*
65 caviarder T – *to censor*
69 **céder** à I, T, Ti – *to give up, to yield (to)*
123 ceindre T – *to put on, to gird on*
123 ceindre (se) P – *to put on, to gird on*
65 ceinturer T – *to encircle, to girdle*
69 célébrer T – *to celebrate, to hold*

T: direct transitive (p. p. variable) – **Ti**: indirect transitive (p. p. invariable) – **I**: intransitive verb (p. p. invariable) **P**: pronominal verb (auxiliary *être*) – **impers.**: impersonal verb – **D**: defective verb – *être*: verb conjugated with the auxiliary *être* – *être* or *avoir*: verbs conjugated with *être* or *avoir* (see paragraph 15)

73 celer T – *to conceal, to hide from*
65 cémenter T – *to cement*
65 cendrer T – *to cinder, to colour ash-grey*
65 censurer T – *to censure, to criticize, to censor, to ban*
65 centraliser T – *to centralize*
65 centrer I, T – *to centre*
67 centrifuger T – *to separate*
65 centupler I, T – *to centuplicate, to make a hundredfold*
65 cercler T – *to ring*
65 cerner T – *to encircle, to close in, to define*
76 certifier T – *to certify, to authenticate*
65 césariser T – *to perform a Caesarean (section) on*
65 cesser de I, T, Ti – *to cease, to stop*
65 chabler T – *to fasten a cable to, to lift, to shake off*
65 chagriner T – *to distress, to upset*
65 chagriner (se) P – *to be distressed, to be upset*
65 chahuter I, T – *to barrack, to create an uproar, to heckle*
65 chaîner/chainer T – *to chain*
67 challenger T – *to challenge*
chaloir D – *to be important, to matter especially in the 3rd person singular of the present indicative*
"peu lui chaut" – *it matters little to him/her, it imports little*
65 chalouper I – *to sway*
65 chamailler (se) P – *to bicker, to squabble*
65 chamarrer T – *to bedeck*
65 chambarder T – *to upset*
65 chambouler T – *to disturb*
65 chambranler québ. I – *to totter, to wobble*
65 chambrer T – *to bring to room temperature*
65 chameauser afr. I – *to make a language mistake*
65 chamoiser T – *to chamois*
65 champagniser T – *to champagnize, to give sparkle to*
68 champlever T – *to cut away*
72 chanceler I – *to totter, to stagger*
65 chancetiquer I – *to change, to replace*
81 chancir I – *to go mouldy*
81 chancir (se) P – *to go mouldy*
65 chanfreiner T – *to bevel*
67 changer de I, T, Ti – *to exchange for*
67 changer (se) P – *to change one's clothes*
65 chansonner T – *to lampoon*
65 chanstiquer I, T – *to change, to replace*
65 chanter I, T – *to sing*
65 chantonner I, T – *to hum*
65 chantourner T – *to cut round a curved outline*
65 chaparder I, T – *to scrounge, to filch*
65 chapeauter T – *to oversee*
65 chaperonner T – *to chaperon, to hood (falcon)*
65 chapitrer T – *to lecture, to reprimand*
65 chaponner T – *to caponize*
65 chaptaliser T – *to chaptalize, to add sugar (to wine)*
65 charbonner I, T – *to char, to blacken with charcoal*
65 charcuter T – *to hack about, to mangle, to cut to bits*
65 charcuter (se) P – *to cut (each other) to bits (figurative)*
67 charger I, T – *to load, to burden*
67 charger (se) P– *to burden oneself, to be responsible for*
65 chariboter I – *to exaggerate, to overestimate*
65 charlater afr. I – *to consult a traditional healer / witch doctor*
65 charmer I, T – *to charm, to delight*
65 charpenter T – *to cut timber, to construct*
76 charrier I, T – *to cart, to joke*
65 charrioter T – *to machine (cylinder)*
78 charroyer T – *to cart*
65 chartériser T – *to charter*
65 chasser I, T – *to chase, to hunt*
65 châtaigner I – *to bash around, to clout, to biff*
65 châtaigner (se) P – *to bash around*
76 châtier T – *to chastise, to punish*
76 châtier (se) P – *to chastise oneself, to punish oneself*
65 chatonner I – *to set a stone*
65 chatouiller T – *to tickle, to excite*
78 chatoyer I – *to shimmer, to glisten*
65 châtrer T – *to castrate, to neuter*
65 chauffer I, T – *to heat up, to warm up*
65 chauffer (se) P – *to warm oneself*
65 chauler T – *to lime*
65 chaumer I, T – *to clear a field of stubble*
65 chausser I, T – *to put on shoes*
65 chausser (se) P – *to put on shoes*
chaut → chaloir
81 chauvir I – *to prick up the ears*
65 chavirer I, T – *to capsize, to tip over*
65 ch(e)linguer I – *to smell foul*
65 cheminer I – *to plod along*
65 chemiser T – *to case, to line*
65 chercher I, T – *to look for, to search for*
65 chercher (se) P – *to feel one's way*
69 chérer I – *to exaggerate*
81 chérir T – *to cherish*
65 cherrer I – *to boast*
65 chevaler T – *to prop up*
65 chevaucher I, T – *to ride, to straddle*
65 chevaucher (se) P – *to overlap*
65 cheviller T – *to pin together, to peg*
70 chevreter I – *to lamb, to give birth to a young sheep*
65 chevretter I – *to lamb, to give birth to a young sheep*
65 chevronner T – *to rafter*
65 chevroter I – *to quaver*
65 chiader T – *to swot*
65 chialer I – *to blubber*
65 chicaner sur I, T, Ti – *to quibble over, to squabble over*
65 chicaner (se) P – *to haggle with*
65 chicorer (se) P – *to fight*
65 chicorner (se) P– *to fight*
65 chicoter I – *to wrangle*
65 chicotter afr. T – *to whip, to flog*
65 chienner I – *to pup*
76 chier I, T – *to shit*
65 chiffonner I, T – *to crumple, to annoy*
65 chiffonner (se) P – *to become crumpled*
65 chiffrer I, T – *to calculate, to number*
65 chiffrer (se) P – *to amount*
65 chigner I – *to blubber*
65 chimer T – *to show anger*
65 chiner T – *to dye the warp of, to kid, to hunt (around) for antiques*

65 chinoiser I – *to be finicky about*
65 chiper T – *to pinch*
65 chipoter I – *to nibble at*
65 chiquer I, T – *to chew (tobacco)*
76 chirographier T – *to draw up a contract*
65 chlinguer I – *to pong, to stink to high heaven*
65 chlorer T – *to chlorinate*
65 chloroformer T – *to chloroform*
65 chlorurer T – *to chlorinate*
65 chofer T – *to drive*
115 choir I, *avoir* (or *être*) – *to fall*
81 choisir T – *to choose, to select*
65 chômer I, T – *to be off work*
65 choper – *to pinch, to steal*
65 chopiner I – *to booze*
65 chopper I – *to pinch, to steal*
65 choquer T – *to shock, to knock*
65 choquer (se) P – *to be angry*
76 chorégraphier I, T – *to choreograph*
65 choser afr. I, T – *to take care of something*
76 chosifier T – *to realize*
65 chouchouter T – *to coddle*
65 chouraver T – *to pinch, to swipe*
65 chourer T – *to pinch, to swipe*
65 chouriner T – *to stab to death*
78 choyer T – *to pet*
65 christianiser T – *to christianize*
65 chromer T – *to chrome*
65 chroniquer I – *to report*
69 chronométrer T – *to time*
65 chuchoter I, T – *to whisper*
65 chuinter I – *to hoot, to hiss*
65 chuter I – *to fall, to fail*
65 cibler T – *to target*
65 cicatriser I, T – *to heal over, to scar*
65 cicatriser (se) P – *to heal over, to scar*
65 cigler T – *to pay*
65 ciller I – *to blink*
65 cimenter T – *to cement*
65 cimenter (se) P – *to become cemented*
76 cinématographier T – *to film*
65 cingler I, T – *to lash, to sting, to sail out (boat)*
65 cingler (se) P – *to lash*
65 cintrer T – *to bend, to take in*
151 circoncire T – *to circumcise*
150 circonscrire T – *to limit*
150 circonscrire (se) P – *to circumscribe*
76 circonstancier T – *to give a full account*
84 circonvenir T – *to thwart, to impose on*
65 circuler I – *to circulate*
65 cirer T – *to wax, to polish*
65 cisailler T – *to shear*
73 ciseler T – *to chisel, to tool*
65 citer T – *to quote, to summon*
65 civiliser T – *to civilize*
65 civiliser (se) P – *to become civilized*
65 clabauder I – *to babble, to gossip*
65 claboter I, T – *to die*
65 clacher belg. T – *to throw something somewhere*
65 claironner I, T – *to trumpet*
66, 68 clamecer I – *to kick the bucket, to snuff it*
65 clamer T – *to exclaim, to proclaim*
65 clamper T – *to clamp*
65 clamser I – *to kick the bucket*
65 claper T – *to eat*
81 clapir I – *to squeal*
81 clapir (se) P – *to squeal*
65 clapoter I – *to chop, to lap against*
65 clapper I – *to click (one's tongue)*
65 clapser I – *to die*
65 claquemurer T – *to coop up*
65 claquemurer (se) P – *to remain cooped up*
65 claquer I, T – *to click, to clap, to slap*
65 claquer (se) P – *to click, to grow tired*
70 claqueter I – *to clapper, to cluck*
76 clarifier T – *to clarify*
76 clarifier (se) P – *to become clarified*
65 classer T – *to file, to classify*
65 classer (se) P – *to be placed*
76 classifier T – *to classify*
65 claudiquer I – *to limp*
65 claustrer T – *to confine*
65 claustrer (se) P – *to become yarded*
65 clavarder québ. I – *to chat*
65 claver T – *to place a keystone*
70 claveter T – *to wedge*
65 clavetter T – *to wedge*
65 clayonner T – *to pile*
65 clicher T – *to stereotype*
65 clienter afr. T – *to make someone a customer*
65 cligner de I, T, Ti – *to blink*
65 clignoter I – *to twinkle*
65 climatiser T – *to air-condition*
65 cliquer I – *to click*
70 cliqueter I – *to jingle, to rattle*
65 cliquoter belg. I – *to jingle*
65 clisser T – *to cover with wicker (work)*
65 cliver T – *to cleave*
65 cliver (se) P – *to cleave*
65 clochardiser T – *to become tramp-like*
65 clochardiser (se) P – *to become run-down*
65 clocher I – *to be amiss*
65 cloisonner T – *to partition*
65 cloîtrer/cloitrer T – *to cloister, to shut away*
65 cloîtrer/cloitrer (se) P – *to shut oneself off*
65 cloner T – *to clone*
65 cloper belg. I – *to smoke*
65 clopiner I – *to hobble, to limp*
65 cloquer I, T – *to blister*
138 clore T – *to close, to close up*
65 clôturer I, T – *to enclose*
65 clouer T – *to nail down*
65 clouter T – *to stud*
65 coaguler I, T – *to coagulate*
65 coaguler (se) P – *to coagulate*
65 coaliser T – *to join forces*
65 coaliser (se) P – *to join forces*
65 coasser I – *to croak*

T: direct transitive (p. p. variable) – **Ti**: indirect transitive (p. p. invariable) – **I**: intransitive verb (p. p. invariable)
P: pronominal verb (auxiliary *être*) – **impers.**: impersonal verb – **D**: defective verb – *être*: verb conjugated with the auxiliary *être* – *être* or *avoir*: verbs conjugated with *être* or *avoir* (see paragraph 15)

65 cocaliser afr. (se) P – *to cocalize*
65 cocher T – *to tick, to check*
65 côcher T – *to check off, to tick off*
65 cochonner I, T – *to botch up*
65 cocot(t)er I – *to stink, to pong*
76 cocufier T – *to cuckold*
65 coder I, T – *to code*
76 codifier T – *to codify*
67 codiriger T – *to co-direct*
65 coéditer T – *to co-publish*
65 coexister I – *to coexist*
65 coffrer T – *to put into prison, to coffer*
69 cogérer T – *to manage jointly*
65 cogiter I, T – *to cogitate*
65 cogner sur T, Ti – *to knock on, to hammer*
65 cogner (se) P – *to bump (into)*
65 cognoter I – *to stink*
65 cohabiter I – *to cohabit*
65 cohériter I – *to inherit jointly*
65 coiffer T – *to do somebody's hair*
65 coiffer (se) P – *to do one's hair*
66 coincer T – *to wedge, to jam*
66 coincer (se) P – *to wedge, to jam*
65 coïncider I – *to coincide*
65 coïter I – *to mate, to copulate*
76 cokéfier T – *to coke*
65 collaborer à I, Ti – *to collaborate with, to contribute*
65 collapser I – *to collapse*
65 collationner I, T – *to collate*
65 collecter T – *to collect*
65 collecter (se) P – *to collect oneself*
65 collectionner T – *to collect, to make collection of*
65 collectiviser T – *to collectivize*
65 coller à I, T, Ti – *to stick, to cling to, to suit*
65 coller (se) P – *to stick oneself*
70 colleter T – *to collar*
70 colleter (se) à P – *to come to grips with*
67 colliger T – *to collect and compare*
65 colloquer T – *to relegate, to foist*
65 colmater T – *to fill in*
65 coloniser T – *to colonize*
65 colorer T – *to colour, to tinge, to dye*
65 colorer (se) P – *to turn red*
76 colorier T – *to colour up*
65 coloriser T – *to colourize*
65 colporter T – *to peddle, to hawk*
65 coltiner T – *to carry*
65 coltiner (se) P – *to burden oneself*
121 combattre pour, contre, avec I, T, Ti – *to fight for, against, with*
65 combiner T – *to combine, to join*
65 combiner (se) P – *to unite with*
65 combler T – *to fill, to fulfil*
65 combler (se) P – *to fill up*
65 commander à I, T, Ti – *to order, to be in command*
65 commander (se) P – *to be ordered or chosen*
65 commanditer T – *to finance, to support*
65 commémorer T – *to commemorate*
66 commencer à I, T, Ti – *to begin, to start to*
66 commencer (se) P – *to begin*
65 commenter T – *to comment, to comment upon*
66 commercer I – *to trade*
65 commercialiser T – *to market*
69 commérer I – *to gossip*
122 commettre T – *to commit, to entrust, to appoint*
122 commettre (se) P – *to lower oneself, to endanger one's reputation*
65 commissionner T – *to commission*
65 commotionner T – *to shock*
65 commuer T – *to commute*
65 communaliser T – *to communalize*
76 communier I – *to receive communion, to be in communion with*
65 communiquer I, T – *to communicate, to pass on*
65 communiquer (se) P – *to spread to*
65 commuter I, T – *to communte*
65 compacter T – *to compact, to compress*
130 comparaître/comparaitre I – *to appear*
65 comparer T – *to compare to*
65 comparer (se) P – *to compare oneself*
comparoir I, D – *to appear in court*
only in the infinitive
"être assigné à comparoir" – *summoned to appear in court*
and present participle "comparant"
65 compartimenter T – *to partition, to divide up*
65 compasser T – *to control rigidly*
81 compatir à Ti – *to sympathize*
65 compenser T – *to compensate, to make up for*
65 compenser (se) P – *to compensate, to make up for*
69 compéter I – *to be within the competence of*
65 compétitionner québ. I – *to compete*
65 compiler T – *to compile*
65 compisser T – *to piss*
129 complaire à Ti – *to (try to) please*
129 complaire (se) P – *to take pleasure in*
p. p. invariable
69 compléter T – *to complete*
69 compléter (se) P – *to be complementary*
65 complexer T – *to give someone a complex*
65 complexer (se) P – *to develop a complex*
76 complexifier T – *to make complex or complicated*
76 complexifier (se) P – *to become complex or complicated*
65 complimenter T – *to compliment, to congratulate on*
65 compliquer T – *to complicate*
65 compliquer (se) P – *to become complicated*
65 comploter contre I, T, Ti – *to plot against*
65 comporter T – *to compose, to consist of, to include*
65 comporter (se) P – *to behave*
65 composer I, T – *to make up, to compose, to dial (phone)*
65 composer (se) P – *to be composed*
65 composter T – *to stamp, to obliterate, to compost*
119 comprendre T – *to understand, to realize, to include*
119 comprendre (se) P – *to understand each other*
65 compresser T – *to compress*
65 comprimer T – *to compress, to restrain*
122 compromettre I, T – *to compromise*
122 compromettre (se) P – *to compromise*
65 comptabiliser T – *to post (accounts)*
65 compter I, T – *to count, to reckon*
65 compter (se) P – *to number*

65 compulser T – *to examine*
65 computer T – *to compute*
65 concasser T – *to grind, to crush*
69 concéder T – *to concede, to admit*
69 concélébrer T – *to celebrate together (Mass)*
65 concentrer T – *to concentrate*
65 concentrer (se) P – *to concentrate*
65 conceptualiser I, T – *to conceptualize*
65 concerner T – *to concern, to affect*
used only in the 3rd person
in the active voice and in all
persons in the passive voice
65 concerter I, T – *to devise*
65 concerter (se) P – *to consult each other*
100 concevoir T – *to imagine, to conceive*
100 concevoir (se) P – *to be conceivable*
76 concilier T – *to reconcile*
76 concilier (se) P – *to win*
139 conclure à I, T, Ti – *to conclude (that), to decide*
139 conclure (se) P – *to conclude, to settle*
65 concocter T – *to concoct*
65 concorder I – *to agree, to tally*
94 concourir à I, Ti – *to converge to, to work towards*
69 concréter T – *to solidify*
65 concrétiser T – *to materialize*
65 concrétiser (se) P – *to take shape*
66 concurrencer T – *to compete*
65 condamner T – *to condemn, to sentence*
65 condenser T – *to condense*
65 condenser (se) P – *to condense*
118 condescendre à Ti – *to condescend to, to yield to*
65 conditionner T – *to condition*
152 conduire T – *to conduct, to drive*
152 conduire (se) P – *to behave*
65 confectionner T – *to make, to prepare*
65 confectionner (se) P – *to be made up of*
69 confédérer T – *to confederate*
69 conférer à I, T, Ti – *to confer to*
65 confesser T – *to confess*
65 confesser (se) P – *to go to confession*
66 confiancer afr. T – *to trust*
76 confier T – *to entrust, to confide*
76 confier (se) P – *to confide oneself*
65 configurer T – *to shape*
65 confiner à Ti – *to confine to*
65 confiner (se) P – *to limit oneself to*
151 confire T – *to preserve*
151 confire (se) P – *to be preserved*
65 confirmer T – *to confirm*
65 confisquer T – *to confiscate*
65 confiturer afr. T – *to spread jam on*
65 confluer I – *to meet, to join*
118 confondre T – *to mistake, to confuse*
118 confondre (se) P – *to merge, to blend*
65 conformer T – *to shape*
65 conformer (se) P – *to conform*
65 conforter T – *to strengthen, to reinforce*
65 conforter (se) P – *to become strenghtened*
65 confronter T – *to confront, to compare*
76 congédier T – *to dismiss*
73 congeler T – *to freeze*
73 congeler (se) P – *to freeze*
65 congestionner T – *to congest*
65 congestionner (se) P – *to become congested*
69 conglomérer T – *to conglomerate*
69 conglomérer (se) P – *to conglomerate*
65 conglutiner T – *to conglutinate*
65 congratuler T – *to congratulate*
65 congratuler (se) P – *to congratulate*
74 congréer T – *to worm*
81 cônir T – *to die, to kill*
65 conjecturer I, T – *to conjecture, to guess*
124 conjoindre T – *to join (in marriage)*
65 conjuguer T – *to conjugate, to combine*
65 conjuguer (se) P – *to conjugate, to combine*
65 conjurer T – *to avert, to plot, to entreat*
65 conjurer (se) P – *to conspire*
130 connaître/connaitre T – *to know, to be acquainted (with)*
130 connaître/connaitre (se) P – *to know oneself, to be acquainted*
65 connecter T – *to connect*
65 con(n)obler T – *to know*
65 connoter T – *to imply, to relate (to)*
65 conobrer T – *to know*
65 coquer T – *to sell out, to denounce, to expose*
85 conquérir T – *to conquer*
85 conquérir (se) P – *to be conquered*
65 consacrer T – *to devote*
65 consacrer (se) P – *to devote (oneself)*
65 conscientiser T – *to sensitize*
65 conseiller à T, Ti – *to advise (someone to do something)*
86 consentir à T, Ti – *to consent to*
65 conserver T – *to keep, to retain, to preserve*
65 conserver (se) P – *to keep, to retain, to preserve*
69 considérer T – *to consider, to regard*
69 considérer (se) P – *to consider oneself, to be considered*
65 consigner T – *to record, to detain, to deposit*
65 consister I – *to consist of*
65 consoler I, T – *to console, to solace*
65 consoler (se) P – *to be consoled, to get over*
65 consolider T – *to consolidate*
65 consolider (se) P – *to grow firm*
65 consommer I, T – *to consume*
65 consommer (se) P – *to be consumed*
65 consoner I – *to harmonize*
65 conspirer contre I, T, Ti – *to conspire against*
65 conspuer T – *to decry, to boo*
65 constater T – *to note, to establish*
65 consteller T – *to spangle, to stud*
65 consterner T – *to dismay*
65 constiper I, T – *to constipate*
65 constituer T – *to constitute, to set up, to make up*
65 constituer (se) P – *to constitute, to set up, to make up*
65 constitutionnaliser T – *to constitutionalize*
152 construire I, T – *to construct, to build*

T: direct transitive (p. p. variable) – **Ti**: indirect transitive (p. p. invariable) – **I**: intransitive verb (p. p. invariable)
P: pronominal verb (auxiliary *être*) – **impers.**: impersonal verb – **D**: defective verb – *être*: verb conjugated with the auxiliary *être* – *être* or *avoir*: verbs conjugated with *être* or *avoir* (see paragraph 15)

152 construire (se) P – *to be constructed*
65 consulter I, T – *to consult*
65 consulter (se) P – *to confer*
65 consumer T – *to consume, to burn*
65 consumer (se) P – *to burn (up), to waste (away)*
65 contacter T – *to contact*
65 contagionner T – *to infect*
65 containeriser T – *to containerize*
65 contaminer T – *to contaminate*
65 contempler T – *to contemplate, to meditate, to gaze at*
65 contempler (se) P – *to be contemplated, to gaze at (oneself)*
65 conteneuriser T – *to containerize*
84 contenir T – *to contain, to suppress*
84 contenir (se) P – *to contain one's feelings*
65 contenter T – *to satisfy*
65 contenter (se) P – *to content oneself, to make do*
65 conter T – *to tell, to relate*
65 contester I, T – *to contest, to challenge*
65 contextualiser T – *to contextualize*
65 contingenter T – *to fix on a quota basis*
65 continuer à, de I, T, Ti – *to continue (to)*
65 continuer (se) P – *to continue*
65 contorsionner T – *to contort*
65 contorsionner (se) P – *to contort*
65 contourner T – *to bypass, to skirt*
65 contracter T – *to contract*
65 contracter (se) P – *to shrink, to tense (up)*
65 contractualiser T – *to put on contract*
65 contracturer T – *to narrow a column, to go into spasms*
125 contraindre T – *to compel, to force*
125 contraindre (se) P – *to restrain*
76 contrarier T – *to annoy, to vex*
76 contrarier (se) P – *to be annoyed*
65 contraster I, T – *to contrast*
65 contr(e-)attaquer I – *to counter-attack*
66 contrebalancer T – *to counterbalance, to offsset*
66 contrebalancer (s'en) P – *not to give a damn*
121 contrebattre T – *to fight back*
65 contrebouter T – *to buttress*
65 contrebraquer T – *to steer into the skid*
65 contrebuter T – *to prop up*
65 contrecarrer T – *to cross, to counteract*
148 contredire T – *to contradict*
148 contredire (se) P – *to contradict*
128 contrefaire T – *to imitate, to counterfeit*
65 contreficher (se) P – *not to care a hoot about*
120 contrefoutre (se) P – *not to give a damn about*
65 contr(e-)indiquer T – *to counter-indicate*
65 contremander T – *to cancel, to call off*
65 contre(-)manifester I – *to demonstrate (against)*
65 contremarquer T – *to counter-mark*
65 contre(-)miner T – *to countermine*
65 contre(-)murer T – *to build a supporting wall*
65 contre(-)passer T – *to return*
65 contre(-)plaquer T – *to laminate*
65 contrer I, T – *to counter*
65 contre(-)sceller T – *to counterseal*
65 contresigner T – *to countersign*
65 contre(-)tirer T – *to counterproof*
84 contrevenir à Ti – *to contravene, to transgress*
65 contribuer à Ti – *to contribute to, to conduce*
65 contrister T – *to sadden*
65 contrôler T – *to control, to inspect, to check*
65 contrôler (se) P – *to control oneself*
65 controuver T – *to fabricate*
65 controverser I, T – *to debate*
65 contusionner T – *to bruise*
126 convaincre T – *to convince*
126 convaincre (se) P – *to convince oneself*
84 convenir à I, Ti, *avoir* – *to suit*
84 convenir de Ti, *avoir* (or *être*)– *to agree, to admit (to)*
84 convenir (se) P, *être* – *to be well-suited (to each other)*
p. p. invariable
67 converger I – *to converge*
65 converser I – *to converse*
81 convertir T – *to convert*
81 convertir (se) P – *to convert*
76 convier T – *to invite*
65 convivialiser I, T – *to make more friendly or convivial*
65 convoiter I, T – *to covet*
65 convoler I – *to marry*
65 convoquer T – *to convene, to invite*
78 convoyer T – *to convoy*
65 convulser T – *to convulse, to distort*
65 convulser (se) P – *to convulse, to distort*
65 convulsionner T – *to convulse*
69 coopérer à I, Ti – *to cooperate to*
65 coopter T – *to co-opt*
65 coordonner T – *to coordinate*
65 copermuter T – *to exchange, to change*
76 copier I, T – *to copy, to reproduce, to crib*
65 copiner I – *to be pally*
69 coposséder T – *to have joint ownership (of)*
65 coprésider T – *to co-chair*
152 coproduire T – *to co-produce*
65 copuler I – *to copulate*
65 coquer T – *to sell our, to denounce*
70 coqueter I – *to flirt, to toy (with)*
65 coquiller I – *to cockle*
65 coraniser afr. T – *to coranize*
72 cordeler T – *to twist*
65 corder T – *to tie up, to string*
65 cordonner T – *to twine*
65 cornancher T – *to thump, to fight*
65 cornancher (se) P – *to fight*
65 cornaquer T – *to show around*
65 corner I, T – *to hoot, to turn down a corner (page)*
65 correctionnaliser T – *to diminish the importance of a crime*
69 corréler T – *to correlate*
118 correspondre à I, Ti – *to correspond to*
118 correspondre (se) P – *to communicate with one another*
67 corriger T – *to correct, to put right*
67 corriger (se) P – *to mend one's ways*
65 corroborer T – *to corroborate*
65 corroder T – *to corrode*
120 corrompre T – *to corrupt, to taint*
120 corrompre (se) P – *to become debased, to decay*
78 corroyer T – *to curry*

65 corser T – *to strengthen, to pep up*
65 corser (se) P – *to strengthen, to pep up*
71 corseter T – *to corset*
65 cosigner T – *to co-sign*
65 cosmétiquer T – *to apply cosmetics*
65 cosser I – *to butt (rams)*
65 costumer T – *to dress (someone) up*
65 costumer (se) P – *to wear fancy-dress*
65 coter I, T – *to mark*
81 cotir T – *to damage, to bruise (a fruit)*
65 cotiser I – *to subscribe*
65 cotiser (se) P – *to get up a subscription*
65 cotonner I, T – *to wad, to fluff up*
65 cotonner (se) P – *to wad, to fluff up*
78 côtoyer T – *to keep close (to)*
78 côtoyer (se) P – *to mix, to rub shoulders*
65 couchailler I – *to sleep around*
65 coucher I, T – *to put to bed, to lay down*
65 coucher (se) P – *to go to bed, to lie down*
65 couder T – *to bend*
78 coudoyer T – *to elbow*
143 coudre T – *to sew, to stitch*
65 couiller afr. T – *to fuck, to bungle*
65 couillonner T – *to swindle*
65 couiner I – *to squeak*
65 couler I, T – *to run, to flow, to sink (boat)*
65 couler (se) P – *to glide, to slip*
65 coulisser I, T – *to slide*
65 coupailler T – *to cut away (at)*
65 coupeller T – *to assay, to cut, to reap*
65 couper à I, T, Ti – *to get out of*
65 couper (se) P – *to cut, to intersect (roads)*
65 coupler T – *to couple*
65 courailler I – *to gallivant*
65 courbaturer T – *to tire (out, to make ache)*
in modern French past participial forms:
"courbaturé, ée, és, ées"
replace old forms
"courbatu, ue, us, ues"
now used as adjectives
65 courber I, T – *to bow, to bend*
65 courber (se) P – *to stoop*
94 courir I, T – *to run*
65 couronner T – *to crown*
65 couronner (se) P – *to crown*
courre T, D – *to hunt*
only in the infinitive
"chasse à courre"
66 courroucer T – *to anger*
66 courroucer (se) P – *to become incensed*
65 courser T – *to chase, to hare after*
65 courtauder T – *to dock*
65 court-circuiter T – *to short-circuit*
65 courtiser T – *to court, to pay court (to)*
65 cousiner I – *to be on familiar terms (with)*
65 couteauner afr. T – *to knife, to stab*
65 coûter/couter à I, T, Ti – *to cost (financially and otherwise)*
65 coutoner afr. T – *to knife, to stab*
78 coutoyer afr. T – *to knife, to stab*
65 couturer T – *to scar*
65 couver I, T – *to brood, to hatch*
88 couvrir T – *to cover (with)*
88 couvrir (se) P – *to become covered, to cover oneself*
65 coxer T – *to catch, to nab*
65 cracher I, T – *to spit, to splutter*
65 crachiner impers. – *to drizzle*
65 crachoter I – *to splutter*
65 crachouiller I, T – *to splutter*
65 crailler I – *to scream, to yell*
125 craindre I, T – *to fear, to be afraid (of)*
65 cramer I, T – *to scorch*
65 cramponner T – *to clamp together*
65 cramponner (se) P – *to hang on (to)*
65 crampser I – *to die*
65 cramser I – *to die*
65 craner T – *to swank, to show off*
65 crâner I – *to swank, to show off*
65 cranter T – *to notch, to wawe (hair)*
65 crapahuter I – *to yomp, to bonk*
65 crapaüter I – *to trudge*
65 crapoter I – *not to inhale (while smoking)*
65 crapuler I – *to be a scumbag*
72 craqueler T – *to crackle, to crack*
72 craqueler (se) P – *to crackle, to crack*
65 craquer I, T – *to crack, to strike, to give up*
70 craqueter I – *to crackle*
65 crasher (se) P – *to crash into*
65 crasser T – *to foul*
65 cravacher I, T – *to flog*
65 cravater (se) afr. P – *to put one's (or a) tie on*
65 cravater T – *to put a tie on*
65 crawler I – *to swim the crawl*
65 crayonner T – *to pencil, to jot down*
69 crécher I – *to live (in)*
65 crédibiliser T – *to back up, to give credibility to*
65 créditer T – *to credit*
74 créer T – *to create*
74 créer (se) P – *to build up, to create (problems) for*
69 crémer I – *to cream*
72 créneler T – *to crenelate*
69 créner T – *to kern*
65 créoliser T – *to creolize*
65 créoliser (se) P – *to creolize*
65 créosoter T – *to creosote*
65 crêper T – *to crimp, to frizz*
65 crêper (se) P – *to crimp, to frizz*
81 crépir T –*to roughcast, to grain*
65 crépiter I – *to crackle, to patter*
65 crétiniser T – *to dull, to make stupid*
65 creuser I, T – *to hollow (out), to delve (into)*
65 creuser (se) P – *to grow hollow, to widen*
65 crevasser T – *to chap, to crack*
65 crevasser (se) P – *to become cracked*
68 crever I, T – *to burst, to puncture, to die*
68 crever (se) P – *to wear oneself out*
65 criailler I – *to squawk*
65 cribler T – *to silt, to hurl (at)*

T: direct transitive (p. p. variable) – **Ti**: indirect transitive (p. p. invariable) – **I**: intransitive verb (p. p. invariable) **P**: pronominal verb (auxiliary *être*) – **impers.**: impersonal verb – **D**: defective verb – *être*: verb conjugated with the auxiliary *être* – *être* or *avoir*: verbs conjugated with *être* or *avoir* (see paragraph 15)

76 **crier** I, T – *to shout, to call out, to proclaim*
65 criminaliser T – *to refer to a criminal court*
65 crisper T – *to contrat, to shrivel (up)*
65 crisper (se) P – *to contrat, to shrivel (up)*
65 crisser I – *to grate, to squeak*
65 cristalliser I, T – *to crystallize*
65 cristalliser (se) P – *to crystallize*
65 criticailler I, T – *to criticize, to run down*
65 critiquer T – *to criticize*
65 croasser I – *to caw, to croak*
65 crocher I, T – *to hook, to grip*
71 crocheter T – *to pick (lock), to crochet*
135 **croire** à, en I, T, Ti – *to believe*
135 croire (se) P – *to think*
65 croiser I, T – *to fold, to cross*
65 croiser (se) P – *to cut across, to intersect*
134 **croître/croitre** I – *to grow*
65 croquer I, T – *to crunch, to munch*
65 crosser T – *to rebuke*
65 crotter I, T – *to soil*
65 crotter (se) P – *to get dirty*
65 crouler I – *to collapse, to crumble*
81 croupir I – *to wallow, to stagnate*
65 croustiller I – *to nibble, to crunch*
65 croûter/crouter I, T – *to have some grub*
76 crucifier T – *to crucify*
65 crypter T – *to encrypt*
76 cryptographier T – *to write in cryptograph*
65 cuber I, T – *to cube*
89 **cueillir** T – *to pick, to gather*
65 cuirasser T – *to armour-plate*
65 cuirasser (se) P – *to harden (against)*
152 **cuire** I, T – *to cook*
65 cuisiner I, T – *to cook, to prepare (dish), to interrogate*
65 cuiter (se) P – *to get plastered*
65 cuivrer T – *to copperplate*
65 culbuter I, T – *to tumble, to topple, to tip*
65 culer I, T – *to go/veer astern*
65 culminer I – *to culminate*
65 culotter T – *to season (pie)*
65 culotter (se) P – *to put trousers on*
65 culpabiliser I, T – *to make someone feel guilty*
65 culpabiliser (se) P – *to feel guilty*
65 cultiver T – *to cultivate*
65 cultiver (se) P – *to improve one's mind*
65 cumuler T – *to accumulate*
65 curer T – *to clean out, to dredge*
65 curer (se) P – *to pick*
70 cureter T – *to scrape*
72 cuveler T – *to line*
65 cuver I, T – *to ferment, to work off*
65 cylindrer T – *to roll, to mangle*

d

76 dactylographier T – *to type*
65 daigner (+ infinitive) T – *to deign, to be pleased (to)*
65 daller T – *to pave*
65 damasquiner T – *to damascene*
65 damasser T – *to damask*
65 damer I,T – *to pack down*
65 damner I, T – *to damn*
65 damner (se) P – *to incur damnation*
65 dandiner T – *to dandle*
65 dandiner (se) P – *to waddle*
65 danser I, T – *to dance*
65 darder I, T – *to hurl, to shoot*
65 darder (se) P – *to hurl, to shoot*
65 dater I, T – *to date*
65 dauber I, T – *to jeer*
65 déactiver T – *to deactivate*
65 dealer T – *to push drugs*
65 déambuler I – *to stroll about*
65 débâcher I, T – *to uncover*
65 débâcler I, T – *to break up, to unfasten*
65 débagouler I, T – *to vomit*
65 débâillonner T – *to ungag, to unmuzzle*
65 déballer I, T – *to unpack*
65 déballonner (se) P – *to chicken out*
65 débanaliser T – *to make less commonplace*
65 débander I, T – *to unbandage, to disband*
65 débander (se) P – *to disperse*
65 débaptiser T – *to change the name (of)*
65 débarbouiller T – *to wash (face)*
65 débarbouiller (se) P – *to wash (face)*
65 débarder T – *to unload*
65 débarquer I, T – *to disembark, to set down*
65 débarrasser I, T – *to clear*
65 débarrasser (se) P – *to get rid (of)*
65 débarrer T – *to unbar*
65 débâter T – *to unsaddle*
81 débâtir T – *to pull down, to untack*
121 débattre T – *to debate, to argue*
121 débattre (se) P – *to struggle*
65 débaucher T – *to corrupt, to debauch*
65 débaucher (se) P – *to lead a life of debauchery*
65 débecter T – *to disgust*
65 débecter (se) P – *to be disgusted*
70 débe(c)queter T – *to disgust*
70 débe(c)queter (se) P – *to be disgusted*
65 débiliter T – *to debilitate, to weaken*
65 débiner T – *to disparage, to knock*
65 débiner (se) P – *to scram*
65 débiter T – *to debit, to charge*
69 déblatérer I – *to rant and rave*
77 déblayer T – *to clear away*
65 débloquer I, T – *to release, to talk nonsense*
65 débobiner T – *to unwind*
65 déboguer T – *to debug*
65 déboiser T – *to deforest, to clear*
65 déboîter/déboiter I, T – *to dislocate, to disconnect*
65 déboîter/déboiter (se) P – *to come out of joint*
65 débonder T – *to remove the bung/stopper from, to pull the plug out of*
65 débonder (se) P – *to open one's heart, to pour out one's feelings*
65 déborder I, T – *to overflow, to spill out, to burst*
65 déborder (se) P – *to overflow, to spill out, to burst*
72 débosseler T – *to remove dents*
65 débotter T – *to take boots off*
65 débotter (se) P – *to take one's boots off*
65 déboucher I, T – *to emerge, to uncork*
65 déboucler T – *to unbuckle*
65 débouler I, T – *to roll (down), to rush (in)*

65 déboulonner T – *to unbolt, to debunk*
65 débouquer I – *to disembogue*
65 débourber T – *to clean out, to sluice*
65 débourrer I, T – *to remove padding*
65 débourser T – *to spend*
65 déboussoler T – *to disorientate*
65 débouter T – *to dismiss, to reject*
65 déboutonner T – *to unbutton*
65 déboutonner (se) P – *to unbutton*
65 débrailler (se) P – *to loosen clothing*
65 débrancher T – *to disconnect*
65 débrancher (se) P – *to disconnect oneself, to be disconnected*
77 débrayer I, T – *to declutch, to change gear*
65 débrider I, T – *to unbridle*
65 débriefer T – *to debrief*
65 débrocher T – *to unspit, to strip*
65 débrouiller T – *to unravel, to disentangle*
65 débrouiller (se) P – *to manage*
65 débroussailler T – *to clear (of undergrowth)*
65 débucher I, T – *to break cover, to force to break cover*
65 débudgétiser T – *to exclude from budget*
65 débugger T – *to debug*
65 débureaucratiser T – *to do away with the bureaucracy of*
65 débusquer T – *to drive out, to oust*
65 débuter I – *to start, to begin*
70 décacheter T – *to unseal*
65 décadenasser T – *to unpadlock*
65 décaféiner T – *to decaffeinate*
65 décaisser T – *to unbox*
65 décalaminer T – *to decarbonize*
76 décalcifier T – *to decalcify*
76 décalcifier (se) P – *to decalcify*
65 décaler T – *to alter, to shift*
65 décalotter T – *to take (the top) off*
65 décalquer T – *to trace, to transfer*
65 décamper I – *to decamp, to run away*
65 décaniller I – *to clear off*
65 décanter I, T – *to settle, to decant*
65 décanter (se) P – *to become clear*
72 décapeler T – *to unrig*
65 décaper T – *to scour, to scrape*
65 décapiter T – *to decapitate*
65 décapoter T – *to take a hood down*
65 décapsuler T – *to take the cap off (bottle)*
65 décapuchonner T – *to remove (cap)*
65 décarburer T – *to decarburize*
65 décarcasser T – *to flog to death*
65 décarcasser (se) P – *to flog to death*
72 décarreler T – *to take up tiles (from)*
65 décarrer I – *to skedaddle*
65 décartonner T – *to strip (book)*
81 décatir T – *to sponge, to steam*
81 décatir (se) P – *to decay, to age*
65 décauser belg. T – *to denigrate, to run down*
69 décéder I, *être* – *to die, to decease*
73 déceler T – *to discover, to expose*
69 décélérer I – *to decelerate, to slow down*
65 décentraliser T – *to decentralize*
65 décentraliser (se) P – *to become decentralized*
65 décentrer T – *to throw off center*
65 décentrer (se) P – *to throw off center*
65 décercler T – *to unhoop*
69 décérébrer T – *to decerebrate*
65 décerner T – *to award, to bestow*
72 décerveler T – *to make moronic, to brainwash*
100 décevoir T – *to deceive, to disappoint*
65 déchaîner/déchainer T – *to unleash*
65 déchaîner/déchainer (se) P – *to burst out*
65 déchanter I – *to be disillusioned*
65 déchaper T – *to peel (tire)*
65 déchaperonner T – *to unhood*
67 décharger I, T – *to unload, to discharge*
67 décharger (se) P – *to put down, to lay down*
65 décharner T – *to emaciate*
65 déchaumer T – *to plough stubble*
65 déchausser I, T – *to take off (shoes)*
65 déchausser (se) P – *to take off (shoes)*
65 déchevêtrer T – *to unhalter*
65 décheviller T – *to unpin*
65 déchiffonner T – *to smooth out*
65 déchiffrer I, T – *to decipher, to read (music)*
70 déchiqueter T – *to slash*
65 déchirer T – *to tear, to rip*
65 déchirer (se) P – *to tear, to rip*
65 déchlorurer T – *to dechlorinate*
117 **déchoir** de I, Ti, D – *to strip/deprive of*
65 déchristianiser T – *to dechristianize*
65 déchristianiser (se) P – *to dechristianize oneself*
65 déchromer T – *to remove chromiun plating*
65 décider de T, Ti – *to decide to, to persuade to*
65 décider (se) P – *to make up one's mind*
65 déciller T – *to undeceive*
65 décimaliser T – *to decimalize*
65 décimer T – *to decimate*
65 décintrer T – *to discentre*
65 déclamer I, T – *to declaim, to recite*
65 déclarer T – *to declare, to announce*
65 déclarer (se) P – *to state one's opinion*
65 déclasser T – *to lower in status*
70 déclaveter T – *to unkey*
65 déclencher T – *to set off, to trigger off*
65 déclencher (se) P – *to set off, to trigger off*
65 décliner I, T – *to decline, to go down, to refuse*
65 décliner (se) P – *to decline, to go down, to refuse*
65 décloisonner T – *to remove partitions*
138 déclore T, D – *to open up, to throw open*
65 déclouer T – *to unnail*
65 décocher T – *to shoot, to let off*
65 décoder T – *to decode*
65 décoffrer T – *to remove from casing*
65 décoiffer T – *to disarrange hair, to muss*
65 décoiffer (se) P – *to disarrange hair, to muss*
66 décoincer T – *to unjam*
69 décolérer I – *to calm down*
65 décoller I, T – *to unstick, to take off*

T: direct transitive (p. p. variable) – **Ti**: indirect transitive (p. p. invariable) – **I**: intransitive verb (p. p. invariable) **P**: pronominal verb (auxiliary *être*) – **impers.**: impersonal verb – **D**: defective verb – *être*: verb conjugated with the auxiliary *être* – *être* or *avoir*: verbs conjugated with *être* or *avoir* (see paragraph 15)

65 décoller (se) P – *to come unstuck*
70 décolleter T – *to reveal neck and shoulders*
70 décolleter (se) P – *to reveal neck and shoulders*
65 décoloniser T – *to decolonize*
65 décolorer T – *to discolor*
65 décolorer (se) P – *to lose its color*
65 décommander T – *to cancel (order)*
65 décommander (se) P – *to cancel (appointment)*
122 décommettre T – *to unlay (rope)*
65 décommuniser T – *to leave communism behind*
65 décompenser I – *to decompensate, to collapse (emotionally)*
65 décomplexer T – *to remove complexes*
65 décomposer T – *to decompose, to rot, to contort (features)*
65 décomposer (se) P – *to decay*
65 décompresser I, T – *to decompress*
65 décomprimer T – *to decompress*
65 décompter I, T – *to deduct*
65 déconcentrer T – *to disperse*
65 déconcentrer (se) P – *to lose one's concentration*
65 déconcerter T – *to disconcert, to confound*
65 déconcubiner (se) P – *to disconcert, to confound*
65 déconditionner T – *to decondition*
151 déconfire T – *to nonpluss*
73 décongeler T – *to thaw, to defreeze*
65 décongestionner T – *to decongest*
65 déconnecter T – *to disconnect*
65 déconner I – *to talk twaddle*
65 déconseiller T – *to advise against*
69 déconsidérer T – *to discredit*
69 déconsidérer (se) P – *to discredit oneself*
65 déconsigner T – *to take out*
65 déconstiper T – *to relieve constipation*
152 déconstruire T – *to deconstruct, to dismantle*
65 décontaminer T – *to decontaminate*
66 décontenancer T – *to disconcert*
66 décontenancer (se) P – *to disconcert*
65 décontracter T– *to relax*
65 décontracter (se) P – *to relax*
65 décorder T – *to unrope*
65 décorder (se) P – *to unrope*
65 décorer I, T – *to decorate, to do up*
65 décorner T – *to dehorn, to smooth out*
65 décortiquer T – *to shell, to puzzle out*
65 découcher I – *to stay out all night*
143 découdre T – *to unpick*
143 découdre (se) P – *to come unstitched, to come apart*
65 découler de I, Ti – *to ensue from*
65 découper T – *to cut up, to carve*
65 découper (se) P – *to stand out, to show up*
65 découpler T – *to uncouple*
67 décourager T – *to discourage*
67 décourager (se) P – *to lose heart*
65 découronner T – *to discrown*
88 découvrir T – *to find, to discover, to reveal*
88 découvrir (se) P – *to take off (hat), to come to light*
65 décrasser T – *to cleanse*
65 décrasser (se) P – *to cleanse oneself*
65 décrédibiliser T – *to undermine the credibility of*
65 décréditer T – *to bring into disrepute*
65 décréditer (se) P – *to loose one's credit*
65 décrêper T – *to unfrizz*
81 décrépir T – *to strip plaster*
81 décrépir (se) P – *to fall into disrepair*
65 décrépiter I, T – *to decrepitate*
69 décréter T – *to decree, to issue*
76 décrier T – *to decry, to run down*
65 décriminaliser T – *to decriminalize*
150 décrire T – *to describe*
65 décrisper T – *to relax*
65 décrisper (se) P – *to relax oneself*
65 décrocher I, T – *to unhook, to take down, to pick up (phone)*
65 décrocher (se) P – *to come undone, to come away form*
65 décroiser T – *to uncross*
136 décroître/décroitre I – *to decrease*
65 décrotter T – *to remove mud*
65 décroûter/décrouter T – *to skin (casting)*
65 décrypter T – *to decipher*
65 décuivrer T – *to remove copper-plating*
65 déculasser T – *to unbreech*
65 déculotter T – *to take trousers off*
65 déculotter (se) P – *to take one's trousers off, to chicken out*
65 déculpabiliser T – *to exonerate from blame*
65 décupler I, T – *to increase tenfold*
65 décuver T – *to tun (wine)*
65 dédaigner de T, Ti – *to disdain, to scorn*
66 dédicacer T – *to dedicate*
76 dédier T – *to dedicate, to consecrate*
148 dédire T – *to deny*
148 dédire (se) P – *to retract a statement*
67 dédommager T – *to indemnify, to compensate*
67 dédommager (se) P – *to repay*
65 dédorer T – *to remove gilt*
65 dédouaner T – *to clear (customs)*
65 dédouaner (se) P – *to dissociate oneself (from)*
65 dédoubler T – *to unfold, to split in two*
65 dédoubler (se) P – *to unfold, to split in two*
65 dédramatiser I, T – *to reduce dramatic effects*
152 déduire T – *to deduce, to infer*
152 déduire (se) P – *to ensue*
90 défaillir I – *to lose strength, to faint*
128 défaire T – *to dismantle, to undo, to demolish*
128 défaire (se) P – *to come undone, to fall apart*
65 défalquer T – *to deduct*
65 défarder T – *to remove make-up*
65 défatiguer I, T – *to refresh, to rest*
65 défatiguer (se) P – *to refresh, to rest*
65 défaufiler T – *to untack*
65 défausser T – *to discard*
65 défausser (se) P – *to get rid (of)*
65 défavoriser T – *to be unfair (to)*
118 défendre T – *to champion, to forbid*
118 défendre (se) P – *to stand up (for)*
65 défenestrer T – *to throw out of a window, to defenestrate*
65 défenestrer (se) P – *to throw oneself out of a window*
69 déféquer I, T – *to defecate*
69 déférer à T, Ti – *to submit to, to defer to*
65 déferler I, T – *to break out*
65 déferrer T – *to remove iron*

65 défeuiller T – *to defoliate, to strip*
65 défibrer T – *to disintegrate*
72 déficeler T – *to untie*
76 défier T – *to challenge*
76 défier (se) P – *to challenge oneself*
67 défiger T – *to liquefy, to thaw*
65 défigurer T – *to disfigure*
65 défigurer (se) P – *to disfigure oneself*
65 défiler I, T – *to unthread, to parade*
65 défiler (se) P – *to take cover*
81 définir T – *to define*
81 définir (se) P – *to define oneself*
65 défiscaliser T – *to exempt from taxation*
65 déflagrer I – *to deflagrate*
81 défléchir I, T – *to deflect*
81 défleurir I, T – *to lose blossom*
65 défloquer T – *to remove asbestos from*
65 déflorer T – *to deflower, to spoil*
76 défolier T – *to defoliate*
66 défoncer T – *to stave in, to plough deeply*
66 défoncer (se) P – *to collapse, to get high*
66 déforcer afr. T – *to dishearten*
65 déformer T – *to deform*
65 déformer (se) P – *to become deformed*
65 défouler T – *to let off steam*
65 défouler (se) P – *to let off steam*
65 défourailler I, T – *to draw (one's gun)*
65 défourner T – *to take from oven*
65 défourrer T – *to remove fur*
81 défraîchir/défraichir T – *to lose freshness, to fade*
81 défraîchir/défraichir (se) P – *to fade, to become worn*
65 défranciser T – *to remove the French quality*
77 défrayer T – *to defray, to be the subject of*
65 défricher T – *to clear (land), to reclaim*
65 défringuer T – *to undress*
65 défringuer (se) P – *to undress*
65 défriper T – *to smoothe out*
65 défriser T – *to uncurl, to disappoint*
65 défroisser T – *to smoothe out*
66 défroncer T – *to undo gathering*
65 défroquer I, T – *to renounce one's vows*
65 défroquer (se) P – *to renounce one's vows*
65 défruiter T – *to strip (fruit tree)*
67 dégager I, T – *to release, to disengage, to give off*
67 dégager (se) P – *to free oneself, to back out*
65 dégainer T – *to unsheathe*
65 dégalonner T – *to remove braid*
65 déganter (se) P – *to take off one's gloves*
81 dégarnir T – *to empty, to drain*
81 dégarnir (se) P – *to empty, to lose one's hair*
65 dégasoliner T – *to separate liquid hydrocarbons*
81 dégauchir T – *to rough-plane*
65 dégazer I, T – *to remove gas from a liquid*
65 dégazoliner T – *to extract the hydrocarbons from*
65 dégazonner T – *to remorve turf*
73 dégeler I, T – *to thaw*
73 dégeler (se) P – *to get oneself warmed up*
69 dégénérer I – *to degenerate*
65 dégermer T – *to remove germ*
65 dégingander (se) P – *to be ungainly, to be awkward*
65 dégîter/dégiter T – *to dislodge*
65 dégivrer T – *to defrost*
66 déglacer T – *to thaw*
65 déglinguer T – *to dislocate*
65 déglinguer (se) P – *to become dislocated*
65 dégluer T – *to get rid of glue*
81 déglutir I, T – *to swallow*
65 dégobiller I, T – *to puke*
65 dégoiser I, T – *to spout, to rattle on*
65 dégommer T – *to ungum, to unstick*
65 dégonder T – *to unhinge*
65 dégonfler I, T – *to deflate*
65 dégonfler (se) P – *to go flat, to chicken out*
67 dégorger I, T – *to disgorge*
67 dégorger (se) P – *to become disgorge*
65 dégot(t)er I, T – *to unearth*
65 dégoudronner T – *to remove tar*
65 dégouliner I – *to trickle, to roll down*
65 dégoupiller T – *to unpin (grenade)*
81 dégourdir T – *to remove stiffness, to revive*
81 dégourdir (se) P – *to warm up, to restore the circulation, to liven up, to grow smart*
65 dégourrer T – *to malign, to slander*
65 dégoûter/dégouter T – *to disgust*
65 dégoûter/dégouter (se) P – *to disgust oneself*
65 dégoutter I, T – *to drip*
65 dégrader T – *to degrade, to debase*
65 dégrader (se) P – *to become debased, to become dilapidated*
65 dégrafer T – *to unhook, to unfasten*
65 dégrafer (se) P – *to unhook, to unfasten*
65 dégraisser T – *to skim off fat*
78 dégravoyer T – *to damage, to deteriorate*
74 dégréer T – *to unrig*
69 dégréner I, T – *to shell, to pick off*
68 dégrever T – *to reduce (tax), to diminish*
65 dégringoler I, T – *to tumble down*
65 dégripper T – *to unblock, to unchoke*
65 dégriser T – *to sober up*
65 dégriser (se) P – *to sober up*
65 dégrosser T – *to draw*
81 dégrossir T – *to trim*
81 dégrossir (se) P – *to acquire polish*
65 dégrouiller (se) P – *to hurry, to get a move on*
81 déguerpir I, T – *to bolt*
65 dégueulasser T – *to mess up*
65 dégueuler I, T – *to puke*
65 déguiser T – *to disguise, to dress up*
65 déguiser (se) P – *to disguise, to dress up*
65 dégurgiter T – *to vomit*
65 déguster T – *to taste*
65 déhaler T – *to haul out*
65 déhaler (se) P – *to haul out*
65 déhancher T – *to sway one's hips*
65 déhancher (se) P – *to sway one's hips*
65 déharnacher T – *to unharness*
65 déharnacher (se) P – *to become unharnessed*

T: direct transitive (p. p. variable) – **Ti**: indirect transitive (p. p. invariable) – **I**: intransitive verb (p. p. invariable)
P: pronominal verb (auxiliary *être*) – **impers.**: impersonal verb – **D**: defective verb – *être*: verb conjugated with the auxiliary *être* – *être* or *avoir*: verbs conjugated with *être* or *avoir* (see paragraph 15)

76 déifier T – *to deify*
65 déjanter T – *to take a tire off the rim*
67 déjauger I – *to hydroplane*
70 déjeter T – *to make lopsided, to warp*
70 déjeter (se) P – *to grow lopsided*
65 déjeuner I – *to lunch, to breakfast*
65 déjouer T – *to foil*
67 déjuger (se) P – *to reverse one's judgment*
65 délabialiser T – *to delabialize*
65 délabialiser (se) P – *to become delabialized*
65 délabrer T – *to dilapidate, to wreck*
65 délabrer (se) P – *to fall to pieces*
66 délacer T – *to unlace*
65 délainer T – *to shear (sheep)*
65 délaisser T – *to forsake*
65 délaiter T – *to dry (butter)*
65 délarder T – *to unlard*
65 délasser I, T – *to refresh*
65 délasser (se) P – *to relax*
65 délatter T – *to remove slats*
65 délatter (se) P – *to remove slats*
65 délaver T – *to wash out, to dilute*
77 délayer T – *to thin down, to spin out (story)*
65 déléaturer T – *to delete*
65 délecter T – *to delight*
65 délecter (se) P – *to delight (in), to revel (in)*
69 déléguer T – *to delegate*
65 délester T – *to remove ballast, to relieve*
65 délester (se) P – *to relieve oneself*
69 délibérer de I, Ti – *to deliberate*
76 délier T – *to unbind*
76 délier (se) P – *to release oneself*
65 délimiter T – *to delimit*
74 délinéer T – *to delineate*
65 délirer I – *to rave*
65 délisser I, T – *to remove smoothness*
65 déliter T – *to exfoliate*
65 déliter (se) P – *to exfoliate*
65 délivrer T – *to deliver, to free*
65 délivrer (se) P – *to free oneself*
65 délocaliser T – *to relocate*
65 délocaliser (se) P – *to become relocated*
67 déloger I, T – *to remove, to turn out*
65 déloquer T – *to strip off*
65 délover T – *to uncoil*
65 délurer T – *to smarten up*
65 délustrer T – *to remove sheen*
65 démaçonner T – *to undo brickwork*
65 démagnétiser T – *to demagnetize*
81 démaigrir I, T – *to trim*
65 démailler T – *to undo, to unravel*
65 démailler (se) P – *to come apart, to ladder (stocking)*
65 démailloter T – *to unswaddle*
65 démancher T – *to remove handle*
65 démancher (se) P – *to collapse*
65 demander T – *to ask for, to request*
65 demander (se) P – *to wonder*
67 démanger I, T – *to itch*
73 démanteler T – *to dismantle*
65 démantibuler T – *to demolish*
65 démantibuler (se) P – *to fall apart*
65 démaquiller T – *to remove make-up*
65 démaquiller (se) P – *to remove make-up*
65 démarcher T – *to canvass, to sell door-to-door*
76 démarier T – *to obtain a legal separation*
76 démarier (se) P – *to obtain a legal separation*
65 démarquer T – *to remove identity marks*
65 démarquer (se) P – *to distinguish oneself*
65 démarrer I, T – *to start off*
65 démasquer T – *to unmask*
65 démasquer (se) P – *to take off one's mask*
65 démastiquer T – *to remove putty*
65 démâter I, T – *to dismast*
65 dématérialiser T – *to dematerialize*
65 démazouter T – *to remove the oil from*
65 démédicaliser T – *to demedicalize*
65 démêler T – *to unravel*
65 démêler (se) P – *to disentangle, to extricate onself*
65 démembrer T – *to dismember*
67 déménager T, *avoir* – *to move house, to remove, to go batty*
67 déménager I, *avoir* (or être) – *to move, to clear off*
68 démener (se) P – *to trash (about), to struggle (about)*
86 démentir T – *to deny*
86 démentir (se) P – *to contradict oneself*
65 démerder (se) P – *to get out of a mess, to manage*
65 démériter I – *to forfeit, to act in a blameworthy manner*
122 démettre T – *to dislocate*
122 démettre (se) P – *to resign*
65 démeubler T – *to remove furniture*
65 demeurer (habiter) I, *avoir* – *to live somewhere*
65 demeurer (continuer à être) I, *être* – *to remain*
65 démieller T – *to remove honey*
65 démilitariser T – *to demilitarize*
65 déminer T – *to clear of mines*
65 déminéraliser T – *to demineralize*
65 démissionner de I, Ti – *to resign from*
65 démobiliser I, T – *to demobilize, to discharge*
65 démobiliser (se) P – *to become demobilized*
65 démocratiser T – *to democratize*
65 démocratiser (se) P – *to democratize*
65 démoder T – *to make obsolete*
65 démoder (se) P – *to get out of fashion*
65 démoduler T – *to demodulate*
81 démolir T – *to demolish, to knock down*
65 démonétiser T – *to withdraw (a coin) from circulation, to discredit*
65 démonter T – *to unseat, to dismantle*
65 démonter (se) P – *to come apart, to lose countenance*
65 démontrer T – *to demonstrate*
65 démontrer (se) P – *to demostrate oneself*
65 démoraliser T – *to demoralize, to undermine*
65 démoraliser (se) P – *to lose morale*
118 démordre de Ti – *to let go, to give up*
65 démotiver T – *to demotivate*
65 démotiver (se) P – *to become demotivated*
70 démoucheter T – *to take off the button (from foil)*
65 démouler T – *to unmold*
76 démultiplier T – *to gear down, to reduce*
81 démunir T – *to deprive*
81 démunir (se) P – *to part with, to give up*
65 démurer T – *to remove masonry*

67 démurger I, T – *to go off*
72 démuseler T – *to unmuzzle*
76 démystifier T – *to demystify*
76 démythifier T – *to divest of a mythical quality*
65 dénasaliser T – *to deprive of a nasal sound*
65 dénationaliser T – *to denationalize*
65 dénatter T – *to unplait, to unbraid*
65 dénaturaliser T – *to denaturalize*
65 dénaturer T – *to distort, to denature*
65 dénaturer (se) P – *to distort, to denature*
76 dénazifier T – *to denazify*
65 dénébuler T – *to dispel the fog from*
65 dénébuliser T – *to dispel the fog from*
67 déneiger T – *to remove snow*
65 dénerver T – *to remove nerves*
65 déniaiser T – *to initiate*
65 déniaiser (se) P – *to lose one's innocence*
65 dénicher I, T – *to ferret out, to fly away (birds)*
72 dénickeler T – *to remove nickel-plating*
65 dénicotiniser T – *to extract nicotine*
76 dénier T – *to deny, to disclaim*
65 dénigrer T – *to disparage, to run down*
65 dénitrer T – *to remove nitric acid*
76 dénitrifier T – *to remove nitrogen*
72 déniveler T – *to make uneven*
65 dénombrer T – *to enumerate, to count*
65 dénommer T – *to denominate, to name*
66 dénoncer T – *to denounce, to give away*
66 dénoncer (se) P – *to denounce oneself*
65 dénoter I, T – *to denote, to show, to point*
65 dénouer T – *to untie, to undo, to untangle*
65 dénouer (se) P – *to become untied, to wind up*
65 dénoyauter T – *to stone (fruit)*
78 dénoyer T – *to dry (out), to pump (out)*
76 densifier T – *to make denser*
72 denteler T – *to notch, to jag*
65 dénucléariser T – *to free from nuclear effect*
65 dénuder T – *to strip*
65 dénuder (se) P – *to strip*
65 dénuer (se) P – *to deprive oneself*
65 dépailler T – *to strip rush seat (chair)*
65 dépanner T – *to repair, to give a hand, to help*
70 dépaqueter T – *to unpack*
65 déparasiter T – *to rid of parasites*
65 dépareiller T – *to spoil, to break (pair, collection)*
65 déparer T – *to mar*
76 déparier T – *to remove one (of a pair)*
67 départager T – *to decide between*
65 départementaliser T – *to dive the status of department to*
86 départir T – *to assign, to deal out*
86 départir (se) P – *to depart oneself from*
65 dépasser I, T – *to pass, to go beyond, to overtake*
65 dépasser (se) P – *to excel oneself*
65 dépassionner T – *to remove passion from*
65 dépatouiller (se) P – *to get out of (a difficult situation)*
65 dépaver T – *to unpave*
65 dépayser T – *to remove from usual surroundings*
66, 68 dépecer T – *to cut up, to tear up*
65 dépêcher T – *to despatch, to send*
65 dépêcher (se) P – *to hurry*
65 dépeigner T – *to ruffle hair*
123 dépeindre T – *to depict, to picture, to make out*
65 dépelotonner T – *to unwind*
65 dépénaliser T – *to decriminalize*
118 dépendre de T, Ti – *to depend, to hang on*
65 dépenser T – *to spend (money), to expend*
65 dépenser (se) P – *to exert oneself*
81 dépérir I – *to waste away*
65 dépersonnaliser T – *to depersonalize*
65 dépersonnaliser (se) P – *to depersonalize oneself*
65 dépêtrer T – *to extricate*
65 dépêtrer (se) P – *to extricate*
65 dépeupler T – *to depopulate*
65 dépeupler (se) P – *to depopulate*
65 déphaser T – *to put out of touch*
65 déphosphorer T – *to dephosphorate*
65 dépiauter T – *to skin*
65 dépiler I, T – *to depilate*
65 dépingler T – *to unpin*
65 dépiquer T – *to unstitch*
65 dépister T – *to outwit, to track*
65 dépiter T – *to vex*
65 dépiter (se) P – *to vex oneself*
66 déplacer T – *to move, to displace*
66 déplacer (se) P – *to move about, to travel*
65 déplafonner T – *to lift a restriction*
129 déplaire à Ti – *to displease to*
129 déplaire (se) P – *to be displeased p. p. invariable*
65 déplanter T – *to displant*
65 déplâtrer T – *to strip off plaster*
76 déplier T – *to unfold, to open out*
76 déplier (se) P – *to come unfolded*
65 déplisser T – *to unpleat*
65 déplisser (se) P – *to unpleat*
65 déplomber T – *to unseal*
65 déplorer T – *to deplore*
78 déployer T – *to open out, to spread out, to display*
78 déployer (se) P – *to spread out, to unfurl*
65 déplumer T – *to pluck*
65 déplumer (se) P – *to moult*
65 dépoétiser T – *to deprive of poetic quality*
65 dépolariser T – *to depolarize*
81 dépolir T – *to tarnish*
81 dépolir (se) P – *to tarnish*
65 dépolitiser T – *to depoliticize*
65 dépolitiser (se) P – *to become depoliticized*
65 dépolluer T – *to clean up, to rid of pollution*
65 dépolymériser T – *to depolymerize*
65 déporter T – *to deport, to move aside*
65 déporter (se) P – *to deport, to move aside*
65 déposer I, T – *to put down, to deposit (money), to set down, to depose*
65 déposer (se) P – *to settle*
69 déposséder T – *to dispossess, to deprive*
65 dépoter T – *to unpot*

T: direct transitive (p. p. variable) – **Ti**: indirect transitive (p. p. invariable) – **I**: intransitive verb (p. p. invariable) **P**: pronominal verb (auxiliary *être*) – **impers.**: impersonal verb – **D**: defective verb – *être*: verb conjugated with the auxiliary *être* – *être* or *avoir*: verbs conjugated with *être* or *avoir* (see paragraph 15)

65 dépoudrer T – *to remove powder*
65 dépouiller T – *to scrutinize, to peruse, to strip*
65 dépouiller (se) P – *to shed, to divest*
102 dépourvoir T – *to deprive*
102 dépourvoir (se) P – *to deprive*
69 dépoussiérer T – *to remove dust*
65 dépraver T – *to deprave*
76 déprécier T – *to belittle, to disparage*
76 déprécier (se) P – *to depreciate*
119 déprendre (se) P – *to lose one's fondness for*
65 dépressuriser T – *to depressurize*
65 déprimer I, T – *to depress, to lower*
65 déprimer (se) P – *to become depressed*
65 dépriser T – *to undervalue*
65 déprogrammer T – *to take off the air, to cancel*
65 déprolétariser T – *to deproletarianise*
65 dépropaniser T – *to remove propane*
75 déprotéger T – *to unprotect*
72 dépuceler T – *to deflower*
65 dépulper T – *to reduce to pulp*
65 dépurer T – *to purify*
65 députer T – *to delegate*
76 déqualifier T – *to deskill*
65 déquiller T – *to bowl over*
65 déraciner T – *to uproot*
67 dérager I – *to stop being angry*
81 déraidir T – *to make supple*
81 déraidir (se) P – *to make supple*
65 dérailler I – *to go off the rails*
65 déraisonner I – *to talk nonsense*
67 déranger T – *to disturb*
67 déranger (se) P – *to trouble oneself, to become deranged*
65 déraper I – *to skid*
65 déraser T – *to lower the level of*
65 dératiser T – *to get rid of rats*
77 dérayer I, T – *to unscotch*
65 déréaliser T – *to derealize*
65 déréglementer/dérèglementer T – *to deregulate*
69 dérégler T – *to disturb, to upset*
69 dérégler (se) P – *to become unsettled, to go wrong*
65 déresponsabiliser T – *to take away someone's sense of responsibility*
65 dérider T – *to brighten up*
65 dérider (se) P – *to brighten up*
65 dériver de I, T, Ti – *to divert, to derive*
65 dérober T – *to steal, to conceal*
65 dérober (se) P – *to shy away*
65 dérocher I, T – *to fall from rock*
65 déroder T – *to clear land*
67 déroger à Ti – *to go against, to depart from*
65 dérouiller I, T – *to remove rust, to brush up, to catch*
65 dérouiller (se) P – *to polish up*
65 dérouler T – *to unwind, to unreel*
65 dérouler (se) P – *to take place, to happen*
65 dérouter T – *to divert, to lead astray*
65 dérouter (se) P – *to go astray, to be confused*
65 désabonner T – *to give up subscription*
65 désabonner (se) P – *to give up subscription*
65 désabuser T – *to disillusion*
65 désabuser (se) P – *to lose one's illusions*
65 désacclimater T – *to disacclimatize*
65 désaccorder T – *to put out of tune*
65 désaccorder (se) P – *to go out of tune*
65 désaccoupler T – *to unpair*
65 désaccoutumer T – *to lose the habit (of)*
65 désaccoutumer (se) P – *to lose the habit (of)*
65 désacraliser T – *to remove from a pedestal*
65 désactiver T – *to deactivate*
65 désadapter T – *to unadapt*
65 désadapter (se) P – *to become unadapted*
65 désaffecter T – *to put to another purpose*
65 désaffectionner (se) P – *to lose one's affection, to lose one's fondness*
76 désaffilier T – *to break affiliation (from)*
66 désagencer T – *to disorganize*
65 désagrafer T – *to unfasten, to undo, to unstaple*
75 désagréger T – *to disintegrate, to break (up)*
75 désagréger (se) P – *to disintegrate, to break (up)*
65 désaimanter T – *to demagnetize*
65 désaisonnaliser T – *to make seasonal adjustments to*
65 désajuster T – *to unadjust*
69 désaliéner T – *to unalienate*
65 désalper I – *to bring cattle down from the high mountain pastures*
69 désaltérer T – *to quench thirst*
69 désaltérer (se) P – *to quench thirst*
65 désamarrer T – *to unmoor*
65 désambiguïser T – *to disambiguate*
65 désamianter T – *to remove asbestos from*
65 désamidonner T – *to unstarch*
65 désaminer T – *to deaminate*
66 désamorcer T – *to unprime*
66 désamorcer (se) P – *to unprime*
65 désannexer T – *to disannex*
65 désaper T – *to undress*
65 désaper (se) P – *to get undressed*
76 désapparier T – *to split up*
65 désappointer T – *to disappoint*
119 désapprendre T – *to forget how to*
65 désapprouver I, T – *to disapprove*
65 désapprovisionner T – *to remove stock*
65 désarçonner T – *to unseat, to stagger*
65 désargenter T – *to rub off silver*
65 désargenter (se) P – *to rub or wear the silver off*
65 désarmer I, T – *to disarm*
65 désarmer (se) P – *to become disarmed*
65 désarrimer T – *to shift, to cause to shift*
65 désarticuler T – *to dislocate, to disjoint*
65 désarticuler (se) P – *to dislocate, to disjoint*
65 désassembler T – *to dismantle*
65 désassimiler T – *to disassimilate*
81 désassortir T – *to break up*
67 désavantager T – *to handicap, to harm*
65 désaveugler T – *to disabuse*
65 désavouer T – *to disown*
65 désaxer T – *to unbalance*
65 desceller T – *to break the seal off, to loosen*
65 desceller (se) P – *to break the seal off, to loosen*
118 descendre T, *avoir* – *to go down, to come down, to land, to kill*
118 descendre I, *être* (or *avoir*) – *to be descended from*
65 déséchouer T – *to refloat*
65 désectoriser T – *to remove a region's catchment area, to remove a school district's boundaries*

65 désembobiner T – *to unwind, to uncoil*
65 désembourber T – *to extricate from mud*
65 désembourgeoiser T – *to become less bourgeois*
65 désembourgeoiser (se) P – *to lose some of one's bourgeois habits or attitudes*
65 désembouteiller T – *to unblock*
65 désembuer T – *to demist*
65 désemparer I, T – *to quit, to disable*
68 désempeser T – *to unstarch*
81 désemplir I, T – *to empty*
81 désemplir (se) P – *to empty*
65 désemprisonner T – *to release from prison*
65 désencadrer T – *to remove from frame*
65 désencarter T – *to remove inset*
65 désenchaîner/désenchainer T – *to unfetter*
65 désenchanter T – *to disenchant*
65 désenclaver T – *to remove enclosures*
65 désenclaver (se) P – *to open up*
65 désencombrer T – *to clear out*
65 désencombrer (se) P – *to become cleared up*
65 désencrasser T – *to clean out*
65 désendetter (se) P – *to get oneself out of debt*
65 désénerver T – *to calm down*
65 désénerver (se) P – *to calm oneself down*
65 désenfiler T – *to unthread*
65 désenflammer T – *to reduce inflammation*
65 désenfler I, T – *to become less swollen, to deflate*
65 désenfumer T – *to remove smoke*
67 désengager T – *to disengage*
67 désengager (se) P – *to disengage, to withdraw*
67 désengorger T – *to unblock*
65 désenivrer I, T – *to sober up*
66 désenlacer T – *to unlace*
81 désenlaidir I, T – *to make less ugly*
79 désennuyer I, T – *to relieve boredom*
79 désennuyer (se) P – *to while away the time*
77 désenrayer T – *to release a mechanism*
65 désenrhumer T – *to relieve a cold*
65 désensabler T – *to dredge sand*
65 désensibiliser T – *to insensibilize*
65 désensibiliser (se) P – *to become insensibilized*
72 désensorceler T – *to free from a spell*
65 désentoiler T – *to remove cloth*
65 désentortiller T – *to disentangle*
65 désentraver T – *to unshackle*
65 désenvaser T – *to dredge mud*
65 désenvelopper T – *to unwrap*
65 désenvenimer T – *to cleanse (from poison), to calm*
65 désenverguer – *to remove sail*
65 désenvoûter – *to free from a spell, to release from a spell*
81 désépaissir T – *to thin down*
65 déséquilibrer T – *to unbalance*
65 déséquiper T – *to remove equipment*
65 déséquiper (se) P – *to remove one's equipment*
65 déserter I, T – *to desert*
65 déserter (se) P – *to become deserted, to become abandoned*
69 désespérer I, T – *to drive to despair*
69 désespérer (se) P – *to despair*
81 désétablir T – *to disestablish*
65 désétamer T – *to remove tin-plating*
65 désétatiser T – *to denationalize*
65 désexciter T – *to de-energize*
65 désexciter (se) P – *to become de-energized*
65 désexualiser T – *to desexualize*
65 déshabiller T – *to undress*
65 déshabiller (se) P – *to undress*
65 déshabituer T – *to break a habit*
65 déshabituer (se) P – *to break a habit*
65 désherber T – *to weed*
65 déshériter T – *to disinherit*
65 déshonorer T – *to disgrace, to dishonour*
65 déshonorer (se) P – *to disgrace, to dishonour*
65 déshuiler T – *to remove oil*
65 déshumaniser T – *to dehumanize*
65 déshumaniser (se) P – *to dehumanize*
76 déshumidifier T – *to dehumidify*
65 déshydrater T – *to dehydrate*
65 déshydrater (se) P – *to become dehydrated*
69 déshydrogéner T – *to dehydrogenate*
69 déshypothéquer T – *to free from mortgage*
65 désigner T – *to point out, to fix, to nominate*
65 désillusionner T – *to disillusion*
65 désincarner T – *to disembody*
65 désincarner (se) P – *to become disembodied*
65 désincorporer T – *to disincorporate*
65 désincruster T – *to descale*
65 désinculper T – *to withdraw a charge*
65 désindexer T – *to de-index*
65 désindustrialiser T – *to de-industrialize*
65 désindustrialiser (se) P – *to become de-industrialized*
65 désinfecter T – *to disinfect*
65 désinformer T – *to give false information to*
65 désinhiber T – *to rid one for his (or her) inhibitions*
65 désinsectiser T – *to kill insects*
69 désintégrer T – *to split up*
69 désintégrer (se) P – *to disintegrate*
65 désintéresser T – *to pay off*
65 désintéresser (se) P – *to lose interest*
65 désintoxiquer T – *to detoxicate*
65 désintoxiquer (se) P – *to detoxicate*
81 désinvestir I, T – *to cease to invest*
65 désinviter T – *to cancel an invitation*
65 désirer T – *to want, to wish for, to desire*
65 désister (se) P – *to desist, to stand down*
81 désobéir à I, Ti – *to disobey*
67 désobliger T – *to offend*
65 désobstruer T – *to unblock*
65 désocialiser T – *to turn into a social misfit, to turn into a social outcast*
65 désoccuper T – *to unoccupy*
65 désodoriser T – *to deodorize*
65 désoler T – *to distress*
65 désoler (se) P – *to be upset*
65 désolidariser T – *to divide, to separate*
65 désolidariser (se) P – *to do in different directions*

T: direct transitive (p. p. variable) – **Ti**: indirect transitive (p. p. invariable) – **I**: intransitive verb (p. p. invariable) **P**: pronominal verb (auxiliary *être*) – **impers.**: impersonal verb – **D**: defective verb – *être*: verb conjugated with the auxiliary *être* – *être* or *avoir*: verbs conjugated with *être* or *avoir* (see paragraph 15)

65 désoperculer T – *to remove the operculum from*
65 désopiler (se) P – *to roar (with laughter)*
65 désordonner T – *to throw into disorder*
65 désorganiser T – *to disorganize*
65 désorganiser (se) P – *to become disorganized*
65 désorienter T – *to disorientate, to bewilder*
65 désorienter (se) P – *to become disorientated, to become confused*
65 désosser T – *to bone*
65 désosser (se) P – *to twist oneself in every direction*
65 désoxyder T – *to deoxidize*
69 désoxygéner T – *to deoxygenate*
65 desquamer I, T – *to peel, to scale*
65 dessabler T – *to remove sand*
81 dessaisir T – *to dispossess*
81 dessaisir (se) P – *to give up, to part with*
65 dessaler I, T – *to remove salt*
65 dessaler (se) P – *to learn a thing or two, to learn about life*
65 dessangler T – *to ungirth (horse)*
65 dessangler (se) P – *to become ungirthed, to become unstrapped*
65 dess(a)ouler I, T – *to sober up*
65 dess(a)ouler (se) P – *to sober up*
69 dessécher T – *to dry up*
69 dessécher (se) P – *to dry out, to wither*
65 desseller T – *to unsaddle*
65 desserrer T – *to loosen*
65 desserrer (se) P – *to come loose, to slacken*
81 dessertir T – *to unset*
96 desservir T – *to serve, to clear (table), to go against*
65 dessiller T – *to undeceive*
65 dessiner T – *to draw, to show*
65 dessiner (se) P – *to be outlined*
65 dessoler T – *to change the rotation of crops in*
65 dessouder T – *to unsolder*
65 dessouder (se) P – *to come unsoldered*
65 dessoûler/dessouler I, T – *to sober up*
65 dessoûler/dessouler (se) P – *to sober up*
65 dessuinter T – *to scour*
65 déstabiliser T – *to destabilize*
65 destaliniser – *to destalinize*
65 destiner T – *to intend, to mean*
65 destiner (se) P – *to destine oneself*
65 destituer T – *to discharge*
65 destocker I, T – *to sell off, to destock*
65 destructurer T – *to disorganise*
65 destructurer (se) P – *to disintegrate, to become destructured*
65 désulfiter T – *to remove sulphite*
65 désulfurer T – *to desulphurize*
81 désunir T – *to divide*
81 désunir (se) P – *to divide, to come asunder*
65 désynchroniser T – *to desynchronize*
65 détacher T – *to detach, to unfasten, to undo*
65 détacher (se) P – *to come undone, to break loose*
65 détailler T – *to divide up, to retail, to enumerate*
65 détaler I – *to decamp*
65 détaller T – *to scurry*
65 détapisser T – *to remove tapestry*
65 détartrer T – *to descale*
65 détaxer T – *to take off tax*
65 détecter T – *to detect*
123 déteindre I, T – *to fade, to lose colour*
72 dételer I, T – *to unharness*
118 détendre T – *to slacken*
118 détendre (se) P – *to relax, to expand*
84 détenir T – *to hold*
67 déterger T – *to cleanse*
65 détériorer T – *to damage, to spoil*
65 détériorer (se) P – *to deteriorate, to worsen*
65 déterminer T – *to determine, to establish, to decide*
65 déterminer (se) P – *to determine, to establish, to decide*
65 déterrer T – *to unearth*
65 détester T – *to hate*
65 détirer T – *to stretch (linen)*
65 détirer (se) P – *to stretch (linen)*
65 détisser T – *to unweave*
65 détoner I – *to detonate*
72 détonneler T – *to take from barrel*
65 détonner I – *to be out of tune, to jar*
118 détordre T – *to untwist*
65 détortiller T – *to disentangle*
65 détourer T – *to cut out, to outline*
65 détourner T – *to divert, to hijack (aircraft)*
65 détourner (se) P – *to turn away*
65 détoxiquer T – *to detoxicate, to detoxify*
65 détransposer T – *to detranspose*
65 détraquer T – *to put out of order*
65 détraquer (se) P – *to break down*
65 détremper T – *to soak*
65 détresser T – *to unbraid*
65 détricoter T – *to undo knitting*
65 détromper T – *to disabuse, to undeceive*
65 détromper (se) P – *to be disillusionned*
65 détrôner T – *to dethrone*
65 détroquer T – *to detach*
65 détrousser T – *to rob, to rifle*
152 détruire T – *to destroy, to wreck, to ruin*
152 détruire (se) P – *to destroy, to wreck, to ruin*
65 dévaler I, T – *to rush down*
65 dévaliser T – *to burgle*
65 dévaloriser T – *to depreciate*
65 dévaloriser (se) P – *to fall in value*
65 dévaluer T – *to devalue*
65 dévaluer (se) P – *to devalue*
66 devancer T – *to precede*
65 dévaser T – *to dredge*
65 dévaster T – *to devaste*
65 développer T – *to develop, to extend*
65 développer (se) P – *to develop, to extend*
84 devenir I, *être* – *to become, to grow (into), to turn (into)*
65 déventer T – *to spill sail*
81 déverdir I – *to lose greenness*
65 dévergonder (se) P – *to run wild*
65 déverguer T – *to unbend sail*
81 dévernir T – *to remove varnish*
65 déverrouiller T – *to unbolt*
65 déverser T – *to pour, to flow out*
65 déverser (se) P – *to pour, to flow out*
87 dévêtir T – *to undress*
87 dévêtir (se) P – *to undress*
65 dévider T – *to unwind*
65 dévider (se) P – *to unwind*

76 dévier I, T – *to deviate*
65 deviner T – *to guess*
65 deviner (se) P – *to appear, to be obvious*
65 dévirer I, T – *to turn around*
65 déviriliser T – *to emasculate*
67 dévisager T – *to stare (at)*
65 deviser I – *to converse*
65 dévisser I, T – *to unscrew*
65 dévisser (se) P – *to unscrew*
65 dévitaliser T – *to devitalize, to kill a nerve*
76 dévitrifier T – *to devitrify*
65 dévoiler T – *to unveil, to unmask*
65 dévoiler (se) P – *to unveil, to unmask*
104 devoir T – *to owe, to have to*
104 devoir (se) P – *to have, to must*
65 dévolter T – *to reduce voltage*
65 dévorer I, T – *to devour, to consume, to eat up*
65 dévorer (se) P – *to devour, to consume, to eat up*
65 dévouer T – *to sacrifice*
65 dévouer (se) P – *to sacrifice oneself, to devote oneself*
78 dévoyer T – *to lead astray*
78 dévoyer (se) P – *to go astray*
65 dézinguer T – *to kill*
65 diaboliser T – *to demonize*
65 diagnostiquer T – *to diagnose*
65 dialectiser T – *to dialectalize*
65 dialoguer I, T – *to converse*
65 dialyser T – *to dialyze*
65 diamanter T – *to decorate with diamonds*
65 diaphragmer I, T – *to put a diaphragm on*
65 diaprer T – *to mottle*
65 dicter T – *to dictate, to lay down*
69 diéser T – *to raise a semi tone*
65 diffamer T – *to slander*
76 différencier T – *to differentiate*
76 différencier (se) P – *to differ, to become differentiated*
69 différer I, T – *to differ*
65 difformer T – *to deform*
65 diffracter T – *to diffract*
65 diffuser T – *to diffuse, to spread, to broadcast*
65 diffuser (se) P – *to diffuse, to spread*
69 digérer I, T – *to digest*
69 digérer (se) P – *to digest*
65 digitaliser T – *to digitize*
69 dilacérer T – *to put into pieces*
65 dilapider T – *to dilapidate*
65 dilater T – *to expand, to dilate*
65 dilater (se) P – *to distend*
65 diligenter T – *to launch an immediate inquiry, to carry out an (immediate) assessment*
65 diluer T – *to dilute, to thin down*
65 diluer (se) P – *to dilute, to thin down*
65 dimensionner T – *to proportion*
65 diminuer I, T – *to diminish*
65 diminuer (se) P – *to reduce*
65 dindonner T – *to dupe*
65 dîner/diner I – *to dine*
65 dinguer I – *to fall flat on one's face, to go crashing down*
65 diphtonguer T – *to diphthong*
65 diplômer T – *to award a diploma to*
148 dire T – *to say (to), to tell*
148 dire (se) P – *to say to oneself, to claim*
67 diriger T – *to direct, to control, to steer, to aim*
67 diriger (se) P – *to make for, to head for*
65 discerner T – *to discern*
65 discipliner T – *to discipline*
65 discontinuer T, I, D – *to discontinue*
only in the infinitive
84 disconvenir de I, Ti – *to gainsay*
être or *avoir*
65 discorder I – *to clash*
65 discounter T – *to discount, to sell at a discount*
94 discourir I – *to discourse*
65 discréditer T – *to discredit*
65 discréditer (se) P – *to become discredited, to fall into disrepute*
65 discriminer T – *to discriminate*
65 disculper T – *to exonerate (from)*
65 disculper (se) P – *to exonerate (from)*
65 discutailler I, T – *to quibble*
65 discuter I, T – *to discuss, to confer with, to debate about*
65 discuter (se) P – *to discuss, to confer with, to debate about*
76 disgracier T – *to disgrace*
124 disjoindre T – *to take apart*
124 disjoindre (se) P – *to come apart, to separate*
65 disjoncter I, T – *to break circuit*
65 disloquer T – *to dislocate, to dismantle*
65 disloquer (se) P – *to dislocate, to dismantle*
130 disparaître/disparaitre I – *to disappear*
avoir *(or* être*)*
65 dispatcher T – *to dispatch*
65 dispenser T – *to dispense, to exempt (from)*
65 dispenser (se) P – *to get out of, to refrain from*
65 disperser T – *to scatter, to disperse*
65 disperser (se) P – *to scatter, to disperse*
65 disposer de T, Ti – *to have at one's disposal*
65 disposer (se) P – *to prepare to do, to be about to do*
65 disproportionner T – *to make disproportionate*
65 disputailler I – *to argue pointlessly*
65 disputer T, Ti – *to fight (for), to dispute*
65 disputer (se) P – *to fight (over), to contest*
76 disqualifier T – *to disqualify*
76 disqualifier (se) P – *to be disqualified*
65 disséminer T – *to scatter*
65 disséminer (se) P – *to scatter*
69 disséquer T – *to dissect*
65 disserter I – *to hold forth*
65 dissimuler T – *to conceal, to hide*
65 dissimuler (se) P – *to conceal, to hide*
65 dissiper T – *to dissipate, to disperse*
65 dissiper (se) P – *to drift away, to become unruly*
76 dissocier T – *to dissociate*
76 dissocier (se) P – *to break up, to split up*

T: direct transitive (p. p. variable) – **Ti**: indirect transitive (p. p. invariable) – **I**: intransitive verb (p. p. invariable) **P**: pronominal verb (auxiliary *être*) – **impers.**: impersonal verb – **D**: defective verb – *être*: verb conjugated with the auxiliary *être* – *être* or *avoir*: verbs conjugated with *être* or *avoir* (see paragraph 15)

65 dissoner I – *to be dissonant*
141 dissoudre T – *to dissolve*
141 dissoudre (se) P – *to dissolve, to disband*
65 dissuader T – *to dissuade*
66 distancer T – *to outdistance*
66 distancer (se) P – *to become outdistanced*
76 distancier T – *to distance*
76 distancier (se) P – *to distance oneself from*
118 distendre T – *to distend, to stretch*
118 distendre (se) P – *to distend, to stretch*
65 distiller I, T – *to distil*
65 distinguer I, T – *to distinguish, to set apart, to single out*
65 distinguer (se) P – *to distinguish oneself*
118 distordre T – *to twist*
118 distordre (se) P – *to become twisted, to become distorted*
127 distraire I, T, D – *to entertain, to divert*
127 distraire (se) P, D – *to enjoy oneself*
65 distribuer T – *to distribute*
65 distribuer (se) P – *to be distributed*
65 divaguer I – *to ramble*
67 diverger I – *to diverge*
76 diversifier T – *to diversify*
76 diversifier (se) P – *to be diversified, to become more diverse*
81 divertir T – *to amuse, to divert*
81 divertir (se) P – *to enjoy oneself*
65 diviniser T – *to deify*
65 diviser T – *to divide, to share out, to set against*
65 diviser (se) P – *to split up*
66 divorcer I – *to divorce*
65 divulguer T – *to divulge, to disclose*
65 divulguer (se) P – *to divulge, to disclose*
65 documenter T – *to document*
65 documenter (se) P – *to gather information, to gather material*
65 dodeliner I – *to nod (head)*
65 dogmatiser I – *to dogmatize*
65 doigter I, T – *to finger*
65 doler T – *to plane*
65 domestiquer T – *to domesticate, to tame*
76 domicilier T – *to pay by banker's order*
65 dominer I, T – *to dominate, to surpass*
65 dominer (se) P – *to control oneself*
65 dompter T – *to tame*
65 donner I, T – *to give, to grant, to yield, to look out (on)*
65 donner (se) P – *to give oneself, to devote oneself*
65 doper T – *to dope*
65 doper (se) P – *to dope*
65 dorer T – *to gild*
65 dorer (se) P – *to get brown*
65 dorloter T – *to pamper, to mollycoddle*
65 dorloter (se) P – *to pamper, to mollycoddle*
93 dormir I – *to sleep, to be dormant*
65 doser T – *to measure out a dose*
65 doter T – *to provide with a doury*
65 doter (se) P – *to endow oneself*
65 double(-)cliquer I, T – *to double-click*
65 doubler I, T – *to double, to repeat, to understudy (actor), to overtake (car), to dub (film)*
65 doubler (se) P – *to be coupled with*
65 doublonner I – *to duplicate*
65 doucher T – *to shower*
65 doucher (se) P – *to take a shower*
81 doucir T – *to polish a metal*
65 douer T – *to endow with, to bless with especially in the infinitive, the p. p. and the compound tenses*
65 douiller I – *to pay through the nose*
65 douter de I, Ti – *to doubt*
65 douter (se) P – *to suspect*
76 dragéifier T – *to coat with sugar*
65 drageonner I – *to produce suckers*
65 draguer I, T – *to dredge, to search for a partner*
65 drainer T – *to drain*
65 dramatiser I, T – *to dramatize*
65 draper T – *to drape*
65 draper (se) P – *to drape oneself*
65 draver québ. I, T – *to drive, to raft*
65 dresser T – *to draw up, to put up, to erect, to break in (animal)*
65 dresser (se) P – *to stand upright*
65 dribbler I, T – *to dribble*
65 driller T – *to drill*
65 driver I, T – *to drive (golf)*
65 droguer I, T – *to drug*
65 droguer (se) P – *to take drugs*
65 droper I, T – *to drop*
65 drosser T – *to drive, to drift (ship)*
76 dulcifier T – *to sweeten*
65 duper T – *to dupe, to deceive*
65 duper (se) P – *to dupe, to deceive*
65 duplexer T – *to establish a two-way link*
65 dupliquer T – *to duplicate*
81 durcir I, T – *to harden*
81 durcir (se) P – *to harden*
65 durer I – *to last*
70 duveter (se) P – *to become downy*
65 dynamiser T – *to give spirit to, to make dynamic*
65 dynamiter T – *to dynamite*

e

81 ébahir T – *to flabbergast, to astound*
81 ébahir (s') P – *to be dumbfounded, to be astonished*
65 ébarber T – *to trim*
121 ébattre (s') P – *to frolic*
81 ébaubir (s') P – *to gawp (at)*
65 ébaucher T – *to sketch out*
65 ébaucher (s') P – *to take shape*
81 ébaudir T – *to rejoice*
81 ébaudir (s') P – *to rejoice oneself*
65 ébavurer T – *to burr*
65 éberluer T – *to flabbergast*
72 ébiseler T – *to chamfer (carpentry)*
81 éblouir I, T – *to dazzle*
65 éborgner T – *to poke out an eye, to blind*
65 éborgner (s') P – *to blind oneself*
65 ébosser T – *to seed*
65 ébouer T – *to clean out*
65 ébouillanter T – *to scald, to blanch*
65 ébouillanter (s') P – *to scald*

65 ébouler I, T – *to crumble, to collapse*
65 ébouler (s') P – *to crumble*
65 ébourgeonner T – *to remove buds*
65 ébouriffer T – *to ruffle*
65 ébourrer T – *to remove stuffing*
65 ébouter T – *to cut off*
65 ébouzer T – *to bump*
65 ébraiser T – *to rake out embers*
65 ébrancher T – *to prune*
65 ébranler T – *to shake, to rattle*
65 ébranler (s') P – *to move off (vehicule)*
65 ébraser T – *to splay*
69 ébrécher T – *to chip*
69 ébrécher (s') P – *to chip*
65 ébrouer (s') P – *to snort*
65 ébruiter T – *to disclose, to leak (information)*
65 ébruiter (s') P – *to leak*
65 ébruter T – *to brute*
65 écacher T – *to crush*
65 écailler T – *to scale (fish)*
65 écailler (s') P – *to flake off, to peel off*
65 écaler T – *to shell*
65 écaler (s') P – *to shell*
65 écanguer T – *to scutch, to swingle (flax, hemp)*
65 écarquiller T – *to open wide*
73 écarteler T – *to quarter*
65 écarter I, T – *to move apart, to set aside, to ward off*
65 écarter (s') P – *to move away, to draw aside*
65 échafauder I, T – *to erect scaffolding, to build up, to compile*
65 échalasser T – *to stake (vines)*
81 échampir T – *to pick out, to set off*
65 échancrer T – *to Indent, to scallop*
67 échanger T – *to exchange, to swap*
67 échanger (s') P – *to swap, to trade*
65 échantillonner T – *to sample*
65 échapper à, de I, T, Ti, *avoir* – *to let out, to slip out*
65 échapper (dit ou fait par mégarde) à Ti, *avoir* (or *être*) – *to slip, to let slip*
65 échapper (s') P, *être* – *to escape*
65 échardonner T – *to clear of thistles, to pick*
65 écharner T – *to flesh*
65 écharper T – *to tear to pieces*
65 écharper (s') P – *to tear to piece*
65 échauder T – *to scald*
65 échauder (s') P – *to scald oneself*
65 échauffer T – *to make hot, to excite*
65 échauffer (s') P – *to warm up*
65 échauler T – *to whitewash*
65 échaumer T – *to pull out wheat roots*
65 échelonner T – *to space out*
65 échelonner (s') P – *to space out*
65 écheniller T – *to clear out the caterpillars*
72 écheveler T – *to dishevel*
65 échiner T – *to break the back of*
65 échiner (s') P – *to work oneself into the ground*
116 échoir I, D, *être* (or *avoir*) – *to fall due*
65 échopper T – *to gouge*
65 échouer I, T – *to fail, to go aground (boat)*
65 échouer (s') P – *to run aground*
65 écimer T – *to prune a tree*
65 éclabousser T – *to splash, to spatter*
65 éclabousser (s') P – *to splash each other*
81 éclaircir T – *to make lighter, to clear up*
81 éclaircir (s') P – *to brighten up, to clear up*
65 éclairer I, T – *to light up*
65 éclairer (s') P – *to be lit, to be brighter*
65 éclater I, T – *to explode, to burst*
65 éclater (s') P – *to have a ball*
65 éclipser T – *to eclipse*
65 éclipser (s') P – *to slip away*
65 éclisser T – *to put in splints*
65 écloper T – *to lame*
138 éclore I, *avoir* (or *être*)– *to hatch, to blossom, to open out*
65 écluser T – *to knock back (drink), to go through a lock*
65 écobuer T – *to burn weeds, to remove sods*
65 écœurer I, T – *to make sick, to disgust*
65 écœurer (s') québ. P – *to taunt each other*
152 éconduire T – *to dismiss*
65 économiser I, T – *to save up, to husband*
65 écoper I, T – *to be reprimanded, to bail out (water)*
66 écorcer T – *to peel*
65 écorcher T – *to flay, to graze, to grate*
65 écorcher (s') P – *to scrape oneself*
65 écorer T – *to keep tally-sheets, to keep score*
65 écorner T – *to chip the corner (of), to curtail*
65 écornifler T – *to scrounge*
65 écosser T – *to shell*
65 écouler T – *to flow out, to sell*
65 écouler (s') P – *to ooze, to seep, to run (time)*
65 écourter T – *to shorten*
65 écouter I, T – *to listen to*
65 écouter (s') P – *to coddle oneself*
65 écouvillonner T – *to mop out*
65 écrabouiller T – *to squash*
65 écraser I, T – *to crush, to run over (car)*
65 écraser (s') P – *to collapse, to crumble, to keep quiet*
69 écrémer T – *to skim milk*
65 écrêter T – *to decrest*
76 écrier (s') P – *to exclaim, to cry out*
150 écrire à I, T, Ti – *to write*
150 écrire (s') P – *to write to each other, to be written*
65 écrivailler I – *to scribble*
65 écrivasser T – *to scribble*
65 écrouer T – *to imprison, to commit to*
81 écrouir T – *to hammer-harden*
65 écrouler (s') P – *to collapse, to fall down, to flop*
65 écroûter/écrouter T – *to remove crust*
65 écuisser T – *to splinter, to cleave (trees)*
65 éculer T – *to wear out the heel of shoes*
65 écumer I, T – *to skim, to scum, to froth*
65 écurer T – *to scour*
65 écussonner T – *to decorate with a shield or badge*
65 édenter T – *to break the teeth of*
65 édicter T – *to decree*
76 édifier I, T – *to build, to enlighten*

T: direct transitive (p. p. variable) – **Ti**: indirect transitive (p. p. invariable) – **I**: intransitive verb (p. p. invariable) **P**: pronominal verb (auxiliary *être*) – **impers.**: impersonal verb – **D**: defective verb – *être*: verb conjugated with the auxiliary *être* – *être* or *avoir*: verbs conjugated with *être* or *avoir* (see paragraph 15)

65 éditer T – *to publish, to edit*
65 éditionner T – *to do a special edition*
65 édulcorer T – *to sweeten, to water down*
65 éduquer T – *to educate*
65 éfaufiler T – *to unthread*
66 effacer I, T – *to efface, to erase, to outshine*
66 effacer (s') P – *to fade away, to stand aside*
65 effaner T – *to thin out or cut off leaves*
65 effarer T – *to frighten, to alarm*
65 effarer (s') P – *to be frightened, to be alarmed*
65 effaroucher T – *to frighten away*
65 effaroucher (s') P – *to be scared, to take offense*
65 effectuer T – *to carry out, to affect*
65 effectuer (s') P – *to accomplish, to be done*
65 efféminer T – *to effeminize*
65 effeuiller T – *to thin out (leaves)*
65 effeuiller (s') P – *to shed (leaves, petals)*
65 effiler T – *to taper, to sharpen, to streamline*
65 effiler (s') P – *to fray out*
65 effilocher T – *to fray*
65 effilocher (s') P – *to fray*
65 efflanquer T – *to emaciate*
65 efflanquer (s') P – *to emaciate*
65 effleurer T – *to touch lightly, to brush*
81 effleurir I – *to effloresce*
65 effluver I – *to discharge*
65 effondrer T – *to plough up*
65 effondrer (s') P – *to cave in, to fall through*
66 efforcer (s') P – *to try hard, to do one's best*
67 effranger T – *to fringe*
67 effranger (s') P – *to fray*
77 effrayer T – *to scare, to frighten*
77 effrayer (s') P – *to be frightened*
65 effriter T – *to crumble away*
65 effriter (s') P – *to crumble away*
65 égailler (s') P – *to scatter*
65 égaler T – *to equal*
65 égaliser I, T – *equalize*
65 égarer T – *to mislead, to mislay*
65 égarer (s') P – *to get lost, to go astray*
77 égayer T – *to enliven, to cheer up*
77 égayer (s') P – *to make merry*
65 égnaffer T – *to astound (slang)*
67 égorger T – *to slit the throat (of)*
67 égorger (s') P – *to kill each other*
65 égosiller (s') P – *to shout oneself hoarse*
65 égoutter I, T – *to drain, to drip*
65 égoutter (s') P – *to drain, to drip*
65 égrainer T – *to shell*
65 égrainer (s') P – *to drop away*
65 égrapper T – *to pick off (grapes)*
65 égratigner T – *to scratch*
65 égratigner (s') P – *to scratch oneself*
68 égrener T – *to shell, to pod*
68 égrener (s') P – *to shell, to fall from the stalk, to pass (hour)*
65 égriser T – *to grind*
67 égruger T – *to crush*
65 égueuler T – *to break/deform the neck of (pot, bottle, gun)*
65 éjaculer T – *to ejaculate*
65 éjarrer T – *to remove the unwanted parts*
65 éjecter T – *to eject*
65 éjecter (s') P – *to eject oneself*
65 éjointer T – *to clip (wings)*
65 élaborer T – *to develop, to design*
65 élaborer (s') P – *to develop*
65 élaguer T – *to prune*
66 élancer I, T – *to suffer from shooting pains*
66 élancer (s') P – *to dash forward*
81 élargir I, T – *to widen, to stretch*
81 élargir (s') P – *to widen or broaden out*
76 électrifier T – *to electrify*
65 électriser T – *to thrill, to rouse*
65 électrocuter T – *to electrocute*
65 électrocuter (s') P – *to electrocute oneself*
65 électrolyser T – *to electrolyze*
65 électroniser T – *to electronify*
81 élégir T – *to fine down*
68 élever T – *to bring up (child), to rear (animal), to elevate, to raise*
68 élever (s') P – *to rise, to go up*
65 élider T – *to elide*
65 élider (s') P – *to be dropped, to disappear*
65 élimer T – *to wear thin*
65 éliminer I, T – *to eliminate*
65 éliminer (s') P – *to eliminate oneself or each other*
65 élinguer T – *to sling*
147 élire T – *to elect*
65 éloigner T – *to move away, to take away*
65 éloigner (s') P – *to go away, to withdraw*
67 élonger T – *to lengthen, to stretch*
65 élucider T – *to elucidate, to clear*
65 élucubrer T – *to expatiate*
65 éluder T – *to elude, to dodge*
65 éluer T – *to elute*
76 émacier T – *to emaciate*
76 émacier (s') P – *to waste away*
65 émailler T – *to enamel*
65 émanciper T – *to emancipate*
65 émanciper (s') P – *to become emancipated*
65 émaner I – *to emanate*
67 émarger I, T – *to draw out (salary)*
65 émasculer T – *to emasculate*
65 emballer T – *to wrap up*
65 emballer (s') P – *to bolt (horse), to be carried away*
65 emballotter T – *to bale*
65 emballuchonner T – *to bundle (belongings)*
65 embarbouiller T – *to trouble the mind*
65 embarbouiller (s') P – *to get oneself mixed up*
65 embarder T – *to sheer*
65 embarder (s') P – *to sheer*
65 embarquer I, T – *to embark, to board*
65 embarquer (s') P – *to get involved in, to ship off*
65 embarrasser T – *to embarass, to encumber, to hamper, to inconvenience*
65 embarrasser (s') P – *to become confused, to be muddled*
65 embarrer I, T – *to lever, to block (a wheel, mechanism)*
65 embarrer (s') P – *to lock oneself in or out*
65 embastiller T – *to imprison*
65 embastionner T – *to fortify with bastions*
121 embat(t)re T – *to encircle, to ring*
65 embaucher I, T – *to hire (staff)*
65 embaucher (s') P – *to get oneself a job*

65 embaumer I, T – *to embalm, to be fragrant*
65 embecquer T – *to force-feed, to cram*
65 embéguiner (s') P – *to be infatuated*
81 embellir I, T – *to embellish, to beautify*
81 embellir (s') P – *to improve, to grow more beautiful*
65 emberlificoter T – *to bamboozle*
65 emberlificoter (s') P – *to get tangled up*
65 embêter T – *to bother, to worry, to pester*
65 embêter (s') P – *to be bored, to be fed up (with)*
65 embidonner T – *to can, to embazzle (slang)*
65 embistrouiller T – *to bug someone*
65 emblaver T – *to sow, to seed*
65 embobeliner T – *to deceive, to trick*
65 embobiner T – *to hoodwink*
137 emboire (s') P – *to coat oneself*
65 emboîter/emboiter T – *to fit together, to fit into each other*
65 emboîter/emboiter (s') P – *to fit together, to fit into each other*
65 embosser T – *to moor fore and aft (boat), to emboss (print)*
65 embosser (s') P – *to moor fore and aft (boat)*
72 embotteler T – *to truss*
65 emboucaner I – *to be a nuisance, to "stink out"*
65 emboucher T – *to raise to one's lips, to trumpet*
65 embouer I, T – *to bespatter*
65 embouquer I, T – *to enter a strait, or a narrow passage (navigation)*
65 embourber T – *to get stuck in the mud*
65 embourber (s') P – *to get stuck in the mud*
65 embourgeoiser T – *to become middle-class*
65 embourgeoiser (s') P – *to become middle-class*
65 embourrer T – *to stuff*
65 embourrer (s') P – *to stuff (oneself), to wrap oneself in warm clothes*
65 embouteiller T – *to jam, to bottle*
65 embouter T – *to furnish with a tip*
81 emboutir T – *to collide (cars), to ram*
65 embrancher T – *to join up, to connect*
65 embrancher (s') P – *to join up*
65 embraquer T – *to pull a rope (navigation)*
65 embraser T – *to set ablaze, to kindle*
65 embraser (s') P – *to blaze up, to flame up*
65 embrasser T – *to kiss, to embrace*
65 embrasser (s') P – *to kiss, to embrace (one another)*
77 embrayer I, T – *to put into gear*
73 embreler T – *to lash down*
68 embrever T – *to join two pieces of wood*
65 embrigader T – *to recruit*
65 embrigader (s') P – *to enrol (in)*
65 embringuer T – *to involve*
65 embringuer (s') P – *to get involved (in)*
65 embrocher T – *to put on a spit*
65 embroncher T – *to lay down (tiles, shingles, ...)*
65 embrouiller T – *to tangle, to snarl up*
65 embrouiller (s') P – *to become muddled*
65 embroussailler T – *to tousle*
65 embroussailler (s') P – *to be covered with weed*
65 embrumer T – *to cover with mist, to darken*
81 embrunir T – *to darken, to make brown*
65 embuer T – *to mist (over or up)*
65 embuer (s') P – *to mist over*
65 embusquer T – *to ambush*
65 embusquer (s') P – *to lie in ambush, to shirk duty*
69 émécher T – *to make tipsy*
67 émerger I – *to emerge*
65 émerillonner T – *to brighten up*
65 émeriser T – *to coat with emery*
65 émerveiller T – *to fill with wonder*
65 émerveiller (s') P – *to marvel*
122 émettre I, T – *to emit, to put forward, to transmit*
76 émier T – *to reduce to crumbs*
65 émietter T – *to crumble, to break up*
65 émietter (s') P – *to crumble, to break up*
65 émigrer I – *to emigrate*
66 émincer T – *to slice thinly*
65 emmagasiner T – *to store up*
65 emmailloter T – *to swaddle, to wrap up*
65 emmailloter (s') P – *to wrap oneself up*
65 emmancher T – *to fix a handle on*
65 emmancher (s') P – *to get going*
67 emmarger T – *to put in the margin*
65 emmêler T – *to tangle, to mix up*
65 emmêler (s') P – *to get into a muddle*
67 emménager I, T – *to move in*
68 emmener T – *to take away, to lead away*
65 emmerder T – *to be a pain in the neck, to bug*
65 emmerder (s') P – *to be bored stiff*
69 emmétrer T – *to arrange for easy mesuring*
65 emmieller T – *to aggravate*
65 emmitonner T – *to put on mittens, to circumvent (figurative)*
65 emmitoufler T – *to muffle up*
65 emmitoufler (s') P – *to muffle oneself up*
65 emmortaiser T – *to insert in a mortise*
65 emmouscailler T – *to annoy*
65 emmurer T – *to immure*
65 émonder T – *to trim*
65 émorfiler T – *to take the roughness off (metal)*
65 émotionner T – *to agitate, to upset*
65 émotter T – *to break clumps of earth (agriculture)*
65 émoucher T – *to chase flies away*
71 émoucheter T – *to break off point*
144 émoudre T – *to grind, to sharpen*
65 émousser T – *to blunt*
65 émousser (s') P – *to become blunt*
65 émoustiller T – *to rouse*
106 émouvoir I, T – *to move, to affect, to disturb*
106 émouvoir (s') P – *to be moved*
65 empaffer T – *to sodomize (slang), to get drunk*
65 empailler T – *to stuff*
65 empaler T – *to impale*
65 empaler (s') P – *to impale*
65 empalmer T – *to palm*
65 empanacher T – *to decorate with plumes*
65 empanner I – *to change direction (nautical)*
65 empapa(h)outer T – *to bugger*
65 empapilloter T – *to wrap (for cooking)*

T: direct transitive (p. p. variable) – **Ti**: indirect transitive (p. p. invariable) – **I**: intransitive verb (p. p. invariable)
P: pronominal verb (auxiliary *être*) – **impers.**: impersonal verb – **D**: defective verb – *être*: verb conjugated with the auxiliary *être* – *être* or *avoir*: verbs conjugated with *être* or *avoir* (see paragraph 15)

70 empaqueter T – *to pack, to wrap (up)*
65 emparer (s') P – *to grab, to seize*
65 emparquer T – *to fold (sheep)*
65 empâter T – *to paste (over), to coat*
65 empâter (s') P – *to thicken out*
65 empatter T – *to support*
65 empaumer T – *to catch, to get the better (of)*
65 empêcher T – *to prevent*
65 empêcher (s') P – *to stop (from), to refrain (from)*
65 empeigner T – *to warp (loom)*
65 empêner I, T – *to enhance a lock*
65 empenner T – *to feather, to fill empennage*
65 empercher T – *to stick antlers in the ground*
65 emperler T – *to decorate with pearls, to form into pearls*
68 empeser T – *to starch, to give stiffness (to)*
65 empester I, T – *to stink, to reek*
65 empêtrer T – *to get tangled up*
65 empêtrer (s') P – *to get tangled up*
75 empiéger T – *to trap*
65 empierrer T – *to pave with stone*
69 empiéter I – *to encroach on, to overlap with*
65 empiffrer (s') P – *to stuff one's face (with)*
65 empiler T – *to pile up, to stack up*
65 empiler (s') P – *to be piled up, to be stacked up*
65 empirer I, T – *to deteriorate, to grow worse used especially in the 3rd person*
65 empirer (s') afr. P – *to worsen*
65 emplafonner T – *to hit violently*
65 emplafonner (s') P – *to hit violently*
65 emplâtrer T – *to paster, to burden (with)*
81 emplir I, T – *to fill up with*
81 emplir (s') P – *to be filled up with*
78 employer T – *to make use of, to use, to employ*
78 employer (s') P – *to devote onself, to apply oneself*
65 emplumer T – *to feather*
65 empocher T – *to pocket*
65 empoigner T – *to grasp*
65 empoigner (s') P – *to brave, to have a go at one another*
65 empoisonner T – *to poison, to drive someone up the wall*
65 empoisonner (s') P – *to poison oneself*
65 empoisser T – *to cover with something gooey, to cover with peas*
65 empoissonner T – *to stock with fish*
65 emporter T – *to take away, to carry along*
65 emporter (s') P – *to lose one's temper*
65 empoter T – *to pot*
65 empourprer T – *to turn crimson*
65 empourprer (s') P – *to flush*
69 empoussiérer T – *to cover with dust*
69 empoussiérer (s') P – *to get dusty*
123 empreindre T – *to imprint, to stamp*
123 empreindre (s') P – *to show a mark or sign*
65 empresser (s') P – *to bustle about, to hasten*
65 emprésurer T – *to add rennet (to)*
65 emprisonner T – *to imprison*
65 emprunter I, T – *to borrow, to derive, to assume*
81 empuantir T – *to stink out*
65 émuler T – *to emulate*
76 émulsifier T – *to emulsify*
65 émulsionner T – *to emulsion*
65 enamourer (s') P – *to become enamored*
65 énamourer (s') P – *to become enamored*
65 encabaner T – *to put in prison*
65 encadrer T – *to frame, to supervise*
65 encadrer (s') P – *to be in a framelike structure, to appear*
67 encager T – *to cage*
65 encagouler T – *to put a hood on someone*
65 encaisser T – *to collect (money), to take (blow), to stand*
65 encanailler T – *to become vulgar*
65 encanailler (s') P – *to get into low habits*
65 encaper T – *to be between two courses (nautical)*
65 encapuchonner T – *to put on a hood*
65 encapuchonner (s') P – *to put on a hood*
65 encapsuler T – *to encapsulate*
65 encaquer T – *to put in a barrel (fish), to cram or pack (people)*
65 encarrer I – *to enter*
65 encarter T – *to insert*
65 encartonner T – *to put in a box*
65 encartoucher T – *to put gunpowder in a cartridge*
65 encaserner T – *to quarter in barracks*
73 encasteler (s') P – *to be lame (horse)*
65 encastrer T – *to embed*
65 encastrer (s') P – *to be embedded*
65 encaustiquer T – *to polish*
65 encaver T – *to cellar*
123 enceindre T – *to gird*
65 enceinter afr. T – *to get someone pregnant*
65 encenser I, T – *to incense, to flatter*
65 encercler T – *to encircle*
65 enchaîner/enchainer I, T – *to chain up, to enslave, to bind*
65 enchaîner/enchainer (s') P – *to follow on, to be linked*
65 enchanter T – *to enchant, to bewitch, to delight*
65 enchanter (s') P – *to be delighted, enchanted*
65 enchaperonner T – *to hood a falcon*
65 encharner T – *to hinge*
65 enchâsser T – *to enshrine, to set, to mount*
65 enchâsser (s') P – *to be enshrined, to be set, to be mounted*
65 enchatonner T – *to set (a stone)*
65 enchausser T – *to earth up*
65 enchemiser T – *to put a dust-cover*
81 enchérir I – *to raise, to outbid, to surpass*
65 enchevaucher T – *to overlap, to join by overlapping*
65 enchevêtrer T – *to tangle*
65 enchevêtrer (s') P – *to get entangled*
68 enchifrener T – *to have a cold*
65 enchtiber T – *to imprison (slang)*
65 enchtourber T – *to imprison (slang)*
65 encirer T – *to wax*
65 enclaver T – *to hem in*
65 enclaver (s') P – *to be hemmed in*
65 enclencher T – *to engage, to set in motion*
65 enclencher (s') P – *to engage, to set in motion*
70 encliqueter T – *to cog*
65 encloîtrer/encloitrer T – *to cloister*
65 encloquer T – *to impregnate (slang)*
138 enclore T – *to fence in*
65 enclouer T – *to prick*
65 encocher T – *to notch, to insert*

65 encoder T – *to code (in)*
65 encoffrer T – *to lock up*
65 encoller T – *to paste*
65 encombrer T – *to clutter up, to congest*
65 encombrer (s') P – *to be loaded, to be weighed down*
65 encorder T – *to rope up*
65 encorder (s') P – *to rope up*
65 encorner T – *to gore*
67 encourager T – *to encourage, to foster*
94 encourir T – *to incur*
65 encrasser T – *to foul up, to clog up*
65 encrasser (s') P – *to become fouled up, to become clogged up*
65 encrêper T – *to trim with crape*
65 encrer I, T – *to ink*
65 encrister T – *to imprison (slang)*
65 encroumer (s') P – *to put in jail*
65 encroûter/encrouter T – *to encrust*
65 encroûter/encrouter (s') P – *to get into a rut, to stagnate*
65 encuver T – *to put in a vat*
65 endauber T – *to stew (meat)*
65 endenter T – *to join (with teeth)*
65 endetter T – *to get into debt*
65 endetter (s') P – *to get into debt*
65 endeuiller T – *to plunge into grief*
65 endêver I, D – *to enrage*
mainly in the infinitive
65 endiabler I, T – *to infuriate*
65 endiguer T – *to dam, to hold back*
65 endimancher T – *to put on one's Sunday best*
65 endimancher (s') P – *to put on one's Sunday best*
65 endivisionner T – *to form in divisions*
65 endoctriner T – *to indoctrinate*
81 endolorir T – *to make ache*
67 endommager T – *to damage, to injure*
93 endormir T – *to send to sleep, to lull to sleep, to deaden, to dull, to bore stiff*
93 endormir (s') P – *to go to sleep, to slack off*
65 endosser T – *to put on, to shoulder, to endorse*
152 enduire I, T – *to coat*
152 enduire (s') P – *to coat (oneself)*
81 endurcir T – *to toughen*
81 endurcir (s') P – *to become hardened*
65 endurer T – *to endure, to bear*
65 énerver T – *to irritate, to enervate*
65 énerver (s') P – *to get excited, to get worked up*
65 enfaîter/enfaiter T – *to roof*
65 enfanter I, T – *to give birth to, to bring forth*
67 enfarger québ. T – *to trip someone*
67 enfarger (s') québ. I, T – *to trip, to stumble*
65 enfermer T – *to shut up, to imprison, to lock up*
65 enfermer (s') P – *to shut up, to imprison, to lock up*
65 enferrer T – *to mislead*
65 enferrer (s') P – *to tie oneself up in a knot*
65 enficher T – *to plug-in*
65 enfieller T – *to embitter*
69 enfiévrer T – *to give fever, to rouse*
69 enfiévrer (s') P – *to get excited*
65 enfiler T – *to thread, to pull on, to put on, to slip into something*
65 enfiler (s') P – *to down something (food), to go into*
65 enflammer T – *to ignite, to inflame, to blaze*
65 enflammer (s') P – *to ignite, to inflame, to blaze*
69 enflécher T – *to rattle down or to climb up a mast (nautical)*
65 enfler I, T – *to swell, to cause to swell*
65 enfler (s') P – *to swell, to cause to swell*
65 enfleurer T – *to scent (flower)*
65 enfoirer T – *to screw up*
65 enfoirer (s') P – *to screw oneself up*
66 enfoncer I, T – *to drive in, to push in*
66 enfoncer (s') P – *to plunge, to sink into, to penetrate*
81 enforcir I – *to reinforce*
65 enfouiller T – *to bury*
81 enfouir T – *to bury, to conceal*
81 enfouir (s') P – *to retire*
65 enfourailler T – *to arm or to imprison*
65 enfourcher T – *to mount*
65 enfourner T – *to put in the oven*
65 enfourner (s') P – *to wolf down something*
123 enfreindre T – *to infringe*
97 enfuir (s') P – *to flee, to make a getaway*
65 enfumer T – *to fill with smoke*
65 enfumer (s') P – *to fill with smoke*
65 enfutailler T – *to put in a cask*
65 enfûter/enfuter T – *to keg*
67 engager T – *to engage, to take on, to bind, to commit, to start*
67 engager (s') P – *to undertake, to commit oneself (to), to enlist (in)*
65 engainer T – *to sheathe*
65 engamer T – *to swallow the hook (fishing)*
65 engaver T – *to feed*
65 engazonner T – *to turf over*
65 engendrer T – *to beget, to engender*
65 engerber T – *to sheaf, to pile up*
66 englacer T – *to cover with ice*
65 englober T – *to encompass, to include*
81 engloutir T – *to swallow, to gulp, to gobble up*
81 engloutir (s') P – *to be engulfed*
65 engluer T – *to lime, to ensnare*
65 engluer (s') P – *to become gluey*
65 engober T – *to cover with slip*
65 engommer T – *to gum*
66 engoncer T – *to bundle up (in clothes)*
67 engorger T – *to choke, to clog*
67 engorger (s') P – *to become clogged*
65 engouer (s') P – *to have a craze or sudden passion*
65 engouffrer T – *to engulf, to swallow up*
65 engouffrer (s') P – *to rush, to surge (into)*
65 engouler T – *to gobble*
81 engourdir T – *to dull, to numb*
81 engourdir (s') P – *to grow numb*
65 engraisser I, T – *to fatten, to cram, to fertilize (land)*
65 engraisser (s') P – *to put on weight, to thrive (on)*
67 engranger T – *to garner, to put by*
65 engraver T – *to engrave*

T: direct transitive (p. p. variable) – **Ti**: indirect transitive (p. p. invariable) – **I**: intransitive verb (p. p. invariable) **P**: pronominal verb (auxiliary *être*) – **impers.**: impersonal verb – **D**: defective verb – *être*: verb conjugated with the auxiliary *être* – *être* or *avoir*: verbs conjugated with *être* or *avoir* (see paragraph 15)

68 engrener T – *to gear, to start*
68 engrener (s') P – *to be in a mesh*
65 engrosser T – *to make a woman pregnant*
72 engrumeler T – *to curdle, to clot*
72 engrumeler (s') P – *to curdle, to clot*
65 engueuler T – *to bawl out*
65 engueuler (s') P – *to row*
65 enguirlander T – *to garland, to scold*
81 enhardir T – *to embolden*
81 enhardir (s') P – *to pluck up courage*
65 enharnacher T – *to harness*
65 enherber T – *to plant with grass*
65 énieller T – *to get rid of corn-cockle*
65 enivrer I, T – *to intoxicate*
65 enivrer (s') P – *to get drunk, to become intoxicated*
65 enjamber I, T – *to straddle over, to span*
72 enjaveler T – *to gather (corn) in swathes*
124 enjoindre T – *to enjoin, to prescribe*
65 enjôler T – *to wheedle, to coax*
65 enjoliver T – *to embellish*
65 enjoliver (s') P – *to embellish*
66 enjoncer T – *to sow reeds*
65 enjouer T – *to give a pleasant tone*
65 enjuguer T – *to yoke (oxen)*
65 enjuponner T – *to put into petticoats, to flounce*
65 enkikiner T – *to irritate, to bug*
65 enkyster (s') P – *to become encysted*
66 enlacer T – *to entwine, to hug, to clasp*
66 enlacer (s') P – *to entwine, to hug, to clasp*
81 enlaidir I, T – *to make ugly, to disfigure*
81 enlaidir (s') P – *to make ugly, to disfigure*
68 enlever T – *to remove, to take away, to kidnap*
68 enlever (s') P – *to come off, to sell out*
65 enliasser T – *to bundle*
76 enlier T – *to bond*
65 enligner T – *to set in line*
65 enliser T – *to sink, to engulf*
65 enliser (s') P – *to get bogged down*
65 enluminer T – *to illuminate, to colour up*
67 enneiger T – *to block with snow*
81 ennoblir T – *to ennoble, to elevate*
67 ennuager T – *to cloud over*
67 ennuager (s') P – *to cloud over*
79 ennuyer I, T – *to bore, to annoy, to weary, to worry*
79 ennuyer (s') P – *to be bored (with), to miss*
66 énoncer T – *to state, to articulate*
66 énoncer (s') P – *to express*
81 enorgueillir T – *to make proud*
81 enorgueillir (s') P – *to pride oneself*
65 énouer T – *to remove knots (cloth)*
85 enquérir (s') P – *to enquire about*
65 enquêter I – *to investigate*
65 enquêter (s') P – *to inquire*
65 enquiller I – *to put in, to put on, to enter, to do right away, to down (drink)*
65 enquiquiner T – *to aggravate, to bug, to annoy*
65 enquiquiner (s') P – *to be bored (stiff)*
65 enraciner T – *to dig in*
65 enraciner (s') P – *to take root*
67 enrager I – *to be in a rage*
65 enrailler T – *to put on rails*
77 enrayer T – *to jam*
77 enrayer (s') P – *to jam*
65 enrégimenter T – *to enlist, to apply army discipline*
65 enregistrer T – *to record, to register, to score*
65 enregistrer (s') P – *to record oneself, to register oneself*
65 enrêner T – *to put reins on*
65 enrésiner T – *to resin*
65 enrhumer T – *to give a cold*
65 enrhumer (s') P – *to catch a cold*
81 enrichir T – *to enrich*
81 enrichir (s') P – *to make money, to grow rich*
65 enrober T – *to coat*
65 enrocher T – *to riprap, to fortify with rock armour*
65 enrôler T – *to enrol, to recruit*
65 enrôler (s') P – *to enrol, to recruit*
65 enrouer T – *to make hoarse*
65 enrouer (s') P – *to get/make hoarse*
65 enrouiller I – *to get rusty*
65 enrouiller (s') P – *to rust through*
65 enrouler T – *to roll up, to wind*
65 enrouler (s') P – *to wind up, to coil up, to wrap oneself (in a blanket)*
65 enrubanner T – *to trim with ribbon*
65 ensabler T – *to sand up, to silt up, to run aground (ship)*
65 ensabler (s') P – *to sand up, to silt up, to run aground (ship)*
65 ensaboter T – *to put in clogs*
65 ensacher T – *to bag*
65 ensaisiner T – *to recognize a new tenant (feudal)*
65 ensanglanter T – *to stain with blood*
67 ensauvager T – *to make wild*
65 ensauver (s') P – *to get way, to run away*
65 enseigner T – *to teach, to show up*
65 enseigner (s') P – *to teach (oneself), to be taught*
66 ensemencer T – *to sow*
65 enserrer T – *to encompass, to squeeze*
81 ensevelir T – *to bury, to entomb, to shroud*
81 ensevelir (s') P – *to bury, to entomb, to shroud*
65 ensiler T – *to ensilage*
65 ensoleiller T – *to give sunshire (to), to brighten up*
72 ensorceler T – *to bewitch*
65 ensoufrer T – *to sulphurate*
69 enstérer T – *to heap up by the cubic meter*
145 ensuivre (s') P, D – *to ensue, to follow*
65 ensuquer T – *to knock out, to be listless (figurative)*
65 entabler T – *to adjust scissor blades*
65 entabler (s') P – *to sidepass crookedly (horse)*
65 entacher T – *to blemish*
65 entailler T – *to cut, to groove*
65 entailler (s') P – *to cut, to groove*
65 entamer T – *to cut into, to begin, to open*
65 entaquer T – *to join pieces of velvet*
65 entarter T – *to pie someone in the face*
65 entartrer T – *to cause tartar to build up*
65 entartrer (s') P – *to build up tartar (teeth)*
65 entasser T – *to accumulate, to pile up*
65 entasser (s') P – *to accumulate, to pile up*
118 entendre à I, T, Ti – *to mean, to hear, to understand*
118 entendre (s') P – *to agree (with), to understand (one another)*
69 enténébrer T – *to plunge into shadow*
69 enténébrer (s') P – *to become dark*
65 enter T – *to graft*

65 entériner T – *to ratify*
65 enterrer T – *to bury, to inter*
65 enterrer (s') P – *to dig oneself in*
65 entêter T – *to go to the head (of)*
65 entêter (s') P – *to be stubborn*
65 enthousiasmer T – *to enthuse*
65 enthousiasmer (s') P – *to be enthused*
65 enticher (s') P – *to be infatuated*
65 entifler T – *to marry*
65 entifler (s') P – *to get married*
65 entoiler T – *to mount, to cover (with fabric)*
65 entôler T – *to con, to fleece*
65 entonner T – *to intone, to break into (song)*
65 entorser afr. I – *to sprain*
65 entortiller T – *to wind, to twist, to wheedle*
65 entortiller (s') P – *to get tangled up (in)*
65 entourer T – *to surround, to fence in*
65 entourer (s') P – *to surround, to fence in*
65 entourlouper T – *to dupe, to fool*
65 entraccorder (s') P – *to agree with one another*
65 entraccuser (s') P – *to accuse one another*
65 entradmirer (s') P – *to admire one another*
65 entraider (s') P – *to help one another*
65 entraimer (s') P – *to love each other*
65 entraîner/entrainer T – *to drag, to carry off, to seduce, to involve, to entail, to coach*
65 entraîner/entrainer (s') P – *to train*
100 entrapercevoir T – *to catch a glimpse (of)*
100 entrapercevoir (s') P – *to catch a glimpse of one another*
65 entraver T – *to hinder*
65 entrebâiller T – *to half-open*
65 entrebâiller (s') P – *to be half-opened*
121 entrebattre (s') P – *to fight one another*
65 entrechoquer T – *to knock together, to bang together*
65 entrechoquer (s') P – *to collide, to clink together*
65 entrecouper T – *to interrupt, to intersect*
65 entrecouper (s') P – *to interrupt, to intersect*
65 entrecroiser T – *to intersect, to criss-cross*
65 entrecroiser (s') P – *to intersect, to criss-cross*
65 entre(-)déchirer (s') P – *to tear one another to pieces*
152 entre(-)détruire (s') P – *to destroy one another*
65 entre(-)dévorer (s') P – *to tear one another to pieces*
67 entr(e-)égorger (s') P – *to cut one another's throats*
67 entr'égorger (s') P – *to cut one another's throats*
65 entre(-)frapper (s') P – *to hit one another*
82 entre(-)haïr (s') P – *to hate one another*
65 entre(-)heurter (s') P – *to bang into one another*
66 entrelacer T – *to interlace, to interwine*
66 entrelacer (s') P – *to interlace, to interwine*
65 entrelarder T – *to lard, to streak (with fat)*
65 entre(-)louer (s') P – *to praise one another*
67 entre(-)manger (s') P – *to eat one another*
65 entremêler T – *to intermingle*
65 entremêler (s') P – *to become entangled*
122 entremettre (s') P – *to mediate, to interpose*
152 entre(-)nuire (s') P – *to injure one another*
65 entreposer T – *to store*
119 entreprendre I, T – *to undertake, to contract (for)*
65 entrer T, *avoir* – *to take in, to bring in*
65 entrer I, *être* – *to enter*
65 entre(-)regarder (s') P – *to look at one another*
65 entretailler (s') P – *to knock the legs against each other (horse)*
84 entretenir T – *to maintain, to support, to speak to*
84 entretenir (s') P – *to keep fit, to be self-supporting*
65 entretoiser T – *to cross-brace*
65 entre(-)tuer (s') P – *to kill one another*
101 entrevoir T – *to glimpse*
101 entrevoir (s') P – *to glimpse*
67 entrobliger (s') P – *to oblige one another*
88 entrouvrir T – *to half-open*
88 entrouvrir (s') P – *to gape*
65 entuber T – *to con, to rip off*
74 énucléer T – *to enucleate*
69 énumérer T – *to enumerate*
81 envahir T – *to invade*
65 envaser T – *to silt up, to choke up*
65 envaser (s') P – *to silt up, to choke up*
65 envelopper T – *to wrap up, to envelop*
65 envelopper (s') P – *to wrap up, to envelop*
65 envenimer T – *to poison*
65 envenimer (s') P – *to go septic, to fester*
67 enverger T – *to twist (wires)*
65 enverguer T – *to bend (sail)*
65 enviander T – *to sodomize (slang)*
65 envider T – *to spool*
76 envier T – *to envy, to wish for*
81 envieillir T – *to grow old*
81 envieillir (s') P – *to grow old*
65 environner T – *to surround*
65 environner (s') P – *to surround*
67 envisager T – *to face, to consider*
65 envoiler (s') P – *to curve (metal)*
65 envoler (s') P – *to fly away, to take wing*
65 envoûter/envouter T – *to bewitch*
80 envoyer T – *to send, to despatch*
80 envoyer (s') P – *to send one another*
81 épaissir I, T – *to thicken, to deepen*
81 épaissir (s') P – *to grow fat*
65 épaler T – *to use a pot as a unit of measurement*
65 épamprer T – *to thin out*
65 épancher T – *to pour out*
65 épancher (s') P – *to give vent to (feelings)*
118 épandre T – *to pour forth, to scatter, to spread*
118 épandre (s') P – *to pour forth, to scatter, to spread*
72 épanneler T – *to sculpt stone, to carve marble into a rough shape*
65 épanner T – *to flatten the sides of a grounding stone*
81 épanouir T – *to open out, to blossom, to bloom*
81 épanouir (s') P – *to open out, to blossom, to bloom*
65 épargner I, T – *to save (up), to economize*
65 épargner (s') P – *to save (up), to economize*
65 éparpiller T – *to scatter, to disperse*
65 éparpiller (s') P – *to scatter, to disperse*

T: direct transitive (p. p. variable) – **Ti**: indirect transitive (p. p. invariable) – **I**: intransitive verb (p. p. invariable) **P**: pronominal verb (auxiliary *être*) – **impers.**: impersonal verb – **D**: defective verb – *être*: verb conjugated with the auxiliary *être* – *être* or *avoir*: verbs conjugated with *être* or *avoir* (see paragraph 15)

65 épastrouiller T – *to astound, to amaze*
65 épater T – *to amaze*
65 épaufrer T – *to flake, to fragment*
65 épauler I, T – *to support, to take aim (gun)*
65 épauler (s') P – *to help each other*
72 épeler I, T – *to spell*
72 épeler (s') P – *to spell*
65 épépiner T – *to remove pips*
118 éperdre (s') P – *to distract, to make distraught*
65 éperonner T – *to spur*
65 épeuler T – *to remove the strings in a parchment*
65 épeurer T – *to frighten*
66 épicer T – *to spice*
76 épier I, T – *to spy (on)*
76 épier (s') P – *to spy on (one another)*
65 épierrer T – *to remove stones*
65 épiler T – *to remove hair*
65 épiler (s') P – *to remove one's hair*
65 épiloguer sur T, Ti – *to hold forth on, to carp at*
73 épinceler T – *to remove knots (cloth)*
66 épincer T – *to burl, to pinch off*
70 épinceter T – *to remove knots (cloth)*
65 épiner T – *to protect (with thorn)*
65 épingler T – *to pin, to pin up, to catch*
65 épisser T – *to tie two ropes together*
65 épivarder (s') québ. P – *to occupy more room than needed (lit. and figurative)*
78 éployer T – *to spread out*
78 éployer (s') P – *to spread out*
65 éplucher T – *to peel*
65 épointer T – *to blunt*
67 éponger T – *to sponge (up), to mop (up)*
67 éponger (s') P – *to sponge (up), to mop (up)*
65 épontiller T – *to shore up*
65 épouiller T – *to delouse*
65 épouiller (s') P – *to delouse*
65 époumoner (s') P – *to shout (oneself) hoarse*
65 épouser I, T – *to marry, to wed, to fit*
65 épouser (s') P – *to marry*
70 épousseter T – *to dust*
65 époustoufler T – *to flabbergast*
76 époutier T – *to burl*
81 époutir T – *to burl*
65 épouvanter T – *to terrify, to appal*
65 épouvanter (s') P – *to be panic-stricken*
123 épreindre T – *to squeeze out*
119 éprendre (s') P – *to fall in love with*
65 éprouver T – *to feel, to experience, to test*
65 éprouver (s') P – *to feel, to experience, to test*
66 épucer T – *to get rid of fleas*
66 épucer (s') P – *to get rid of fleas*
65 épuiser T – *to exhaust*
65 épuiser (s') P – *to become exhausted, to run out*
65 épurer T – *to purify*
65 épurer (s') P – *to purify*
81 équarrir T – *to square, to quarter*
65 équerrer T – *to square*
65 équeuter T – *to pull the stalk off, to hull*
65 équilibrer T – *to balance*
65 équilibrer (s') P – *to balance*
65 équiper T – *to equip, to fit out*
65 équiper (s') P – *to equip, to fit out*
109 équivaloir à Ti – *to be equivalent to, to amount to*
109 équivaloir (s') P – *to be equivalent p. p. invariable*
65 équivoquer I – *to quibble*
65 éradiquer T – *to eradicate*
65 érafler T – *to graze, to scratch*
65 érafler (s') P – *to graze oneself*
65 érailler T – *to scratch, to make hoarse*
65 érailler (s') P – *to make hoarse, to scratch*
77 érayer T – *to plough pushing the slice on the outside*
65 éreinter T – *to break the back of, to criticize*
65 éreinter (s') P – *to exhaust oneself*
65 ergoter I – *to split hair*
67 ériger T – *to erect*
67 ériger (s') P – *to set oneself up*
65 éroder T – *to erode*
65 éroder (s') P – *to erode*
65 érotiser T – *to eroticize*
65 errer I – *to ramble, to err*
65 éructer I, T – *to belch, to eruct*
81 esbaudir (s') P – *to divert oneself*
65 esbigner (s') P – *to skedaddle*
65 esbroufer T – *to bluff*
65 escalader T – *to climb*
65 escamoter T – *to conjure away, to skip*
65 escarmoucher I – *to skirmish*
65 escarper T – *to steepen*
76 escarrifier T – *to form a scab*
65 escher T – *to bait*
65 esclaffer (s') P – *to guffaw, to shake (with laughter)*
67 esclavager T – *to enslave*
76 escoffier T – *to kill (archaic)*
65 escompter T – *to anticipate, to discount*
65 escorter T – *to escort*
65 escrimer (s') P – *to strive to do somethinf (figurative)*
65 escroquer T – *to swindle*
65 esgourder T – *to listen*
66 espacer T – *to space out*
66 espacer (s') P – *to space out*
65 espagnoliser T – *to Spanishize*
69 espérer I, T – *to hope (for)*
65 espionner T – *to spy*
65 espoliner T – *to spool*
65 espouliner T – *to spool*
65 esquicher I – *to squeeze*
65 esquinter T – *to mess up*
65 esquinter (s') P – *to knock oneself out*
65 esquisser T – *to sketch, to outline*
65 esquisser (s') P – *to sketch, to outline*
65 esquiver T – *to dodge, to avoid*
65 esquiver (s') P – *to slip away*
65 essaimer I, T – *to swarm*
67 essanger T – *to prewash (clothes)*
65 essarter T – *to clear (land)*
77 essayer T – *to try (to)*
77 essayer (s') P – *to try*
65 essorer T – *to wring, to mangle*
65 essorer (s') P – *to wring, to mangle*
65 essoriller T – *to cut someone's ear*
65 essoucher T – *to rip out stocks/stumps*
65 essouffler T – *to wind, to make breathless*
65 essouffler (s') P – *to be puffed, to be winded*
79 essuyer T – *to wipe, to dry*
79 essuyer (s') P – *to wipe, to dry*

65 estamper T – *to swindle*
65 estampiller T – *to stamp*
65 ester I, D – *to stand to court*
only in the infinitive
76 estérifier T – *to estrify*
65 esthétiser I, T – *to estheticize*
65 estimer T – *to estimate, to value, to assess*
65 estimer (s') P – *to be estimated, to be assessed*
65 estiver I, T – *to summer*
65 estomaquer T – *to flabbergast*
65 estomper T – *to dim, to blur, to stump*
65 estomper (s') P – *to become dimmed, to become blurry*
65 estoquer T – *to deal (the bull) the death-blow*
81 estourbir T – *to stun, to knock out*
65 estrapader T – *to torture by strappado*
65 estrapasser T – *to exhaust a horse*
76 estropier T – *to cripple*
76 estropier (s') P – *to cripple oneself*
65 établer T – *to stable, to stall*
81 établir T – *to establish, to prove, to construct, to draw up*
81 établir (s') P – *to establish oneself, to set oneself up as, to become customary*
67 étager T – *to lay out in tiers or to stack*
67 étager (s') P – *to rise in tiers*
67 étalager T – *to display*
65 étaler I, T – *to spread, to set on (goods)*
65 étaler (s') P – *to spread, to stretch out*
65 étalinguer T – *to moor (nautical)*
65 étalonner T – *to calibrate*
65 étamer T – *to tin*
65 étamper T – *to stamp (metal)*
65 étancher T – *to check (flow), to quench*
65 étançonner T – *to prop*
65 étarquer T – *to hoist taut*
65 étatiser T – *to establish state control*
77 étayer T – *to prop up, to shore up*
77 étayer (s') P – *to be propped up*
123 éteindre T – *to extinguish, to put out, to switch off*
123 éteindre (s') P – *to go out, to die out, to die*
118 étendre T – *to spread, to stretch, to extend, to dilute*
118 étendre (s') P – *to stretch*
65 éterniser T – *to perpetuate, to drag out*
65 éterniser (s') P – *to become interminable*
65 éternuer I – *to sneeze*
65 étêter T – *to cut the head off*
76 éthérifier T – *to turn into ether*
65 éthériser T – *to etherize*
65 éthniciser T – *to ethnicize*
72 étinceler I – *to sparkle*
65 étioler T – *to blanch, to etiolate (agriculture)*
65 étioler (s') P –*to become blanched or whitened*
70 étiqueter T – *to label*
65 étirer T – *to stretch, to draw out*
65 étirer (s') P – *to stretch*
65 étoffer T – *to enrich, to fill out, to pad*
65 étoffer (s') P – *to fill out*
65 étoiler T – *to stud, to bespangle*
65 étoiler (s') P – *to light up (with stars)*
65 étonner T – *to stun, to surprise*
65 étonner (s') P – *to be surprised*
65 étouffer I, T – *to suffocate, to choke, to smother, to muffle (noise)*
65 étouffer (s') P – *to feel stifled, to die of suffocation*
65 étouper T – *to tow (linen)*
65 étoupiller T – *to fuse*
81 étourdir T – *to stun, to daze*
81 étourdir (s') P – *to cause to forget*
65 étrangler T – *to strangle, to throttle*
65 étrangler (s') P – *to choke*
61 être I – *to be, to exist*
81 étrécir T – *to narrow*
81 étrécir (s') P – *to narrow*
123 étreindre T – *to clasp, to embrace*
123 étreindre (s') P – *to clasp, to embrace*
65 étrenner I, T – *to use for the first time*
65 étrésillonner T – *to strut (construction)*
65 étriller T – *to curry (horse), to thrash*
65 étripailler I, T – *to assassinate*
65 étriper T – *to disembowel, to gut*
65 étriper (s') P – *to make mincemeat of each other*
65 étriquer T – *to shorten or to narrow*
65 étronçonner T – *to prune*
76 étudier I, T – *to study*
76 étudier (s') P – *to analyse oneself*
65 étuver T – *to steam, to stew*
65 euphoriser I, T – *to make euphoric*
65 européaniser T – *to Europeanize*
65 européaniser (s') P – *to become Europeanized*
76 euthanasier T – *to put down, to help to die, to euthanize*
65 évacuer T – *to evacuate, to clear*
65 évacuer (s') P – *to be evacuated*
65 évader (s') P – *to escape*
65 évaluer T – *to evaluate*
65 évangéliser T – *to preach the Gospel*
81 évanouir (s') P – *to faint*
65 évaporer T – *to evaporate*
65 évaporer (s') P – *to evaporate*
65 évaser T – *to widen*
65 évaser (s') P – *to widen*
65 éveiller T – *to awaken*
65 éveiller (s') P – *to wake up*
65 éventer T – *to air*
65 éventer (s') P – *to fan oneself*
65 éventrer T – *to disembowel*
65 éventrer (s') P – *to disembowel oneself, to burst open*
65 évertuer (s') P – *to strive, to do one's utmost*
65 évider T – *to hollow out*
66 évincer T – *to evict, to oust*
65 éviter à, de T, Ti – *to avoid, to dodge, to evade, to save/spare someone something*
65 éviter (s') P – *to avoid one another, to spare oneself something*
65 évoluer I – *to evolve*
65 évoluer (s') afr. P – *to evolve*

T: direct transitive (p. p. variable) – **Ti**: indirect transitive (p. p. invariable) – **I**: intransitive verb (p. p. invariable) **P**: pronominal verb (auxiliary *être*) – **impers.**: impersonal verb – **D**: defective verb – *être*: verb conjugated with the auxiliary *être* – *être* or *avoir*: verbs conjugated with *être* or *avoir* (see paragraph 15)

65 évoquer T – *to evoke*
65 exacerber T – *to exacerbate*
65 exarcerber (s') P – *to exacerbate*
69 exagérer I, T – *to exaggerate*
69 exagérer (s') P – *to exaggerate*
65 exalter T – *to exalt, to extol*
65 exalter (s') P – *to enthuse (over)*
65 examiner I, T – *to examine, to investigate*
65 examiner (s') P – *to examine one's conscience*
69 exaspérer T – *to exasperate*
69 exaspérer (s') P – *to lose one's patience*
66 exaucer T – *to fulfill*
65 excaver T – *to excavate*
69 excéder T – *to exceed, to go beyond*
65 exceller I – *to excel*
65 excentrer T – *to throw off center*
65 excepter T – *to except*
65 exciper de Ti – *to plead, to allege*
65 exciser T – *to excise*
65 exciter T – *to excite, to arouse, to thrill*
65 exciter (s') P – *to get worked up*
65 exclamer (s') P – *to exclaim, to cry out*
139 exclure T – *to expel, to exclude*
139 exclure (s') P – *to expel, to exclude*
76 excommunier T – *to excommunicate*
76 excorier T – *to peel off*
65 excracher T – *to spread scandal, to speak ill*
69 excréter T – *to excrete*
65 excursionner I – *to go touring*
65 excuser T – *to make excuse, to apologise, to pardon*
65 excuser (s') P – *to apologise, to send excuses (for)*
69 exécrer T – *to loathe*
65 exécuter T – *to execute, to carry out*
65 exécuter (s') P – *to comply, to submit, to pay up*
76 exemplifier T – *to exemplify*
65 exempter T – *to exempt*
65 exempter (s') P – *to abstain*
66 exercer I, T – *to exercise, to train*
66 exercer (s') P – *to practise*
65 exfiltrer T – *to smuggle so into another country*
76 exfolier T – *to exfoliate*
76 exfolier (s') P – *to exfoliate*
65 exhaler T – *to exhale, to emit*
65 exhaler (s') P – *to exhale, to emit*
65 exhausser T – *to raise up*
69 exhéréder T – *to disinherit*
65 exhiber T – *to exhibit, to show*
65 exhiber (s') P – *to show off*
65 exhorter T – *to exhort, to urge*
65 exhumer T – *to exhume*
67 exiger T – *to demand, to require*
65 exiler T – *to exile, to banish*
65 exiler (s') P – *to go in exile, to withdraw*
65 exister I – *to exist*
65 exonder (s') P – *to emerge (land)*
69 exonérer T – *to exonerate*
65 exorciser T – *to exorcize*
76 expatrier T – *to expatriate*
76 expatrier (s') P – *to leave one's country*
65 expectorer I, T – *to expectorate*
76 expédier T – *to dispatch, to expedite*
65 expérimenter I, T – *to test*
65 expertiser T – *to value*
76 expier T – *to expiate, to atone for*
76 expier (s') P – *to be expiated*
65 expirer I, T – *to expire, to breathe out*
65 expliciter T – *to make explicit*
65 expliquer T – *to explain, to account (for)*
65 expliquer (s') P – *to explain oneself*
65 exploiter I, T – *to exploit, to work, to take advantage (of)*
65 explorer T – *to explore*
65 exploser I – *to explode*
65 exporter I, T – *to export*
65 exposer T – *to exhibit, to display*
65 exposer (s') P – *to expose oneself*
65 exprimer T – *to express, to show, to squeeze (out)*
65 exprimer (s') P – *to express oneself, to put it, to be articulate*
76 exproprier T – *to take over, to expropriate*
65 expulser T – *to expel, to turn out*
67 expurger T – *to expurgate*
65 exsuder I, T – *to exude*
76 extasier (s') P – *to go into raptures (over)*
65 exténuer T – *to extenuate, to exhaust*
65 exténuer (s') P – *to tire oneself out*
65 extérioriser T – *to show*
65 extérioriser (s') P – *to reveal oneself outwardly*
65 exterminer T – *to exterminate*
65 externaliser T – *to outsource*
65 externer afr. T – *to make someone an extern/ a non-resident*
65 extirper T – *to extirpate*
65 extirper (s') P – *to drag oneself, to haul oneself, to extricate oneself*
65 extorquer T – *to extort*
65 extourner T – *to reverse an entry (accounting)*
65 extrader T – *to extradite*
127 extraire T, D – *to extract, to draw out*
127 extraire (s') P, D – *to extract, to draw out*
65 extrapoler I, T – *to extrapolate*
65 extravaguer I – *to rave*
65 extravaser T – *to exude*
65 extravaser (s') P – *to exude*
65 extruder T – *to extrude*
69 exulcérer T – *to superficially ulcerate*
65 exulter I – *to exult, to rejoice*

f

65 fabriquer I, T – *to make, to forge, to manufacture*
65 fabriquer (se) P – *to make for oneself, to forge for oneself, to manufacture for oneself*
65 fabuler I – *to fabricate (stories)*
65 facetter T – *to facet*
65 fâcher T – *to make angry, to anger*
65 fâcher (se) P – *to lose one's temper*
65 faciliter T – *to facilitate, to make easier*
65 faciliter (se) P – *to facilitate for oneself, to make easier for oneself*
65 façonner T – *to shape*
65 factoriser T – *to factorize*
65 facturer T – *to invoice, to charge*
65 fader T – *to share the loot (slang), to use profusely*

65 fagoter T – *to botch (work), to bundle up (wood), to be dressed strangely*
65 fagoter (se) P – *to dress oneself strangely*
81 faiblir I – *to weaken, to fail, to flag*
65 faignanter I – *to loaf about*
65 failler (se) P – *to fault (geological)*
91 faillir I, D – *to nearly miss*
now patterned after finir *in the future and conditional; obsolete in the present indicative and the* imparfait.
65 fainéanter I – *to loaf about*
65 fainéantiser I – *to loaf*
128 faire I, T – *to make, to do, to form*
128 faire (se) P – *to develop, to become, to mature, to make oneself*
65 faisander T – *to hang (meat)*
65 faisander (se) P – *to get high, to go bad*
108 falloir T – *to have to, should*
impers.: " il faut"
108 falloir (s'en) P – *to come close to, to nearly miss*
impers.: "il s'en faut"
or "il s'en est fallu"
65 faloter I – *to singe, to burn*
76 falsifier T – *to falsify*
65 faluner T – *to fertilize with shell marl*
65 familiariser T – *to get used to*
65 familiariser (se) P – *to become familiar (with)*
65 fanatiser T – *to rouse, to fanaticize*
65 fanatiser (se) P – *to rouse, to fanaticize*
65 faner T – *to make hay, to fade*
65 faner (se) P – *to fade, to wither*
65 fanfaronner I – *to brag (about)*
65 fanfrelucher T – *to frill*
65 fantasmer I, T – *to fantasize*
81 farcir T – *to stuff (with), to cram (with)*
81 farcir (se) P – *to have to put up with*
65 farder I, T – *to disguise, to mask*
65 farder (se) P – *to make up*
65 farfouiller I, T – *to rummage about*
65 farguer T – *to accuse, to charge (slang)*
65 fariner I, T – *to flour*
65 farter T – *to wax (skis)*
65 fasciner T – *to fascinate*
65 fasciser T – *to make fascist*
77 faseyer I – *to be untaut because of a lack of wind (sail)*
65 fatiguer I, T – *to tire, to wear out*
65 fatiguer (se) P – *to get tired, to tire oneself out*
69 faubérer afr. I – *to mop*
65 faucarder T – *to reap, to mow down (river, swamp)*
65 faucher I, T – *to reap, to mow down*
65 fauconner I – *to go hawking*
65 faufiler I, T – *to tack, to baste*
65 faufiler (se) P – *to weave through, to slip through*
65 fausser T – *to distort, to warp, to strain*
65 fausser (se) P – *to become strained*
65 fauter I – *to sin*
65 favoriser T – *to favour*
65 faxer T – *to fax*
65 fayot(t)er I – *to suck up, to lick someone's boot*
65 féconder T – *to impregnate*
65 féculer T – *to remove starch*
65 fédéraliser T – *to federalize*
65 fédéraliser (se) P – *to federalize*
69 fédérer T – *to federate*
69 fédérer (se) P – *to federate*
65 feignanter I – *to loaf about*
123 feindre I, T – *to feign, to sham*
65 feinter I, T – *to feint*
65 fêler T – *to crack*
65 fêler (se) P – *to crack*
65 féliciter T – *to congratulate*
65 féliciter (se) P – *to congratulate*
65 féminiser T – *to feminize*
65 féminiser (se) P – *to become effeminate*
65 fendiller T – *to fissure*
65 fendiller (se) P – *to fissure*
118 fendre T – *to split, to crack*
118 fendre (se) P – *to split, to crack*
65 fenestrer T – *to make windows*
65 fenêtrer T – *to put in windows*
férir T, D – *to strike*
used only in the expressions "sans coup férir" *(= without meeting any opposition) or* "féru de" *(= keen on, with a keen interest in)*
65 ferler T – *to furl*
65 fermenter I – *to ferment*
65 fermer I, T – *to close, to shut up*
65 fermer (se) P – *to close, to shut up*
65 ferrailler I – *to clash swords*
65 ferrer T – *to shoe (a horse)*
65 ferrouter T – *to railroad transport (combining truck and trains)*
65 fertiliser T – *to fertilize*
65 fesser T – *to spank*
65 féticher afr. T – *to use magic on someone*
65 festonner T – *to scallop, to festoon*
78 festoyer I, T – *to feast*
65 fêter T – *to celebrate*
65 fétichiser T – *to make into a fetish*
65 feuiller I, T – *to grow leaves*
70 feuilleter T – *to leaf (through), to make flaky*
65 feuilletiser T – *to make an edged contour (diamond)*
65 feuler I – *to growl*
65 feutrer I, T – *to line with felt*
65 feutrer (se) P – *to become matted*
65 fiabiliser T – *to safeguard, to guarantee the accuracy*
66 fiancer T – *to betroth*
66 fiancer (se) P – *to get engaged*
72 ficeler T – *to tie up*
65 ficher T – *to file, to do, to drive in*
65 ficher (se) P – *to get oneself into, to do oneself in*
65 fiche (se) P – *to kid someone, to tease someone*
"je me fiche de…" – *I don't give a damn about …,*
past participle "fichu, ue, us, ues"
65 fidéliser T – *to make faithful/loyal/true, to foster loyalty*

T: direct transitive (p. p. variable) – **Ti**: indirect transitive (p. p. invariable) – **I**: intransitive verb (p. p. invariable)
P: pronominal verb (auxiliary *être*) – **impers.**: impersonal verb – **D**: defective verb – *être*: verb conjugated with the auxiliary *être* – *être* or *avoir*: verbs conjugated with *être* or *avoir* (see paragraph 15)

65 fieffer T – *to enfeoff*
65 fienter I – *to excrete*
76 fier (se) P – *to trust*
67 figer I, T – *to congeal, to set*
67 figer (se) P – *to congeal, to set*
65 fignoler T – *to polish, to touch up*
65 figurer I, T – *to represent, to act, to appear*
65 figurer (se) P – *to imagine, to fancy*
65 filer I, T – *to spin, to run*
65 filer (se) P – *to spin, to run*
71 fileter T – *to thread*
65 filigraner T – *to filigree*
65 filmer I, T – *to film*
65 filocher I, T – *to tail (so), to skedaddle*
65 filouter I, T – *to cheat*
65 filtrer I, T – *to filter*
65 finaliser T – *to finalize*
66 financer I, T – *to finance*
65 financiariser T – *to base on finance*
65 finasser I, T – *to use trickery*
81 finir I, T – *to finish, to end, to get over*
65 finlandiser T – *to make Finnish*
65 finlandiser (se) P – *to make something Finnish*
65 fiscaliser T – *to make subject to tax*
65 fissionner T – *to undergo fission, to provoke a nuclear fission*
65 fissurer T – *to crack, to fissure*
65 fissurer (se) P – *to crack, to fissure*
65 fixer T – *to fix, to fasten*
65 fixer (se) P – *to settle*
65 flageller T – *to flog*
65 flageller (se) P – *to flog*
65 flageoler I – *to shake, to give way*
65 flagorner T – *to fawn upon, to flatter*
65 flairer T – *to sniff*
65 flamber I, T – *to blaze, to singe, to squander*
78 flamboyer I – *to flare up, to blaze up*
65 flancher I, T – *to flinch, to break down*
65 flâner I – *to dawdle, to stroll*
65 flânocher I – *to stroll slowly*
65 flanquer T – *to flank, to fling*
65 flanquer (se) P – *to fall flat, to take a tumble*
65 flaquer I – *to splash*
65 flasher I, T – *to flash*
65 flatter T – *to flatter*
65 flatter (se) P – *to pride oneself, to delude oneself*
65 flauper T – *to beat, to hit (slang)*
69 flécher T – *to arrow*
81 fléchir I, T – *to bend, to flex*
81 fléchir (se) P – *to bend, to flex*
65 flemmarder I – *to lounge about*
81 flétrir T – *to wither, to fade, to wilt*
81 flétrir (se) P – *to wither, to fade, to wilt*
65 fleurer I, T – *to smell, to be fragrant*
81 fleurir I, T – *to blossom, to thrive, to flourish*
for "orner de fleurs" – *to blossom, the stem is* fleur;
for "prospérer" *to thrive, to flourish, the stem is* flor
in the imparfait (il florissait) *and in the present participle* (florissant)
81 fleurir (se) P – *to deck with flowers*
65 flexibiliser T – *to make flexible, to become flexible*
65 flibuster I, T – *to buccaneer*
65 flingoter T – *to shot (gun) (slang)*
65 flinguer I, T – *to gun down*
65 flinguer (se) P – *to shoot oneself*
65 flipper I – *to flip*
65 fliquer T – *to police*
65 flirter I – *to flirt*
65 floconner I – *to fleck, to make fluffy*
65 floculer I – *to flocculate*
65 floquer T – *to make a surface velvety, to paint (cars)*
65 flotter I, T, impers. – *to float, to stream, to rain (familiar)*
impers.: "il flotte"
65 flouer T – *to swindle, to cheat*
65 flouser I – *to pass wind, to fart*
65 fluber I – *to be scared*
65 fluctuer I – *to fluctuate*
65 fluer I – *to flow, to flux, to creep*
76 fluidifier T – *to fluidize*
65 fluidiser T – *to fluidize*
65 fluoriser T – *to fluorize*
65 flûter/fluter I, T – *to flute*
65 fluxer T – *to add oil*
65 focaliser T – *to focus*
65 focaliser (se) P – *to focus on, to be focused*
65 foirer I – *to fail*
65 foisonner I – *to abound*
65 folâtrer I – *to frolic*
65 folichonner I – *to lark*
65 folioter T – *to folio, to foliate*
65 folkloriser T – *to make folk*
65 fomenter T – *to foment, to foster*
66 foncer I, T – *to rush, to tear along, to darken*
65 fonctionnariser T – *to officialize, to make a civil servant (of)*
65 fonctionner I – *to work*
65 fonder I, T – *to set up, to found*
65 fonder (se) P – *to be based, to be founded*
118 fondre I, T – *to melt, to cast (metal), to blend (colour)*
118 fondre (se) P – *to merge (into), to fade (into)*
66 forcer I, T – *to force, to compel, to strain*
66 forcer (se) P – *to make an effort*
81 forcir I – *to broaden out*
138 forclore T, D – *to foreclose*
infinitive and p. p. "forclos(e)"
65 forer T – *to drill*
128 forfaire à I, T, Ti, D – *to forfeit, to be false to*
only in the infinitive,
the present indicative singular,
the p. p. and at compound tenses
67 forger I, T – *to forge*
67 forger (se) P – *to forge, to earn a reputation*
70 forjeter I, T – *to be out of alignment (architecture)*
66 forlancer T – *to make an animal come out of its lair (hunting)*
65 forligner I – *to act as to shame one's forefathers*
67 forlonger T – *to distance (hunting), to leave the usual pasture (animal)*
65 formaliser T – *to formalize*
65 formaliser (se) P – *to take offence*
65 formater T – *to format*
65 former T – *to form, to train*
65 former (se) P – *to form, to train*
65 formoler T – *to disinfect with formol*
65 formuler T – *to formulate*

65 formuler (se) P – *to be enunciated, to be formulated, to be expressed*
65 forniquer I – *to fornicate*
76 fortifier T – *to strengthen, to fortify*
76 fortifier (se) P – *to grow stronger*
65 fossiliser T – *to fossilize*
65 fossiliser (se) P – *to fossilize*
78 fossoyer T – *to dig graves, to trench*
65 fouailler T – *to lash*
78 foudroyer T – *to strike (thunder), to crush*
65 fouetter I, T – *to whip*
67 fouger I – *to unearth roots with one's snout (boar), to overturn grass roots (agriculture)*
65 fouiller I, T – *to search, to rummage*
65 fouiller (se) P – *to go through one's pockets, to do without*
65 fouiner I – *to go through, to be noisy*
81 fouir T – *to dig*
65 fouler T – *to press*
65 fouler (se) P – *to put oneself out*
65 fourailler I, T – *to whip*
65 fourber I, T – *to cheat*
81 fourbir T – *to furbish, to polish up*
65 fourcher I, T – *to fork*
65 fourgonner I – *to poke about*
65 fourguer T – *to flog*
65 fourmiller I – *to swarm*
81 fournir à T, Ti – *to supply, to provide (to)*
81 fournir (se) P – *to get supplies from*
67 fourrager I, T – *to rummage*
65 fourrer T – *to tuck, to line with fur*
65 fourrer (se) P – *to hide oneself*
78 fourvoyer T – *to mislead*
78 fourvoyer (se) P – *to lose one's way*
120 foutre T – *to do*
p. p. "foutu", "c'est foutu !" – *it's all up*
120 foutre (se) P – *to get on, to line one's pocket (money), to blow it*
65 fracasser T – *to smash, to crash, to shatter*
65 fracasser (se) P – *to smash, to crash, to shatter*
65 fractionner T – *to split up, to divide*
65 fractionner (se) P – *to split up, to divide*
65 fracturer T – *to fracture*
65 fracturer (se) P – *to fracture*
65 fragiliser T – *to render fragile*
65 fragmenter T – *to break up*
81 fraîchir/fraichir I – *to freshen*
65 fraiser T – *to mill*
65 framboiser T – *to add rasberry juice*
81 franchir T – *to clear, to cross*
65 franchiser T – *to franchise*
65 franciser T – *to Frenchify*
65 francophoniser québ. T – *to become francophone*
67 franger T – *to edge with fringe*
65 fransquillonner belg. I – *to speak French without an accent*
65 frapper I, T – *to knock, to strike*
65 frapper (se) P – *to hit oneself, to hit each other, to be worried*
65 fraterniser I – *to fraternize*
65 frauder I, T – *to defraud*
77 frayer I, T – *to clear (road), to spawn (fish), to associate*
77 frayer (se) P – *to open up, to force one's way through*
65 fredonner I, T – *to hum*
65 frégater T – *to give the shape of a frigate*
65 freiner I, T – *to brake, to slow down*
65 freiner (se) P – *to slow oneself down (figurative)*
65 frelater T – *to adulterate*
81 frémir I – *to quiver, to rustle, to shiver*
65 fréquenter I, T – *to frequent, to keep company (with)*
65 fréquenter (se) P – *to date, to see each other*
69 fréter T – *to charter*
65 frétiller I – *to wriggle, to wag (tail), to fidget*
65 fretter T – *to fret*
65 fricasser T – *to fricassee*
65 fricoter I, T – *to cook up*
65 frictionner T – *to rub*
65 frictionner (se) P – *to rub*
76 frigorifier T – *to refrigerate*
67 frigorifuger T – *to insulate to keep cold*
65 frimer I, T – *to pretend*
65 fringuer I, T – *to get dressed*
65 fringuer (se) P – *to get dressed*
65 friper T – *to crumple*
65 friper (se) P – *to crumple*
65 friponner I, T – *to be mischievous*
65 friquer afr. T – *to give money*
151 frire I, T, D – *to fry*
65 friser I, T – *to curl, to be close to*
65 frisot(t)er I, T – *to curl slightly*
65 frissonner I – *to shiver, to shudder*
65 fristouiller belg. I, T – *to cook*
65 fritter I, T – *to calcine*
81 froidir I – *to make cold*
65 froisser T – *to crease, to offend*
65 froisser (se) P – *to crush, to crease, to take offence*
65 frôler T – *to brush against, to skim*
65 frôler (se) P *to brush against, to skim*
66 froncer T – *to frown, to pucker, to gather (cloth)*
66 froncer (se) P – *to wrinkle*
65 fronder I, T – *to scoff at, to use a sling*
65 frotter I, T – *to rub*
65 frotter (se) P – *to rub*
65 frouer I – *to mimic the calls of birds (hunting)*
65 froufrouter I – *to rustle*
65 frousser afr. I – *to be scared*
76 fructifier I – *to be productive, to bear fruit*
65 frusquer T – *to dress*
65 frusquer (se) P – *to dress oneself*
65 frustrer T – *to frustrate*
65 fuguer I – *to abscond*
97 fuir I, T – *to flee, to run away, to shun, to leak*
97 fuir (se) P – *to avoid each other, to avoid oneself (figurative)*
65 fuiter T – *to leak (information)*

T: direct transitive (p. p. variable) – **Ti**: indirect transitive (p. p. invariable) – **I**: intransitive verb (p. p. invariable) **P**: pronominal verb (auxiliary *être*) – **impers.**: impersonal verb – **D**: defective verb – *être*: verb conjugated with the auxiliary *être* – *être* or *avoir*: verbs conjugated with *être* or *avoir* (see paragraph 15)

65 fulgurer I, T – *to flash*
65 fulminer I, T – *to fulminate*
65 fumer I, T – *to smoke, to steam*
67 fumiger T – *to fumigate*
71 fureter I – *to ferret (around)*
72 fuseler T – *to taper*
65 fuser I – *to burst forth*
65 fusiller T – *to shoot*
65 fusionner I, T – *to merge*
67 fustiger T – *to denounce, to strike*

g

76 gabarier T – *to make from a template, to maximize loading capacity*
65 gabionner T – *to fortify with gabion*
65 gâcher I, T – *to spoil, to squander, to mix*
65 gadgétiser T – *to gadgetize*
65 gaffer I, T – *to blunder*
65 gafouiller T – *to do bad work*
67 gager T – *to wager, to bet*
65 gagner I, T – *to win, to gain, to earn*
65 gagner (se) P – *to win, to gain, to earn*
65 gainer T – *to sheath, to cover*
65 galber T – *to curve*
69 galéjer I – *to spin a yarn, to joke*
69 galérer I – *to work hard, to slave away, to waste time*
65 galipoter T – *to coat with resin (boat)*
65 galonner T – *to trim with braid*
65 galoper I, T – *to gallop*
65 galvaniser T – *to galvanize, to give new life (to)*
65 galvauder I, T – *to botch, to loaf about*
65 galvauder (se) P – *to demean oneself*
65 gambader I – *to caper*
67 gamberger I, T – *to think*
65 gambiller I – *to skip about*
72 gameler T – *to eat, to fall*
72 gameler (se) P – *to fall or to fail (figurative)*
65 gaminer I – *to be playful*
68 gangrener T – *to gangrene*
68 gangrener (se) P – *to become gangrenous*
69 gangréner T – *to gangrene*
69 gangréner (se) P – *to become gangrenous*
65 ganser T – *to braid*
65 ganter I, T – *to glove*
65 ganter (se) P – *to put on/to slip on gloves*
66 garancer T – *to dye bright red*
81 garantir T – *to guarantee, to warrant, to protect*
65 garder T – *to keep, to look after, to guard*
65 garder (se) P – *to keep*
65 garer T – *to park (car), to take cover*
65 garer (se) P – *to park (car), to take cover*
65 gargariser (se) P – *to gargle, to boast*
65 gargoter I – *to eat cheaply*
65 gargouiller I – *to gurgle*
81 garnir T – *to fit out, to fill, to garnish*
81 garnir (se) P – *to fill up*
65 garrocher québ. T – *to throw carelessly*
65 garrot(t)er T – *to pinion, to garrotte*
65 gasconner I – *to boast*
65 gaspiller T – *to waste, to squander*
65 gâter T – *to spoil, to go bad*
65 gâter (se) P – *to go off/bad (food)*
76 gâtifier I – *to become a dodderer*
81 gauchir I, T – *to warp, to distort*
81 gauchir (se) P – *to warp, to distort*
65 gaufrer T – *to emboss, to crinkle*
65 gauler T – *to shake fruit (from tree)*
65 gausser (se) P – *to mock*
65 gaver T – *to force-feed*
65 gaver (se) P – *to stuff oneself*
76 gazéifier T – *to gasify*
65 gazer I, T – *to gas, to get on*
65 gazonner I, T – *to plant with grass*
65 gazouiller I – *to chirp (birds), to gurgle (babies), to babble (river)*
123 geindre I – *to groan*
65 gélatiner T – *to make gelatinous*
65 gélatiniser T – *to make gelatinous*
73 geler I, T – *to freeze*
73 geler (se) P – *to freeze*
76 gélifier T – *to gel, to make into jelly*
76 gélifier (se) P – *to become gel/jelly*
65 géminer T – *to geminate, to twin*
81 gémir I, T – *to groan, to moan, to squeak*
65 gemmer T – *to tap pine trees*
65 gendarmer (se) P – *to flare up, to kick up a fuss*
65 gêner T – *to hinder, to bother, to inconvenience*
65 gêner (se) P – *to put oneself out*
65 généraliser T – *to generalize*
65 généraliser (se) P – *to become widespread*
69 générer T – *to generate*
65 géométriser T – *to make geometric*
65 gerber I, T – *to sheave, to vomit*
66 gercer I, T – *to chap, to crack*
66 gercer (se) P – *to chap, to crack*
69 gérer T – *to manage*
65 germaniser I, T – *to Germanize*
65 germaniser (se) P – *to become Germanized*
65 germer I – *to sprout, to spring up*
99 gésir I, D – *to be lying down*
only in the present participle
the present and the imparfait *of the indicative*
65 gesticuler I – *to gesticulate*
78 giboyer T – *to hunt*
65 gicler I – *to spurt*
65 gifler T – *to slap*
65 gigoter I – *to kick about*
65 giguer québ. I – *to jig*
65 gironner T – *to round edges (metal)*
65 girouetter I – *to veer*
"gisant" (*to lie montionless, to be laid to rest*) *see* "gésir"
"gît, il gît, ci-gît" *see* "gésir"
"git, il git, ci-git" *see* "gésir"
65 gîter/giter I – *to lodge, to list (ship)*
65 givrer T – *to frost*
65 givrer (se) P – *to frost up, to ice up*
66 glacer I, T, impers. – *to freeze, to chill, to ice*
impers.: "il glace"
66 glacer (se) P – *to freeze, to become numb*
65 glaglater I – *to shiver*
65 glairer T – *to glair*
65 glaiser T – *to clay*

65 glander I – *to hang about*
65 glandouiller I – *to hang about*
65 glaner I, T – *to glean, to gather*
81 glapir I, T – *to yap, to yeld*
81 glatir I – *to cry (eagle)*
65 glaviot(t)er I – *to spit*
65 glaviotter I – *to spit*
69 gléner T – *to coil (rope)*
65 gletter belg. I – *to salivate, to drool*
65 glisser I, T – *to slide, to slip*
65 glisser (se) P – *to slide, to slip*
65 globaliser T – *to globalize*
76 glorifier T – *to praise*
76 glorifier (se) P – *to praise oneself, to boast, to brag*
65 gloser sur I, T, Ti – *to annotate, to gloss, to ramble on*
65 glouglouter I – *to gurgle*
65 glousser I – *to chuckle*
65 gloutonner I, T – *to guzzle*
65 glycériner T – *to add glycerine*
65 gober T – *to swallow, to gulp*
67 goberger (se) P – *to indulge oneself*
70 gobeter T – *to bemsear a wall*
65 godailler I – *to drink, to be ill-fitted*
65 goder I – *to pucker, to bag*
65 godiller I – *to scull, to single*
65 godronner T – *to edge with tar*
65 goguenarder I – *to mock*
65 goinfrer I – *to make a pig of*
65 goinfrer (se) P – *to guzzle*
65 gominer (se) P – *to put hair cream on*
65 gommer T – *to erase, to rub out, to stick*
65 gonder T – *to hinge*
65 gondoler I – *to crinkle, to warp*
65 gondoler (se) P – *to crinkle, to laugh*
65 gonfler I, T – *to pump (up), to inflate, to swell, to irritate*
65 gonfler (se) P – *to be puffed up (with)*
65 gorgeonner (se) P – *to get drunk, to guzzle (alcohol)*
67 gorger T – *to fill up*
67 gorger (se) P – *to be filled up, to gorge oneself (eating)*
65 gouacher T – *to paint with gouache*
65 gouailler I – *to banter*
65 goualer I, T – *to sing*
65 gouaper I – *to lead a life of debauchery (archaic)*
65 goudronner T – *to tar*
67 gouger T – *to work with a gouge*
65 gougnot(t)er T – *to perform cunnilingus (slang)*
65 goujonner T – *to pin, to assemble with gudgeon*
65 goupiller T – *to pin, to fix*
65 goupiller (se) P – *to turn out*
65 goupillonner T – *to clean with a bottle-brush*
66 gourancer (se) P – *to make a mistake*
65 gourer (se) P – *to make a mistake*
65 gourmander T – *to rebuke, to chide*
65 goûter/gouter à, de I, T, Ti – *to taste, to take a little, to sample*
65 goutter I – to drip
65 gouttiner belg. I – *to leak a drop at a time impers.*
65 gouverner I, T – *to govern, to rule, to steer (ship)*
65 gouverner (se) P – *to govern, to rule, to steer (ship)*
76 gracier T – *to pardon*
65 graduer T – *to graduate, to grade*
65 graffiter I, T – *to make graffitis*
65 grafigner québ. T – *to scratch, to scrape*
65 grailler I, T – *to eat*
65 graillonner I – *to cough*
65 grainer T – *to granulate*
65 graisser I, T – *to grease, to lubricate*
65 grammaticaliser T – *to make grammatical*
65 grammaticaliser (se) P – *to grammaticalize*
81 grandir I, T – *to grow, to increase, to magnify*
81 grandir (se) P – *to grow, to increase, to magnify*
65 graniter T – *to make granite-like*
65 granuler T – *to granulate*
65 graphiter T – *to graphitize*
65 grappiller I, T – *to glean, to cadge*
77 grasseyer I, T – *to speak with a strong emphasis on R the y remains throughout the conjugation*
65 graticuler T – *to grid*
76 gratifier T – *to confer, to ascribe*
65 gratiner I, T – *to cook au gratin, to brown*
65 grat(t)ouiller T – *to itch, to scratch*
65 gratter I, T – *to scratch, to scrape, to itch*
65 gratter (se) P – *to scratch oneself*
65 graver I, T – *to engrave*
65 graver (se) P – *to engrave*
65 gravillonner T – *to cover with grit/fine gravel*
81 gravir sur, à T, Ti – *to climb*
65 graviter I – *to gravitate*
65 gréciser T – *to Hellenize*
65 grecquer T – *to sawbind*
74 gréer T – *to rig*
65 greffer T – *to graft, to transplant (organ)*
65 greffer (se) P – *to add, to attach*
65 grêler T, impers. – *to hail (weather) impers.*: "il grêle"
65 grelot(t)er I – *to shiver*
65 grenailler T – *to granulate*
72 greneler T – *to grain*
68 grener I, T – *to granulate*
65 grenouiller I – *to act in an underhand fashion, to plot*
69 gréser T – *to polish, to rub with sandstone*
65 grésiller I, impers. – *to sizzle, to sputter impers.*: "il grésille"
68 grever T – *to burden*
69 gréver afr. I – *to be on strike*
65 gribouiller I, T – *to scribble*
65 griffer I, T – *to claw, to scratch*
65 griffonner I, T – *to scribble*
65 grigner I – *to pucker*
65 grignoter I, T – *to nibble, to pick at*
65 grigriser afr. T – *to bewitch using a fetish*
67 grillager T – *to put wire netting (on)*
65 griller I, T – *to grill, to toast, to scorch, to singe, to jump (traffic light)*

T: direct transitive (p. p. variable) – **Ti**: indirect transitive (p. p. invariable) – **I**: intransitive verb (p. p. invariable) **P**: pronominal verb (auxiliary *être*) – **impers.**: impersonal verb – **D**: defective verb – *être*: verb conjugated with the auxiliary *être* – *être* or *avoir*: verbs conjugated with *être* or *avoir* (see paragraph 15)

65 griller (se) P – *to grill, to toast, to scorch, to singe, to jump (traffic light)*
66 grimacer I – *to grimace, to make faces*
65 grimer T – *to make up*
65 grimer (se) P – *to make up*
65 grimper I, T – *to climb*
66 grincer I – *to grate, to squeak, to grit*
65 grincher T – *to creak, to squeak, to grit*
65 gringuer I – *to flirt, to sweet-talk*
65 gripper I, T – *to jam, to seize up*
65 gripper (se) P – *to jam, to seize up*
65 grisailler I, T – *to turn grey*
65 griser T – *to make tipsy*
65 griser (se) P – *to get drunk*
65 grisoler I – *to sing (lark)*
65 grisoller I – *to sing (lark)*
65 grisonner I – *to be going grey*
72 griveler I, T – *to sneak (a meal)*
65 grognasser I – *to grumble, to growl, to grunt*
65 grogner I, T – *to grumble, to growl, to grunt*
65 grognonner I – *to grumble*
72 grommeler I, T – *to mutter*
65 gronder I, T – *to scold, to rumble (storm)*
81 grossir I, T – *to enlarge, to swell, to grow fat*
78 grossoyer T – *to engross (document)*
65 grouiller I – *to swarm, to teem, to mill about*
65 grouiller (se) P – *to hurry*
65 groûler/grouler belg. I – *to growl*
65 groumer I – *to grumble, to growl, to grunt (sailor)*
65 grouper I, T – *to group*
65 grouper (se) P – *to gather together*
67 gruger T – *to dupe*
72 grumeler (se) P – *to curdle*
74 guéer T – *to ford*
81 guérir I, T – *to cure, to heal*
81 guérir (se) P – *to get better, to cure oneself*
78 guerroyer I, T – *to wage war*
65 guêtrer T – *to wear gaiters*
65 guêtrer (se) P – *to put on gaiters*
65 guetter I, T – *to watch, to be on the look out (for)*
65 guetter (se) P – *to watch one another*
65 gueuler I, T – *to bawl*
65 gueuletonner I – *to feast*
65 gueuser I, T – *to beg*
65 guider T – *to guide*
65 guider (se) P – *to guide*
65 guigner T – *to eye, to sneak a peek*
70 guillemeter T – *to put in inverted commas*
65 guillocher T – *to chequer*
65 guillotiner T – *to guillotine*
65 guincher I – *to dance*
65 guindailler afr. + belg. I – *to party (involving heavy drinking)*
65 guinder T – *to make stilted*
65 guinder (se) P – *to make oneself appear of a higher status (figurative), to elevate oneself socially*
65 guiper T – *to insulated with tape (wires)*

h

(* = aspirate *h*)
65 habiliter T – *to enable*
65 habiller T – *to dress*
65 habiller (s') P – *to dress, to get dressed, to dress up*
65 habiter I, T – *to live, to occupy*
65 habituer T – *to accustom*
65 habituer (s') P – *to get use to, to become use to*
65 * hâbler I – *to boast*
65 * hacher T – *to chop, to mince*
65 * hachurer T – *to hatch*
82 haïr I, T – *to hate*
82 haïr (se) P – *to hate oneself/each other*
68 halener T – *to smell so's breath, to exhale, to pick up the scent (hunting dogs)*
65 * haler T – *to tow, to pull, to haul*
65 * hâler T – *to turn brown, to tan*
65 hâler (se) P – *to get a tan*
71 * haleter I – *to gasp, to pant*
65 * halkiner belg. I – *to hesitate, to talk it over*
65 halluciner T – *to hallucinate*
65 hameçonner T – *to hook (fish)*
65 * hancher I, T – *to swing (hips)*
73 handeler belg. T – *to care for animals (farm)*
65 * handicaper T – *to handicap*
65 * hannetonner I, T – *to kill cockchafer*
65 * hanter T – *to haunt*
65 * happer I, T – *to snap up*
65 * haranguer T – *to harangue, to lecture*
65 * harasser T – *to harass, to tire*
73 * harceler T – *to harry, to torment*
65 * harder T – *to leash (hounds)*
65 haricoter T – *to speculate underhandedly (dishonest)*
65 harmoniser T – *to harmonize (with)*
65 harmoniser (s') P – *to match*
65 * harnacher T – *to harness*
65 harnacher (se) P – *to get equiped*
65 * harpailler I – *to quarrel*
65 * harper T – *to clutch, to grab*
65 * harponner T – *to harpoon, to clutch*
65 * hasarder T – *to risk, to venture*
65 hasarder (se) P – *to risk, to venture*
65 * hâter T – *to hasten, to hurry*
65 hâter (se) P – *to hasten, to hurry*
65 * haubaner T – *to stabilize a vertical part with ropes*
65 * hausser T – *to raise, to heighten*
65 hausser (se) P – *to raise, to reach up*
65 * haver I, T – *to under-cut, to channel*
81 * havir I, T – *to cook meat over a large fire*
67 héberger T – *to lodge, to entertain (somebody)*
69 hébéter T – *to stupefy*
65 hébraïser I, T – *to assimilate into Jewish culture*
69 * héler T – *to hail, to call*
69 * héler (se) P – *to hail, to call out each other (sailor)*
65 hélitreuiller T – *to winch up (helicopter)*
65 helléniser I, T – *to Hellenize*
81 * hennir I – *to neigh*
67 herbager T – *to put out to grass*
65 herber T – *to exhibit on the grass*
65 herboriser I – *to botanize*
65 hercher I – *to manually push carts (mining)*
65 * hérisser T – *to bristle, to stand on end*
65 hérisser (se) P – *to bristle, to stand on end*
65 * hérissonner I, T – *to cover wall with mortar*
65 hérissonner (se) P – *to straighten up fur/spikes/feathers*

65 hériter de I, T, Ti – *to inherit*
65 * herser T – *to harrow*
65 hésiter I – *to hesitate, to waver, to falter*
65 * heurter I, T – *to strike, to hit, to knock*
65 heurter (se) P – *to collide, to bump or to run into each other*
65 hiberner I, T – *to hibernate*
65 * hiérarchiser T – *to organize into hierarchy*
65 * hisser T – *to hoist*
65 hisser (se) P – *to have oneself up*
76 historier T – *to illustrate, to embellish*
65 hiverner I, T – *to winter*
65 * hocher T – *to nod*
76 holographier T – *to write one's own will*
76 homogénéifier T – *to homogenize*
65 homogénéiser T – *to homogenize*
65 homologuer T – *to endorse, to ratify*
65 * hongrer T – *to geld, to castrate*
78 * hongroyer T – *to work leather in an Hungarian way*
81 * honnir T – *to disgrace, to revile, to despise*
65 honorer T – *to honour, to esteem, to be a credit to*
65 honorer (s') P – *to gain honour*
70 * hoqueter I – *to hiccup*
76 horrifier T – *to horrify*
65 horripiler T – *to exasperate*
65 hospitaliser T – *to hospitalize*
65 * houblonner T – *to hop (beer)*
65 * houer T – *to hoe*
65 * houpper T – *to trim (with tassles)*
65 * hourder T – *to rough-cast*
81 * hourdir T – *to do rough stoneworking*
65 * houspiller T – *to abuse, to bully*
65 * housser T – *to cover up (furniture)*
65 houssiner T – *to beat with a stick (horse, carpets)*
65 * hucher T – *to call*
65 * huer I, T – *to boo, to hoot*
65 huiler T – *to oil, to lubricate*
81 * huir I, D – *to cry, to scream (birds of prey) only in the infinitive, the present indicative and the compound tenses*
65 (h)ululer I – *to hoot*
65 humaniser T – *to humanize*
65 humaniser (s') P – *to humanize*
65 humecter T – *to dampen, to moisten*
65 humecter (s') P – *to dampen, to moisten*
65 * humer T – *to smell, to inhale*
76 humidifier T – *to humidify*
76 humilier T – *to humiliate*
76 humilier (s') P – *to humiliate*
65 * hurler I, T – *to scream*
65 hybrider T – *to hybridize*
65 hybrider (s') P – *to hybridize*
65 hydrater T – *to hydrate*
65 hydrater (s') P – *to become hydrated*
67 hydrofuger T – *to waterproof*
69 hydrogéner T – *to hydrogenate*
65 hydrolyser T – *to hydrolyse*
76 hypertrophier T – *to enlarge abnormally*
76 hypertrophier (s') P – *to hypertrophy*
65 hypnotiser T – *to hypnotize*
65 hypnotiser (s') P – *to be mesmerized*
76 hypostasier T – *to hypostasize*
69 hypothéquer T – *to mortgage*

i

65 iconiser T – *to iconize*
65 idéaliser T – *to idealize*
65 idéaliser (s') P – *to idealize*
76 identifier T – *to identify*
76 identifier (s') P – *to be identified*
65 idéologiser T – *to make into an ideology*
65 idiotiser T – *to reduce to imbecility, to make idiotic*
65 idolâtrer T – *to idolize*
65 idolâtrer (s') P – *to idolize oneself*
67 ignifuger T – *to fireproof*
65 ignorer T – *to ignore, to be unaware (of)*
65 ignorer (s') P – *to ignore each other*
65 illuminer T – *to light up, to illuminate, to enlighten*
65 illuminer (s') P – *to light up, to illuminate, to enlighten*
65 illusionner T – *to delude*
65 illusionner (s') P – *to delude, to deceive oneself*
65 illustrer T – *to illustrate*
65 illustrer (s') P – *to become famous*
67 imager T – *to add images*
65 imaginer T – *to imagine, to devise, to think up*
65 imaginer (s') P – *to imagine oneself, to devise, to think up, to picture*
65 imbiber T – *to moisten, to soak*
65 imbiber (s') P – *to become soaked*
65 imbriquer T – *to be linked*
65 imbriquer (s') P – *to overlap*
65 imiter T – *to imitate*
65 immatérialiser T – *to immaterialize*
65 immatérialiser (s') P – *to immaterialize*
65 immatriculer T – *to register*
67 immerger T – *to immerge, to submerge*
67 immerger (s') P – *to dive (in/into)*
65 immigrer I – *to immigrate*
66 immiscer (s') P – *to interfere, to enter subtlely*
65 immobiliser T – *to immobilize*
65 immobiliser (s') P – *to stop, to stand still*
65 immoler T – *to immolate, to sacrifice*
65 immoler (s') P – *to immolate, to sacrifice*
65 immortaliser T – *to immortalize*
65 immortaliser (s') P – *to win eternal fame*
65 immuniser T – *to immunize*
65 immuniser (s') P – *to immunize oneself*
65 impacter T – *to impact*
81 impartir T – *to assign especially in the present indicative, the past participle and at compound tenses*
65 impatienter T – *to irritate, to annoy*
65 impatienter (s') P – *to grow/become impatient*

T: direct transitive (p. p. variable) – **Ti**: indirect transitive (p. p. invariable) – **I**: intransitive verb (p. p. invariable) **P**: pronominal verb (auxiliary *être*) – **impers.**: impersonal verb – **D**: defective verb – *être*: verb conjugated with the auxiliary *être* – *être* or *avoir*: verbs conjugated with *être* or *avoir* (see paragraph 15)

65 impatroniser T – *to gain enough power to rule*
65 impatroniser (s') P – *to establish oneself as master*
65 imperméabiliser T – *to waterproof*
69 impétrer T – *to receive by authority*
65 implanter T – *to introduce, to set up, to implant*
65 implanter (s') P – *to become established*
65 implémenter T – *to implement*
65 impliquer T – *to implicate, to involve*
65 impliquer (s') P – *to implicate oneself, to involve oneself*
65 implorer T – *to implore*
65 imploser I – *to implode*
65 importer à I, T, Ti – *to matter, to import*
65 importuner T – *to bother, to pester, to trouble*
65 imposer T – *to impose, to set, to tax*
65 imposer (s') P – *to impose oneself, to stand out, to be necessary*
69 imprégner T – *to impregnate, to permeate*
69 imprégner (s') P – *to become imbued, to become soaked, to become impermated*
65 impressionner T – *to impress*
65 imprimer T – *to print, to stamp*
65 imprimer (s') P – *to print, to stamp*
65 improuver T – *to disapprove (of)*
65 improviser I, T – *to improvise*
65 improviser (s') P – *to improvise*
65 impulser T – *to impulse*
65 imputer à T, Ti – *to attribute to, to charge (expenses)*
65 inactiver T – *to inactivate*
65 inaugurer T – *to inaugurate*
69 incarcérer T – *to incarcerate*
65 incarner T – *to embody, to incarnate*
65 incarner (s') P – *to become incarnate (religion), to be embodied*
76 incendier T – *to set fire (to)*
69 incinérer T – *to incinerate, to cremate*
65 inciser T – *to incise*
65 inciter T – *to prompt, to encourage, to incite*
65 incliner I, T – *to incline, to tilt, to lean*
65 incliner (s') P – *to bow, to yield*
140 inclure T – *to enclose, to insert*
65 incomber à Ti – *to fall to, to devolve upon used in 3rd person singular and plural*
65 incommoder T – *to disturb*
65 incorporer T – *to integrate*
65 incorporer (s') P – *to incorporate*
65 incrémenter T – *to increment*
65 incriminer T – *to incriminate*
65 incruster T – *to inlay*
65 incruster (s') P – *to become imbedded (in), to take root, to stick around*
65 incuber T – *to incubate*
65 inculper T – *to charge*
65 inculquer T – *to instil (into)*
65 incurver T – *to form into a curve, to bend*
65 incurver (s') P – *to form into a curve, to bend*
65 indaguer belg. I – *to investigate*
65 indemniser T – *to indemnify, to compensate*
65 indemniser (s') P – *to indemnify oneself*
65 indexer T – *to index*
66 indicer T – *to subscript, to allocate an index*
69 indifférer T – *to be indifferent*
65 indigner T – *to make indignant*
65 indigner (s') P – *to be indignant*
65 indiquer T – *to point to, to point out, to indicate*
65 indisposer T – *to upset*
65 individualiser T – *to individualize*
65 individualiser (s') P – *to acquire an identity of one's own*
152 induire T – *to infer, to induce*
65 indurer T – *to harden*
65 industrialiser T – *to industrialize*
65 industrialiser (s') P – *to become industrialized*
65 infantiliser T – *to make infantile, to retard*
65 infatuer T – *to infatuate*
65 infatuer (s') P – *to be conceited, to be infatuated*
65 infecter T – *to infect, to contaminate*
65 infecter (s') P – *to become septic*
65 inféoder T – *to enfeoff*
65 inféoder (s') P – *to become the vassal of a lord*
69 inférer T – *to infer*
65 inferioriser T – *to make so feel inferior, to minimize the importance of something*
65 infester T – *to infest*
65 infiltrer T – *to infiltrate*
65 infiltrer (s') P – *to seep, to filter in, to infiltrate*
65 infirmer T – *to invalidate*
81 infléchir T – *to bend, to sag, to inflect*
81 infléchir (s') P – *to bend, to curve, to shift (opinion)*
67 infliger à T, Ti – *to inflict*
66 influencer T – *to influence*
65 influer I – *to have an influence over, to affect*
65 informatiser T – *to computerize*
65 informatiser (s') P – *to become computerized*
65 informer I, T – *to inform*
65 informer (s') P – *to ask, to inquire*
65 infuser I, T – *to infuse*
76 ingénier (s') P – *to seek, to endeavour, to attempt*
69 ingérer T – *to ingest*
69 ingérer (s') P – *to interfere, to meddle*
65 ingurgiter T – *to swallow, to gulp down*
65 inhaler T – *to inhale*
65 inhiber T – *to inhibit*
65 inhumer T – *to inter*
65 initialer québ. T – *to sign with one's inital especially to indicate approval, to endorse*
65 initialiser T – *to initialize*
76 initier T – *to initiate*
76 initier (s') P – *to learn/study the basis, to initiate*
65 injecter T – *to inject*
65 injecter (s') P – *to become injected*
76 injurier T – *to insult, to abuse*
76 injurier (s') P – *to insult each other*
65 innerver T – *to innervate*
65 innocenter T – *to prove innocent*
65 innover I, T – *to innovate*
65 inoculer T – *to inoculate, to infect*
65 inoculer (s') P – *to be inoculated or to inoculate oneself, to infect oneself*
65 inonder T – *to inundate, to flood*
65 inonder (s') P – *to splash/spary/douse oneself*
69 inquiéter T – *to disturb*
69 inquiéter (s') P – *to worry, to be worried*
150inscrire T – *to note down, to write down, to register*
150 inscrire (s') P – *to register, to join*

65 insculper T – *to hallmark, to engrave with a stylus/ chisel*
65 inséminer T – *to inseminate*
65 insensibiliser T – *to anaesthetize, to dull*
69 insérer T – *to insert*
69 insérer (s') P – *to join, to integrate*
65 insinuer T – *to insinuate, to imply*
65 insinuer (s') P – *to creep in, to filter, to seep in*
65 insister I – *to insist*
65 insoler T – *to insolate*
65 insolubiliser T – *to make insoluble*
65 insonoriser T – *to soundproof*
65 inspecter T – *to inspect*
65 inspirer I, T – *to breathe in, to inspire*
65 inspirer (s') P – *to draw inspiration, to imitate*
65 installer T – *to install, to settle*
65 installer (s') P – *to settle down*
65 instaurer T – *to institute*
65 instaurer (s') P – *to establish oneself, to base oneself*
65 instiguer belg. T – *to incite to bad behaviour*
65 instiller T – *to instil*
65 instituer T – *to institute, to appoint*
65 instituer (s') P – *to institute, to appoint*
65 institutionnaliser T – *to institutionalize*
65 institutionnaliser (s') P – *to institutionalize*
152 instruire T – *to teach, to educate*
152 instruire (s') P – *to become educated*
65 instrumentaliser T – *to use, to manipulate*
65 instrumenter I, T – *to orchestrate*
65 insuffler T – *to inspire*
65 insulter à I, T, Ti – *to insult, to give credit, to not give what is due*
65 insulter (s') P – *to insult each other*
65 insupporter T – *to annoy, to aggravate*
used only with a pronoun complement
ex: "Paul m'insupporte" – *I can't stand Paul*
67 insurger T – *to rise against, to rebel*
67 insurger (s') P – *to rise against, to rebel*
65 intailler T – *to intaliate*
69 intégrer à I, T, Ti – *to integrate to, to combine to, to add to*
69 intégrer (s') P – *to fit (into), to become part*
65 intellectualiser T – *to intellectualize*
76 intensifier T – *to intensify*
76 intensifier (s') P – *to intensify*
65 intenter T – *to bring an action*
81 interagir I – *to interact*
65 intercaler T – *to insert, to inset*
65 intercaler (s') P – *to fit between, to come between*
69 intercéder I – *to intercede*
65 intercepter T – *to intercept*
65 interclasser T – *to interfile, to merge*
65 interconnecter T – *to interconnect*
148 interdire T – *to forbid, to ban*
148 interdire (s') P – *to abstain, to deny oneself*
65 intéresser T – *to interest, to affect*
65 intéresser (s') P – *to have interest*
69 interférer I – *to interfere*
76 interfolier T – *to interpage*
65 intérioriser T – *to internalize*
70 interjeter T – *to lodge (an appeal)*
65 interligner T – *to interline*
65 interloquer T – *to dumbfound*
65 internationaliser T – *to internationalize*
65 internationaliser (s') P – *to become internationalize*
65 interner T – *to intern*
72 interpeler T – *to hail in order to question or insult, to arrest*
72 interpeler (s') P – *to hail one another to question or insult*
65 interpeller T – *to call out, to hail*
65 interpeller (s') P – *to call out or hail one another*
69 interpénétrer (s') P – *to interpenetrate*
65 interpoler T – *to interpolate*
65 interposer T – *to interpose*
65 interposer (s') P – *to intervene*
69 interpréter T – *to interpret, to perform (part)*
69 interpréter (s') P – *to be interpreted, to be performed (part)*
67 interroger T – *to interrogate, to question*
67 interroger (s') P – *to wonder, to be uncertain*
120 interrompre T – *to interrupt, to break into*
120 interrompre (s') P – *to break off*
84 intervenir I, être – *to intervene*
81 intervertir T – *to invert, to reverse the order*
65 interviewer T – *to interview*
65 intimer T – *to order, to instruct, to summon (law)*
65 intimider T – *to intimidate*
65 intituler T – *to entitle, to call*
65 intituler (s') P – *to be called*
65 intoxiquer T – *to poison, to intoxicate, to brainwash*
65 intoxiquer (s') P – *to be poisoned, to be intoxicated, to be brainwashed*
65 intriguer I, T – *to intrigue*
65 intriquer T – *to criss-cross*
152 introduire T – *to introduce, to insert*
152 introduire (s') P – *to introduce oneself, to work one's way (into)*
65 introniser T – *to enthrone*
65 intuber T – *to insert a tube*
65 invaginer (s') P – *to fold inwards*
65 invalider T – *to invalidate*
65 invectiver I, T – *to curse, to insult*
65 inventer I, T – *to invent*
65 inventer (s') P – *to invent*
76 inventorier T – *to make an inventory*
65 inverser T – *to inverse, to reverse*
65 inverser (s') P – *to inverse, to reverse*
81 invertir T – *to invert*
81 investir I, T – *to invest*
81 investir (s') P – *to be involve in*
69 invétérer (s') P – *to be inveterate*
65 inviter T – *to invite*
65 inviter (s') P – *to invite oneself*
65 invoquer T – *to invoke*
65 ioder T – *to iodize*
65 iodler I – *to yodel*
65 ioniser T – *to ionize*

T: direct transitive (p. p. variable) – **Ti**: indirect transitive (p. p. invariable) – **I**: intransitive verb (p. p. invariable) **P**: pronominal verb (auxiliary *être*) – **impers.**: impersonal verb – **D**: defective verb – *être*: verb conjugated with the auxiliary *être* – *être* or *avoir*: verbs conjugated with *être* or *avoir* (see paragraph 15)

65 iouler I, T – *to yodel*
65 iriser T – *to make irridescent*
65 iriser (s') P – *to become irridescent*
65 ironiser I – *to be ironic*
76 irradier I, T – *to irridiate*
76 irradier (s') P – *to irridiate*
65 irriguer T – *to irrigate*
65 irriter T – *to irriate, to annoy*
65 irriter (s') P – *to get irritated/annoyed*
65 islamiser T – *to Islamize*
65 islamiser (s') P – *to become Islamized*
65 isoler T – *to isolate, to insulate*
65 isoler (s') P – *to isolate oneself, to distance oneself*
issir I, D – *to stem from*
only in the past partciple:
"issu, ue, us, ues"
65 italianiser I, T – *to Italianize*
69 itérer T – *to iterate*
65 ivoiriser afr. T – *to bring/give the ambiance of the Côte d'Ivoire*
65 ixer T – *to classify as pornographic*

j, k

65 jabler T – *to make a groove (barrel)*
65 jaboter I, T – *to jabber*
65 jacasser I – *to chatter*
65 jacter I, T – *to jabber*
65 jaffer I – *to eat (slang)*
81 jaillir I – *to spring (from)*
65 jalonner I, T – *to mark off*
65 jalouser T – *to be jealous of*
65 jalouser (se) P – *to be jealous of one another*
65 jambonner T – *to attack the legs (hunting dogs)*
65 japoniser T – *to Japanize*
65 japoniser (se) P – *to become Japanized*
65 japonner T – *to reheat porcelain to create Japanese imitation (archaic)*
65 japper I – *to yap, to bark*
65 jardiner I, T – *to garden*
65 jargonner I – *to utter jargon, to jargonize*
70 jarreter I, T – *to wear a garter*
65 jaser I – *to prattle, to chatter, to gossip*
65 jasper T – *to give the appearance of jasper*
65 jaspiner I, T – *to chat (slang)*
67 jauger I, T – *to gauge*
67 jauger (se) P – *to measure oneself against, to pit oneself against*
81 jaunir I, T – *to yellow, to fade*
72 javeler I, T – *to lay in swathes*
65 javelliser T – *to chlorinate, to bleach*
65 javer afr. T – *to danse (java)*
70 jeter T – *to throw, to plunge*
70 jeter (se) P – *to throw oneself, to flow (river)*
65 jeûner/jeuner I – *to fast*
the circumflex is mandatory only in
"je/elle/il jeûne, tu jeûnes, jeûne, jeûnes".
Note however: "nous jeûnons" *or* "jeunons",
"je jeûnais" *or* "jeunais", *etc.*
65 jobarder T – *to dupe*
65 jodler I – *to yodel*
65 jogger I – *to jog*
124 joindre I, T – *to join, to link, to enclose*
124 joindre (se) P – *to join, to link, to enclose*
78 jointoyer T – *to joint*
66 joncer T – *to put on a ring*
65 joncher T – *to strew*
65 jongler I – *to juggle*
65 jouailler I – *to play for fun, to play badly (music)*
65 jouer – *to play, to act (theatre), to gamble* I, T
65 jouer (se) P – *to be on, to be performed, to be played, to be at stake*
81 jouir de I, Ti – *to enjoy*
65 jouter I – *to joust*
65 jouxter T – *to adjoin*
65 jubiler I – *to jubilate*
65 jucher I, T – *to perch*
65 jucher (se) P – *to perch*
65 judaïser I, T – *to Judaize*
67 juger de I, T, Ti – *to judge, to try, to decide*
67 juger (se) P – *to judge, to try, to decide*
65 juguler T – *to strangle, to put a stop (to)*
72 jumeler T – *to pair, to twin (town)*
65 juponner I, T – *to put on a petticoat/underskirt*
65 jurer I, T – *to swear, to vow*
65 jurer (se) P – *to swear/vow to one antoher*
76 justifier de T, Ti – *to justify, to back up, to prove*
76 justifier (se) P – *to justify oneself*
65 juter I – *to be juicy, to drip juice*
65 juxtaposer T – *to juxtapose*
65 kératiniser T – *to make comparable to kératin*
65 kératiniser (se) P – *to infiltrate/inject of keratin*
65 kidnapper T – *to kidnap*
69 kilométrer T – *to measure in kilometers*
65 klaxonner I, T – *to hoot (horn)*
65 koter belg. I – *to live in a dorm or "en chambre"*

l

65 labelliser T – *to guarantee by a marking (of quality)*
65 labialiser T – *to labialize*
65 labialiser (se) P – *to become labialized*
65 labourer T – *to plough, to go through hard times (figurative)*
65 labourer (se) P – *to be plough*
65 lacaniser I, T – *to follow the words of Jacques Lacan*
66 lacer T – *to lace (up)*
66 lacer (se) P – *to lace*
69 lacérer T – *to lacerate*
65 lâcher I, T – *to release, to slacken, to give up*
65 laïciser T – *to secularize*
65 laïciser (se) P – *to secularize*
65 lainer T – *to teasel*
65 laisser T – *to leave, to let*
65 laisser (se) P – *to leave, to let*
65 laitonner T – *to brass-plate*
65 laïusser I – *to make a long speech*
65 lambiner I – *to dawdle*
65 lambrisser T – *to wainscot*
65 lamenter I, T – *to lament, to moan, to groan*
65 lamenter (se) P – *to moan, to whine*
65 lamer T – *to spangle*
65 laminer T – *to laminate*
65 lamper T – *to swig*

65 lancequiner I – *to rain, to urinate*
66 lancer T – *to throw, to launch (ship)*
66 lancer (se) P – *to launch out, to dash*
65 lanciner I, T – *to throb*
67 langer T – *to change a baby's nappy, diaper*
65 langueyer T – *to examine a pig's tongue*
81 languir I – *to languish*
81 languir (se) P – *to languish*
65 lansquiner I – *to rain, to urinate*
65 lanterner I, T – *to dawdle*
65 laper I, T – *to lap*
65 lapider T – *to stone*
76 lapidifier T – *to turn to stone*
76 lapidifier (se) P – *to turn to stone*
65 lapiner I – *to give birth (rabbit)*
65 laquer T – *to lacquer*
65 larder T – *to lard*
65 lardonner T – *to dicing bacon*
65 larguer T – *to cast off, to let loose*
78 larmoyer I – *to whimper*
65 lasser I, T – *to weary to get tired*
65 lasser (se) P – *to get tired, to be weary*
65 latiniser I, T – *to latinize*
65 latter T – *to lath*
65 laver T – *to wash, to bathe*
65 laver (se) P – *to wash oneself*
77 layer T – *to trace, to toll*
69 lécher T – *to lick*
69 lécher (se) P – *to lick*
65 légaliser T – *to legalize*
65 légender T – *to caption*
69 légiférer I – *to legislate*
65 légitimer T – *to legitimate, to justify*
69 léguer T – *to bequeath, to hand down*
69 léguer (se) P – *to be bequeathed, to be handed down*
65 lemmatiser T – *to lemmatize*
76 lénifier T – *to calm, to assuage*
69 léser T – *to wrong, to encroach*
65 lésiner I – *to act parsimoniously*
65 lessiver T – *to wash*
65 lester T – *to ballast*
65 lester (se) P – *to ballast, to eat and drink (figurative), to be more thoughtful (figurative)*
65 leurrer T – *to lure, to delude*
65 leurrer (se) P – *to delude onseself, to deceive oneself*
68 lever I, T – *to raise, to lift, to levy*
68 lever (se) P – *to rise, to get up (tax)*
67 léviger T – *to process to obtain powder (pharm.)*
65 léviter I – *to levitate*
65 levretter I – *to hunt with greyhounds*
65 lexicaliser (se) P – *to become lexicalized*
65 lézarder I, T – *to crack*
65 lézarder (se) P – *to crack*
65 liaisonner T – *to bond stone*
65 liarder I – *to pinch and scrape*
65 libaniser (se) afr. P – *to be divided in parts/pieces*
65 libeller T – *to draw up, to word, to fill in (cheque)*
65 libéraliser T – *to liberalize*
65 libéraliser (se) P – *to become liberalized*
69 libérer T – *to free, to release*
69 libérer (se) P – *to free oneself, to release oneself*
76 licencier T – *to make redundant, to fire*
65 licher I, T – *to lick, to become drunk*
65 lichetrogner I, T – *to become drunk*
65 liciter T – *to sell (by auction), to auction*
75 liéger T – *to buoy (with cork floats)*
76 lier T – *to bind, to tie up, to link*
76 lier (se) P – *to become friend*
65 lifter T – *to put topspin on the ball*
65 ligaturer T – *to bind*
65 ligner T – *to mark (by a line)*
76 lignifier (se) P – *to lignify*
65 ligoter T – *to bind hand and foot*
65 liguer T – *to unite against*
65 liguer (se) P – *to form a league*
65 limander T – *to wrap ropes with tarred strips (nautical), to lay on a thin piece of wood (carpentry)*
65 limer I, T – *to file down*
65 limer (se) P – *to browse through thoughts (figurative), to file (one's nail)*
65 limiter T – *to limit*
65 limiter (se) P – *to restraint oneself*
67 limoger T – *to supersede, to dismiss*
65 limoner T – *to scald (fish)*
65 limousiner T – *to build with rubble stone and mortar*
67 linger (se) P – *to fit oneself out*
76 liquéfier T – *to liquify*
76 liquéfier (se) P – *to liquify*
65 liquider T – *to wind up, to close (transaction), to liquidate*
147 **lire** I, T – *to read*
147 lire (se) P – *to read*
68 liserer T – *to edge with ribbon*
69 lisérer T – *to edge*
65 lisser T – *to smooth*
65 lister T – *to list*
65 liter T – *to arrange in layers*
76 lithographier T – *to lithograph*
65 livrer T – *to deliver, to hand over*
65 livrer (se) P – *to give oneself over, to devote oneself*
65 lober T – *to lob*
65 lobotomiser T – *to lobotomize*
65 localiser T – *to localize, to confine*
65 localiser (se) P – *to localize, to confine*
65 locher I, T – *to shake, to hurt, to hit*
65 lock(-)outer T – *to lock out*
65 lofer I – *to luff*
67 loger I, T – *to lodge (in)*
67 loger (se) P – *to find a place to live, to get stuck*
65 loguer afr. I – *to do logarithmic exercises*
67 longer T – *to pass along, to skirt, to coast along*
65 loquer T – *to dress (popular)*
65 loquer (se) P – *to dress oneself (popular)*
65 lorgner T – *to ogle*
65 lotionner T – *to apply (lotion)*
81 lotir T – *to divide into lots*

T: direct transitive (p. p. variable) – **Ti**: indirect transitive (p. p. invariable) – **I**: intransitive verb (p. p. invariable) **P**: pronominal verb (auxiliary *être*) – **impers.**: impersonal verb – **D**: defective verb – *être*: verb conjugated with the auxiliary *être* – *être* or *avoir*: verbs conjugated with *être* or *avoir* (see paragraph 15)

67 louanger T – *to flatter*
65 loucher I – *to squint, to be cross-eyed*
81 louchir I – *to turn cloudy (liquid)*
65 louer T – *to praise, to rent, to hire*
65 louer (se) P – *to be rented, to be hired*
65 loufer I – *to fart*
65 louper I, T – *to flunk, to miss, to bungle*
65 louper (se) P – *to miss, to bungle*
65 louquer T – *to dress fashionably*
65 lourder T – *to kick out, to throw out, to fire*
65 lourer T – *to connect, to link (music)*
70 louveter I – *to whelp (wolf)*
78 louvoyer I – *to beat about, to scheme*
65 lover T – *to coil*
65 lover (se) P – *to coil up*
76 lubrifier T – *to lubricate*
67 luger I – *to toboggan*
153 luire I – *to shine, to gleam*
65 luncher I – *to attend a buffet-party*
65 lustrer T – *to gloss, to polish*
65 luter T – *to lute*
65 lutiner T – *to tease*
65 lutter I – *to wrestle, to contend*
65 luxer T – *to dislocate*
65 luxer (se) P – *to dislocate*
65 lyncher T – *to lynch*
65 lyophiliser T – *to lyophilize*
65 lyrer québ. I – *to whine, to lament*
65 lyser T – *to dissolve*

m

65 macadamiser T – *to tarmac*
69 macérer I, T – *to steep, to macerate*
65 mâcher T – *to chew, to mince (words)*
65 machicoter I – *to sing (Gregorian chant)*
65 machiner T – *to contrive, to plot*
65 mâchonner T – *to munch, to mumble*
65 mâchouiller T – *to chew*
65 mâchurer T – *to bruise, to soil*
65 macler I, T – *to mix-stir glass, to crystalize (cross crystalization)*
65 maçonner T – *to build*
65 macquer T – *to brake flax, to supervise*
65 maculer T – *to stain*
76 madéfier T – *to dampen (pharmaceutical)*
65 madériser T – *to oxidize, to maderize*
65 madériser (se) P – *to oxidize, to maderize*
65 madrigaliser I – *to make pretty speeches, to pay compliments*
65 maganer québ. T – *to ruin, to injure, to wear out*
65 maganer (se) québ. P – *to injure oneself, to wear out oneself*
65 magasiner québ. I, T – *to shop, to negotiate*
65 magner (se) P – *to get a move on*
65 magnétiser T – *to magnetize*
65 magnétoscoper T – *to video-tape*
76 magnifier T – *to magnify*
65 magoter afr. T – *to get one's share (money)*
65 magouiller I, T – *to scheme, to graft*
81 maigrir I, T – *to lose weight*
65 mailler I, T – *to net, to beat (with a mallet)*
122 mainmettre T – *to set free serf (archaic)*
84 maintenir T – *to maintain, to keep up*
84 maintenir (se) P – *to persist, to hold one's own*
65 maîtriser/maitriser T – *to control, to master*
65 maîtriser/maitriser (se) P – *to exercise self-control*
65 majorer T – *to increase*
65 malaxer T – *to knead*
128 malfaire I, D – *to do evil, to wrong only in the infinitive*
65 malléabiliser T – *to make malleable*
65 mallouser T – *to abandon (slang)*
68 malmener T – *to manhandle*
65 malter T – *to malt*
65 maltraiter T – *to ill-treat*
65 mamelonner T – *to undulate*
67 manager T – *to manage*
65 manchonner T – *to connect with a sleeve (technical)*
65 mandater T – *to commission*
65 mander T – *to instruct, to summon*
75 manéger T – *to train (animals)*
65 mangeot(t)er T – *to nibble*
67 manger T – *to eat*
67 manger (se) P – *to eat, to be eaten*
76 manier T – *to handle*
76 manier (se) P – *to handle*
69 maniérer T – *to affect with mannierism*
69 maniérer (se) P – *to become affected with mannierism*
65 manifester I, T – *to show, to demonstrate*
65 manifester (se) P – *to emerge, to appear*
66 manigancer T – *to scheme*
66 manigancer (se) P – *to be schemed, to be plotted*
65 manipuler T – *to manipulate*
65 mannequiner T – *to dispose, to show, to present (unnaturally)*
65 manœuvrer I, T – *to manoeuvre*
65 manoquer T – *to bundle, to sheaf (tobacco)*
65 manquer à, de I, T, Ti – *to miss, to be absent (from), to neglect, to fail, to break (promise, word), to lack*
65 manquer (se) P – *to miss each other, to fail (suicide)*
65 mansarderT – *to convert the attic into a room*
65 manucurer T – *to manicure*
65 manufacturer T – *to manufacture*
65 manutentionner T – *to handle*
65 mapper T – *to map (computer, mathematics)*
65 maquer T – *to have a common-law spouse, to pimp*
65 maquer (se) P – *to get into a relationship, to get a pimp*
65 maquetter T – *to build models, to design an interface (computer)*
65 maquignonner T – *to rig, to fake up*
65 maquiller T – *to make up, to fake*
65 maquiller (se) P – *to make up*
65 marabouter afr. T – *to throw a spell on someone (through a wizard)*
65 marauder I, T – *to pilfer*
65 maraver I, T – *to demolish, to dismantle*
65 marbrer T – *to mottle*
65 marchander I, T – *to bargain, to haggle (over)*
65 marcher I – *to walk, to work*
65 marcotter T – *to layer*
65 margauder I – *to scream (quail)*
67 marger I, T – *to edge*

65 marginaliser T – *to give little importance (to)*
65 marginaliser (se) P – *to opt out of society*
65 marginer T – *to make notes in margin*
65 margot(t)er I – *to scream (quail)*
76 marier T – *to marry, to wed*
76 marier (se) P – *to marry, to get married*
65 mariner I, T – *to marinate*
65 marivauder I – *to banter, to flirt*
65 marmiter T – *to shell*
65 marmonner T – *to mumble*
65 marmoriser T – *to turn to marble*
65 marmotter I, T – *to mutter*
65 marner I, T – *to marl, to work hard*
65 maronner I – *to grumble*
65 maroquiner T – *to give leather a morocco-finish, to tool (leather)*
65 maroufler T – *to glue, to stick on a wall (painting)*
65 marquer I, T – *to mark, to note, to score*
65 marquer (se) P – *to mark*
70 marqueter T – *to inlay*
65 marrer (se) P – *to have a good laugh*
65 marronner I – *to live in hiding, to wait*
65 marsouiner I – *to sway from side to side (airplane)*
73 marteler T – *to hammer*
65 martyriser T – *to make a martyr of*
65 marxiser T – *to make Marxist*
65 masculiniser T – *to make masculine, to turn mannish*
65 masquer I, T – *to hide*
65 masquer (se) P – *to put on a mask*
65 massacrer T – *to massacre*
65 massacrer (se) P – *to be massacred, to massacre one another*
65 masser T – *to assemble, to massage*
65 masser (se) P – *to assemble, to massage*
65 massicoter T – *to guillotine (paper)*
76 massifier T – *to adapt to the masses*
69 mastéguer I, T – *to eat (slang)*
65 mastiquer I, T – *to chew, to cement*
65 masturber T – *to masturbate*
65 masturber (se) P – *to masturbate*
65 matabicher afr. T – *to bribe*
65 matcher I, T – *to match*
65 matelasser T – *to pad, to upholster*
65 mater I, T – *to bring down, to humble, to stare*
65 mâter T – *to mast*
65 matérialiser T – *to make, to materialize*
65 matérialiser (se) P – *to materialize*
65 materner T – *to mother*
65 materniser T – *to make suitable for infants*
65 mathématiser T – *to deal mathematically (with)*
65 mâtiner T – *to cross*
81 matir T – *to matt, to dull*
65 matouser I, T – *to humble, to stare, to watch*
65 matraquer T – *to club, to bludgeon, to browbeat*
66 matricer T – *to stamp out*
65 matriculer T – *to register*
65 maturer T – *to ripen, to mature*
81 maudire T – *to curse*
p. p.: "maudit, te, ts, tes"
74 maugréer I, T – *to grouse*
65 maximaliser T – *to maximize*
65 maximiser T – *to maximize*
65 mazouter I, T – *to refuel, to pollute*
65 mécaniser T – *to mechanize*
69 mécher T – *to fumigate*
65 mécompter (se) P – *to disappoint*
152 méconduire (se) belg. P – *to be mean, bad*
130 méconnaître/méconnaitre T – *to disregard, to ignore*
65 mécontenter T – *to dissatisfy*
135 mécroire T – *to disbeleive*
65 médailler T – *to award a medal*
65 médiatiser T – *to mediatize*
65 médicaliser T – *to provide health care*
65 médicamenter T – *to administer medicine*
148 médire de Ti – *to speak ill of, to slander*
65 médiser I – *to speak ill, to slander*
65 méditer I, T – *to meditate, to think of*
65 méduser T – *to dumbfound*
128 méfaire I, D – *to do harm, to wrong*
only in the infinitive
76 méfier (se) P – *to be wary, to be careful, to mistrust, to distrust*
81 mégir T – *to tan sheep skin*
65 mégisser T – *to tan sheep skin*
65 mégoter I, T – *to quibble (over)*
67 méjuger de T, Ti – *to misjudge, to underrate*
67 méjuger (se) P – *to underestimate oneself*
67 mélanger T – *to mix, to blend*
67 mélanger (se) P – *to get mixed up, to mix, to get mixed with*
65 mêler T – *to mix, to muddle, to shuffle (cards)*
65 mêler (se) P – *to mix, to muddle, to shuffle (cards)*
69 mémérer québ. I, T – *to gossip*
65 mémoriser I, T – *to memorize*
66 menacer I, T – *to threaten*
67 ménager T – *to handle carefully, to treat tactfully*
67 ménager (se) P – *to handle carefully, to treat tactfully*
76 mendier I, T – *to beg*
65 mendigoter I, T – *to beg*
68 mener I, T – *to lead, to conduct*
65 menotter T – *to handcuff*
65 mensualiser T – *to pay monthly*
65 mensurer T – *to measure*
65 mentionner T – *to mention*
86 mentir à I, Ti – *to lie, to belie to*
86 mentir (se) P – *to fool oneself*
p. p. invariable
65 menuiser T – *to do woodwork*
119 méprendre (se) P – *to misjudge, to make a mistake, to be mistaken*
65 mépriser T – *to scorn, to disregard*
65 mépriser (se) P – *to scorn oneself*
65 mercantiliser T – *to make mercantile, to commercialise*
65 merceriser T – *to mercerize*
65 merder I – *to mess up, to have difficulty with, to fail miserably*

T: direct transitive (p. p. variable) – **Ti**: indirect transitive (p. p. invariable) – **I**: intransitive verb (p. p. invariable) **P**: pronominal verb (auxiliary *être*) – **impers.**: impersonal verb – **D**: defective verb – *être*: verb conjugated with the auxiliary *être* – *être* or *avoir*: verbs conjugated with *être* or *avoir* (see paragraph 15)

78 merdoyer I – *to be in a mess*
65 meringuer T – *to coat with meringue*
65 mériter de T, Ti – *to deserve to*
76 mésallier (se) P – *to marry below oneself*
65 mésestimer T – *to underestimate*
113 mess(e)oir I, D – *to be unbecoming*
used only in the past participle, the present, the infinitive, the 3rd person of the present subjunctive, the present indicative, the imparfait, *the simple future and the present conditional.*
65 mesurer I, T – *to measure, to assess, to limit*
65 mesurer (se) P – *to size each other up*
65 mésuser de Ti – *to misuse*
65 métaboliser T – *to metabolize*
65 métalliser T – *to plate*
65 métamorphiser T – *to metamorph*
65 métamorphoser T – *to metamorphose*
65 métamorphoser (se) P – *to turn into, to be metamorphosed into*
65 métaphoriser T – *to use metaphors*
65 météoriser T – *to distend*
65 métisser T – *to crossbreed (human)*
69 métrer T – *to measure, to survey*
122 mettre T – *to put, to set*
122 mettre (se) P – *to put oneself*
65 meubler T – *to furnish (room)*
65 meubler (se) P – *to get some furniture*
65 meugler I – *to moo*
65 meuler T – *to grind down*
81 meurtrir T – *to bruise*
118 mévendre T – *to sell at a loss*
65 miauler I – *to mew*
65 michetonner I – *to prostitute (non-professional)*
65 microfilmer T – *to microfilm*
65 microniser T – *to micronise*
65 mignarder T – *to fondle*
65 mignoter T – *to treat gently, to cuddle*
65 mignoter (se) P – *to treat gently, to cuddle*
65 migrer I – *to migrate*
65 mijoler belg. I – *to flirt (slang)*
65 mijoter I, T – *to simmer, to hatch (plot)*
65 mijoter (se) P – *to simmer, to hatch (plot)*
65 militariser T – *to militarize*
65 militer I – *to be militant*
65 millésimer T – *to be of vintage*
65 mimer T – *to mime*
65 minauder I – *to simper, to smirk*
81 mincir I – *to get thinner*
65 miner T – *to mine, to wear out*
65 minéraliser T – *to mineralize*
65 miniaturer T – *to paint in miniature*
65 miniaturiser T – *to make on a miniature scale*
65 minimiser T – *to minimize*
65 minorer T – *to reduce*
65 minuter T – *to time*
65 mirer T – *to mirror*
65 mirer (se) P – *to gaze (at), to be reflected*
65 miroiter I – *to sparkle*
65 miser I, T – *to stake, to bet*
69 misérer afr. I – *to live in poverty*
65 mitarder T – *to be put in solitary confinement*
65 miter I – *to be moth-eathen*
65 miter (se) P – *to become moth-eaten*
65 mithridatiser T – *to get use to poison*
65 mithridatiser(se) P – *to get oneself use to poison*
67 mitiger T – *to mitigate*
65 mitonner I, T – *to simmer, to nurse (plan)*
65 mitonner (se) P – *to be simmered, to be nursed*
65 mitrailler I, T – *to machine-gun*
65 mixer T – *to mix, to blend*
65 mixtionner T – *to blend (drug)*
65 mobiliser T – *to mobilize*
65 mobiliser (se) P – *to become active*
73 modeler T – *to model, to fashion, to mould*
73 modeler (se) P – *to model oneself*
65 modéliser T – *to design*
69 modérer T – *to moderate, to restrain*
69 modérer (se) P – *to calm down, to control oneself*
65 moderniser T – *to modernize*
65 moderniser (se) P – *to modernize*
76 modifier T – *to modify, to alter*
76 modifier (se) P – *to modify, to alter*
65 moduler I, T – *to modulate*
65 mofler belg. T – *to fail an exam*
65 moirer T – *to mottle*
65 moiser T – *to fix with struts*
81 moisir I – *to go mouldy*
65 moissonner T – *to harvest*
65 moiter I – *slighty damp*
81 moitir T – *to make clammy*
65 molester T – *to molest*
70 moleter T – *to mill*
65 mollarder I, T – *to spit*
65 molletonner T – *to line (with padding)*
81 mollir I, T – *to yield*
76 momifier T – *to mummify*
76 momifier (se) P – *to atrophy, to shrivel up*
65 monder T – *to blanch*
65 mondialiser T – *to bring world-wide*
65 mondialiser (se) P – *to spread throughout the word*
65 monétiser T – *to mint, to monetize*
77 monnayer T – *to coin, to convert into cash*
65 monologuer I – *to talk to oneself*
65 monopoliser T – *to monopolize*
65 monter T, *avoir* – *to go up, to take up, to turn up*
65 monter I, *être* (or *avoir*) – *to go up, to board, to rise*
65 monter (se) P, *être* – *to amount, to equip*
65 montrer T – *to show, to display*
65 montrer (se) P – *to appear, to prove oneself*
65 moquer T – *to mock*
65 moquer (se) P – *to jest*
65 moquetter T – *to carpet*
65 moraliser I, T – *to moralize*
72 morceler T – *to parcel out*
66 mordancer T – *to mordant*
65 mordiller I, T – *to nibble*
65 mordorer T – *to bronze*
118 mordre à I, T, Ti – *to bite (on), to gnaw*
118 mordre (se) P – *to bite (on), to gnaw*
65 morfaler I – *to stuff oneself*
65 morfiler T – *to remove excess metal (when sharpening), to stuff oneself*
65 morfler T – *to take (punishment, hits)*
118 morfondre (se) P – *to mope, to fret*
69 morigéner T – *to reprimand*
65 mornifler T – *to slap (backhand) (slang)*

65 mortaiser T – *to slot, to mortise*
76 mortifier T – *to mortify*
76 mortifier (se) P – *to mortify*
65 motionner I – *to propose a motion, to put forward*
65 motiver T – *to justify, to motivate*
65 motiver (se) P – *to motivate oneself, to be motivated*
65 motoriser T – *to motorize*
65 motter (se) P – *to hide behind*
65 moucharder I, T – *to sneak (on)*
65 moucher I, T – *to snuff, to snub*
65 moucher (se) P – *to blow one's nose*
65 moucheronner I – *to catch insects which are on the water's surface (fish)*
70 moucheter T – *to fleck*
144 moudre T – *to mill, to grind*
65 mouetter I – *to stink, to be scared (slang)*
70 moufeter I, D – *to protest especially in the infinitive and at compound tenses*
65 moufter I, D – *to protest especially in the infinitive, the* imparfait *of the indicative and at compound tenses*
65 mouiller I, T – *to wet, to moisten, to water down, to anchor (ship)*
65 mouiller (se) P – *to get wet, to become implicated*
65 mouler I, T – *to cast, to mould*
65 mouliner I, T – *to put through a mill*
65 moulurer T – *to decorate with mouldings*
95 mourir I, *être* – *to die (from)*
95 mourir (se) P, D – *to die (from)*
65 mouronner I – *to worry*
65 mouronner (se) P – *to worry*
65 mousser I – *to froth, to lather*
65 moutonner I – *to foam, to cloud over*
65 mouvementer T – *to liven up*
65 mouver I – *to turn over earth (in a pot, box) (gardening)*
106 mouvoir T – *to drive*
106 mouvoir (se) P – *to move*
65 moyenner I, T – *to bring about*
65 mucher T – *to hide*
65 muer I, T – *to moult*
65 muer (se) P – *to change, to transform*
81 mugir I – *to bellow, to roar*
70 mugueter T – *to flirt, to charm (archaic)*
65 muloter I – *to dig, to unearth (done by animals)*
65 multiplexer T – *to transmit too many simultaneously*
76 multiplier I, T – *to multiply, to increase*
76 multiplier (se) P – *to multiply, to increase*
65 municipaliser T – *to municipalize*
81 munir T – *to provide, to equip*
81 munir (se) P – *to take with oneself, to prepare oneself*
65 munitionner T – *to munition*
65 murailler T – *to wall*
65 murer T – *to wall up, to wall in*
65 murer (se) P – *to wall up, to wall in*
81 mûrir/murir I, T – *to ripen, to mature*
65 murmurer I, T – *to murmur, to whisper*
65 musarder I – *to waste time*
65 muscler T – *to develop muscle*
72 museler T – *to muzzle*
65 muser I – *to dawdle*
65 musiquer I, T – *to set to music*
65 musquer T – *to scent with musk*
65 musser T – *to hide (archaic)*
65 musser (se) P – *to hide (archaic)*
65 muter I, T – *to transfer*
65 mutiler T – *to mutilate*
65 mutiler (se) P – *to mutilate oneself*
65 mutiner (se) P – *to mutiny*
65 mutualiser T – *to regroup for economic purposes*
76 mystifier T – *to fool, to hoax*
76 mythifier I, T – *to mythicize*

n

65 nacrer T – *to give a pearly gloss*
65 nacrer (se) P – *to become glossy*
67 nager I, T – *to swim, to float (on/in)*
131 naître/naitre I, *être* – *to be born*
76 nanifier T – *to keep small, to prevent growth*
81 nantir T – *to secure*
81 nantir (se) P – *to secure as a precaution, to provide oneself with*
65 napper T – *to coat*
65 narguer T – *to flout*
65 narrer T – *to narrate*
65 nasaliser T – *to nasalize*
65 nasaliser (se) P – *to be nasalized*
65 nasiller I, T – *to speak with a nasal twang*
65 natchaver I – *to run off, to run away*
65 nationaliser T – *to nationalize*
65 natter T – *to plait*
65 naturaliser T – *to naturalize*
67 naufrager I – *to shipwreck*
65 naviguer I – *to sail, to navigate*
65 navrer T – *to grieve, to distress*
65 néantiser T – *to reduce to nothing*
65 néantiser (se) P – *to reduce to nothing*
65 nécessiter T – *to necessitate*
65 nécroser T – *to necrose*
65 nécroser (se) P – *to necrose*
67 négliger T – *to neglect, to disregard*
67 négliger (se) P – *to not look after oneself*
76 négocier I, T – *to negociate*
76 négocier (se) P – *to negociate*
65 neigeoter impers. – *to snow (lightly) impers.:* "il neigeote"
67 neiger impers. – *to snow impers.:* "il neige"
65 nervurer T – *to rib*
78 nettoyer T – *to clean, to clean up*
65 neutraliser T – *to neutralise*
65 neutraliser (se) P – *to neutralise*
65 niaiser I – *to play the fool*

T: direct transitive (p. p. variable) – **Ti**: indirect transitive (p. p. invariable) – **I**: intransitive verb (p. p. invariable) **P**: pronominal verb (auxiliary *être*) – **impers.**: impersonal verb – **D**: defective verb – *être*: verb conjugated with the auxiliary *être* – *être* or *avoir*: verbs conjugated with *être* or *avoir* (see paragraph 15)

65 nicher I, T – *to nest, to nestle*
65 nicher (se) P – *to nest, to nestle*
72 nickeler T – *to nickel-plate*
65 nicotiniser T – *to add nicotine*
76 nidifier I – *to nest*
65 nieller T – *to blight, to smut*
76 nier I, T – *to deny*
65 nigérianiser afr. T – *to Nigerianize*
65 nimber T – *to put a halo (on)*
65 nimber (se) P – *to be given a halo*
65 nipper T, P – *to deck out*
65 nipper (se) P – *to deck out*
65 niquer I, T – *to have sex (slang/vulgar), to steal (slang), to scam (slang)*
65 nitrater T – *to add nitrogen*
65 nitrer T – *to treat with nitric acid*
76 nitrifier T – *to nitrify*
76 nitrifier (se) P – *to be covered with nitrate*
65 nitrurer T – *to nitride*
65 nivaquiner afr. I – *to take "nivaquine" (antimalarial drugs)*
72 niveler T – *to level, to even out*
65 nobscuriter afr. I – *to make love in darkness*
66 nocer I – *to overindulge (wine/food)*
81 noircir I, T – *to blacken*
81 noircir (se) P – *to grow dark, to turn dark*
65 noliser T – *to charter*
65 nomadiser I – *to nomadize*
65 nombrer T – *to number, to count*
65 nominaliser T – *to nominalize*
65 nommer T – *to name, to call*
65 nommer (se) P – *to appoint, to be called*
65 noper T – *to remove knots (cloth)*
81 nordir I – *to veer North (wind)*
65 normaliser T – *to normalize*
65 normaliser (se) P – *to normalize*
65 noter T – *to note down, to take notice of, to mark*
76 notifier T – *to notify*
65 nouer I, T – *to knot, to tie*
65 nouer (se) P – *to join, to gather momentum*
81 nourrir I, T – *to feed, to nurse (child)*
81 nourrir (se) P – *to feed, to eat*
65 nover I, T – *to renew (obligation)*
65 noyauter T – *to infiltrate*
78 noyer T – *to flood, to swamp*
78 noyer (se) P – *to drown*
66 nuancer T – *to shade, to tone down*
65 nucléariser T – *to nuclearize*
74 nucléer T – *to nucleate*
65 nuer T – *to match colors (archaic)*
152 nuire à Ti – *to harm, to injure*
152 nuire (se) P – *to harm, to injure*
p. p. invariable
65 numériser T – *to digitize*
65 numéroter T – *to number*
65 numéroter (se) P – *to number off*

O

81 obéir à Ti – *to obey*
69 obérer T – *to burden (with debt)*
69 obérer (s') P – *to burden (with debt)*
65 objecter T – *to object*
65 objectiver T – *to objectify*
65 objectiver (s') P – *to objectify*
65 objurguer I – *to plea*
67 obliger T – *to force someone, to bind, to oblige*
67 obliger (s') P – *to force oneself, to bind oneself, to oblige oneself*
65 obliquer I – *to turn at an oblique angle, to edge to*
69 oblitérer T – *to obliterate*
65 obnubiler T – *to obsess*
65 obombrer T – *to darken, to shadow*
81 obscurcir T – *to darken, to obscure*
81 obscurcir (s') P – *to grow dark*
69 obséder T – *to obsess*
65 observer T – *to observe, to watch*
65 observer (s') P – *to be observed, to watch one antoher*
65 obstiner (s') P – *to persist*
65 obstruer T – *to obstruct*
65 obstruer (s') P – *to be obstructed*
69 obtempérer à I, Ti – *to comply with*
84 obtenir T – *to gain, to obtain*
84 obtenir (s') P – *to gain, to obtain*
65 obturer T – *to seal, to stop off*
84 obvenir I, *être* – *to revert*
76 obvier à Ti – *to prevent*
65 occasionner T – *to cause*
65 occidentaliser T – *to westernize*
65 occidentaliser (s') P – *to westernize*
occire T, D – *to slay*
only in the infinitive,
at compound tenses
and in the p. p.: "occis, e, es"
140 occlure T – *to occlude*
65 occulter T – *to hide*
65 occuper T – *to occupy, to take up (space/time)*
65 occuper (s') P – *to keep busy*
65 ocrer T – *to ochre*
76 octavier I, T – *to play on the octave up*
78 octroyer T – *to bestow, to grant*
78 octroyer (s') P – *to treat oneself to*
65 octupler T – *to mulitply by eight*
65 œilletonner T – *to remove buds (gardening)*
65 œuvrer I – *to work (at)*
65 offenser T – *to offend*
65 offenser (s') P – *to take offense, to be offended*
65 officialiser T – *to take official*
76 officier I – *to officiate*
88 offrir T – *to give, to offer, to present*
88 offrir (s') P – *to treat oneself (to)*
65 offusquer T – *to offend*
65 offusquer (s') P – *to take offense, to be offended*
124 oindre T, D – *to anoint*
124 oindre (s') P – *to anoint oneself*
72 oiseler I, T – *to go bird-catching*
67 ombrager T – *to shade, to overshadow*
65 ombrer T – *to shade*
122 omettre T – *to omit*
78 ondoyer I, T – *to ripple, to christen*
65 onduler I, T – *to undulate, to wave (hair)*
76 opacifier T – *to make opaque*
76 opacifier (s') P – *to become opaque*
65 opaliser T – *to make opal-like*

69 opérer I, T – *to operate, to implement, to proceed*
69 opérer (s') P – *to operate, to implement, to proceed*
66 opiacer T – *to opiate*
65 opiner I – *to be in favor (of)*
65 opiniâtrer (s') P – *to be opinionated*
65 opposer T – *to oppose*
65 opposer (s') P – *to confront each other*
65 oppresser T – *to oppress*
65 opprimer T – *to oppress*
65 opter I – *to opt*
65 optimaliser T – *to optimize*
65 optimiser T – *to optimize*
65 oraliser T – *to express orally*
67 oranger T – *to make orange*
65 orbiter I – *to orbit*
65 orchestrer T – *to orchestrate*
66 ordonnancer T – *to pass (account)*
65 ordonner I, T – *to organize, to order*
65 ordonner (s') P – *to sort out*
65 organiser T – *to organize, to arrange*
65 organiser (s') P – *to organize, to arrange*
65 organsiner T – *to shear silk and mill it twice*
65 orientaliser – *to orientalize*
65 orientaliser (s') – *to become orientalized*
65 orienter T – *to orientate, to position*
65 orienter (s') P – *to find one's bearing*
65 oringuer T – *to raise the anchor*
65 ornementer T – *to ornament*
65 orner T – *to decorate*
65 orner (s') P – *to be decorated*
76 orthographier I, T – *to spell*
76 orthographier (s') P – *to be spelled*
65 osciller I – *to oscillate*
65 oser T – *to dare*
76 ossifier T – *to ossify*
76 ossifier (s') P – *to become ossified*
65 ostraciser T – *to ostracize*
65 ôter T – *to take away, to remove*
65 ôter (s') P – *to take away, to remove*
65 ouater T – *to quilt*
65 ouatiner T – *to quilt*
76 oublier I, T – *to forget, to neglect*
76 oublier (s') P – *to forget oneself*
65 ouiller I, T – *to add the same wine to a barrel to compensate for what has evaporated*
98 **ouïr** T, D – *to hear*
especially in the infinitive, the imperative and at compound tenses
81 ourdir T – *to hatch*
81 ourdir (s') P – *to be hatched*
65 ourler T – *to hem*
65 outiller T – *to equip, to fit out*
65 outiller (s') P – *to equip, to fit out*
67 outrager T – *to offend gravely*
65 outrepasser T – *to go beyond, to exceed, to exagerate*
65 outrer T – *to carry to excess*
67 ouvrager T – *to work with skill*
65 ouvrer I, T – *to make, to fashion*
88 ouvrir I, T – *to open (up)*
88 ouvrir (s') P – *to be opened, to become open*
65 ovaliser T – *to make oval*
65 ovationner T – *to give an ovation*
65 ovuler I – *to ovulate*
65 oxyder T – *to oxidize*
65 oxyder (s') P – *to oxidize*
69 oxygéner T – *to oxygenate*
69 oxygéner (s') P – *to oxygenate*
65 ozoniser T – *to ozonize*

p

67 pacager I, T – *to pasture, to graze*
76 pacifier T – *to pacify*
65 pacquer T – *to sort out fish for transport*
65 pactiser I – *to compound, to compromise*
65 paddocker (se) P – *to go to bed (slang)*
65 paganiser I, T – *to paganize*
77 pagayer I – *to paddle*
67 pager I – *to page (pager)*
67 pager (se) P – *to go to bed (slang)*
65 pageoter (se) P – *to turn in*
65 paginer T – *to paginate*
65 pagnoter (se) P – *to turn in*
65 paillarder I – *to live lewdly, to laugh*
65 paillarder (se) P – *to live lewdly, to laugh*
65 paillassonner T – *to straw (plants)*
65 pailler T – *to straw*
70 pailleter T – *to spangle, to flake*
65 paillonner T – *to melt tin in order to tin something*
72 paisseler T – *to put poles for the vines to grow on*
132 **paître/paitre** I, T, D – *to feed (animals)*
no passé simple *nor* subjonctif imparfait*; used only in simple forms.*
65 pajoter (se) P – *to turn in*
65 palabrer I – *to palaver*
65 palancrer T – *to fish using a line with multiple hooks*
65 palangrer T – *to fish using a line with multiple hooks*
65 palanguer I, T – *to browse*
65 palanquer I, T – *to browse*
65 palataliser T – *to palatalize*
70 paleter T – *to flatten to tip of a hook to tie it to the line*
65 palettiser T – *to load on a pallet*
81 pâlir I, T – *to grow pale, to grow dim*
65 palissader T – *to palissade*
65 palisser T – *to nail up, to train (branches)*
76 pallier T – *to palliate*
65 palmer T – *to flatten the end of a needle to create the eye*
65 paloter T – *to spade trench between colza plants*
65 palper T – *to feel, to finger, to receive (money)*
65 palpiter I – *to flutter, to throb, to thrill*
65 pâmer (se) P – *to swoon*
65 panacher I, T – *to plume, to variegate*
65 panacher (se) P – *to plume, to variegate*
65 paner T – *to coat with crumbs*
76 panifier T – *to turn into bread*

T: direct transitive (p. p. variable) – **Ti**: indirect transitive (p. p. invariable) – **I**: intransitive verb (p. p. invariable) **P**: pronominal verb (auxiliary *être*) – **impers.**: impersonal verb – **D**: defective verb – *être*: verb conjugated with the auxiliary *être* – *être* or *avoir*: verbs conjugated with *être* or *avoir* (see paragraph 15)

65 paniquer I, T – *to panic*
65 paniquer (se) P – *to get panicky*
65 panneauter I, T – *to panel*
65 panner T – *to hammer out*
65 panoramiquer I – *to pan (out)*
65 panser T – *to groom, to dress (wound)*
72 panteler I – *to pant*
65 pantoufler I – *to leave the civil service for private business*
65 papillonner I – *to flit about*
65 papilloter I, T – *to wrap in curlpaper, to have wandering eyes (unable to focus to tire the eyes), (too bright, too colorful) (figurative)*
65 papoter I – *to gossip*
65 papouiller T – *to cover with kisses*
68 parachever T – *to complete*
65 parachuter T – *to parachute*
65 parader I – *to parade, to show off*
65 parafer T – *to initial, to sign*
65 paraffiner T – *to paraffin*
65 paraisonner T – *to blow glass (glassblower)*
130 paraître/paraître I – *to appear, to come out, to seem, to look*
avoir *(or* être*)*
65 paralléliser T – *to make parallel*
65 paralyser T – *to paralyze, to incapacitate*
69 paramétrer T – *to parameterize*
65 parangonner T – *to be a paragon*
65 parapher T – *to initial, to sign*
65 paraphraser T – *to paraphrase*
65 parasiter T – *to sponge (on), to bug (radio)*
65 parcellariser T – *to divide into lots*
65 parceller T – *to divide into lots*
65 parcelliser T – *to divide into lots*
65 parcelliser (se) P – *to be divided into lots*
65 parcheminer T – *to give the appearance of a parchment*
65 parcheminer (se) P – *to shrivel up*
94 parcourir T – *to go over, to cover (distance), to examine*
65 pardonner à I, T, Ti – *to forgive, to excuse*
65 pardonner (se) P – *to be forgiven, to be excused*
65 parementer T – *to facet (wall)*
65 parer à T, Ti – *to avoid, to ward off, to defend, to embellish, to prepare*
65 parer (se) P – *to prepare oneself, to adorn oneself, to be embellished*
65 paresser I – *to idle, to loll*
128 parfaire T – *to finish off, to complete*
present indicative, infinitive and p. p.
65 parfiler T – *to pick (threads)*
118 parfondre T – *to fuse evenly*
65 parfumer T – *to scent, to flavour*
65 parfumer (se) P – *to wear perfume*
76 parier I, T – *to bet, to back (a horse)*
65 parjurer (se) P – *to perjure oneself*
65 parkériser T – *to treat with phosphate (metal)*
65 parlementer I – *to parley*
65 parler de, à I, T, Ti – *to speak about, to speak to, to talk about, to talk to*
65 parler (se) P – *to be spoken, to speak to one another, to speak to oneself*
p. p. often invariable
65 parloter I – *to chat*
76 parodier T – *to parody, to travesty*
65 parquer I, T – *to pen (cattle), to park (car)*
70 parqueter T – *to parquet*
65 parrainer T – *to sponsor*
68 parsemer T – *to sprinkle, to scattered, to strew*
67 partager T – *to share, to divide*
67 partager (se) P – *to share, to divide*
65 participer à, de Ti – *to participate, to share in, to contribute to, to partake of*
65 particulariser T – *to particularize*
65 particulariser (se) P – *to be distinguished by*
86 partir I, *être* – *to leave, to go (off), to depart, to proceed*
partir (partager) T, D – *to share*
used in the expression "avoir maille à partir" *(= to have a bone to pick with sb)* in the infinitive only
65 partouzer I – *to carouse*
84 parvenir à I, Ti, *être* – *to reach*
65 passementer T – *to trim (garment)*
65 passepoiler T – *to braid*
65 passer T, *avoir* – *to go (by/through), to pass (by), to drop (in, by), to pass, to be on (television), to get through*
65 passer I, *être* (or *avoir*) – *to pass (by), to get through*
65 passer (se) P, *être* – *to take place, to do without*
65 passionner T – *to fascinate, to excite*
65 passionner (se) P – *to have a passion for*
65 pasteller I, T – *to colour in pastels*
65 pasteuriser T – *to pasteurize*
65 pasticher T – *to imitate, to copy*
65 pastiller T – *to pellet (packing, plastic)*
65 pastiquer I – *(slang of "passer"), to pass, to go (through, by), to get through, to drop (in, by), to be on (television)*
65 patafioler T – *to confuse*
67 patauger I – *to splash, to flounder*
65 pateliner I, T – *to butter up*
65 patenter T – *to license*
65 pâter I – *to paste together (leather)*
65 patienter I – *to be patient, to wait for*
65 patienter (se) afr. P – *to wait*
65 patiner I, T – *to skate, to skid*
65 patiner (se) P – *to acquire patina*
81 pâtir I – *to suffer*
65 pâtisser I – *to make pastry*
65 patoiser I – *to speak patois*
65 patouiller I, T – *to flounder*
65 patronner T – *to sponsor, to give patronage (to)*
65 patrouiller I – *to patrol*
65 patter T – *to leave footprints*
65 pâturer I, T – *to graze*
65 paumer T – *to smack, to lose*
65 paumer (se) P – *to get lost*
78 paumoyer T – *to pass a rope from one hand to the other (nautical), to sew using a leather palm (nautical), to use one's hand to mesure (rural)*
65 paupériser T – *to impoverish*
65 pauser I – *to pause*
65 pavaner (se) P – *to strut*
65 paver T – *to pave*
65 pavoiser I, T – *to put out (flags)*

77 **payer** I, T – *to pay, to pay for, to stand*
77 payer (se) P – *to pay oneself, to be paid*
65 peaufiner T – *to perfect*
65 peausser I – *to disguise as, to appear to be (archaic)*
69 pécher I – *to sin, to err, to trespass*
65 pêcher I, T – *to fish, to angle, to catch*
65 pecquer afr. I – *to pay (salary)*
65 pédaler I – *to pedal*
65 peigner T – *to comb, to smooth out*
65 peigner (se) P – *to comb one's hair*
123 **peindre** I, T – *to paint*
123 peindre (se) P – *to portray oneself*
65 peiner I, T – *to work hard, to pain*
65 peinturer T – *to coat with paint*
65 peinturlurer T – *to daub (colours)*
73 peler I, T – *to peel, to skin*
73 peler (se) P – *to peel, to skin*
65 peller T – *to shovel*
70 pelleter T – *to shovel*
65 peloter I, T – *to paw, to cuddle*
65 pelotonner T – *to huddle*
65 pelotonner (se) P – *to curl into a ball*
65 pelucher I – *to become fluffy*
65 pembeniser afr. I – *to discard, to dismiss, to relegate*
65 pénaliser T – *to penalize*
65 pencher I, T – *to lean, to tilt, to tip up*
65 pencher (se) P – *to lean down, to bend down*
65 pendiller I – *to dangle*
65 pendouiller I – *to hang loose*
118 pendre I, T – *to hang*
118 pendre (se) P – *to hang oneself, to cling to*
65 penduler I – *to swing like a pendulum (climbing)*
69 pénétrer I, T – *to enter, to penetrate*
69 pénétrer (se) P – *to become imbued with*
65 penser à I, T, Ti – *to think, to have in mind, to agree, to imagine*
65 pensionner T – *to pension*
76 pépier I – *to cheep, to chirp*
66 percer I, T – *to pierce, to go through*
100 percevoir T – *to perceive*
65 percher I, T – *to perch*
65 percher (se) P – *to perch*
65 percuter I, T – *to strike*
118 perdre I, T – *to lose, to waste*
118 perdre (se) P – *to lose one's way, to be lost (in)*
65 perdurer I – *to be perturable*
65 pérégriner I – *to peregrinate*
65 pérenniser T – *to make durable*
65 péréquater belg. T – *to adjust (inflation)*
65 perfectionner T – *to improve, to perfect*
65 perfectionner (se) P – *to improve, to perfect*
65 perforer T – *to perforate*
65 perfuser T – *to put so on a drip*
65 péricliter I – *to be in a bad way, to decline*
65 périmer (se) P – *to become out of date*
65 périphraser I – *to expatiate*
81 périr I – *to perish*
65 perler I, T – *to pearl, to work with care, to bead (sugar)*
65 permanenter T – *to perm hair*
65 perméabiliser T – *to make permeable*
122 permettre T – *to permit, to allow*
122 permettre (se) P – *to venture, to permit oneself*
65 permuter I, T – *to change (over), to exchange (with)*
65 permuter (se) P – *to substitute one for another*
65 pérorer I – *to hold forth*
65 peroxyder T – *to peroxydize*
69 perpétrer T – *to perpetrate*
69 perpétrer (se) P – *to be perpetrated*
65 perpétuer T – *to perpetuate*
65 perpétuer (se) P – *to survive, to continue, to perpetuate*
65 perquisitionner I – *to search*
65 persécuter T – *to persecute*
69 persévérer I – *to persevere*
65 persi(f)fler T – *to banter*
65 persiller T – *to season with parsley*
65 persister I – *to persist*
65 personnaliser T – *to personalize*
76 personnifier T – *to impersonate, to personify*
65 persuader T – *to persuade, to convince*
65 persuader (se) P – *to become convinced*
65 perturber T – *to perturb*
81 pervertir T – *to pervert*
81 pervertir (se) P – *to become perverted*
65 pervibrer T – *to vibrate freash concrete*
68 **peser** I, T – *to weigh, to ponder*
68 peser (se) P – *to be weighed, to weigh oneself*
65 pesteller belg. I – *to stamp one's foot*
65 pester I – *to curse (figurative)*
69 pestiférer T – *to plague*
65 pétarader I – *to bang, to pop*
65 pétarder I, T – *to blast, to back-fire*
69 péter I, T – *to fart, to break*
69 péter (se) P – *to break*
65 pétiller I – *to crackle*
65 petit-déjeuner I – *to have breakfast*
65 pétitionner I – *to petition*
65 pétocher I – *to be scared*
65 pétrarquiser I – *to imitate Pétrarque (poetry)*
76 pétrifier T – *to petrify*
76 pétrifier (se) P – *to petrify*
81 pétrir T – *to knead*
65 pétuner I – *to smoke*
65 peupler T – *to people, to populate*
65 peupler (se) P – *to people, to populate*
65 phagocyter T – *to absorb (by phagocytosis), to distroy*
65 phantasmer I, T – *to have a fantasy*
65 philosopher I – *to philosophize*
65 phosphater T – *to phosphate*
65 phosphorer I – *to phosphorate*
76 photocopier T – *to photocopy*
76 photographier T – *to photograph*
65 phraser I, T – *to phrase*
65 piaffer I – *to paw (the ground)*
65 piailler I – *to squeal*
65 pianoter I, T – *to strum*

T: direct transitive (p. p. variable) – **Ti**: indirect transitive (p. p. invariable) – **I**: intransitive verb (p. p. invariable)
P: pronominal verb (auxiliary *être*) – **impers.**: impersonal verb – **D**: defective verb – *être*: verb conjugated with the auxiliary *être* – *être* or *avoir*: verbs conjugated with *être* or *avoir* (see paragraph 15)

65 piauler I – *to cheep, to whine*
65 picoler I, T – *to tipple*
65 picorer I, T – *to peck*
65 picoter T – *to prick tiny holes*
75 piéger T – *to trap*
65 pierrer T – *to smooth a surface with abrasive stone (technical)*
69 piéter I – *to toe the line*
69 piéter (se) P – *to stand firm, to dig one's heels*
65 piétiner I, T – *to trample*
65 pieuter (se) P – *to turn in, to hit the sack*
65 pif(f)er T – *to tolerate*
65 pigeonner T – *to dupe*
67 piger I, T – *to understand*
65 pigmenter T – *to pigment*
65 pignocher I, T – *to pick at (food)*
65 piler I, T – *to pound, to ground*
65 pîler/piler belg. I – *to mash (potatoes)*
65 piller T – *to pillage*
65 pilonner T – *to pulp*
65 piloter T – *to steer, to pilot*
65 pimenter T – *to add spice (to)*
65 pinailler I – *to quibble (over)*
66 pincer I, T – *to pinch, to squeeze, to nab*
66 pincer (se) P – *to pinch oneself*
65 pindariser I – *to write in an affected style*
65 pinter I – *to booze*
65 pinter (se) P – *to booze*
65 piocher I, T – *to pick, to swot*
67 pioger I – *to live in, to put up (slang)*
66 pioncer I – *to sleep*
65 pionner I – *to take pawns (chess)*
65 piper I, T – *to peep, to dupe, to load (dice)*
65 pique(-)niquer I – *to picnic*
65 piquer I, T – *to sting, to bite, to prick, to steal*
65 piquer (se) P – *to sting oneself, to take offence*
70 piqueter T – *to mark out, to picket*
65 piquouser T – *to take offence (slang)*
65 pirater I, T – *to pirate*
65 pirouetter I – *to pirouette*
65 pisser I, T – *to pee*
65 pissoter I – *to urinate (little by little)*
65 pistacher (se) P – *to become intoxicated (slang)*
65 pister T – *to track*
65 pistonner T – *to back, to push*
65 pitancher T – *to drink (slang)*
65 piter belg. I – *to kick (literal), to expel, to evict (figurative)*
65 pitonner I – *to use pegs (in mountaineering)*
65 pivoter I – *to hinge on*
65 placarder T – *to post up, to stick up*
66 **placer** T – *to put, to place, to post, to invest (money)*
66 placer (se) P – *to take up (position), to find a job, to be placed (sport)*
65 placoter québ. I – *to chat*
65 plafonner I, T – *to reach the top of*
76 plagier I, T – *to crib*
65 plaider I, T – *to plead*
125 plaindre T – *to be sorry (for), to pity*
125 plaindre (se) P – *to complain*
65 plainer T – *to even (out)*
129 **plaire** à I, Ti – *to please*
129 plaire (se) P – *to be attracted, to like oneself, to take pleasure in*
p. p. invariable
65 plaisanter I, T – *to joke*
76 planchéier T – *to board*
65 plancher I – *to swot*
65 planer I, T – *to soar, to hang over, to be above care, to be happy*
76 planifier T – *to plan*
65 planquer I, T – *to stash away*
65 planquer (se) P – *to hide, to take cover*
65 planter T – *to plant, to pitch*
65 planter (se) P – *to take stand, to fail*
65 plaquer T – *to chuck, to veneer*
65 plaquer (se) P – *to lie flat*
76 plasmifier T – *to transform gaz into plasma*
76 plastifier T – *to plasticize*
65 plastiquer T – *to blast*
65 plastronner I, T – *to strut, to boast about*
65 platiner T – *to plate, to dye blond (hair)*
65 platiniser T – *to platinize*
65 plâtrer T – *to plaster*
65 plébisciter T – *to vote by plebiscite*
65 pleurer I, T – *to cry, to weep, to mourn*
65 pleurnicher I – *to snivel*
65 pleuvasser impers. – *to drizzle*
impers.: "il pleuvasse"
65 pleuviner impers. – *to drizzle*
impers.: "il pleuvine"
65 pleuvioter impers. – *to rain (familiar)*
impers.: "il pleuviote"
107 **pleuvoir** I, impers. – *to rain*
impers.: "il pleut"
65 pleuvoter impers. – *to drizzle*
impers.: "il pleuvote"
76 plier I, T – *to fold (up)*
76 plier (se) P – *to bend, to submit*
65 plisser I, T – *to pleat, to crease*
65 plisser (se) P – *to screw up (eyes)*
65 plomber T – *to lead, to close (tooth)*
65 plomber (se) P – *to become lead colored*
67 plonger I, T – *to dive, to plunge*
67 plonger (se) P – *to get absorbed into*
65 ploquer T – *to cover with "ploc" (a mix of hair and tar) (nautical), to mix diferent colors (wool)*
65 ploquer (se) P – *to pile wool*
78 ployer I, T – *to bend, to give way*
65 plucher I – *to shed fluff*
65 plumer I, T – *to pluck, to fleece*
65 plumer (se) P – *to pluck, to fleece*
65 pluviner impers. – *to drizzle*
impers.: "il pluvine"
65 pocharder (se) P – *to become tipsy*
65 pocher I, T – *to poach (egg), to blacken (eye), to bag (clothes)*
65 podzoliser T – *to turn into podzol (geological)*
65 poêler T – *to cook in frying-pan*
65 poétiser T – *to make poetic*
65 pogner T – *to catch, to take, to grasp, to get (popular)*
65 poignarder T – *to stab*
65 poiler (se) P – *to guffaw*
65 poinçonner T – *to punch*
124 poindre I, T – *to dawn*

65 pointer I, T – *to tick off (list), to check in, to point, to soar, to thrust at*
65 pointer (se) P – *to turn up*
65 pointiller I, T – *to dot*
65 poireauter I – *to wait (familiar)*
65 poiroter I – *to wait (familiar)*
65 poisser I, T – *to pitch*
65 poivrer T – *to pepper*
65 poivrer (se) P – *to get peppered*
65 poivroter (se) P – *to booze*
65 polariser T – *to center upon, to polarize*
65 polariser (se) P – *to concentrate (on), to focus (on)*
65 polémiquer I – *to enter into polemics*
66 policer T – *to bring order, to civilize*
66 policer (se) P – *to become civilized*
81 polir T – *to polish, to refine*
81 polir (se) P – *to become polished*
65 polissonner I – *to be bawdy*
65 politiquer I – *to talk politics*
65 politiser T – *to give a political angle*
65 politiser (se) P – *to become politically involved, to become political*
65 polluer I, T – *to pollute*
76 polycopier T – *to duplicate*
65 polymériser T – *to polymerize*
65 pommader T – *to pomade, to flatter*
65 pommader (se) P – *to apply a pomade*
72 pommeler (se) P – *to become dappled*
65 pommer I – *to form a head (vegetables)*
65 pomper I, T – *to pump*
65 pomponner T – *to adorn, to titivate*
65 pomponner (se) P – *to smarten oneself up*
66 poncer T – *to sand paper*
65 ponctionner T – *to puncture, to tap*
65 ponctuer T – *to punctuate, to dot*
69 pondérer T – *to balance*
118 pondre I, T – *to lay*
65 ponter I, T – *to make a bridge*
76 pontifier I – *to pontificate*
65 pontiller T – *to polish with a round punt (glass)*
65 populariser T – *to make popular, to popularize*
65 populariser (se) P – *to become popular*
65 poquer I – *to throw high so it will not move upon landing (petanque)*
65 porphyriser T – *to grind (stone)*
65 porter sur I, T, Ti – *to carry, to bring, to wear (clothes), to be about (theme, subject)*
65 porter (se) P – *to feel (health)*
65 portraiturer T – *to portray*
65 poser I, T – *to pose, to put down, to lay down*
65 poser (se) P – *to arise (question), to land (aircraft), to settle*
65 positionner T – *to position*
65 positionner (se) P – *to position oneself*
65 positiver I, T – *to make positive, to be confident*
69 posséder T – *to possess, to own*
69 posséder (se) P – *to control own*
65 postdater T – *to postdate*
65 poster T – *to post*
65 poster (se) P – *to take up a position*
65 posticher I – *to patter (salesman)*
65 postillonner I – *to splutter*
65 postposer T – *to place after*
65 postsynchroniser T – *to postsynchronize*
65 postuler I, T – *to solicit, to apply for*
65 potasser I, T – *to swot*
65 potentialiser T – *to make more potent (pharm.)*
65 poter belg. I – *to drink (from a pot), to choose using a nursery rhyme (games)*
65 potiner I – *to gossip*
65 poudrer T – *to powder*
65 poudrer (se) P – *to powder*
78 poudroyer I – *to be covered in dust, to whirl up*
65 pouffer I – *to guffaw*
65 pouliner I – *to foal*
65 pouponner I – *to coddle*
65 pourchasser T – *to pursue, to be after*
118 pourfendre T – *to cleave (in twain), to defeat*
69 pourlécher T – *to lick*
69 pourlécher (se) P – *to smack one's lip*
65 pourprer (se) P – *to turn purple*
81 pourrir I, T – *to rot, to go bad*
81 pourrir (se) P – *to rot, to go bad*
145 poursuivre T – *to pursue, to chase*
145 poursuivre (se) P – *to continue*
102 pourvoir à T, Ti – *to provide (for)*
102 pourvoir (se) P – *to provide oneself with*
65 pousser I, T – *to push, to urge on, to grow*
65 pousser (se) P – *to make one's way*
65 poutser T – *to polish, to scour (fam.)*
105 pouvoir I, T – *to be able to*
105 pouvoir (se) P, impers. – *to be able to impers.:* "il se peut"
65 praliner T – *to brown (in sugar), to crisp*
65 pratiquer I, T – *to put into practice*
65 pratiquer (se) P – *to be usual, to be the practice*
71 préacheter T – *to pre-buy*
65 préaviser T – *to forewarn*
65 précariser T – *to make precarious/insecure*
65 précariser (se) P – *to become precarious/insecure*
65 précautionner T – *to take precautions*
65 précautionner (se) P – *to take precautions*
69 précéder I, T – *to precede*
65 préchauffer T – *to preheat*
65 prêcher I, T – *to preach*
65 précipiter T – *to throw down, to hurry*
65 précipiter (se) P – *to hurry, to rush, to speed up*
65 préciser I, T – *to make clear, to clarify, to specify*
65 préciser (se) P – *to take shape, to become clearer*
65 précompter T – *to deduct beforehand*
65 préconiser T – *to recommend*
152 précuire T – *to precook*
65 prédestiner T – *to predestinate*
65 prédéterminer T – *to predetermine*
65 prédiquer T – *to predicate*
148 prédire T – *to predict*
65 prédisposer I, T – *to predispose*
65 prédominer I – *to predominate, to prevail*

T: direct transitive (p. p. variable) – **Ti**: indirect transitive (p. p. invariable) – **I**: intransitive verb (p. p. invariable) **P**: pronominal verb (auxiliary *être*) – **impers.**: impersonal verb – **D**: defective verb – *être*: verb conjugated with the auxiliary *être* – *être* or *avoir*: verbs conjugated with *être* or *avoir* (see paragraph 15)

65 préempter T – *to pre-empt*
81 préétablir T – *to pre-establish*
65 préexister I – *to pre-exist*
65 préfabriquer T – *to prefabricate*
66 préfacer T – *to write a preface*
69 préférer I, T – *to prefer, to like better, would rather*
69 préférer (se) P – *to prefer oneself*
65 préfigurer T – *to freshadow*
65 préfixer T – *to prefix*
65 préformer T – *to preform*
76 préjudicier I – *to be detrimental (to)*
67 préjuger de T, Ti – *to prejudge*
65 prélasser (se) P – *to loll*
68 prélever T – *to deduct, to set apart*
65 préluder à I, Ti – *to prelude to*
65 préméditer de T, Ti – *to premeditate*
81 prémunir T – *to warn, to protect*
81 prémunir (se) P – *to protect oneself*
119 prendre I, T – *to take, to seize, to catch, to capture*
119 prendre (se) P – *to be seized, to be grasped, to be caught*
65 prénommer T – *to name*
65 prénommer (se) P – *to be called (Christian name)*
65 préoccuper T – *to preoccupy*
65 préoccuper (se) P – *to be worrying, to concern*
65 préparer T – *to prepare to, to get ready for*
65 préparer (se) P – *to prepare, to get ready for*
77 prépayer T – *to prepay*
65 prépensionner belg. T – *to put in pre-retirement*
65 préposer T – *to appoint*
69 prérégler T – *to preset*
67 présager T – *to forebode, to predict*
150 prescrire I, T – *to prescribe, to stipulate*
150 prescrire (se) P – *to lapse*
65 présélectionner T – *to preselect*
65 présenter I, T – *to present, to display, to introduce*
65 présenter (se) P – *to appear, to arise, to introduce oneself*
65 préserver T – *to protect (from), to preserve*
65 préserver (se) P – *to protect oneself, to preserve oneself*
65 présider à I, T, Ti – *to preside over*
86 pressentir T – *to guess, to predict*
65 presser I, T – *to squeeze, to press*
65 presser (se) P – *to hurry up, to be in a rush, to throng*
65 pressurer T – *to press (strongly), to extort (money)*
65 pressurer (se) P – *to ponder, to reflect (intensely)*
65 pressuriser T – *to pressurize*
65 prester belg. T – *to work on*
65 présumer de T, Ti – *to presume*
65 présupposer T – *to presuppose*
65 présurer T – *to curdle (milk)*
118 prétendre à T, Ti – *to claim*
118 prétendre (se) P – *to assert oneself as*
65 prêter I, T – *to lend, to attribute*
65 prêter (se) P – *to consent, to accept, to adapt*
65 prétexter T – *to pretext*
109 prévaloir I – *to prevail*
109 prévaloir (se) P – *to take advantage, to pride oneself*
65 prévariquer I – *to prevaricate*
84 prévenir T – *to anticipate, to inform*
101 prévoir T – *to foresee, to forecast*
76 prier I, T – *to pray, to beg, to request*
65 primariser T – *to make a connection (between preschool and elementary school, or elementary school and secondary school)*
65 primer I, T – *to excel (in), to award a prize*
65 priser I, T – *to snuff, to appraise, to treasure*
65 privatiser T – *to privatize*
65 priver T – *to deny, to deprive*
65 priver (se) P – *to abstain, to refrain oneself*
76 privilégier T – *to privilege*
65 prober belg. T – *to try*
69 procéder à, de I, Ti – *to proceed, to initiate, to originate from*
65 processionner I – *to walk in procession*
65 proclamer T – *to proclaim*
65 proclamer (se) P – *to proclaim oneself*
74 procréer T – *to procreate*
65 procurer T – *to gain, to obtain*
65 procurer (se) P – *to gain, to obtain*
65 prodiguer T – *to lavish, to squander*
65 prodiguer (se) P – *to be lavished, to be squandered*
152 produire I, T – *to produce, to make, to bring about*
152 produire (se) P – *to happen, to appear (on stage)*
65 profaner T – *to profane*
69 proférer T – *to utter*
65 professer I, T – *to profess, to teach*
65 professionnaliser T – *to professionalize*
65 professionnaliser (se) P – *to become professionalized*
65 profiler T – *to profile, to shape*
65 profiler (se) P – *to present one's profile, to emerge*
65 profiter à, de Ti – *to profit, to make a profit, to take advantage of*
65 programmer I, T – *to program*
65 progresser I – *to progress, to advance*
65 prohiber T – *to prohibit*
70 projeter T – *to project, to show (film), to plan*
70 projeter (se) P – *to jut out*
65 prolétariser T – *to proletarianize*
69 proliférer I – *to proliferate*
67 prolonger T – *to prolong, to extend*
67 prolonger (se) P – *to last, to persist*
68 promener T – *to take for a walk*
68 promener (se) P – *to go for a walk, to wander*
122 promettre I, T – *to promise*
122 promettre (se) P – *to promise oneself*
65 promotionner T – *to promote*
106 promouvoir T – *to promote*
65 promulguer T – *to issue (decree)*
65 prôner I, T – *to extol*
66 prononcer I, T – *to utter, to pronounce*
66 prononcer (se) P – *to reach a decision*
65 pronostiquer T – *to forecast*
67 propager T – *to propagate*
67 propager (se) P – *to spread, to reproduce*
65 prophétiser I, T – *to prophesy*
65 proportionner T – *to proportion*
65 proportionner (se) P – *to be proportioned*
65 proposer I, T – *to suggest, to propose*
65 proposer (se) P – *to set oneself, to intend, to offer one's services*
65 propulser T – *to propel*
65 propulser (se) P – *to propel*

67 proroger T – *to adjourn*
67 proroger (se) P – *to give oneself an extension*
150 proscrire T – *to outlaw*
76 prosodier T – *to follow the rules of prose-writing*
65 prospecter I, T – *to prospect*
69 prospérer I – *to prosper*
65 prosterner T – *to bow, to prostrate*
65 prosterner (se) P – *to bow, to prostrate oneself*
65 prostituer T – *to prostitute*
65 prostituer (se) P – *to prostitute*
75 protéger T – *to protect, to shelter, to patronize*
75 protéger (se) P – *to protect oneself, to be protected*
65 protester de I, T, Ti – *to protest*
65 prouter I – *to fart*
65 prouver T – *to prove*
65 prouver (se) P – *to prove oneself, to prove to oneself*
84 provenir I, *être* – *to arise from*
65 proverbialiser T – *to make into a proverb*
65 provigner I, T – *to plant a stem so it can take roots without separating it from the main plant*
65 provisionner T – *to provision*
65 provoquer T – *to provoke, to induce, to arouse*
65 provoquer (se) P – *to provoke*
65 pruner T – *to prune*
76 psalmodier I, T – *to chant*
65 psychanalyser T – *to psychoanalyze*
65 psychiatriser T – *to interpret according to psychiatry*
76 publier I, T – *to publish, to proclaim*
65 puddler T – *to puddle*
65 puer I, T – *to stink*
rare: past historic
imparfait *of the subjunctive,*
and compound tenses
65 puiser I, T – *to draw, to derive*
65 pulluler I – *to pullulate, to swarm*
65 pulser T – *to pulse*
65 pulvériser T – *to grind*
65 punaiser T – *to tack*
81 punir T – *to punish*
67 purger T – *to purge*
67 purger (se) P – *to purge (bowels)*
76 purifier T – *to purify*
76 purifier (se) P – *to be purified, to purify oneself*
76 putréfier T – *to putrefy*
76 putréfier (se) P – *to putrefy*
65 pyramider I – *to make a pyramid*
65 pyrograver T – *to pyrograph*

q, r

65 quadriller T – *to cross-rule, to divide into cros-sections*
65 quadrupler I, T – *to quadruple*
76 qualifier T – *to qualify, to term*
76 qualifier (se) P – *to be qualified, to label oneself*
76 quantifier T – *to quantify*
65 quarderonner T – *to quarter-round*
65 quarrer T – *to quadrate*
67 quartager T – *to give the fourth plowing (vineyards)*
65 quémander I, T – *to beg (from)*
65 quereller T – *to scold*
65 quereller (se) P – *to quarrel (with one another)*
85 quérir T, D – *to fetch*
65 questionner T – *to question*
65 questionner (se) P – *to question (oneself)*
65 quêter I, T – *to collect*
65 queuter I – *to push a billiard ball*
65 quiller afr. T – *to nest*
65 quimper I – *to fall, to fail (Belg), to be dressed to the nines*
76 quintessencier T – *to be quintessential*
65 quintupler I, T – *to quintuple*
66 quittancer T – *to give a receipt, to discharge*
65 quitter I, T – *to leave, to vacate, to desert*
65 quitter (se) P – *to part*
65 rabâcher I, T – *to repeat, to harp on*
65 rabaisser T – *to debase, to belittle*
65 rabaisser (se) P – *to humble oneself*
65 rabanter T – *to make fast, to tie up (vessel)*
121 rabattre I, T – *to shut down, to deduct (sum)*
121 rabattre (se) P – *to cut in (car)*
65 rabibocher T – *to reconcile*
65 rabibocher (se) P – *to bring together*
65 rabioter I, T – *to scrounge*
65 rabistoquer belg. T – *to mend*
65 râbler T – *to stir (fire)*
81 rabonnir I, T – *to improve*
65 raboter T – *to plane*
81 rabougrir I, T – *to shrivel up*
81 rabougrir (se) P – *to become stunted*
65 rabouter T – *to join together*
65 rabrouer T – *to scold, to snap at*
92 racabouillir belg. I – *to overboil*
65 raccommoder T – *to mend, to repair*
65 raccommoder (se) P – *to make it up, to be reconciled*
65 raccompagner T – *to take back*
65 raccorder T – *to link up (to), to join up (to)*
65 raccorder (se) P – *to link up (to), to join up (to)*
81 raccourcir I, T – *to shorten*
81 raccourcir (se) P – *to shorten*
65 raccoutrer T – *to repair (clothes)*
65 raccoutumer T – *to reaccustom*
65 raccoutumer (se) P – *to become reaccustiomed*
65 raccrocher I, T – *to hang up (phone)*
65 raccrocher (se) P – *to cling*
65 raccuser belg. I – *to tattletale*
65 raccuspoter belg. I – *to tell tales*
71 racheter T – *to buy (back), to atone (for)*
71 racheter (se) P – *to redeem oneself*
65 raciner T – *to take root*
65 racketter T – *to extort money (from so)*
65 racler T – *to scrape, to rake*
65 racler (se) P – *to scrape, to rake*
65 racoler T – *to recruit, to solicit*
65 raconter T – *to tell, to relate*
65 raconter (se) P – *to talk about oneself*

T: direct transitive (p. p. variable) – **Ti**: indirect transitive (p. p. invariable) – **I**: intransitive verb (p. p. invariable)
P: pronominal verb (auxiliary *être*) – **impers.**: impersonal verb – **D**: defective verb – *être*: verb conjugated with the auxiliary *être* – *être* or *avoir*: verbs conjugated with *être* or *avoir* (see paragraph 15)

81 racornir T – *to shrivel up, to harden*
81 racornir (se) P – *to shrivel up, to harden*
65 racrapoter (se) belg. P – *to curl up*
65 rader T – *to cut (marble or rock)*
65 radicaliser T – *to toughen, to radicalize*
65 radicaliser (se) P – *to toughen, to radicalize*
76 radier T – *to strike off*
65 radiner I – *to show up, to turn up*
65 radiner (se) P – *to turn up*
65 radiobaliser T – *to transmit signal*
65 radiodiffuser T – *to broadcast*
76 radiographier T – *to X-ray*
65 radioguider T – *to control by radio*
65 radioscoper T – *to X-ray*
76 radiotélégraphier T – *to telegraph by radio*
65 radoter I, T – *to drivel, to ramble on*
65 radouber T – *to repair (ship) in dry dock*
81 radoucir I, T – *to soften, to grow mild*
81 radoucir (se) P – *to soften, to grow mild*
65 rafaler québ. I – *to squall*
81 rafantir belg. I – *to become senile, to return to infancy*
81 raffermir T – *to strengthen, to harden*
81 raffermir (se) P – *to strengthen, to harden*
65 raffiner I, T – *to refine*
65 raffoler de Ti – *to adore*
65 raffûter/raffuter T – *to reset*
65 rafistoler T – *to patch up*
65 rafler T – *to sweep off, to round up*
81 rafraîchir/rafraichir I, T – *to cool down, to chill, to brigthen up*
81 rafraîchir/rafraichir (se) P – *to refresh oneself, to take a drink*
81 ragaillardir T – *to perk up*
67 rager I – *to fume*
65 ragoter I – *to gossip (about)*
65 ragoûter/ragouter T – *to restore (appetite)*
65 ragrafer T – *to hook up*
74 ragréer T – *to smooth (masonry), to finish*
65 raguer I – *to wear out, to chafe*
81 raidir T – *to stiffen*
81 raidir (se) P – *to stiffen*
65 railler I, T – *to scoff (at), to make fun (of)*
65 railler (se) P – *to scoff (at), to make fun (of)*
65 rainer T – *to groove*
70 raineter T – *to trace saw-lines*
65 rainurer T – *to groove*
127 raire I, D – *to bell (deer)*
65 raisonner de, sur I, T, Ti – *to reason (with), to argue about*
65 raisonner (se) P – *to reason (with)*
81 rajeunir I, T – *to rejuvenate, to update*
81 rajeunir (se) P – *to make oneself younger*
65 rajouter T – *to add, to add more (of)*
65 rajuster T – *to straighten*
65 rajuster (se) P – *to straighten one's clothes*
81 ralentir I, T – *to slow down*
81 ralentir (se) P – *to slow down*
65 râler I – *to fume, to rattle*
65 ralinguer I, T – *to rope (sail boat)*
75 ralléger I – *to lighten*
76 rallier I, T – *to join, to side with*
76 rallier (se) P – *to join*
67 rallonger I, T – *to lenghten, to extend*
67 rallonger (se) P – *to lenghten, to extend*
65 rallumer I, T – *to rekindle, to revive*
65 rallumer (se) P – *to come on again (light)*
67 ramager I, T – *to warble*
65 ramailler T – *to chamoize*
65 ramander I, T – *to make fast*
65 ramarrer T – *to make fast again (vessel)*
65 ramasser T – *to gather, to pick up*
65 ramasser (se) P – *to gather, to pick up, to come a cropper*
65 rambiner I – *to reconcile*
65 ramender T – *to mend, to repair*
68 ramener T – *to take back, to bring back*
68 ramener (se) P – *to come down*
65 ramer I, T – *to row, to flounder*
70 rameter belg. I – *to chatter*
65 rameuter T – *to gather together, to round up*
65 rameuter (se) P – *to gather together, to round up*
76 ramifier T – *to branch out, to ramify*
76 ramifier (se) P – *to branch out, to ramify*
81 ramollir T – *to soften*
81 ramollir (se) P – *to grow soft*
65 ramoner I, T – *to sweep (chimney)*
65 ramper I – *to crawl, to trail (plant), to cringe*
65 rancarder T – *to tip off*
65 rancarder (se) P – *to arrange to meet*
81 rancir I – *to grow rancid*
81 rancir (se) P – *to go rancid*
65 rançonner T – *to hold to ransom*
65 randonner I – *to trek*
67 ranger T – *to arrange, to tidy, to put away*
67 ranger (se) P – *to pull over (car), to stand aside, to mend one's way*
65 ranimer T – *to revive, to renew*
65 ranimer (se) P – *to revive, to renew*
65 rapailler québ. T – *to bring together*
65 rapapilloter T – *to reconcile*
76 rapatrier T – *to repatriate*
76 rapatrier (se) P – *to repatriate*
65 râper T – *to grate*
65 rapetasser T – *to patch up*
65 rapetisser I, T – *to shorten, to diminish*
65 rapetisser (se) P – *to shrink*
66,69 rapiécer T – *to patch*
71 rapiéceter/rapièceter T – *to darn, to repair*
65 rapiner I – *to pillage, to graft*
81 raplatir T – *to flatten out*
65 raplomber québ. T – *to put back in shape (figurative)*
65 raplomber (se) québ. P – *to regain shape*
81 rap(p)ointir P – *to sharpen*
65 rappareiller T – *to match*
76 rapparier T – *to match*
72 rappeler I, T – *to call back, to remind, to phone (back)*
72 rappeler (se) P – *to recall, to remember*
65 rapper I – *to rap (sing)*
65 rappliquer I – *to re-apply, to turn up*
65 rapporter I, T – *to bring back, to return, to report, to call off, to give a good return* (money)
65 rapporter (se) P – *to relate*
119 rapprendre T – *to relearn*
65 rapprocher I, T – *to bring near, to come nearer*

65 rapprocher (se) P – *to bring near, to come nearer*
76 rapproprier T – *to clean up, to tidy up*
65 rapprovisionner T – *to renew or restock supplies*
65 rapprovisionner (se) P – *to renew or restock supplies*
65 raquer I, T – *to fork out*
76 raréfier T – *to rarefy*
76 raréfier (se) P – *to rarefy*
65 raser T – *to shave, to bore*
65 raser (se) P – *to shave, to be bored*
76 rassasier T – *to satisfy (hunger)*
76 rassasier (se) P – *to eat one's fill*
65 rassembler T – *to reassemble, to gather*
65 rassembler (se) P – *to reassemble, to gather*
112 rass(e)oir I, T – *to reseat, to sit down again*
past participle: "rassis, ise, ises"
112 rass(e)oir (se) P – *to reseat, to sit down again*
69 rasséréner T – *to restore to serenity, to clear up*
69 rasséréner (se) P – *to recover one's spirit*
81 rassir I – *to grow stale*
rare and especially in the infinitive and past participle "rassi, ie, is, ies"
81 rassir (se) P – *to go stale*
111 rassoir/rasseoir I, T – *to sit back up*
111 rassoir/rasseoir (se) P – *to sit back up*
81 rassortir T – *to reorder*
65 rassurer T – *to reassure*
65 rassurer (se) P – *to feel reassured*
65 ratatiner T – *to shrivel up*
65 ratatiner (se) P – *to shrivel up*
65 ratatouiller I – *to stew*
72 râteler T – *to rake up*
65 rater I, T – *to fail, to miss*
65 rater (se) P – *to miss*
65 ratiboiser T – *to be broke, to swindle, to gamble away*
76 ratifier T – *to ratify*
65 ratiner T – *to frieze (textiles)*
65 ratiociner I – *to split hairs*
65 rationaliser T – *to rationalize*
65 rationner T – *to ration*
65 rationner (se) P – *to ration*
65 ratisser T – *to rake*
65 rattacher T – *to fasten again*
65 rattacher (se) P – *to be connected*
65 rattraper T – *to recapture, to recoup*
65 rattraper (se) P – *to save oneself, to make good*
65 raturer T – *to erase*
65 raugmenter I, T – *to increase again*
65 rauquer I – *to yell in a hoarse voice*
67 ravager T – *to ravage*
65 ravaler T – *to reduce, to swallow again, to renovate*
65 ravaler (se) P – *to debase oneself*
65 ravauder I, T – *to mend*
65 ravigoter T – *to revive*
81 ravilir T – *to degrade, to vivify*
65 raviner T – *to hollow out*
81 ravir T – *to ravish, to enrapture*
65 raviser (se) P – *to change one's mind*
65 ravitailler T – *to refill, to resupply*
65 ravitailler (se) P – *to get fresh supplies*
65 raviver T – *to revive*
65 raviver (se) P – *to revive*
ravoir T, D – *to have again, to clean*
used only in the infinitive
77 rayer T – *to scratch, to cross out (word)*
77 rayer (se) P – *to scratch, to cross out (word)*
65 rayonner I, T – *to radiate*
76 razzier T – *to raid*
65 réabonner T – *to renew one's subscription (to)*
65 réabonner (se) P – *to renew one's subscription (to)*
65 réabsorber T – *to reabsorb*
65 r(é)accoutumer T – *to reaccustom*
65 r(é)accoutumer (se) P – *to become reaccustomed*
65 réactiver T – *to reactivate*
65 réactualiser T – *to update*
65 réadapter T – *to readjust*
65 réadapter (se) P – *to readjust*
122 réadmettre T – *to readmit*
65 réaffirmer T – *to reaffirm*
65 r(é)affûter/réaffuter T – *to regrind*
81 réagir à I, Ti – *to react to*
65 r(é)ajuster T – *to readjust*
65 r(é)ajuster (se) P – *to straighten oneself up, to readjust*
69 réaléser T – *to rebore*
65 réaliser T – *to realize, to fulfil, to produce (film)*
65 réaliser (se) P – *to come true*
67 réaménager T – *to reorganize*
66 réamorcer T – *to revive*
65 réanimer T – *to revive*
130 réapparaître/réapparaitre I – *to reappear*
être *(or* avoir*)*
119 r(é)apprendre T – *to relearn*
65 r(é)approvisionner T – *to stock up again*
65 r(é)approvisionner (se) P – *to stock up again*
65 réargenter T – *to replate*
65 réargenter (se) P – *to replenish the coffers*
65 réarmer I, T – *to refit (boat), to reload (camera)*
65 réarmer (se) P – *to rearm*
67 réarranger T – *to rearrange*
65 réassigner T – *to resummon*
81 r(é)assortir T – *to rematch, to re-stock*
81 réassortir (se) P – *to re-match*
65 réassurer T – *to reassure, to reinsure*
65 réassurer (se) P – *to reassure, to reinsure*
65 rebaisser I, T – *to lower again*
65 rebander T – *to re-bandage*
65 rebaptiser T – *to rebaptize, to rename*
81 rebâtir T – *to rebuild*
121 rebattre T – *to beat again, to reshuffle (cards)*
65 rebecter T – *to nurse back to health, to help out of a tight situation (financial)*
65 rebeller (se) P – *to rebel*
65 rebiffer (se) P – *to bristle up, to strike back*
65 rebiquer I – *to restore*
81 reblanchir T – *to whiten again*
65 reboiser T – *to reforest*

T: direct transitive (p. p. variable) – **Ti**: indirect transitive (p. p. invariable) – **I**: intransitive verb (p. p. invariable) **P**: pronominal verb (auxiliary *être*) – **impers.**: impersonal verb – **D**: defective verb – *être*: verb conjugated with the auxiliary *être* – *être* or *avoir*: verbs conjugated with *être* or *avoir* (see paragraph 15)

81 rebondir I – *to rebound*
70 rebonneter T – *to flatter ironically, to improve*
65 reborder T – *to put a new edge*
65 reboucher T – *to recork, to fill up*
65 reboucher (se) P – *to recork, to fill up*
92 rebouillir I – *to reboil*
65 rebouiser T – *to lustre*
65 rebouter T – *to set up (broken bone)*
65 reboutonner T – *to button up again*
65 reboutonner (se) P – *to button up again*
65 rebraguetter T – *to rezip (pants)*
65 rebraguetter (se) P – *to rezip one's pants*
65 rebroder T – *to re-embroider*
65 rebrousser I, T – *to brush up (hair)*
65 rebrousser (se) P – *to turn up, to bend back*
65 rebuter I, T – *to put off, to rebuff*
65 rebuter (se) P – *to lose heart*
70 recacheter T – *to seal again*
65 recadrer T – *to crop (photography)*
76 recalcifier T – *to recalcify*
65 recaler T – *to fail (somebody), to reset*
65 récapituler T – *to recapitulate*
65 recarder T – *to re-card*
72 recarreler T – *to repave*
65 recaser T – *to resettle, to palm off*
65 recaser (se) P – *to resettle, to palm off*
65 recauser I – *to recause, to chat again*
69 recéder T – *to resell*
73 receler I, T – *to receive stolen goods, to harbour*
69 recéler I, T – *to conceal*
65 recenser T – *to take a census, to count*
65 recentrer T – *to refocus*
69 recéper T – *to cut down*
65 réceptionner T – *to take delivery (of)*
65 recercler T – *to rehoop (cask)*
100 recevoir I, T – *to receive, to welcome*
100 recevoir (se) P – *to land (on)*
81 rechampir T – *to set off*
81 réchampir T – *to recoat (wood)*
67 rechanger T – *to exchange*
67 rechanger (se) P – *to change one's clothes*
65 rechanter T – *to sing again, to repeat*
65 rechaper T – *to retread*
65 réchapper I – *to come through*
67 recharger T – *to recharge*
65 rechasser I, T – *to drive back*
65 réchauffer T – *to reheat, to warm up*
65 réchauffer (se) P – *to get warmer*
65 rechausser T – *to put on one's shoes again*
65 rechausser (se) P – *to put on one's shoes again*
65 rechercher T – *to search for*
65 rechigner à I, Ti – *to jib, to balk at*
65 rechristianiser T – *to rechristianize*
65 rechuter I – *to bakcslide, to have a relapse*
65 récidiver I – *to recur, to relapse*
65 réciproquer belg. I, T – *to reciprocate*
65 réciter T – *to recite*
65 réclamer I, T – *to ask for, to claim, to complain (about)*
65 réclamer (se) P – *to refer*
65 reclaper belg. T – *to reclose*
65 reclasser T – *to reclassify*
65 récliner I – *to tilt backwards*
138 reclore T – *to reclose*
138 reclore (se) P – *to reclose*
65 reclouer T – *to nail up again*
140 reclure T – *to seclude*
140 reclure (se) P – *to confine*
65 recoiffer T – *to re-arrange hair*
65 recoiffer (se) P – *to re-arrange one's hair*
65 récoler T – *to check*
65 recoller à T, Ti – *to restick*
65 recoller (se) P – *to mend, to glue*
65 recolorer T – *to recolour*
65 récolter T – *to harvest*
65 récolter (se) P – *to harvest*
65 recommander T – *to recommend, to register (letter)*
65 recommander (se) P – *to refer*
66 recommencer I, T – *to recommence*
130 recomparaître/recomparaitre I – *to reappear*
65 récompenser T – *to reward*
65 récompenser (se) P – *to recompense, to compensate*
65 recomposer T – *to recompose*
65 recomposer (se) P – *to recompose*
65 recompter T – *to recount*
76 réconcilier T – *to reconcile*
76 réconcilier (se) P – *to reconcile (oneself)*
65 recondamner T – *to recondemn*
152 reconduire T – *to escort home, to reconfirm*
65 réconforter T – *to comfort*
65 réconforter (se) P – *to take comfort in, to take refreshment*
73 recongeler T – *to refreeze*
130 reconnaître/reconnaitre T – *to recognize, to reconnoitre, to admit, to acknowledge*
130 reconnaître/reconnaitre (se) P – *to recognize (one another), to get one's bearing, to own oneself*
65 reconnecter T – *to reconnect*
65 reconnecter (se) P – *to reconnect*
85 reconquérir T – *to recover, to regain*
69 reconsidérer T – *to reconsider*
65 reconsolider T – *to reconsolidate*
65 reconstituer T – *to reconstitue*
65 reconstituer (se) P – *to regenerate*
152 reconstruire T – *to rebuild*
81 reconvertir T – *to reconvert*
81 reconvertir (se) P – *to take up a new activity, to redeploy*
76 recopier T – *to re-copy*
65 recoquiller T – *to shrivel*
65 recoquiller (se) P – *to shrivel*
65 recorder T – *to retie*
67 recorriger T – *to revise*
65 recoucher T – *to put back to bed*
65 recoucher (se) P – *to go back to bed*
143 recoudre T – *to resew*
143 recoudre (se) P – *to be resewed*
65 recouper T – *to cut again, to cross-check*
65 recouper (se) P – *to intersect, to match up*
65 recouponner T – *to reset a coupon rate (securities)*
65 recourber T – *to bend back*
65 recourber (se) P – *to bend back*
94 recourir à T, Ti – *to resort to*
65 recouvrer T – *to recover*
88 recouvrir T – *to re-cover*

88 recouvrir (se) P – *to be covered (with)*
65 recracher I, T – *to spit out*
65 recracher (se) – *to spit out*
74 recréer T – *to recreate*
74 récréer T – *to entertain, to amuse*
74 récréer (se) P – *to entertain, to amuse*
81 recrépir T – *to replaster*
65 recreuser T – *to hollow out again*
76 récrier (se) P – *to exclaim*
65 récriminer I – *to recriminate*
150 récrire T – *to write again*
65 recristalliser T – *to re-crystallize*
65 recroiser T – *to recross*
136 recroître/recroitre I – *to grow again*
65 recroller belg. I – *to fold, to curl*
65 recroqueviller (se) P – *to shrivel up*
65 recruter I, T – *to recruit*
65 recruter (se) P – *to recruit*
76 rectifier T – *to rectify*
89 recueillir T – *to collect, to gather*
89 recueillir (se) P – *to collect one's thoughts*
152 recuire I, T – *to cook again*
65 reculer I, T – *to move back, to step back, to be on the decline*
65 reculer (se) P – *to draw back*
65 reculotter T – *to put pants back on*
65 reculotter (se) P – *to put one's pants back on*
69 récupérer T – *to recover, to recoup*
65 récurer T – *to scour*
65 récuser T – *to challenge*
65 récuser (se) P – *to decline to give an opinion*
65 recycler T – *to recycle*
65 recycler (se) P – *to retrain (for)*
65 redécouper T – *to cut again*
88 redécouvrir T – *to rediscover*
128 redéfaire T – *to undo again*
81 redéfinir T – *to redefine*
65 redemander T – *to ask again (for)*
65 redémarrer I – *to restart*
81 redémolir T – *to redemolish*
78 redéployer T – *to redeploy*
118 redescendre T, *avoir* – *to go or to come down again*
118 redescendre I, *être* (or *avoir*) – *to take down again*
84 redevenir I, *être* – *to become … again, to grow … again*
104 redevoir T – *to owe (a balance) of*
65 rediffuser T – *to rerun*
67 rédiger I, T – *to draft, to write out*
65 rédimer T – *to redeem*
65 rédimer (se) P – *to redeem*
148 redire à T, Ti – *to say again, to repeat, to criticize*
67 rediriger T – *to redirect*
65 rediscuter T – *to discuss again*
65 redistribuer T – *to re-distribute*
65 redonder I – *to be redundant*
65 redonner I, T – *to give again, to fall into*
65 redonner (se) P – *to restore, to reshape*
65 redorer T – *to regild*
65 redoubler de I, T, Ti – *to redouble, to repeat (class)*
65 redouter T – *to fear*
65 redresser T – *to re-erect, to rectify*
65 redresser (se) P – *to sit up again, to stand up straight*
152 réduire T – *to reduce*
152 réduire (se) P – *to be reduced*
150 ré(e)écrire T – *to rewrite*
76 réédifier T – *to rebuild*
65 rééditer T – *to republish*
65 rééduquer T – *to re-educate*
147 réélire T – *to re-elect*
65 réembaucher T – *to re-engage*
78 r(é)employer T – *to re-use, to re-employ*
65 remprunter T – *to re-borrow*
67 r(é)engager T – *to re-enlist*
67 r(é)engager (se) P – *to re-enlist*
66 réensemencer T – *to resow*
118 réentendre T – *to hear again*
65 rééquilibrer T – *to rebalance*
74 réer I – *to bellow (stag)*
65 réescompter T – *to rediscount*
77 r(é)essayer T – *to try again*
65 réévaluer T – *to revalue*
65 réexaminer T – *to reexamine*
76 réexpédier T – *to send back*
65 réexporter T – *to re-export*
65 refaçonner T – *to refashion*
128 refaire T – *to redo, to renew, to make again*
128 refaire (se) P – *to recuperate, to make up one's losses (money)*
118 refendre T – *to split again*
66 référencer T – *to refer (to)*
69 référer (en) à Ti – *to refer, to submit*
69 référer (se) à P – *to consult*
65 refermer T – *to close again*
65 refermer (se) P – *to close again*
65 refiler T – *to palm off*
81 réfléchir à, sur, dans I, T, Ti – *to think about, to reflect (light)*
81 réfléchir (se) P – *to be reflected, to reverberate (sound)*
69 refléter T – *to reflect, to mirror*
69 refléter (se) P – *to reflect, to mirror*
81 refleurir I, T – *to flower again*
65 refluer I – *to flow back, to surge back*
118 refondre I, T – *to remelt, to remodel*
67 reforger T – *to reforge*
65 reformer T – *to re-shape*
65 reformer (se) P – *to re-shape*
65 réformer T – *to reform, to reverse, to discharge (soldier)*
65 réformer (se) P – *to mend one's way*
65 reformuler T – *to reformulate*
65 refouiller T – *to hollow out*
65 refouler I, T – *to force back, to repress*
65 refourguer T – *to reflog*
65 refourrer T – *to re-stick, to put again*
120 refoutre T – *to redo*
65 réfracter T – *to refract*

T: direct transitive (p. p. variable) – **Ti**: indirect transitive (p. p. invariable) – **I**: intransitive verb (p. p. invariable) **P**: pronominal verb (auxiliary *être*) – **impers.**: impersonal verb – **D**: defective verb – *être*: verb conjugated with the auxiliary *être* – *être* or *avoir*: verbs conjugated with *être* or *avoir* (see paragraph 15)

69 refréner/réfréner T – *to curb, to bridle*
69 refréner/réfréner (se) P – *to curb, to check*
69 réfrigérer T – *to refrigerate*
81 refroidir I, T – *to cool down*
81 refroidir (se) P – *to turn cold*
76 réfugier (se) P – *to take refuge*
65 refuser I, T – *to refuse*
65 refuser (se) P – *to refuse (to)*
65 réfuter T – *to refute*
65 regagner T – *to win back*
65 régaler T – *to treat*
65 régaler (se) P – *to feast (on)*
65 regarder à I, T, Ti – *to look at, to watch, to think about*
65 regarder (se) P – *to look at oneself, to look at each other*
81 regarnir T – *to restock*
65 régater I – *to participate in a regatta (marine sport)*
65 regazonner T – *to replant (grass)*
73 regeler I, T – *to freeze again*
69 régénérer T – *to regenerate*
69 régénérer (se) P – *to regenerate*
65 régenter I, T – *to rule over*
65 regimber I – *to rebel (against)*
65 regimber (se) P – *to rebel (against)*
65 régionaliser T – *to regionalize*
81 régir T – *to govern*
65 réglementer T – *to regulate*
69 régler T – *to settle, to adjust, to pay off*
69 régler (se) P – *to settle, to adjust*
69 régner I – *to reign, to prevail*
65 regonfler I, T – *to reinflate*
67 regorger I – *to abound*
65 regratter I, T – *to scratch again, to huckster*
74 regréer T – *to replace rigging*
65 regreffer T – *to regraft*
65 régresser I – *to regress*
65 regretter T – *to regret*
65 regrimper I, T – *to climb again*
81 regrossir I – *to put weight back (on)*
65 regrouper T – *to re-assemble, to gather together*
65 regrouper (se) P – *to re-assemble, to gather together*
65 régulariser T – *to regularise, to straighten out*
65 réguler T – *to regulate*
65 réguler (se) P – *to regulate*
65 régurgiter T – *to regurgitate*
65 réhabiliter T – *to rehabilitate, to restore*
65 réhabiliter (se) P – *to rehabilitate, to restore*
65 réhabituer T – *to get used to again*
65 réhabituer (se) P – *to reaccustom (to)*
65 rehausser T – *to heighten, to enhance*
65 rehausser (se) P – *to heighten, to enhance*
65 rehydrater T – *to rehydrate*
76 réifier T – *to reify*
65 réimperméabiliser T – *to reproof*
65 réimplanter T – *to reimplant*
65 réimporter T – *to reimport*
65 réimposer T – *to reimpose*
65 réimprimer T – *to reprint*
69 réincarcérer T – *to reimprison*
65 réincarner (se) P – *to be reincarnated*
65 réincorporer T – *to reincorporate*
65 réinfecter T – *to reinfect*
65 réinfecter (se) P – *to reinfect*
65 réinjecter T – *to reinject*
150 réinscrire T – *to reinscribe*
150 réinscrire (se) P – *to re-register*
69 réinsérer T – *to reinsert*
69 réinsérer (se) P – *to reinsert*
65 *réinstaller* T – *to put back*
65 réinstaller (se) P – *to settle down again*
69 réintégrer T – *to reintegrate*
69 réinterpréter T – *to reinterpret*
152 réintroduire T – *to reintroduce*
65 réinventer T – *to reinvent*
81 réinvestir T – *to reinvest*
65 réinviter T – *to invite again*
69 réitérer I, T – *to reiterate*
81 rejaillir I – *to splash back, to rebound*
70 rejeter T – *to reject, to throw back, to discard, to transfer*
70 rejeter (se) P – *to jump or to leap back*
124 rejoindre T – *to rejoin, to reunite*
124 rejoindre (se) P – *to meet (again)*
78 rejointoyer T – *to regrout*
65 rejouer I, T – *to replay*
81 réjouir T – *to delight, to thrill*
81 réjouir (se) P – *to be delighted*
65 relâcher I, T – *to relax, to slacken off, to release*
65 relâcher (se) P – *to become slack*
65 relaisser (se) P – *to let oneself (followed by infinitive) again*
66 relancer I, T – *to throw back*
81 rélargir T – *to widen further*
65 relater T – *to relate*
65 relativiser T – *to put in perspective*
65 relaver I, T – *to rewash*
65 relaxer T – *to release*
65 relaxer (se) P – *to relax*
77 relayer I, T – *to relay, to relieve*
77 relayer (se) P – *to take turns*
69 reléguer T – *to relagate*
68 relever de I, T, Ti – *to raise, to pick up, to relieve (troops), to take up (challenge)*
68 relever (se) P – *to get back on one's feet, to recover*
76 relier T – *to bind, to connect (to)*
147 relire T – *to read again*
147 relire (se) P – *to read over what one has written*
67 reloger T – *to rehouse*
67 reloger (se) P – *to rehouse*
65 relooker T – *to relook*
65 relouer T – *to rent again*
153 reluire I – *to shine*
65 reluquer T – *to eye up*
65 remâcher T – *to ruminate*
65 remailler T – *to darn*
67 remanger T – *to eat some more*
76 remanier T – *to reshape*
65 remaquiller T – *to reapply make-up*
65 remaquiller (se) P – *to redo one's makeup (one's face)*
65 remarcher I – *to walk again, to work again*
76 remarier T – *to remarry*
76 remarier (se) P – *to remarry*
65 remarquer T – *to notice, to observe*
65 remarquer (se) P – *to notice, to observe*

65 remastiquer T – *to remasticate*
65 remballer T – *to repack, to rebuff*
65 rembarquer I, T – *to re-embark*
65 rembarquer (se) P – *to re-embark*
65 rembarrer T – *to rebuff*
65 rembaucher T – *to rehire*
65 rembiner I – *to comfort, to make feel better*
65 rembiner (se) P – *to comfort, to make feel better*
65 remblaver T – *to re-sow, to plant again*
77 remblayer T – *to bank up, to fill up*
65 rembobiner T – *to rewind*
65 remboîter/remboiter T – *to reassemble*
67 rembouger T – *to top up (liquid)*
65 rembourrer T – *to stuff*
65 rembourser T – *to repay*
65 rembroquer T – *to look*
81 rembrunir T – *to cloud over*
81 rembrunir (se) P – *to become gloomy*
65 rembucher I, T – *to track (animal)*
65 rembucher (se) P – *to return to its lair*
76 remédier à Ti – *to cure, to remedy*
65 remembrer T – *to regroup*
65 remémorer T – *to recall, to recollect*
65 remémorer (se) P – *to recall, to recollect*
76 remercier T – *to thank (for), to dismiss*
122 remettre T – *to put back (on), to replace, to hand over, to postpone*
122 remettre (se) P – *to recover*
65 remeubler T – *to refurnish*
65 remilitariser T – *to remilitarize*
65 remilitariser (se) P – *to remilitarize*
65 remiser T – *to put away, to put under cover*
65 remiser (se) P – *to take cover*
65 remmailler T – *to mend*
65 remmailloter T – *to swaddle again*
65 remmancher T – *to rehandle*
68 remmener T – *to take back*
73 remodeler T – *to remodel*
65 remonter T, *avoir* – *to go/come back up*
65 remonter I, *être* (or *avoir*) – *to go/come back up*
65 remonter (se) P, *être* – *to recover one's spirits*
65 remontrer à I, T, Ti – *to reshow*
65 remontrer (se) P – *to reappear*
118 remordre T – *to bite again*
65 remorquer T – *to tow*
65 remoucher T – *to wipe another's nose, to spot (colloq)*
65 remoucher (se) P – *to blow one's nose again*
144 remoudre T – *to regrind*
65 remouiller I, T – *to wet again*
65 rempailler T – *to re-cane (chair)*
70 rempaqueter T – *to rewrap*
65 remparer T – *to reseize, to fortify*
69 rempiéter T – *to re-foot*
65 rempiler I, T – *to re-engage, to volunteer for the second time round*
66 remplacer T – *to replace*
66 remplacer (se) P – *to relieve, to delete, to substitute*
76 remplier T – *to fold, to fold in*
81 remplir T – *to fill*
81 remplir (se) P – *to fill*
78 remployer T – *to use again*
65 remplumer T – *to get new feather*
65 remplumer (se) P – *to fill out again*
65 rempocher T – *to put back in pocket*
65 rempoissonner T – *to restock (fish)*
65 remporter T – *to take back, to win*
65 rempoter T – *to repot*
65 remprunter T – *to borrow again*
65 remuer I, T – *to stir, to move*
65 remuer (se) P – *to stir, to move*
69 rémunérer T – *to remunerate*
65 renâcler I – *to show reluctance, to snort (animal)*
131 renaître/renaitre à, de I, Ti – *to be reborn*
être, *rare in the past participle and in compound forms*
65 renarder I – *to play the fox, to vomit (slang)*
65 renauder I – *to complain*
65 rencaisser T – *to rebox*
65 rencarder T – *to tip off*
65 renchaîner/renchainer T – *to tie up again*
81 renchérir I, T – *to get dearer*
65 rencogner T – *to corner*
65 rencogner (se) P – *to huddle up*
65 rencontrer T – *to meet*
65 rencontrer (se) P – *to meet, to collide*
93 rendormir T – *to put back to sleep*
93 rendormir (se) P – *to go back to sleep*
65 rendosser T – *to put on again*
118 rendre I, T – *to give back (to), to pay back (money), to yield (crop), to vomit*
118 rendre (se) P – *to surrender*
67 reneiger I – *to snow again*
impersonal construction: "il reneige" – *it's snowing again*
65 renfaîter/renfaiter T – *to repair (roof)*
65 renfermer T – *to contain*
65 renfermer (se) P – *to withdraw into oneself*
65 renfiler T – *to restring, to put on again (clothes)*
65 renflammer T – *to rekindle*
65 renfler I, T – *to blow out*
65 renfler (se) P – *to bulge out*
65 renflouer T – *to refloat*
65 renflouer (se) – *to recoup one's losses (financially)*
66 renfoncer T – *to indent*
66 renforcer T – *to reinforce, to strengthen*
66 renforcer (se) P – *to reinforce, to strengthen*
81 renformir T – *to strengthen (construction)*
65 renfrogner (se) P – *to scowl*
67 rengager I, T – *to re-enlist, to re-engage*
67 rengager (se) P – *to re-enlist, to re-engage*
65 rengainer T – *to sheathe, to harpon*
67 rengorger (se) P – *to puff oneself up*
76 rengracier I – *to become honest*
65 rengraisser I – *to make fat again*
68 rengrener T – *to regrain*
69 rengréner T – *to refill with grain*
76 renier T – *to renounce*

T: direct transitive (p. p. variable) – **Ti**: indirect transitive (p. p. invariable) – **I**: intransitive verb (p. p. invariable)
P: pronominal verb (auxiliary *être*) – **impers.**: impersonal verb – **D**: defective verb – *être*: verb conjugated with the auxiliary *être* – *être* or *avoir*: verbs conjugated with *être* or *avoir* (see paragraph 15)

76 renier (se) P – *to deny*
65 renifler I, T – *to sniff, to sniff up*
65 renommer T – *to rename*
66 renoncer à T, Ti – *to renounce, to give up*
65 renouer T – *to tie up (knot)*
65 renouer (se) P – *to tie up (knot)*
72 renouveler I, T – *to renew*
72 renouveler (se) P – *to recur, to rejuvenate*
65 rénover T – *to renovate*
65 renquiller T – *to pocket again*
65 renseigner T – *to inform*
65 renseigner (se) P – *to make inquiries*
65 rentabiliser T – *to make profitable*
65 rentamer T – *to begin again*
65 renter T – *to endow*
65 rentoiler T – *to remount (picture)*
127 rentraire T, D – *to darn, to finedraw*
77 rentrayer T – *to darn*
65 rentrer T, *avoir* – *to bring in*
65 rentrer I, *être* – *to go in*
88 rentrouvrir T – *to half-open again*
65 renvelopper T – *to rewrap*
65 renvenimer T – *to poison again*
67 renverger T – *to cross warp (silk) threads again*
65 renverser T – *to spill, to knock over, to reverse*
65 renverser (se) P – *to overturn (car), to capsize (boat)*
65 renvider T – *to wind on spool*
80 renvoyer T – *to send back, to dismiss, to refer to*
80 renvoyer (se) P – *to send back, to dismiss, to refer to*
65 réoccuper T – *to reoccupy*
69 réopérer T – *to reoperate*
65 réorchestrer T – *to reorchestrate*
66 réordonnancer T – *to reauthorize*
65 réordonner T – *to order again*
65 réorganiser T – *to reorganize*
65 réorganiser (se) P – *to reorganize*
65 réorienter T – *to reorientate*
65 réorienter (se) P – *to reorientate*
65 repairer I – *to spot*
133 repaître/repaitre T – *to feed*
133 repaître/repaitre (se) P – *to feed*
118 répandre T – *to spill, to shed*
118 répandre (se) P – *to spread out*
130 reparaître/reparaitre I, *avoir* (or *être*) – *to reappear*
65 réparer T – *to repair*
65 reparler I – *to speak again (of)*
65 reparler (se) P – *to speak again*
67 repartager T – *to share out again*
86 repartir (partir à nouveau) I, *être* – *to leave*
86 repartir (répondre) T, *avoir* – *to retort, to reply*
86 répartir (répondre) T, *avoir* – *to retort, to reply*
81 répartir (distribuer) T, *avoir* – *to distribute*
81 répartir (se) (se distribuer) P, *être* – *to distribute*
65 repasser T, *avoir* – *to rehearse, to iron*
65 repasser I, *être* or *avoir* – *to rehearse, to iron*
65 repasser (se) P, *être* – *to pass from hand to hand*
65 repatiner T – *to skate again*
65 repaver T – *to repave*
77 repayer T – *to repay*
65 repêcher T – *to fish out*
65 repeigner T – *to comb again*
65 repeigner (se) P – *to comb again*
123 repeindre T – *to repaint*
118 rependre T – *to rehang*
65 repenser I, T – *to rethink*
86 repentir (se) P – *to regret, to be sorry (for)*
66 repercer T – *to pierce again*
65 répercuter T – *to echo, to reverberate*
65 répercuter (se) P – *to echo*
118 reperdre T – *to lose again*
69 repérer T – *to spot, to find*
69 repérer (se) P – *to find one's way around*
76 répertorier T – *to itemize*
69 répéter I, T – *to repeat, to rehearse*
69 répéter (se) P – *to recur, to be repeated*
65 repeupler T – *to repopulate*
65 repeupler (se) P – *to repopulate*
66 repincer T – *to pinch again, to catch*
65 repiquer I, T – *to restitch, to thin out (plants), to pick up again*
66 replacer T – *to replace*
66 replacer (se) P – *to replace*
65 replanter I, T – *to replant*
65 replanter (se) P – *to transplant*
65 replâtrer T – *to replaster*
107 repleuvoir impers. – *to rain again*
impers.: "il repleut"
76 replier T – *to fold up again, to withdraw (troops)*
76 replier (se) P – *to curl up*
65 répliquer I, T – *to reply*
65 répliquer (se) P – *to answer*
65 replisser T – *to pleat again*
67 replonger I, T – *to dive back*
67 replonger (se) P – *to immerse oneself again (in)*
78 reployer T – *to fold again*
81 repolir T – *to repolish*
118 répondre à, de I, T, Ti – *to answer, to reply, to respond, to meet*
118 répondre (se) P – *to anwser, to respond*
65 reporter T – *to take back, to put off, to defer, to transfer*
65 reporter (se) P – *to refer*
65 reposer I, T – *to rest, to put down again*
65 reposer (se) P – *to rest, to rely (on)*
65 repositionner T – *to reposition*
65 repositionner (se) P – *to reposition*
65 repousser I, T – *to push away, to reject, to repel*
65 repousser (se) P – *to push away, to reject, to repel*
119 reprendre I, T – *to take back, to recapture, to take up again, to resume*
119 reprendre (se) P – *to pull oneself together, to correct oneself*
65 représenter I, T – *to represent, to depict, to perform (play)*
65 représenter (se) P – *to present oneself again, to bring to mind, to imagine, to recur*
65 réprimander T – *to reprimand*
65 réprimer T – *to quell, to repress*
65 repriser T – *to darn*
65 reprocher T – *to reproach (for)*
65 reprocher (se) P – *to blame oneself*
152 reproduire T – *to reproduce, to copy*
152 reproduire (se) P – *to breed, to happen again*
65 reprogrammer T – *to reschedule*
76 reprographier T – *to reproduce*
65 reprouver T – *to reprove*

65 réprouver T – *to reprobate, to reject*
65 républicaniser T – *to republicanize*
76 répudier T – *to repudiate*
65 répugner à T, Ti – *to feel reluctant*
65 réputer T – *to repute, to be considered*
76 requalifier T – *to requalify*
76 requalifier (se) P – *to re-consider*
85 requérir T – *to ask for, to demand, to claim*
65 requinquer T – *to perk up*
65 requinquer (se) P – *to perk up*
65 réquisitionner T – *to requisition*
65 resaler T – *to add salt*
81 resalir T – *to dirty again*
81 resalir (se) P – *to get dirty again*
65 resaluer T – *to greet again*
65 rescinder T – *to annul, to cancel*
68 resemer T – *to resow*
68 resemer (se) P – *to resow*
69 reséquer T – *to resect*
65 réserver T – *to reserve, to keep*
65 réserver (se) P – *to bide one's time, to keep for oneself*
65 résider I – *to reside*
65 résigner T – *to resign to*
65 résigner (se) P – *to resign (oneself) to*
76 résilier T – *to cancel*
65 résiner T – *to resinate*
76 résinifier T – *to resinify*
65 résister à Ti – *to resist*
65 résonner I – *to reverberate*
65 résorber T – *to bring down gradually*
65 résorber (se) P – *to bring down gradually*
142 résoudre T – *to resolve, to settle (on)*
142 résoudre (se) P – *to be resolved*
65 respecter T – *to respect*
65 respecter (se) P – *to be respected, to be self-respecting*
65 respirer I, T – *to breathe*
81 resplendir I – *to shine*
65 responsabiliser T – *to give responsibility*
65 resquiller I, T – *to avoid paying*
65 ressaigner I, T – *to bleed again*
81 ressaisir T – *to recapture*
81 ressaisir (se) P – *to regain one's self-control*
65 ressasser T – *to hark*
65 ressauter I, T – *to jump again*
77 ressayer T – *to try again*
65 ressembler à Ti – *to ressemble*
65 ressembler (se) P – *to look alike*
p. p. invariable
72 ressemeler T – *to resole*
68 ressemer T – *to resow*
68 ressemer (se) P – *to resow*
86 ressentir T – *to feel, to resent*
86 ressentir (se) P – *to feel the effects*
65 resserrer T – *to tighten, to contract*
65 resserrer (se) P – *to tighten*
96 resservir I, T – *to serve again, to use again*
96 resservir (se) P – *to help oneself again (food)*
86 ressortir (sortir à nouveau) T, *avoir* – *to get out again*
86 ressortir (sortir à nouveau) I, *être* – *to come/go out again*
81 ressortir (être du ressort de) à Ti, *avoir* – *to be within the competence of*
65 ressouder T – *to resolder*
65 ressouder (se) P – *to join again*
66 ressourcer T – *to get fresh ideas*
66 ressourcer (se) P – *to get fresh ideas*
84 ressouvenir (se) P – *to remember again*
65 ressuer I, T – *to sweat again*
81 res(s)urgir I – *to re-emerge*
65 ressusciter T, *avoir* – *to resuscitate*
65 ressusciter I, *être* (or *avoir*) – *to revive, to come to life again*
79 ressuyer T – *to wipe again*
79 ressuyer (se) P – *to air dry*
65 restaurer T – *to restore*
65 restaurer (se) P – *to take some refreshment*
65 rester I, *être* – *to remain, to stay*
65 restituer T – *to return, to refund (money)*
123 restreindre T – *to restrict, to limit*
123 restreindre (se) P – *to cut down (on)*
65 restructurer T – *to restructure*
65 restyler T – *to get a new image*
65 résulter I, D – *to result*
avoir *(or* être*),*
only in the 3rd person,
the infinitive, present and past participles
65 résumer T – *to summarize*
65 résumer (se) P – *to sum up*
81 resurgir I – *to reappear*
81 rétablir T – *to re-establish*
81 rétablir (se) P – *to recover*
65 retailler T – *to recut*
65 rétamer T – *to re-silver*
65 rétamer (se) P – *to retaliate, to come a cropper (colloquial)*
65 retaper T – *to do up, to buck up*
65 retaper (se) P – *to get back on one's feet*
65 retapisser T – *to repaper*
65 retarder I, T – *to delay, to lose (clock)*
65 retâter à T, Ti – *to retry*
123 reteindre T – *to re-dye*
65 retéléphoner à Ti – *to phone again*
118 retendre T – *to stretch again*
84 retenir I, T – *to hold back, to keep back*
84 retenir (se) P – *to control oneself, to hang on to, to refrain from*
65 retenter T – *to try again*
81 retentir I – *to ring*
66 retercer T – *to plough again (vineyard)*
65 reterser T – *to plough again (vineyard)*
65 réticuler T – *to cross-link*
65 retirer T – *to take off, to withdraw*
65 retirer (se) P – *to take leave, to retire from*
65 retisser T – *to reweave*

T: direct transitive (p. p. variable) – **Ti**: indirect transitive (p. p. invariable) – **I**: intransitive verb (p. p. invariable)
P: pronominal verb (auxiliary *être*) – **impers.**: impersonal verb – **D**: defective verb – *être*: verb conjugated with the auxiliary *être* – *être* or *avoir*: verbs conjugated with *être* or *avoir* (see paragraph 15)

65 retomber I, *être* – *to fall again*
118 retondre T – *to shear again, to mow again*
65 retoquer T – *to retort*
118 retordre T – *to twist again*
65 rétorquer T – *to retort*
65 retoucher à T, Ti – *to retouch*
65 retourner T, *avoir* – *to return (something)*
65 retourner I, *être* – *to return*
65 retourner (se) P, *être* – *to overturn, to turn over, to turn round*
66 retracer T – *to retrace, to relate*
65 rétracter T – *to retract*
65 rétracter (se) P – *to retract*
152 retraduire T – *to retranslate*
127 retraire T, D – *to redeem*
65 retraiter T – *to pension off*
65 retrancher T – *to substract (from), to cut off*
65 retrancher (se) P – *to dig in*
150 retranscrire T – *to recopy*
122 retransmettre T – *to retransmit*
65 retravailler à I, T, Ti – *to touch up, to start a new job, to work again on*
65 retraverser T – *to recross, to cross again*
81 rétrécir I, T – *to narrow, to take in*
81 rétrécir (se) P – *to shrink*
123 retreindre T – *to hammer out, to shape (metal)*
123 rétreindre T – *to hammer out (metal)*
65 retremper T – *to resoak, to reinvigorate*
65 retremper (se) P – *to acquire new strength*
65 rétribuer T – *to pay*
81 rétroagir I – *to have a retroactive effect*
69 rétrocéder I, T – *to redimise*
65 rétrograder I, T – *to retrogress, to retrograde*
65 retrousser T – *to hitch up, to roll up*
65 retrousser (se) P – *to hitch up, to roll up*
65 retrouver T – *to meet again*
65 retrouver (se) P – *to find again*
65 retuber T – *to retube*
76 réunifier T – *to reunify*
81 réunir T – *to reunite, to gather together*
81 réunir (se) P – *to gather, to merge (societies), to have a get-together*
81 réussir à I, T, Ti – *to succeed in*
65 réutiliser T – *to reuse*
65 revacciner T – *to revaccinate*
109 revaloir T – *to pay back*
65 revaloriser T – *to revalue*
65 revancher (se) P – *to avenge*
65 rêvasser I – *to daydream*
65 réveiller T – *to wake up, to rouse*
65 réveiller (se) P – *to wake up, to rouse*
65 réveillonner I – *to have a midnight meal (for Christmas and New Year's Eve)*
69 révéler T – *to reveal, to disclose*
69 révéler (se) P – *to appear, to reveal one's character*
65 revendiquer I, T – *to claim*
65 revendiquer (se) P – *to claim*
118 revendre T – *to resell*
118 revendre (se) P – *to resell*
84 revenir I, *être* – *to come back (to), to return (to), to recover (from)*
84 revenir (s'en) P, *être* – *to return*
65 rêver à, de I, T, Ti – *to dream of*
69 réverbérer T – *to reverberate*
69 réverbérer (se) P – *to send back*
81 reverdir I, T – *to grow green again*
69 révérer T – *to revere*
81 revernir T – *to revarnish*
65 reverser T – *to pour out again, to shift, to transfer*
87 revêtir T – *to don*
87 revêtir (se) P – *to don*
65 revigorer T – *to invigorate*
65 revirer I – *to turn around*
65 réviser I, T – *to revise*
65 revisiter T – *to revisit*
65 revisser T – *to screw back*
65 revitaliser T – *to revitalize*
76 revivifier T – *to regenerate*
146 revivre I, T – *to revive*
101 revoir T – *to see again, to meet again*
101 revoir (se) P – *to see again, to meet again*
65 revoler I, T – *to re-steal, (to re-fly)*
65 révolter T – *to revolt, to rebel*
65 révolter (se) P – *to revolt, to rebel*
65 révolutionner T – *to revolutionize, to upset*
65 révolvériser T – *to shoot with a revolver*
65 révoquer T – *to call off, to dismiss*
65 revoter I, T – *to vote again*
110 revouloir T – *to want again*
65 révulser T – *to disgust, to contort*
65 révulser (se) P – *to upset*
65 rewriter T – *to rewrite (journalism)*
65 rhabiller T – *to dress again*
65 rhabiller (se) P – *to dress again*
65 rhumer T – *to add rum*
65 ribler T – *to go through streets at night*
65 ribouler I – *to roll*
65 ricaner I – *to sneer, to snigger*
65 ricocher I – *to rebound*
65 rider T – *to wrinkle*
65 rider (se) P – *to become wrinkled*
65 ridiculiser T – *to ridicule*
65 ridiculiser (se) P – *to make a fool of oneself*
65 riffauder I, T – *to warm, to burn*
65 rifler T – *to plane*
76 rigidifier T – *to rigidify*
65 rigoler I – *to laugh*
65 rimailler I – *to dabble in verse-making*
65 rimer I, T – *to versify, to rhyme*
66 rincer T – *to rinse, to rinse out*
66 rincer (se) P – *to rinse, to rinse out*
65 ringarder T – *to poke (furnace)*
65 ripailler I – *to feast*
65 riper I, T – *to scrape*
65 ripoliner T – *to enarnel*
65 riposter à I, T, Ti – *to retort, to counteract*
149 rire de I, Ti – *to laugh at*
149 rire (se) de P – *to make light of, to make fun of p. p. invariable*
65 risquer T – *to risk*
65 risquer (se) P – *to take a risk*
65 rissoler I, T – *to brown*
65 ritualiser T – *to ritualize*
65 rivaliser I – *to rival*
65 river T – *to rivet*
70 riveter T – *to rivet*

65 rober T – *to wrap*
65 robotiser T – *to robotize*
65 rocher I – *to rock*
65 rôdailler I – *to roam*
65 roder T – *to run in (car), to break in*
65 rôder I – *to prowl, to hang about, to loiter*
65 rogner I, T – *to pare, to cut down, to trim*
65 rognonner I – *to grumble*
81 roidir T – *to stiffen*
81 roidir (se) P – *to stiffen*
66 romancer T – *to embellish, to make into a fiction*
65 romaniser I, T – *to romanize*
65 romaniser (se) P – *to Romanize*
120 rompre I, T – *to break off, to snap*
120 rompre (se) P – *to break off, to snap*
65 ronchonner I – *to grumble*
65 ronéoter T – *to roneo*
65 ronéotyper T – *to roneotype*
81 rondir T – *to make round*
65 ronfler I – *to snore*
67 ronger T – *to gnaw (at), to eat away (at)*
67 ronger (se) P – *to be worried sick*
65 ronronner I – *to purr*
65 ronsardiser I – *to Ronsardize*
65 roquer I – *to castle (chess move)*
65 roser T – *to make pink*
81 rosir I, T – *to blush*
65 rosser T – *to thrash*
65 roter I – *to belch*
81 rôtir I, T – *to roast*
81 rôtir (se) P – *to scorch (sun)*
65 roucouler I, T – *to coo*
65 rouer T – *to coil*
78 rougeoyer I – *to turn red, to glow*
81 rougir I, T – *to redden*
65 rougnotter I – *to blush, to go red*
65 rouiller I, T – *to rust, to go rusty*
65 rouiller (se) P – *to rust, to go rusty*
81 rouir I, T – *to steep (flax)*
65 rouler I, T – *to roll, to run (car), to roam, to cheat*
65 rouler (se) P – *to turn over*
65 roulot(t)er T – *to roll a hem*
65 roupiller I – *to snooze*
65 rouscailler I – *to complain (about)*
69 rouspéter I – *to protest*
72 rousseler québ. I, T – *to freckle*
81 roussir I, T – *to turn brown, to singe*
81 roustir T – *to cheat*
65 router T – *to route*
88 rouvrir I, T – *to reopen*
88 rouvrir (se) P – *to reopen*
65 rubaner T – *to ribbon*
76 rubéfier T – *to redden*
65 rucher T – *to quill, to frill*
65 rudenter T – *to denten*
78 rudoyer T – *to treat roughly*
65 ruer I – *to kich at, to lash out*
65 ruer (se) P – *to rush in*
81 rugir I, T – *to bellow*
65 ruiler T – *to grout*
65 ruiner T – *to ruin*
65 ruiner (se) P – *to ruin oneself, to go bankrupt*
72 ruisseler I – *to stream down, to drip*
65 ruminer I, T – *to ruminate, to brood (over)*
65 rupiner I – *to work hard, to succeed with flying colours*
65 ruser I – *to use trickery*
76 russifier T – *to Russify*
65 rustiquer T – *to rusticate*
65 rûter/ruter belg. I – *to be in heat*
65 rutiler I – *to glow, to gleam red*
65 rythmer T – *to put rhythm (into)*

S

65 sabler I, T – *to sand*
65 sablonner T – *to scour with sand*
65 saborder T – *to shut down, to scuttle (ship)*
65 saborder (se) P – *to scuttle (ship)*
65 saboter T – *to sabotage*
65 sabouler T – *to jostle, to scold*
65 sabouler (se) P – *to jostle, to scold*
65 sabrer I, T – *to cut down, to slash*
65 sacagner T – *to stab*
65 saccader T – *to jerk*
67 saccager T – *to ransack, to pillage*
76 sacc(h)arifier T – *to saccharify*
65 sa(c)quer T – *to kick out, to fire somebody, to sack or fire*
65 sacraliser T – *to make sacred, to regard as sacred, to sacralize*
65 sacrer I, T – *to crown, to curse*
76 sacrifier T – *to sacrifice, to give up*
76 sacrifier (se) P – *to sacrifice oneself*
65 safraner T – *to flavour with saffron*
65 saietter T – *to bristle-brush*
65 saigner I, T – *to bleed*
65 saigner (se) P – *to sacrifice oneself (for), to bleed oneself dry for somebody*
90 saillir (sortir, s'élancer) I, D – *to bulge*
81 saillir (jaillir avec force) I, D – *to spurt*
81 saillir (s'accoupler) T, D – *to mate*
81 saisir T – *to seize, to grab*
81 saisir (se) P – *to take up (an issue)*
65 saisonner I – *to give an abundant yield*
76 salarier T – *to put on salary*
65 saler T – *to salt*
76 salifier T – *to salinize*
65 saligoter T – *to botch*
81 salir T – *to dirty*
81 salir (se) P – *to (get) dirty*
65 saliver I – *to salivate*
65 saloper T – *to botch*
65 salpêtrer T – *to add saltpetre*
65 saluer T – *to greet, to salute*
65 saluer (se) P – *to greet each other, to salute*
76 sanctifier T – *to sanctify, to keep holy*

T: direct transitive (p. p. variable) – **Ti**: indirect transitive (p. p. invariable) – **I**: intransitive verb (p. p. invariable) **P**: pronominal verb (auxiliary *être*) – **impers.**: impersonal verb – **D**: defective verb – *être*: verb conjugated with the auxiliary *être* – *être* or *avoir*: verbs conjugated with *être* or *avoir* (see paragraph 15)

65 sanctionner T – *to approve, to penalize*
65 sanctuariser T – *to sanctuarize*
65 sandwicher T – *to sandwich*
65 sangler T – *to strap up*
65 sangler (se) P – *to be buttoned up tight*
65 sangloter I – *to sob*
65 santonner T – *to place figurines (in a Christmas tree)*
65 s(a)ouler T – *to make someone drunk*
65 s(a)ouler (se) P – *to get drunk*
65 saper T – *to undermine, to sap*
65 saper (se) P – *to get all gussied up*
76 saponifier T – *to saponify*
65 saquer (sacquer) T – *to give someone the sack, to kick somebody out*
65 sarcler T – *to weed, to hoe*
65 sarter T – *to slash-and-burn (agriculture)*
65 sasser T – *to sift, to screen*
65 sataner T – *to damn*
65 sataniser T – *to satanize*
65 satelliser T – *to put into orbit*
65 satelliser (se) P – *to make a satellite of*
65 satiner T – *to satinize, to give a satin-like gloss*
65 satiriser T – *to satirize*
128 satisfaire à T, Ti – *to comply with*
128 satisfaire (se) P – *to satisfy oneself*
65 satonner T – *to strike, to kick*
65 saturer I, T – *to saturate*
66 saucer T – *to dip (bread), to souse, to drench*
65 saucissonner I, T – *to picnic, to truss up, to chop up, to slice up*
65 saumurer T – *to pickle*
65 sauner I – *to produce salt*
65 saupoudrer T – *to sprinkle*
65 saurer T – *to smoke, to cure*
81 saurir T – *to smoke-dry*
65 sauter I, T – *to jump, to skip*
65 sautiller I – *to hop*
65 sauvegarder T – *to safeguard*
65 sauver I, T – *to save*
65 sauver (se) P – *to save oneself (from), to leave in a hurry*
65 savater T – *to kick (kickboxing)*
103 savoir I, T – *to know, to know of*
103 savoir (se) P – *to know, to be aware*
65 savonner T – *to soap*
65 savonner (se) P – *to soap*
65 savourer T – *to savour*
65 scalper T – *to scalp*
65 scandaliser I, T – *to scandalize*
65 scandaliser (se) P – *to be deeply shocked*
65 scander T – *to chant*
65 scanner T – *to scan*
65 scannériser T – *to scan*
76 scarifier T – *to scarify*
65 sceller T – *to seal*
65 scénariser T – *to script*
65 schématiser I, T – *to schematize*
65 schlinguer I – *to pong*
65 schlitter T – *to sledge*
65 schmecter I – *to smell*
65 schnouffer (se) P – *to inhale drugs*
65 schnouper T – *to take snuff*
65 schpiler I – *to complete a task*
76 scier I, T – *to saw*
65 scinder T – *to split up (into)*
65 scinder (se) P – *to split up (into)*
65 scintiller I – *to sparkle*
65 sciotter T – *to saw with a small saw*
65 scissionner I – *to split away*
65 scléroser T – *to sclerose*
65 scléroser (se) P – *to become sclerotic*
65 scolariser T – *to school*
76 scorifier T – *to scorify*
65 scotcher T – *to apply scotch tape*
65 scrafer T – *to kill (slang)*
65 scratcher I, T – *to scratch*
65 scribouiller T – *to scribble*
65 scruter T – *to scrutinize, to scan, to search*
65 sculpter I, T – *to sculpt*
69 sécher I, T – *to dry*
69 sécher (se) P – *to dry*
65 seconder T – *to assist*
65 secouer T – *to shake*
65 secouer (se) P – *to shake oneself, to bestir oneself*
94 secourir T – *to help*
69 secréter T – *to secrete*
69 sécréter T – *to secrete, to exude*
65 sectionner T – *to sever*
65 sectionner (se) P – *to be severed*
65 sectoriser T – *to divide into sectors*
65 séculariser T – *to secularize*
65 sécuriser T – *to give security to sb, to reassure*
65 sédentariser T – *to settle, to stay put*
65 sédentariser (se) P – *to settle, to stay put*
65 sédimenter T – *to deposit sediment*
152 séduire I, T – *to seduce*
65 segmenter T – *to segment*
65 segmenter (se) P – *to break into segments*
69 ségréguer T – *to segregate*
65 séjourner I – *to stay*
65 séjourner (se) afr. P – *to stay*
65 sélecter T – *to place in a high position, to select*
65 sélectionner T – *to select*
65 seller T – *to saddle*
65 sembler I – *to seem, to appear*
68 semer I, T – *to sow*
66 semoncer T – *to lecture*
65 sénégaliser afr. T – *to give a Senegalese flavour, to Senegalese*
65 sensibiliser T – *to sensitize, to make aware (of)*
65 sensibiliser (se) P – *to be made sensitive to ..., to sensitize oneself*
86 sentir I, T – *to feel, to sense, to smell, to taste*
86 sentir (se) P – *to feel, to be conscious (of)*
111 seoir I, D – *to fit, to suit*
Inexistent in the passé simple *and in the* imparfait *of the subjunctive. Used only in the present participle, the infinitive simple forms and 3rd person, also in the imperative and the past participle*
65 séparer T – *to separate*
65 séparer (se) P – *to break up, to separate*
65 septupler I, T – *to increase seven-fold*
66 séquencer T – *to sequence*
65 séquestrer T – *to sequestre, to seclude, to confine*

66 sérancer T – *to comb linen*
81 serfouir T – *to weed*
65 sérialiser T – *to serialize*
76 sérier T – *to classify*
65 seriner T – *to drum into, to bore*
65 seringuer T – *to syringe*
65 sermonner T – *to preach, to lecture*
65 serpenter I – *to wind, to snake*
65 serrer I, T – *to squeeze, to tighten, to close up, to shake (hand)*
65 serrer (se) P – *to stick together, to crowd, to tighten*
81 sertir T – *to set (stone), to embed*
96 servir à I, T, Ti – *to be of use (to)*
96 servir (se) P – *to help oneself*
81 sévir I – *to act ruthlessly*
68 sevrer T – *to wean*
65 sextupler I, T – *to increase six-fold*
65 sexualiser T – *to sexualize*
65 shampooiner T – *to shampoo*
65 shampouiner T – *to shampoo*
65 shooter I, T – *to shoot*
65 shunter T – *to shunt*
69 sidérer T – *to be dumbfounded*
75 siéger I – *to sit*
65 siester afr. I – *to have a siesta, to take a nap*
65 siffler I, T – *to whistle*
65 siffloter I, T – *to whistle*
65 sigler T – *to put the initials of a designer on a product*
65 signaler T – *to signal, to indicate*
65 signaler (se) P – *to distinguish oneself by*
65 signaliser T – *to put up signs*
65 signer I, T – *to sign*
65 signer (se) P – *to cross oneself*
76 signifier T – *to mean, to signify*
65 silhouetter T – *to silhouette*
65 silhouetter (se) P – *to be silhouetted*
65 silicatiser (se) P – *to make silicate*
65 siliconer T – *to add silicone*
65 sillonner T – *to furrow, to travel around*
65 simiiliser T – *to imitate*
76 simplifier I, T – *to simplify*
76 simplifier (se) P – *to simplify*
65 simuler T – *to simulate*
67 singer T – *to ape, to monkey*
65 singulariser T – *to single out*
65 singulariser (se) P – *to call attention to oneself*
65 siniser T – *to make Chinese*
65 siniser (se) P – *to become sinicized*
65 siphonner T – *to siphon*
65 siroter T – *to sip*
65 situer T – *to site, to locate*
65 situer (se) P – *to be situated*
76 skier I – *to ski*
65 slalomer I – *to slalom*
65 slaviser T – *to make Slav-like*
66 slicer T – *to cut into slices*
65 smasher I – *to smash*
65 smurfer I – *to break dance*
65 smiller T – *to sand a cimented surface with a special hammer*
65 sniffer T – *to sniff (drugs, glue)*
65 snober T – *to snub*
65 socialiser T – *to socialize*
65 socratiser I – *to socratize*
65 sodomiser T – *to sodomize*
65 soigner I, T – *to treat, to nurse, to look after*
65 soigner (se) P – *to take care of oneself*
65 soirer belg. I – *to spend the evening*
65 solariser T – *to undergo solarisation*
65 solder T – *to sell off*
65 solder (se) P – *to show, to end in*
65 solenniser T – *to solemnize*
76 solfier T – *to sol-fa*
65 solidariser T – *to solidarize*
65 solidariser (se) P – *to show solidarity*
76 solidifier T – *to solidify*
76 solidifier (se) P – *to solidify*
65 solifluer I – *to landslide*
65 soliloquer I – *to soliloquize, to talk to oneself*
65 solliciter T – *to request, to apply for (job), to solicit*
65 solmiser T – *to sing naming the note*
65 solubiliser T – *to make soluble*
65 solutionner T – *to solve*
65 somatiser I, T – *to make somatic*
65 sombrer I – *to sink*
65 sommeiller I – *to doze*
65 sommer T – *to summon*
65 somnoler I – *to drowse off*
65 sonder T – *to sound*
67 songer à I, Ti – *to dream of, to imagine*
65 sonnailler I – *to ring on and on*
65 sonner de I, T, Ti – *to ring, to chime, to sound*
65 sonoriser T – *to add sound-effects*
65 sonrer belg. I – *to fall asleep*
65 sophistiquer T – *to sophisticate*
65 sophistiquer (se) P – *to become (more) sophisticated*
70 soqueter belg. I – *to fall asleep*
86 sortir T, *avoir* – *to take out*
86 sortir I, *être* – *to go out*
86 sortir (se) P, *être* – *to manage to get out of, from*
121 soubattre T – *to stimulate teats before milking (agriculture)*
65 soubresauter I – *to leap*
70 soucheter T – *to sort out*
68 souchever T – *to cut away (into rock)*
76 soucier T – *to cause worry*
76 soucier (se) P – *to care about*
65 souder T – *to solder, to weld*
65 souder (se) P – *to solder, to weld*
78 soudoyer T – *to bribe*
65 souffler I, T – *to blow, to prompt*
70 souffleter T – *to slap mildly (in the face)*
88 souffrir I, T – *to suffer, to endure*
88 souffrir (se) P – *to suffer, to endure*
65 soufrer T – *to sulphur*
65 souhaiter T – *to wish*

T: direct transitive (p. p. variable) – **Ti**: indirect transitive (p. p. invariable) – **I**: intransitive verb (p. p. invariable) **P**: pronominal verb (auxiliary *être*) – **impers.**: impersonal verb – **D**: defective verb – *être*: verb conjugated with the auxiliary *être* – *être* or *avoir*: verbs conjugated with *être* or *avoir* (see paragraph 15)

65 souiller T – *to soil*
67 soulager T – *to relieve, to soothe*
67 soulager (se) P – *to relieve oneself, to ease one's feelings*
65 soûler/souler T – *to surfeit*
65 soûler/souler (se) P – *to get drunk*
68 soulever T – *to lift up, to arouse*
68 soulever (se) P – *to rise*
65 souligner T – *to underline*
122 soumettre T – *to subject*
122 soumettre (se) P – *to submit to*
65 soumissionner I, T – *to tender for, to bid*
65 soupçonner T – *to suspect*
65 souper I – *to have supper*
68 soupeser T – *to try the weight (of)*
65 soupirer I, T – *to sigh, to long (for)*
65 souquer I, T – *to haul, to pull away (at)*
65 sourciller I – *to frown, to wince*
65 sourdiner T – *to mute*
118 sourdre I, D – *to spring (water), to result, to arise*
only in the infinitive and
3rd person of the indicative
("sourd/sourdent, sourdait/
sourdaient, sourdit/sourdirent,
sourdra/sourdront, sourdrait/
sourdraient")
149 sourire à I, Ti – *to smile at, to appeal to*
149 sourire (se) P – *to be pleased with, to smile at each other*
invariable past participle
65 sous-alimenter T – *to underfeed*
150 souscrire à I, T, Ti – *to subscribe*
78 sous-employer T – *to underuse*
118 sous-entendre T – *to imply*
65 sous-estimer T – *to underestimate*
65 sous-évaluer T – *to undervalue*
65 sous-exploiter T – *to underexploit*
65 sous-exposer T – *to underexpose*
81 sous-investir I – *to underinvest*
65 sous-louer T – *to sublet*
77 sous-payer T – *to under-pay*
69 sous-rémunérer T – *to under-remunerate*
118 sous-tendre T – *to subtend*
65 sous-titrer T – *to subtitle*
127 soustraire T, D – *to substract, to withdraw*
127 soustraire (se) P, D – *to shirk*
65 sous-traiter I, T – *to subcontract*
65 sous-utiliser T – *to underuse*
65 sous-virer I – *to under-steer*
65 soutacher T – *to braid*
84 soutenir T – *to sustain, to support*
84 soutenir (se) P – *to maintain oneself, to support oneself*
65 soutirer T – *to squeeze or get (money) out of (someone), to extract*
84 souvenir impers., *être* – *to remember, to recall*
"il m'en souvient" – *I remember or recall*
"il lui est souvenu que…" – *he remembered or recalled that…*
84 souvenir (se) P – *to remember*
65 soviétiser T – *to sovietize*
76 spathifier T – *to convert into spar*
65 spatialiser T – *to spatialize*
65 spatialiser (se) P – *to spatialize*
65 spécialiser T – *to specialize*
65 spécialiser (se) P – *to specialize*
76 spécifier T – *to specify*
65 spéculer I – *to speculate*
65 speeder I, T – *to accelerate, (to be hyped up)*
69 sphacéler T – *to detach, to sphacelate*
65 spiritualiser T – *to spiritualize*
65 spitter T – *to splatter*
65 splitter T – *to split*
76 spolier T – *to despoil*
65 sponsoriser T – *to sponsor*
65 sporuler I – *to produce spores*
65 sprinter I – *to sprint*
65 squatter T – *to squat*
65 squeezer T – *to squeeze (bridge)*
65 stabiliser T – *to stabilize*
65 stabiliser (se) P – *to stabilize*
65 staffer T – *to construct in staff*
65 stagner I – *to stagnate*
65 staliniser T – *to stalinize*
65 standardiser T – *to standardize*
65 stariser T – *to make somebody a star*
65 stater belg. T – *to evaluate (money, gold)*
65 stationner T – *to park, to stop, to stand*
65 statuer sur T, Ti – *to pronounce judgment on*
76 statufier T – *to erect a statue (to)*
76 sténographier T – *to write in shorthand*
65 sténotyper T – *to stenotype*
65 stéréotyper T – *to stereotype*
69 stérer T – *to measure by the stere*
65 stériliser T – *to sterilize*
65 stigmatiser T – *to stigmatize*
65 stimuler T – *to stimulate, to spur*
65 stimuler (se) P – *to stimulate (oneself), each other*
76 stipendier T – *to hire (the services of)*
65 stipuler T – *to stipulate*
65 stocker T – *to stock*
65 stopper I, T – *to stop, to mend*
65 stranguler T – *to strangulate, to strangle*
76 stratifier T – *to stratify*
65 stresser I, T – *to put under stress, to stress out*
65 stresser (se) P – *to stress oneself out*
65 striduler I, T – *to chirr*
76 strier T – *to flute, to scratch, to streak*
65 stripper T – *to strip*
65 striquer T – *to give the finish*
65 structurer T – *to structure*
65 structurer (se) P – *to form*
128 stupéfaire T, D – *to stupefy*
used only in the 3rd person singular in the indicatif présent, *compound forms and past participle:*
"stupéfait, te, ts, tes"
76 stupéfier T – *to stupefy, to astound*
65 stuquer T – *to stucco*
65 styler T – *to train, to school*
65 styliser T – *to stylize*
69 subdéléguer T – *to subdelegate*
65 subdiviser T – *to subdivide*
65 subdiviser (se) P – *to be subdivided*
81 subir I, T – *to undergo, to go through, to put up with*
65 subjuguer T – *to subjugate, to subdue*

65 sublimer I, T – *to sublimate*
67 submerger T – *to submerge*
65 subodorer T – *to suspect*
65 subordonner T – *to subordinate*
65 subordonner (se) P – *to submit to authority*
65 suborner T – *to suborn, to seduce, to bribe, to tamper (with)*
67 subroger T – *to subrogate*
76 subsidier belg. T – *to subsidize*
65 subsister I – *to subsist*
65 substantiver T – *to use as a noun*
65 substituer T – *to entail*
65 substituer (se) P – *to substitute (oneself) for somebody*
65 subsumer T – *to subsume*
65 subtiliser I, T – *to subtilize, to sneak*
65 subtiliser (se) P – *to steal, to subtilize*
84 subvenir à Ti – *to provide for*
65 subventionner T – *to subsidize*
81 subvertir T – *to subvert*
69 succéder à Ti – *to succeed, to follow after*
69 succéder (se) P – *to follow one another invariable past participle*
65 succomber à I, Ti – *to succumb to, to die of, to fall*
66 sucer I, T – *to suck*
66 sucer (se) P – *to suck*
65 suçoter T – *to suck*
65 sucrer I, T – *to sugar, to sweeten*
65 sucrer (se) P – *to help oneself to sugar, to line one's pocket, to satisfy a craving for sweet*
65 suer I, T – *to sweat*
151 suffire à I, Ti – *to be enough, to suffice*
151 suffire (se) P – *to be self-sufficient invariable past participle*
65 suffixer T – *to suffix*
65 suffoquer I, T – *to suffocate*
69 suggérer I, T – *to suggest*
65 suggestionner T – *to influence by suggestion, to put an idea in someone's head*
65 suicider (se) P – *to commit suicide*
65 suif(f)er T – *to tallow*
65 suinter I, T – *to seep, to ooze*
145 suivre I, T – *to follow, to attend (course)*
145 suivre (se) P – *to follow each other, to follow in the right order*
72 sukkeler belg. I – *to have difficulty*
65 sulfater T – *to sulphate*
65 sulfiter T – *to apply sulfite*
65 sulfoner T – *to sulfonate*
65 sulfurer T – *to sulphurize*
81 superfinir T – *to superfinish*
65 superposer T – *to superimpose*
65 superposer (se) P – *to superimpose*
65 superviser T – *to supervise*
65 supplanter T – *to supplant*
65 supplanter (se) P – *to supplant (one another)*
74 suppléer à T, Ti – *to make up for, to take the place of*
65 supplémenter T – *to supplement*
76 supplicier T – *to execute (criminal)*
76 supplier T – *to implore*
65 supporter T – *to support, to bear, to endure*
65 supporter (se) P – *to stand, to put up with each other*
65 supposer T – *to suppose, to imply, to assume*
65 supprimer T – *to suppress, to delete, to remove*
65 supprimer (se) P – *to commit suicide*
65 suppurer I – *to suppurate*
65 supputer T – *to calculate*
65 surabonder I – *to overabound, to be superabundant*
65 surajouter T – *to superadd*
65 surajouter (se) P – *to add to*
65 suralimenter T – *to overfeed*
65 suralimenter (se) P – *to overfeed*
65 surarmer T – *to overarm*
65 surbaisser T – *to depress, to drop*
65 surboucher T – *to overcap*
65 surbroder T – *to elaborate excessively on a subject*
67 surcharger T – *to overburden*
65 surchauffer T – *to overheat*
65 surclasser T – *to outclass*
65 surcoller belg. I – *to paste (something) over something else (posters)*
65 surcomprimer T – *to overcompress*
65 surcontrer T – *to redouble (cards)*
65 surcoter T – *to over-quote*
65 surcouper I – *to overtrump (cards)*
65 surcreuser T – *to overdig out*
65 surdorer T – *to double-gild*
76 surédifier T – *to build over*
68 surélever T – *to heighten*
81 surenchérir I – *to overbid, to go one better*
65 surentraîner/surentrainer T – *to over-train*
65 suréquiper T – *to overequip*
65 surestimer T – *to overestimate*
65 surestimer (se) P – *to overestimate one's abilities*
65 surévaluer T – *to overvalue*
65 surexciter T – *to overexcite*
65 surexploiter T – *to overexploit, to overwork*
65 surexposer T – *to overexpose*
66 surfacer I, T – *to surface*
65 surfacturer T – *to overbill*
128 surfaire T, D – *to overestimate especially in the infinitive and in the singular of the* indicatif présent, *past participle and compound forms*
65 surfer I – *to surf*
81 surfleurir T – *to over-blossom*
65 surfiler T – *to overcast, to seam in*
65 surfrapper T – *to over strike (money)*
73 surgeler T – *to deep-freeze*
65 surgeonner I – *to sucker*
81 surgir I, *avoir* (or *être*) – *to rise, to loom up*
66 surglacer T – *to ice, to glaze*
65 surgreffer T – *to double graft*
65 surhausser T – *to heighten*
65 surimposer T – *to superimpose*
65 surimposer (se) P – *to overtax*

T: direct transitive (p. p. variable) – **Ti**: indirect transitive (p. p. invariable) – **I**: intransitive verb (p. p. invariable)
P: pronominal verb (auxiliary *être*) – **impers.**: impersonal verb – **D**: defective verb – *être*: verb conjugated with the auxiliary *être* – *être* or *avoir*: verbs conjugated with *être* or *avoir* (see paragraph 15)

65 suriner T – *to stab*
69 surinterpréter T – *to over-interpret*
81 surinvestir I – *to overinvest*
81 surir I – *to turn sour*
65 surjaler I – *to over-anchor*
70 surjeter T – *to overcast (seam)*
76 surlier T – *to over-tie up*
65 surligner T – *to highlight*
65 surmédicaliser T – *to overmedicalize*
68 surmener T – *to overwork*
68 surmener (se) P – *to overwork*
65 surmonter T – *to surmount, to overcome, to rise above*
65 surmonter (se) P – *to master, to control*
65 surmouler T – *to retread*
67 surnager I – *to float on the surface, to survive*
65 surnommer T – *to name, to nickname*
65 suroxyder T – *to overoxidize*
65 surpasser T – *to surpass, to exceed*
65 surpasser (se) P – *to surpass, to exceed*
77 surpayer T – *to overpay*
65 surpeupler T – *to overpopulate*
65 surpiquer T – *to topstitch*
65 surplomber I, T – *to overhang*
119 surprendre T – *to surprise*
119 surprendre (se) P – *to catch oneself*
152 surproduire T – *to overproduce*
75 surprotéger T – *to over protect*
65 sursaturer T – *to oversaturate*
65 sursauter I – *to jump, to start*
68 sursemer T – *to oversow*
114 surs(e)oir à T, Ti – *to suspend, to delay*
65 sursouffler T – *to over-blow*
65 surtailler T – *to over-cut*
65 surtaxer T – *to overtax*
118 surtondre T – *to clip*
65 surveiller T – *to oversee, to supervise*
65 surveiller (se) P – *to watch one's step*
84 survenir I, *être* – *to happen, to occur*
87 survêtir T – *to overdress*
65 survirer T – *to oversteer*
146 survivre à I, T, Ti – *to survive*
146 survivre (se) P – *to live on in, to outlive one's talent*
65 survoler T – *to fly over*
65 survolter T – *to step up, to boost*
65 susciter T – *to raise up, to arouse*
65 suspecter T – *to suspect*
65 suspecter (se) P – *to suspect oneself…*
118 suspendre T – *to hang, to suspend*
118 suspendre (se) P – *to hang from*
65 sustenter T – *to sustain*
65 sustenter (se) P – *to take sustenance*
65 susurrer I, T – *to whisper*
65 suturer T – *to stitch up, to suture*
65 swinguer I – *to swing*
65 syllaber T – *to syllabify*
65 symboliser T – *to symbolize*
65 symétriser I, T – *to arrange symmetrically*
65 sympathiser I – *to hit it off, to get on well, to sympathize (politics)*
65 synchroniser T – *to synchronize*
65 syncoper I, T – *to syncopate, to amaze*
65 syncristalliser I – *to cristallize*
65 syndicaliser T – *to syndicalize*
65 syndiquer T – *to unionize*
65 syndiquer (se) P – *to form a trade union*
65 synthétiser I, T – *to synthetize*
65 syntoniser T – *to tune in*
65 systématiser I, T – *to systematize*
65 systématiser (se) P – *to become the rule*

t

65 tabasser T – *to beat up, to hit*
65 tabasser (se) P – *to have a fight, to punch up*
65 tabler sur Ti – *to reckon on, to count on*
65 tabouiser T – *to taboo*
65 tabuler I, T – *to tabulate*
65 tacher I, T – *to stain, to sully*
65 tacher (se) P – *to stain, to sully*
65 tâcher de T, Ti – *to try, to strive*
70 tacheter T – *to speckle*
65 taguer I, T – *to tag*
65 taillader T – *to gash, to slash*
65 tailler I, T – *to cut, to sharpen*
65 tailler (se) P – *to buzz off*
129 taire T – *to keep silent about*
129 taire (se) P – *to keep silent*
65 taler T – *to bruise (fruit)*
65 taller I – *to sucker*
65 talocher T – *to cuff, to clout*
65 talonner I, T – *to pursue closely*
65 talquer T – *to talc*
65 tambouriner I, T – *to drum*
65 tamiser I, T – *to sieve*
65 tamponner T – *to dab, to stamp*
65 tamponner (se) P – *to crash into each other*
66 tancer T – *to scold, to berate*
65 tanguer I – *to pitch*
65 tan(n)iser T – *to treat with tannin*
65 tanner T – *to tan, to pester*
67 tapager I – *to kick up a row*
65 taper I, T – *to beat, to type, to hit, to hammer, to borrow*
65 taper (se) P – *to put away*
65 tapiner I – *to hustle*
81 tapir (se) P – *to crouch*
65 tapisser T – *to paper, to cover*
65 taponner T – *to screw up*
65 tapoter I, T – *to pat, to thrum, to tap*
65 taquer T – *to plane*
65 taquiner T – *to tease, to toy with*
65 taquiner (se) P – *to tease (one another)*
65 tarabiscoter T – *to add trimmings, to overadorn*
65 tarabuster T – *to huff, to snub*
65 tarauder T – *to thrash*
65 tarder à I, Ti – *to delay, to defer*
65 tarer T – *to spoil, to damage, to tare*
65 targuer (se) P – *to boast about*
65 tarifer T – *to fix price*
81 tarir I, T – *to run dry*
81 tarir (se) P – *to run dry*
65 tartiner I, T – *to spread, to ramble on*
81 tartir I – *to annoy*
65 tasser I, T – *to pack down, to cram, to compress*

65 tasser (se) P – *to subside, to crowd, to settle down*
65 tâter de, y T, Ti – *to feel, to touch, to try one's hand at…*
65 tâter (se) P – *to be in two minds, to think over, to feel (muscles)*
65 tatillonner I – *to niggle*
65 tâtonner I – *to grope, to fumble about*
65 tatouer T – *to tattoo*
65 tauper T – *to squeeze money out of someone*
72 taveler T – *to speckle*
72 taveler (se) P – *to speckle*
65 taveller T – *to wind silk (on a reel)*
65 taxer T – *to tax*
65 tayloriser T – *to taylorize, to organise work*
65 tchadiser afr. T – *to chadicize*
65 tchatcher I – *to yack*
65 techniciser T – *to technify*
65 techniser T – *to technify*
65 technocratiser T – *to make technocratic, to technocratize*
65 technocratiser (se) P – *to make technocratic*
65 tecker afr. I – *to relieve oneself*
65 teiller T – *to remove linen from the lime tree*
123 teindre T – *to dye*
123 teindre (se) P – *to dye*
65 teinter T – *to tint*
65 teinter (se) P – *to become tinged with*
67 télécharger T – *to download*
65 télécommander T – *to operate by remote control*
76 télécopier T – *to fax*
65 télédiffuser T – *to broadcast by television*
76 télégraphier I, T – *to telegraph, to wire, to cable*
65 téléguider T – *to operate by remote control*
69 télémétrer I, T – *to telemeter*
65 téléphoner à I, T, Ti – *to ring, to telephone*
65 téléphoner (se) P – *to telephone each other*
65 téléporter T – *to teleport*
65 téléporter (se) P – *to teleport oneself*
65 télescoper T – *to crash into, to collide with*
65 téléscoper (se) P – *to collide, to crash*
65 téléviser T – *to televise*
65 télexer T – to telex
65 témoigner à, de T, Ti – *to testify, to show*
69 tempérer T – *to temper, to moderate*
69 tempérer (se) P – *to temper, to moderate*
65 tempêter I – *to rage, to fume*
65 temporiser I, T – *to temporize, to put off deliberately*
65 tenailler T – *to rack, to gnaw*
118 tendre à, vers T, Ti – *to tighten, to hang, to stretch, to strain, to aim at, to tend towards*
118 tendre (se) P – *to become taut, to become strained*
84 tenir à I, T, Ti – *to hold, to occupy, to care about, to hold on*
84 tenir (se) P – *to remain, to behave, to stand, to sit*
65 tenonner T – *to tenon*
65 ténoriser I – *to sing tenor*
65 tenter T – *to tempt*
66 tercer T – *to tierce*
65 tergiverser I – *to hum and haw*
65 terminer T – *to terminate, to end*
65 terminer (se) P – *to come to an end*
81 ternir I, T – *to tarnish*
81 ternir (se) P – *to tarnish*
65 terrasser I, T – *to crush, to bring down, to bank up (soil)*
65 terreauter T – *to compost*
65 terrer I, T – *to crouch down, to burrow*
65 terrer (se) P – *to crouch down, to burrow*
76 terrifier T – *to terrify*
81 terrir I – *to approach land*
65 terroriser T – *to terrorize*
65 terser T – *to tierce*
65 tester I, T – *to test, to make out a will*
65 tétaniser T – *to tetanize*
65 tétaniser (se) P – *to tetanize oneself*
69 téter I, T – *to suck*
65 textualiser T – *to textualize*
65 texturer T – *to texturize*
65 texturiser T – *to texturize*
65 théâtraliser I, T – *to dramatize*
65 thématiser T – *to make thematic*
65 théoriser I, T – *to theorize*
65 thésauriser I, T – *to hoard (money)*
65 tictaquer I – *to tick*
81 tiédir I, T – *to cool down*
66 tiercer T – *to tierce*
65 tigrer T – *to stripe*
65 tiller T – *to separate the linen from the skin of the lime tree*
65 timbrer T – *to stamp*
65 tinter I, T, Ti – *to ring, to chime*
65 tintinnabuler I – *to tinkle*
65 tiquer I – *to twitch, to wince, to turn a hair*
65 tirailler I, T – *to pull about, to shoot in disarray, to be torn between*
65 tire(-)bouchonner I, T – *to curl up, to twist*
65 tire(-)bouchonner (se) P – *to guffaw*
65 tirer à, sur I, T, Ti – *to pull at or on, to shoot at*
65 tirer (se) P – *to shoot at each other*
65 tisaner T – *to nurse with tea, to drink (alcohol), to flog*
65 tiser T – *to hit*
65 tisonner I, T – *to poke*
65 tisser T – *to weave*
ti(s)tre T, D – *to weave*
p. p.: "tissue, ue, us, ues" and compound tenses
65 titiller I, T – *to titillate*
65 titrer T – *to confer a title on, to show alcohol content*
65 tituber I – *to stagger*
65 titulariser T – *to confirm in (job)*
65 toaster I, T – *to toast*
65 togoliser afr. T – *to togolize*
65 toiler T – *to mount on canvas*
65 toiletter T – *to groom*
65 toiletter (se) afr. P – *to groom*
65 toiser T – *to eye from head to foot, to size up*

T: direct transitive (p. p. variable) – **Ti**: indirect transitive (p. p. invariable) – **I**: intransitive verb (p. p. invariable)
P: pronominal verb (auxiliary *être*) – **impers.**: impersonal verb – **D**: defective verb – *être*: verb conjugated with the auxiliary *être* – *être* or *avoir*: verbs conjugated with *être* or *avoir* (see paragraph 15)

65 toiser (se) P – *to estimate*
69 tolérer T – *to tolerate*
69 tolérer (se) P – *to accept one self as*
65 tomber (rare) T, *avoir* – *to beat, to seduce (lady killer)*
65 tomber I, *être* – *to fall, to fall down, to drop, to subside, to fail*
65 tomer T – *to divide into parts*
118 tondre T – *to shear, to cut (grass)*
76 tonifier T – *to tone up*
65 tonitruer I – *to thunder*
65 tonner (il) I – *to thunder*
65 tonsurer T – *to tonsure*
65 tontiner T – *to wrap up (plant)*
65 toper I – *to agree*
65 topicaliser T – *to topicalize*
65 toquer I – *to rap*
65 toquer (se) P – *to become infatuated*
65 torcher T – *to wipe clean, to botch*
65 torcher (se) P – *to wipe oneself*
65 torchonner T – *to scour, to do a botched-up job*
118 tordre T – *to wring, to twist, to contort*
118 tordre (se) P – *to sprain, to be doubled up with laughter*
74 toréer I – *to fight a bull*
65 toronner T – *to wring strands*
65 torpiller T – *to torpedo, to sink*
76 torréfier T – *to roast (coffee)*
65 torsader T – *to twist*
65 tortiller I, T – *to twist, to wriggle*
65 tortiller (se) P – *to twist, to wriggle*
65 tortorer T – *to eat*
65 torturer T – *to torture, to torment*
65 torturer (se) P – *to torture, to torment*
65 tosser I – *to toss*
65 totaliser T – *to total*
65 toubabiser afr. T – *to act white*
65 toucher à T, Ti – *to touch, to affect, to adjoin, to be close to, to concern*
65 toucher (se) P – *to adjoin, to meet*
65 touer T – *to warp, to tow, to haul*
65 touer (se) P – *to be warped*
65 touiller T – *to stir*
65 toupiller I, T – *to spin*
65 toupiner I – *to spin, to coil up*
65 tourber I – *to peat*
65 tourbillonner I – *to swirl*
65 tourillonner I – *to revolve*
65 tourmenter T – *to torment*
65 tourmenter (se) P – *to distress oneself, to worry*
65 tournailler I – *to prowl*
65 tournasser T – *to spin (pottery)*
65 tournebouler T – *to put in a whirl*
65 tourner I, T – *to turn, to shape (clay), to shoot (film)*
65 tourner (se) P – *to turn round, to turn towards somebody*
65 tournicoter I – *to wander up and down*
65 tourniller I – *to wander*
65 tourniquer I – *to wander up and down*
78 tournoyer I – *to whirl, to spin*
65 toussailler I – *to keep on coughing*
65 tousser I – *to cough*
65 toussoter I – *to hem*
65 trabouler I – *to walk through*
65 tracaner I, T – *to reel silk*
65 tracasser T – *to worry, to bother*
65 tracasser (se) P – *to worry, to bother*
66 tracer I, T – *to trace, to lay out, to draw*
65 tracter T – *to tow*
152 traduire T – *to translate*
152 traduire (se) P – *to translate into*
65 traficoter I – *to doctor, to fiddle with*
65 trafiquer de T, Ti – *to deal in, to trade in*
81 trahir T – *to betray, to misrepresent*
81 trahir (se) P – *to reveal oneself*
65 traînailler/trainailler I – *to dawdle*
65 traînasser/trainasser I, T – *to dawdle*
65 traîner/trainer I, T – *to drag, to pull, to crawl along*
65 traîner/trainer (se) P – *to crawl along*
127 traire T, D – *to milk*
inexistent in the passé simple, subjonctif imparfait
65 traiter de T, Ti – *to treat, to negotiate, to call, to concern*
65 traiter (se) P – *to be negociated*
65 tramer T – *to weave (plot)*
65 tramer (se) P – *to weave (plot)*
65 tranchefiler T – *to place a band around the head*
65 trancher I, T – *to slice, to settle, to contrast*
65 tranquilliser T – *to reassure*
65 tranquilliser (se) P – *to calm down*
65 transbahuter T – *to shift, to lug along*
65 transborder T – *to transfer*
65 transcender T – *to transcend*
65 transcender (se) P – *to transcend oneself*
65 transcoder T – *to transcode*
150 transcrire T – *to transcribe*
69 transférer T – *to transfer*
65 transfigurer T – *to transfigure, to change (into)*
65 transfiler T – *to bring two pieces together*
65 transformer T – *to transform*
65 transformer (se) P – *to be transformed*
65 transfuser T – *to transfuse*
65 transgresser T – *to transgress*
65 transhumer I, T – *to move to new pastures*
67 transiger I – *to compromise, to transact*
81 transir I, T – *to benumb, to paralyze*
65 transistoriser T – *to transistorize*
65 transiter I, T – *to be in transit, to convey in transit*
65 translater T – *to transfer*
69 translittérer T – *to transliterate*
122 transmettre T – *to transmit, to pass on*
122 transmettre (se) P – *to pass on*
65 transmigrer I – *to transmigrate*
65 transmu(t)er T – *to transmute (into)*
65 transmu(t)er (se) P – *to transmute*
130 transparaître/transparaitre I – *to show through*
66 transpercer T – *to transfix*
65 transpirer I, T – *to perspire, to transpire*
65 transplanter T – *to transplant, to carry away*
65 transplanter (se) P – *to transplant, to carry away*
65 transporter T – *to carry*
65 transporter (se) P – *to take oneself off*
65 transposer T – *to transpose*
76 transsubstantier T – *to transubstantiate*
65 transsuder I, T – *to ooze through*

65 transvaser T – *to decant*
65 transvider T – *to pour into another container*
65 traquer T – *to track down*
65 traumatiser T – *to traumatize*
65 travailler à, sur I, T, Ti – *to work on, to labour*
65 travailler (se) P – *to work on, to labour*
65 travailloter I – *to work a little*
65 traverser T – *to cross, to go through*
81 travestir T – *to dress up, to disguise*
81 travestir (se) P – *to put on fancy dress*
65 trébucher I, T – *to stumble*
65 tréfiler T – *to wiredraw*
118 tréfondre I – *to shake deeply, to the core*
67 treillager T – *to trellis*
65 treillisser T – *to trellis*
65 trémater T – *to overtake (ship)*
65 trembler I – *to tremble, to shake, to shiver*
65 trembloter I – *to quiver, to flicker*
65 trémousser (se) P – *to wiggle*
65 tremper I, T – *to soak*
65 tremper (se) P – *to soak, to steep oneself (in)*
65 trémuler I, T – *to tremble*
65 trépaner T – *to trepan*
65 trépasser I, *être* or *avoir* – *to pass away*
65 trépider I – *to vibrate*
65 trépigner I, T – *to stamp feet*
90 tressaillir I – *to thrill, to shudder*
65 tressauter I – *to jump, to jolt*
65 tresser T – *to plait*
65 treuiller T – *to winch up*
65 trévirer T – *to haul up (cylinder)*
65 trianguler T – *to triangulate*
65 triballer T – *to soften (animal skins)*
65 tricher I – *to cheat*
65 tricocher I – *to be a mole*
65 tricoter I, T – *to knit*
76 trier T – *to sort (out)*
65 trifouiller I, T – *to rummage*
65 triller I, T – *to trill*
65 trimarder I, T – *to walk the roads*
65 trimbal(l)er T – *to lug around*
65 trimbal(l)er (se) P – *to trail along*
65 trimer I – *to slave away (at)*
65 tringler T – *to line out, to fuck*
65 trinquer I – *to clink (glasses), to catch it*
65 triompher de I, Ti – *to triumph, to get the better of*
65 tripatouiller T – *to fiddle*
65 tripler I, T – *to triple, to triplicate*
65 tripoter I, T – *to play with, to finger*
65 triquer T – *to cudgel*
69 triséquer T – *to divide into three*
65 trisser I, T – *to skedaddle*
65 trisser (se) P – *to skedaddle*
65 triturer T – *to grind (up), to masticate*
65 troler afr. T – *to roam*
65 tromper T – *to deceive, to mislead*
65 tromper (se) P – *to make a mistake, to be mistaken*
70 trompeter I, T – *to trumpet abroad*
65 tronçonner T – *to saw up, to chop up*
65 trôner I – *to throne, to lord over*
65 tronquer T – *to truncate*
65 tropicaliser T – *to tropicalize*
65 troquer T – *to barter, to swop (for)*
65 trotter I – *to trot (horse)*
65 trotter (se) P – *to dash off*
65 trottiner I – *to jog along*
65 troubler T – *to disturb*
65 troubler (se) P – *to become confused, to become overcast (weather)*
65 trouer T – *to make a hole*
65 trouer (se) P – *to open up*
65 trouilloter I – *to scare*
65 troussequiner T – *to cantle*
65 trousser T – *to truss*
65 trousser (se) P – *to pick up one's skirts*
65 trouver T – *to find, to discover, to invent*
65 trouver (se) P – *to find oneself, to be situated, to happen*
65 truander I, T – *to swindle*
65 trucider T – *to knock off*
65 truffer T – *to garnish (with truffles)*
65 truquer I, T – *to fake, to rig, to cook (account), to create special effects (film)*
65 trusquiner T – *to draw with a marking gauge*
65 truster T – *to monopolize*
65 tuber T – *to tube*
65 tuberculiner T – *to tuberculinize*
65 tuberculiniser T – *to tuberculinize*
65 tuberculiser T – *to tubercle*
65 tuer I, T – *to kill*
65 tuer (se) P – *to commit suicide, to get killed*
65 tuiler T – *to tile (roof)*
76 tuméfier T – *to tumefy, to swell*
76 tuméfier (se) P – *to tumefy, to swell*
65 turbiner I, T – *to slog away*
65 turlupiner T – *to worry*
65 turluter québ. I, T – *to hum*
65 tûter/tuter belg. I, T – *to suck on a pacifier*
65 tuteurer T – *to provide with a guardian*
65 tutorer T – *to tutor*
78 tutoyer T – *to address someone using "tu"*
78 tutoyer (se) P – *to address someone using "tu"*
65 tututer I – *to drink alcohol*
65 tuyauter I, T – *to flute*
65 twister I – *to dance the twist*
65 tympaniser T – *to repeat on and on*
65 typer T – *to typify*
65 typiser T – *to typify*
76 typographier T – *to type*
65 tyranniser T – *to tyrannize*

u

69 ulcérer T – *to ulcerate*
69 ulcérer (s') P – *to ulcerate*
65 (h)ululer I – *to hoot (owl)*
76 unifier T – *to unify*

T: direct transitive (p. p. variable) – **Ti**: indirect transitive (p. p. invariable) – **I**: intransitive verb (p. p. invariable) **P**: pronominal verb (auxiliary *être*) – **impers.**: impersonal verb – **D**: defective verb – *être*: verb conjugated with the auxiliary *être* – *être* or *avoir*: verbs conjugated with *être* or *avoir* (see paragraph 15)

76 unifier (s') P – *to unify*
65 uniformiser T – *to standardize*
81 unir T – *to unite, to unite (to), to combine (with)*
81 unir (s') P – *to unite, to marry*
65 universaliser T – *to universalize*
65 universaliser (s') P – *to universalize*
65 urbaniser T – *to urbanize*
65 urbaniser (s') P – *to become urbanized*
67 urger I, D – *to be urgent*
only in the 3rd person
65 uriner I, T – *to urinate, to pass water*
65 user de T, Ti – *to make use of*
65 user (s') P – *to wear out*
65 usiner T – *to manufacture*
65 usurper I, T – *to usurp*
65 utiliser T – *to use*

V

65 vacciner T – *to vaccinate*
65 vaciller I – *to wobble*
65 vacuoliser T – *to transform into vacuoles*
65 vadrouiller I – *to rove around, to go on a spree*
65 vagabonder I – *to roam*
81 vagir I – *to cry (baby)*
65 vaguer I, T – *to wander, to dream*
126 vaincre I, T – *to overcome, to defeat*
126 vaincre (se) P – *to overcome, to defeat*
65 vaironner I – *to fish (trout) using minnows as bait*
65 valdinguer I – *to topple*
70 valeter I – *to act as a valet*
65 valider T – *to validate*
65 valiser I, T – *to leave, to abandon*
65 vallonner (se) P – *to undulate*
109 valoir I, T – *to be worth*
109 valoir (se) P – *to be equal*
65 valoriser T – *to add value (to), to enhance*
65 valoriser (se) P – *to valorize*
65 valouser T – *to fire, to drop (an issue)*
65 valser I, T – *to waltz*
65 vamper T – *to vamp*
65 vampiriser T – *to vampirize*
65 vandaliser T – *to vandalize*
65 vanner T – *to fan, to exhaust*
65 vanter T – *to praise*
65 vanter (se) P – *to boast*
65 vaporiser T – *to spray*
65 vaquer à I, Ti – *to attend to*
65 varapper I – *to rock-climb*
76 varier I, T – *to vary, to change*
65 varloper T – *to plane*
65 vaseliner T – *to coat with vaseline*
65 vaser impers. : *il vase* – *to rain*
65 vasouiller I – *to muddle through*
65 vassaliser T – *to subjugate*
65 vaticiner I – *to vaticinate*
65 vautrer (se) P – *to wallow*
69 végéter I – *to vegetate*
65 véhiculer T – *to convey, to transport*
65 véhiculer (se) P – *to convey oneself*
65 veiller à I, T, Ti – *to stay awake, to sit up, to keep vigil, to see to*
65 veiner T – *to vein, to grain*
65 vélariser T – *to velarize*
65 vêler I – *to calve*
65 velouter T – *to soften*
65 velouter (se) P – *to take on a velvety texture*
67 vendanger I, T – *to harvest (grapes)*
118 vendre I, T – *to sell*
118 vendre (se) P – *to sell*
69 vénérer T – *to venerate*
67 venger T – *to avenge*
67 venger (se) P – *to avenge*
84 venir I, *être* – *to come*
84 venir (s'en) P – *to come along*
65 venter impers. – *to blow (wind)*
il vente – *it's windy*
65 ventiler T – *to ventilate*
65 ventouser T – *to cup (patient)*
65 verbaliser I, T – *to verbalize, to put into words*
67 verbiager I – *to be wordy*
81 verdir I, T – *to turn green*
78 verdoyer I – *to become verdant*
65 verduniser T – *to chlorinate*
67 verger belg. I – *to measure with a yardstick, to hit*
66 verglacer impers. – *to be icy*
il verglace – *it's icy*
76 vérifier T – *to check, to ascertain*
76 vérifier (se) P – *to be proved*
65 verjuter T – *to sour*
65 vermiculer I – *to be vermiculated*
65 vermiller I – *to snout*
65 vermillonner I, T – *to vermilion*
65 vermouler (se) P – *to be worm-eaten*
81 vernir T – *to varnish, to gloss*
65 vernisser T – *to glaze*
65 verrouiller T – *to close, to lock up*
65 verrouiller (se) P – *to close, to lock up*
65 verser I, T – *to pour, to shed, to pay (money), to overturn*
65 verser (se) P – *to pay (oneself), to spread*
76 versifier I, T – *to versify, to write poetry*
65 vesser I – to fart
65 vétiller I – *to be concerned with trivial things*
87 vêtir T – *to clothe, to dress*
87 vêtir (se) P – *to clothe, to dress*
65 vexer T – *to provoke*
65 vexer (se) P – *to be annoyed*
65 viabiliser T – *to make viable*
65 viander I – *to graze*
65 viander (se) P – *to graze*
65 vibrer I, T – *to vibrate*
65 vibrionner I – *to breed, to propagate*
76 vicier I, T – *to foul, to taint*
67 vidanger T – *to clean, to empty (oil)*
65 vider T – *to empty, to vacate*
65 vider (se) P – *to empty, to vacate*
65 vidimer T – *to certify as accurate*
81 vieillir I, T – *to age*
81 vieillir (se) P – *to make oneself look older*
65 vieller I – *to play the hurdy-gurdy*
65 vigiler afr. T – *to watch, to guard*
65 vilipender T – *to revile*
65 villégiaturer I – *to be on holiday*
65 vinaigrer T – *to season with vinegar*

65 viner T – *to add alcohol*
76 vinifier T – *to convert into wine*
66 violacer T – *to turn purple*
66 violacer (se) P – *to turn purple*
65 violenter T – *to assault, to batter*
65 violer T – *to rape, to transgress*
65 violoner I, T – *to play the violin*
81 vioquir I – *to grow old*
65 virer à I, T, Ti – *to turn, to give the sack, to turn to*
65 virevolter I – *to twirl around*
65 virguler T – *to punctuate with commas*
65 viriliser T – *to make manly*
65 viroler T – *to ferrule*
65 viser à I, T, Ti – *to aim to*
65 visionner T – *to view*
65 visiter T – *to visit*
65 visser T – *to screw (on)*
65 visser (se) P – *to screw on*
65 visualiser T – *to visualize*
65 vitrer T – *to glaze*
76 vitrifier T – *to vitrify*
65 vitrioler T – *to vitriolize, to insult*
69 vitupérer I, T – *to vituperate, to rage against*
76 vivifier T – *to invigorate*
65 vivoter I – *to struggle along*
146 vivre I, T – *to live*
65 vocaliser I, T – *to vocalize*
69 vociférer I, T – *to vociferate*
65 voguer I – *to sail*
65 voiler I, T – *to veil, to warp*
65 voiler (se) P – *to wear a veil, to mist over (weather)*
101 voir à I, T, Ti – *to see, to see to*
101 voir (se) P – *to find oneself/itself*
65 voisiner I – *to be neighbourly, to be placed side by side*
65 voiturer T – *to convey*
65 volatiliser T – *to volatilize*
65 volatiliser (se) P – *to disappear*
65 volcaniser T – *to bring to volcanic state*
65 voler I, T – *to fly, to steal, to rob*
70 voleter I – *to flutter*
67 voliger T – *to nail laths*
77 volleyer I – *to volley*
65 volter I – *to make a horse circle*
67 voltiger I – *to flutter about*
81 vomir I, T – *to vomit*
65 voter I, T – *to vote*
65 vouer T – *to dedicate to*
65 vouer (se) P – *to dedicate oneself to*
110 vouloir de I, T, Ti – *to want, to wish, to want of something*
110 vouloir (en) à Ti – *to have something against, to resent*
110 vouloir (se) P – *to want, to wish*
110 vouloir (s'en) P – *to reproach to oneself invariable past participle*
78 vous(s)oyer T – *to address sb using "vous" (pl)*
78 vous(s)oyer (se) P – *to address each other using "vous"*
65 voûter/vouter T – *to vault, to arch*
65 voûter/vouter (se) P – *to vault, to arch*
78 vouvoyer T – *to address somebody using "vous"*
78 vouvoyer (se) P – *to address each other using "vous"*
67 voyager I – *to travel*
65 vriller I, T – *to pierce*
81 vrombir I – *to hum*
65 vulcaniser T – *to vulcanize*
65 vulgariser T – *to make popular, to coarsen*

w, x, y, z

65 warranter T – *to warrant*
65 week(-)ender afr. I – *to spend the weekend*
65 wolofiser afr. T – *to wolofize*
65 yailler afr. T – *to mock someone*
65 yodiser T – *to yod*
65 yoyoter I – *to yo-yo*
65 zaïrianiser afr. T – *to Zairianize*
65 zapper I, T – *to channel up*
69 zébrer T – *to stripe, to streak*
65 zerver T – *to cry*
65 zester T – *to zest (lemon)*
77 zézayer I – *to lisp*
65 ziber T – *to dodge a difficulty*
65 zieuter T – *to eye*
65 zigouiller T – *to do in*
65 zigzaguer I – *to zigzag*
65 zinguer T – *to treat with zinc*
65 zinzinuler I – *to warble*
65 zipper T – *to zip up*
65 zoner I, T – *to wander about*
65 zoner (se) P – *to be divided into zones*
65 zonzonner I – *to buzz, to hum*
65 zoomer sur T, Ti – *to zoom on*
65 zouaver afr. T – *to cheat*
65 zouker I – *to zouk*
65 zozoter I – *to lisp*
65 zûner/zuner belg. I – *to squint*
65 zwanzer belg. I – *to joke*
65 zyeuter T – *to stare at*

T: direct transitive (p. p. variable) – **Ti**: indirect transitive (p. p. invariable) – **I**: intransitive verb (p. p. invariable) **P**: pronominal verb (auxiliary *être*) – **impers.**: impersonal verb – **D**: defective verb – *être*: verb conjugated with the auxiliary *être* – *être* or *avoir*: verbs conjugated with *être* or *avoir* (see paragraph 15)

GLOSSARY OF SELECTED TERMS

Adjective phrase (Adj-Phr): A syntactic unit containing an adjective (the core element or head) and all elements modifying the head (adverb phrases, prepositional phrases).

Adverb phrase (Adv-Phr): A syntactic unit containing an adverb (the core element or head) and all elements modifying the head (adverb phrases).

Affix: A morpheme that is added to a word (a base). An affix can be either a prefix (in front of the word), infix (in the middle of the word), suffix (at the end of the word) or discontinuous (around the word).

Antecedent: The noun phrase to which a pronoun refers. In the text, it normally precedes the pronoun.

Aspect: Traditionally defined as the grammatical way to express the internal temporal structure of a situation or how the situation occurs, it is most commonly reflected in the form of the verb. The most common categories of aspect are **perfective**, **imperfective**, **perfect**, **progressive**, **habitual**, **durative**, **punctual** and **iterative**.

Attributive verb: A verb that is accompanied by a syntactic unit that indicates an attribute or quality of the subject of the verb. The verb "to be" is the main attributive verb ("John is tall." John = tall), but other attributive verbs are "smell" ("This dish smells good." The smell of the dish = good), "look" ("That dress looks nice." The look of that dress = nice), etc.

Circumstantial complement: The complement of a verb that is not the object directly acted on by the subject (not a DO), but which indicates information beyond the action, such as time, place, cause, goal, etc. In "The book weighs five kilograms", "five kilograms" is not the DO, it is not what is weighed by the book. Similarly, in "They left on Sunday", "on Sunday" plays a similar role. This feature, also referred to as an **adjunct** by some grammarians, is designated as a **Sentence complement** in this book.

Complement: A syntactic element seen as completing the construction of another element. It generally comes after the verb and "completes" the sentence. This term is originally from French, but usage in the two languages differs.

Direct complement (DC): The term "direct complement" is used here instead of **direct object (DO)**. A direct object is defined as the beneficiary or recipient of the action of a transitive verb. In French, when a noun is the core element of the DC, the syntactic unit that forms the DC is a noun phrase (no preposition).

Indirect complement (IC): The term "indirect complement" is used here instead of **indirect object (IO)**. An indirect object is defined as the beneficiary or recipient for whom or on whose behalf an action is carried out. In inflected languages it is usually marked by a preposition or word order. In French, when a noun is the core element of the IC, the syntactic unit that forms the IC is a prepositional phrase (with a preposition).

Inflection: Variations in form determined by syntactic properties (singular, plural, present, past, etc.).

Lexical verb: A verb with real semantic content, as opposed to auxiliary verbs, and whose semantic content can found in its definition in a dictionary.

Morpheme: Traditionally defined as the smallest physical unit (form) which expresses meaning or grammatical function.

Noun phrase (NP): A syntactic unit containing a noun or a pronoun (the core element or head) and all elements modifying the head (determiners, adjective phrases, prepositional phrases, clauses, etc.).

Obsolete form: A physical form (a conjugated form of a verb or a specific morphological form) that is no longer currently used in the language. In modern language, their use is typically limited to literary use or in fixed expressions.

Participle (or participial) adjective: The present or past participle of a verb used as a modifier of a noun: une porte *coulissante*, une porte *fermée* (= a sliding door, a closed door).

Prepositional phrase (Prep-Phr): A syntactic unit containing a preposition (the core element or head) and its complement (a noun phrase).

Verb form: It is the morphological forms a lexical verb takes when marked for tense and aspect (when conjugated).

Verb phrase (VP): A syntactic unit containing a lexical verb (the core element or head) and all elements modifying the head (auxiliary verb, adverb phrases, prepositional phrases, noun phrases, clauses, etc.).

BIBLIOGRAPHY

REFERENCES – REVISED FRENCH EDITION

PRINCIPAL SOURCES: *Le Trésor de la Langue Française*, the *Littré*, the *Dictionnaire général de la langue française*, *Le Grand Larousse* and *Le Grand Robert*.

OTHER SOURCES:

Antidote Prisme. Dictionnaire et conjugueur, version 5 (logiciel), Druide informatique, 2005

Belgicismes. Inventaire des particularités lexicales du français en Belgique, Duculot, 1994

Dictionnaire de l'argot, Larousse, 1995

Dictionnaire du français non conventionnel, Jacques Cellar et Alain Rey, Hachette, 1991

Dictionnaire Franqus (français québécois – usage standard), Université de Sherbrooke, 2006

Inventaire des particularités du français en Afrique Noire, 2ᵉ édition, EDICEF-AUPELF, 1998

Multidictionnaire de la langue française, 4ᵉ édition, Marie-Éva de Villers, Québec Amérique, 2003

SELECTED REFERENCES – ENGLISH TRANSLATION

BOOKS AND ARTICLES

Belgicismes, inventaire des particularités lexicales du français en Belgique, Albert Doppagne et alii, Duculot, Louvain, 1994

Grammaire méthodique du français, Martin Riegel et alii, Quadrigue / PUF, 1994

The Grammar Book, Marianne Celce-Murcia, Diane Larsen-Freeman, Heinle & Heinle Publishers, 1999

"Le lexique français de Côte d'Ivoire. Appropriation et créativité", Cécile Canut, Suzanne Lafage, *Cahiers d'études africaines*, numéro 181, 2006, http://etudesafricaines.revues.org/index5903.html

Meaning and the English Verb, Geoffrey N. Leech, Longman, London, 1994

Practical English Usage, Michael Swan, Oxford University Press, 2005

Stylistique différentielle et traduction, Egan Valentine et Marie-Christine Aubin, Sodilis, Montréal, 2004

"Les verbes dénominaux en français d'Afrique : rôles thématiques et grilles argumentales", Anne Dagnanc, *Morphologie et Lexique*, pp. 163-182, www.univ-tlse2.fr/erss/textes/publications/CDG/28/CG28-9-Dagnac.pdf

DICTIONARIES

Le Dictionnaire québécois d'aujourd'hui, Dicorobert inc, Montréal, 1993

Le grand dictionnaire terminologique, Office québécois de la langue française, www.granddictionnaire.com/btml/fra/r_motclef/index1024_1.asp

Le Grand Robert de la langue française, version électronique, 2007

Le Grand Robert & Collins, nouvelle génération DVD - ROM, 2008

The Merriam Webster Online Dictionary, www.merriam-webster.com

Lexilogos, www.lexilogos.com

Médiadico, Dictionnaire de langue française & dictionnaire de langue anglaise, www.mediadico.com

Oxford Concise Dictionary of Linguistics, Oxford University Press, 2007

Termium, Government of Canada, Secretary of State, Ottawa, 1989

The Oxford English Dictionary, Oxford University Press, 1989

 Imprimé en France par I.M.E - Dépôt légal : Juin 2009